NEW PRACTICE READERS

THIRD EDITION

BOOK A

DONALD G. ANDERSON
Associate Superintendent, Retired
Oakland Public Schools
Oakland, California

CLARENCE R. STONE

ARDIS EDWARDS BURTON
Teacher-Librarian, Retired
John Swett Union High School
Crockett, California

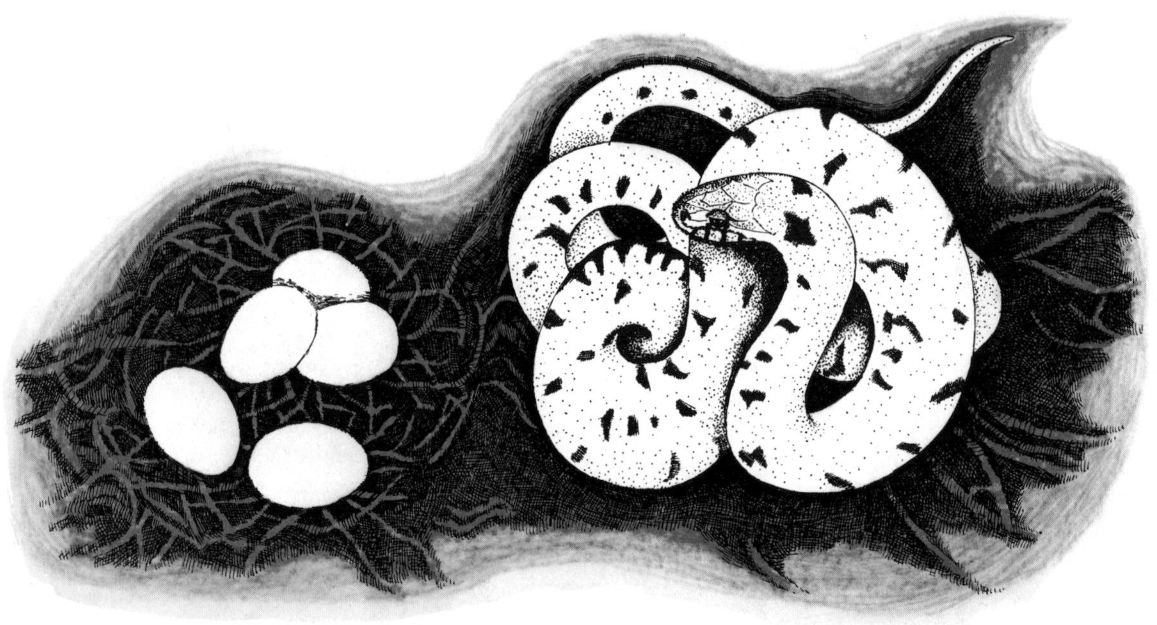

NEW PRACTICE READERS

THIRD EDITION

BOOK A

Phoenix Learning Resources

NEW PRACTICE READERS
THIRD EDITION
BOOK A

Project Management and Production: Kane Publishing Services, Inc.
Cover Design: Pencil Point Studios
Text Design: Craven and Evans, Inc.
Illustrators: Carolyn Bently, Shana Gregor, William Harmuth, Lady McRady, William Singleton, Wayne Anthony Still

—

ISBN 0-7915-2117-6

7 8 9 0 05

TABLE OF CONTENTS

TO THE TEACHER

This book is one of a seven-book series. It is intended to provide reading interest along with comprehension skill development for readers who need additional practice material to achieve mastery. The controlled reading level of each book makes it possible to assign students to the text most suitable for individual reading comfort.

Readabilities for this book are 2.0–2.5, consistent with the Spache Readability Formula. The reading level should be comfortable for students whose reading skills are adequate for completing second grade according to standardized tests.

Words not on the formula's list of familiar words were largely limited to words in use in primary basal materials.

In some cases, the content required the use of unfamiliar words. In such cases, these words appear in the readiness exercises or are supported by strong context clues in the articles themselves.

This book contains eight units, labeled A–H. Within each unit, there are eight reading selections about factual material. Subject matter is widely varied, but at this level the greater part of the content deals with plant and animal life.

There are many selections about wild life: reptiles, mammals, insects, and birds. There are also articles about domestic animals and about caring for pets. Other articles provide views of different cultures and of problems in today's world.

Before each article, there is a readiness activity to introduce new words. This work should be carefully supervised by the teacher before the pupils begin the article itself.

The words are defined in multiple choice or completion situations. Students must consider every word on the readiness list as they answer the preliminary questions. If this section is not handled as oral group work, pupils should have access to individual dictionaries.

Following each regular article is a test which is especially designed to improve specific skills in study reading. There are charts at the end of these workbooks on which to record success on each skill tested. Thus, the teacher and the pupil can make a diagnosis of specific skill weaknesses as well as keep track of progress in each aspect of reading skill.

The skills tested are consistent with the skills measured on widely accepted reading-achievement tests. At this level, the six follow-up skills practiced throughout this book are:

1. Finding specific answers and giving details. In questions of this type, particular words from the article must be used to complete the sentence. Students gain practice in remembering details from their study reading. Questions 1 and 2 are always of this type.
2. Meaning of the whole. These questions require that the student select the answer which best describes the central theme of the story. Question 3 is of this type.
3. Determining whether a given idea has been stated affirmatively, negatively, or not at all within the reading matter. To answer these questions, pupils need to verify that the information is correctly stated. Questions 4 and 5 give practice with this skill.
4. Recognition of the meaning of a word in context. Question 6 is this type.

At the conclusion of each unit A–G, there is a longer story prepared for recreational reading. These stories come from folktales and are intended both as pleasure reading and as a basis for group discussion. *The Thinking It Over* questions following each story may be used to launch the discussions. In certain cases, it is possible to ask students to write whole-sentence answers for additional skill development.

All the selections may be used with average or better readers to develop reading speed when desired. If a time limit is used, it should be standardized. Have all students read the first article and take the following test. Then fix the time limit based on the time taken by 90 percent of the students. For timing, use a watch or clock with a second hand. Announce, "Begin," when the second hand is at 12. Record the time in minutes and seconds. The recreational reading selections have word counts for determining speed. Students should be urged to increase their speed only in terms of their own results.

A sample exercise follows. The directions given in color explain the procedure.

Ideally, the teacher will work through the sample exercise in some detail, directing and modeling the desired behavior. Thereafter, most pupils will be able to proceed independently.

Read-along cassettes to help the most dependent students are available for Books A, B, C, and D.

HOW TO USE THIS BOOK

There are three parts to each lesson.
1. Questions to help you get ready.
   Read them. Write the answers.

Getting Ready for the Next Story

SAY AND KNOW	Draw a line under the right word or fill in the blank.
tall	**1.** It means **part of a tree.** **head** **branch** **bones**
tallest think	**2.** It begins with the same sound as **throw.** **tie** **tall** **three**
three	**3.** It rhymes with **win.** **world** **thin** **legs**
giraffe branch	**4.** Write the word that means **most tall.** ______________

---

2. A story to read.

Sample A Tall Story

The tallest animal in the world is the giraffe. It grows to be three times as tall as people do. It has no more bones in its neck than a person has. But the giraffe's bones are very large.

The giraffe has long, thin legs. It can run very fast. It can sleep standing up. It rests its head on the branch of a tree.

3. Questions to tell how well you read.
   Read them. Write the answers.
   Put the number of your right answers in the box.

Sample Testing Yourself

NUMBER RIGHT

1. The giraffe has large ________________.

2. The giraffe can sleep ________________.
   Draw a line under the right answer.

3. The story as a whole is about
   a. a short animal.
   b. a noisy animal.
   c. tall animals.
   d. the giraffe.

4. The giraffe is almost as tall as a person. Yes No Does not say

5. The giraffe has fat legs. Yes No Does not say

6. What word in line five of the story means **not thick?** ________________

Answers for the Sample

Check your work. If you made a mistake, find out why. Count the number you got right and mark it on your paper.

Getting Ready for the Next Story

1. branch
2. three
3. thin
4. tallest

Testing Yourself

1. bones
2. standing up
3. d. (the giraffe)
4. No (The giraffe is much taller than a person.)
5. No (The giraffe has long, thin legs.)
6. thin

Keeping Track of How You Are Doing

At the back of your book, beginning on page 144, there are record charts. Turn to the chart on page 144 and read the directions. After you finish each of your lessons, put your total score into the right block on page 144.

Then turn to page 146. Read the directions there. On pages 147 and 148, you will be keeping track of how well you do on each type of question. Work to do better each time.

If your teacher asks you not to mark in your book, get help to make a copy of the record charts.

NEW PRACTICE READERS

THIRD EDITION

BOOK A

Getting Ready for the First Story

SAY AND KNOW	Write **yes** or **no** for each.
thin thick	**1.** Are some books **thick?** ____________
	2. Is some paper **thin?** ____________
thin skin	**3.** Does **skin** rhyme with **thin?** ____________
smooth	**4.** Does **thick** rhyme with **thin?** ____________
rough toads	**5.** Are some roads **rough?** ____________

A-1 A Hop and a Jump

The toad is like the frog in many ways. But they are not as much alike as people think.

The toad is short and thick. Its skin is dry and rough. The frog is long and thin. Its skin is wet and smooth. The toad cannot jump as high as the frog. It cannot jump as far or as fast.

Both frogs and toads can live on land or in water. Both sleep in the mud in winter. Both lay their eggs in the water, and both eat bugs.

Children find that both frogs and toads can be very hard to catch. Try it and see!

A-1 Testing Yourself **NUMBER RIGHT**

1. Toads lay their eggs in the ______________.

2. What kind of skin does the toad have? ______________.

Draw a line under the right answer.

3. The story as a whole is about
   a. frog skins.
   b. jumping toads.
   c. how to catch frogs and toads.
   d. how toads and frogs are alike.

4. Frogs are like toads in some ways. Yes No Does not say

5. Toads can jump as high as frogs. Yes No Does not say

6. What word in the last line of the story means **to get hold of?** ______________

Getting Ready for the Next Story

SAY AND KNOW	Write **yes** or **no** for each.
slow blow	**1.** Do children like to blow bubbles? ______________
boat float	**2.** Do **water** and **waves** rhyme? ______________
	3. Does **boat** rhyme with **float?** ______________
can cannot	**4.** Do fish live in trees? ______________
water waves	**5.** Do **blow** and **float** begin with the same sound? ______________
bubble different	**6.** Do **slow** and **blow** rhyme? ______________
	7. What two words put together make **cannot?** ______________ ______________

A-2 A Fish Story

Fish lay their eggs in different kinds of places. Some lay their eggs in mud. Others lay their eggs on stones or underwater roots. Still others lay their eggs on top of the water.

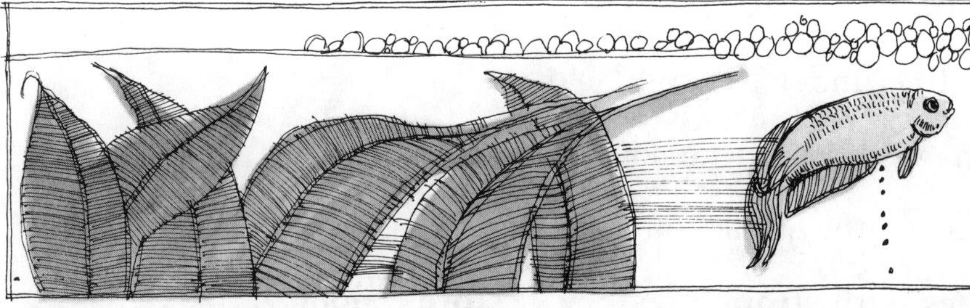

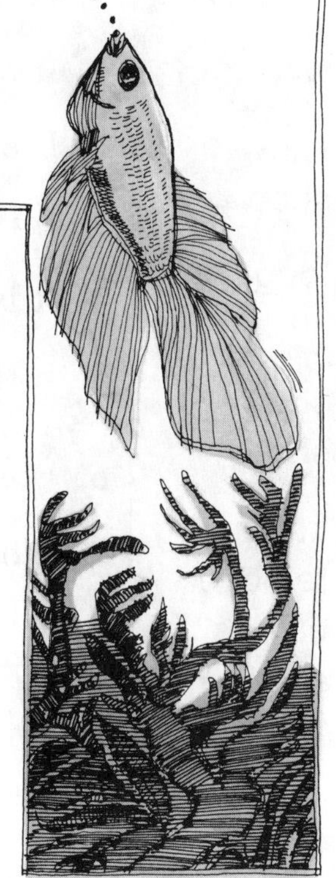

One fish swims around blowing bubbles. These bubbles stick together and make a nest. The bubble nest floats to the top of the water, like an umbrella. The nest is strong. Wind and waves cannot break it.

Into this bubble nest, the fish puts the eggs that a mother fish has laid. Then he watches over the nest. He takes care of the eggs. When an egg falls out, the fish puts it back again.

A-2 Testing Yourself

NUMBER RIGHT

1. Some fish lay their eggs on top of the ________________.

2. What does the fish put into the bubble nest? ________________

Draw a line under the right answer.

3. The story as a whole is about
   a. a bubble nest.
   b. how fish lay eggs.
   c. how fish live.
   d. a fine pet.

4. Wind and waves can break the bubble nest. Yes No Does not say

5. All fish build the same kind of nest. Yes No Does not say

6. In the first line of the story, what word means **not like each other?**

Getting Ready for the Next Story

SAY AND KNOW

warm

show
snow

long
strong

show
shoe

Lapland
reindeer
horses
sheep

Draw a line under the right word.

1. It begins with the same sound as **show.** **see** **sheep** **was**
2. It ends with the same sound as **warm.** **war** **were** **form**
3. It rhymes with **strong.** **story** **store** **long**
4. It is an animal. **rain** **reindeer** **shell**
5. It rhymes with **show.** **shoe** **strong** **snow**
6. Does the milk we drink come from cows? ______________
7. What two words put together make **Lapland?**

______________ ______________

A-3 An "All-Around" Animal

Reindeer are strong, fast-moving animals. In the cold country of Lapland, reindeer take the place of horses. They can pull heavy sleds over the snow.

Reindeer also take the place of sheep. Their skins make warm clothes for the people of the North. Some babies in Lapland drink reindeer milk. So reindeer take the place of cows, too.

Today, many Laplanders live in cities. But many others live in the countryside. It is a good thing that they have reindeer. Our farm animals could not stand the cold. But reindeer can. They love the cold. They can find their own food under the snow.

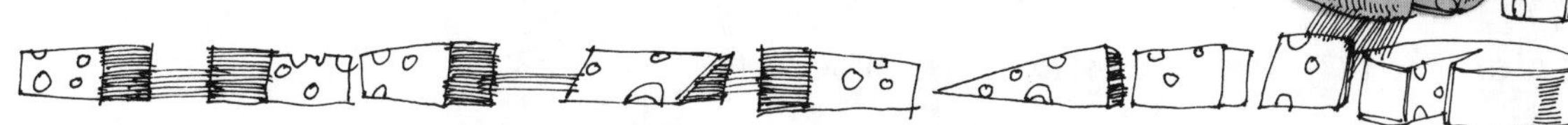

A-3 Testing Yourself

NUMBER RIGHT

1. Reindeer can pull ____________________
2. Where can reindeer find food in the winter?

   ____

Draw a line under the right answer.

3. The story as a whole is about
   a. the people in Lapland.
   b. drinking reindeer milk.
   c. living in the cold.
   d. how reindeer help people in the North.
4. Lapland people make clothes of reindeer skins. Yes No Does not say
5. Some Lapland babies drink cows' milk. Yes No Does not say
6. What word in line seven of the story means **more than one baby**?

   ____

Getting Ready for the Next Story

SAY AND KNOW

dry
wet

ever
every

wide
side

grow
know

life
age
center

Draw a line under the right word.

1. It means **how old you are.** **age** **life** **time**
2. It rhymes with **ring.** **know** **grow** **sing**
3. Does **dry** rhyme with **wet?** ______________
4. Do **wide** and **side** begin with the same sound? ______________
5. Have you ever seen a tree ring? ______________
6. Is a tree trunk something to carry clothes in? ______________
7. Is the **center** of the room the corner? ______________

A-4 Tree Rings Can Tell

Did you ever see a tree trunk that had been cut with a saw? Next time you see one, look at the tree rings on the end.

The rings begin in the center. They move out to the bark. Trees make one ring for every year they grow.

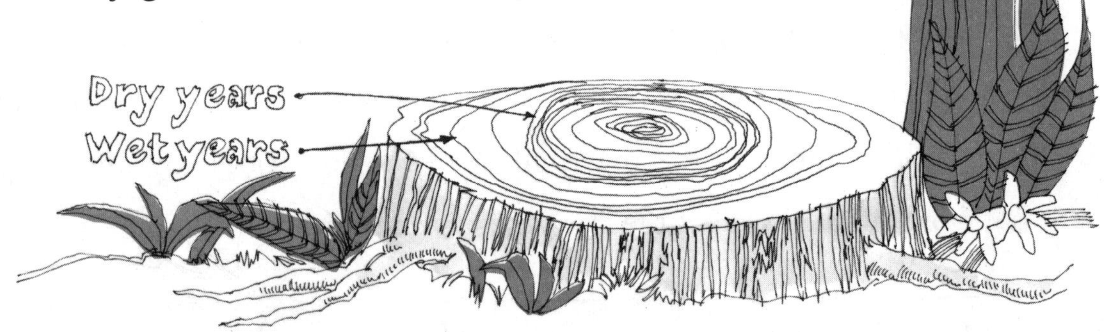

Tree rings tell the story of a tree's life. Some years are dry years. The tree does not grow much. Rings that are close together tell the story of dry years. Other years are wet years. The tree grows fast. Wide tree rings tell the story of wet years.

Count the rings of a tree, and you will know its age.

A-4 Testing Yourself

NUMBER RIGHT

1. Trees grow one new ring every ______________.
2. What do wide tree rings show?

____

Draw a line under the right answer.

3. The story as a whole is about
   a. how tall a tree grows.
   b. how rain makes a tree grow.
   c. what tree rings tell about trees.
   d. cutting down trees.
4. Is there any way to tell the age of a tree that is still standing?
   Yes No Does not say
5. A tree grows more in dry years than in wet years.
   Yes No Does not say
6. What word in line two of the story means **something you cut a tree with?**

____

Getting Ready for the Next Story

SAY AND KNOW

nice
rice

eat
wheat

tall
short

bread
breakfast

pass
grass

Draw a line under the right word

1. It begins with the same sound as **grow.** **row** **pass** **grass**

2. What word at the side rhymes with **nice?** ________________

3. What three-letter word is in **wheat?** ________________

4. Do people **eat** hay? ________________

5. What word in the list means **not short?** ________________

6. Write the two small words in **breakfast.**

________________ ________________

A-5 Grasses We Eat

Did you know there are many kinds of grasses? Some grasses are short. Some are tall.

The kind that grows around your house is a short grass. But field grasses often grow as tall as a man or woman.

Some foods that we eat come from plants of the grass family. Wheat and rice are two of them. We use wheat to make bread. We use both wheat and rice to make breakfast foods. In some lands, people eat more rice than any other food.

Animals as well as people get food from the grass family. Cows eat hay. Do you know the kind of grass that horses like to eat?

A-5 Testing Yourself

NUMBER RIGHT

1. Some grasses grow as tall as a ______________.
2. What are two foods that come from plants of the grass family?

   ______________ and ______________

   Draw a line under the right answer.

3. The story as a whole is about
   a. how grasses grow.
   b. wheat and rice.
   c. foods from the grass family.
   d. how green grass is.
4. The grass that grows around your house is good to eat. Yes No Does not say
5. Some kinds of grasses are good to eat. Yes No Does not say
6. What word in line two of the story means **not long?** ______________

Getting Ready for the Next Story

SAY AND KNOW

penguins
southern

largest
smallest

emperor
feathers

ground

Draw a line under the right word.

1. They are birds. **penguins** **fish** **nests**
2. It means **most little.** **largest** **smallest** **big**
3. It means **in the south.** **feathers** **emperor** **southern**
4. It is **a kind of penguin.** **funny** **emperor** **south**
5. It means **biggest.** **largest** **funny** **penguin**
6. It rhymes with **found.** **funny** **emperor** **ground**
7. They grow on birds. **penguins** **feathers** **pins**

A-6 A Bird That Swims

Penguins have wings but they cannot fly. They use their wings to help them swim. The legs of a penguin are short. Penguins have a funny walk.

Penguins live only near the cold southern seas. They eat fish. Some kinds of penguins lay their eggs in small holes in the ground. One kind of penguin lays its eggs on the ice.

There are many kinds of penguin. The largest kind is the emperor penguin. It is about four feet tall. The smallest is the fairy penguin. It stands less than a foot high.

Penguins have white feathers in front. Their dark backs and wings look like a dress coat.

A-6 Testing Yourself

NUMBER RIGHT 

1. Penguins have short ________________.

2. Penguins live where it is ________________.

Draw a line under the right answer.

3. The story as a whole is about
   a. birds with long legs.
   b. birds building nests.
   c. birds with strong wings.
   d. penguins.

4. Penguins have wings, and they use them to fly. Yes No Does not say

5. The largest penguin is the emperor. Yes No Does not say

6. What word in line six of the story means **oceans?** ________________

Getting Ready for the Next Story

SAY AND KNOW	Draw a line under the right word.
trader explorer guide	**1.** It means **to show the way.** **provide** **help** **guide** **2.** It means **a person who finds new places.** **trader** **warring** **explorer**
Idaho Indians warring	**3.** It means **more than one Indian.** **Idaho** **Indians** **Sacajawea** **4.** It is a Northwest state. **people** **Idaho** **Sacajawea**
language provide	**5.** It means **the words that people speak.** **language** **mountains** **trader** **6.** It means **one who buys and sells.** **explorer** **sold** **trader**
Sacajawea mountains	**7.** **To get** or **to supply** is **to** ____________.

A-7 Sacajawea

Sacajawea (Sak′ ə ja wā′ ə) means Bird Woman. Sacajawea was a Shoshone (Shə sho′ nē) Indian woman. Warring Indians took her from her home in Idaho. They sold her to a trader.

Near the Missouri River, Sacajawea and the trader met the explorers Lewis and Clark. Lewis and Clark were trying to reach the Pacific Ocean. Sacajawea helped to guide the explorers over the land to the West.

Sacajawea knew Indian languages. She could talk with the Indians along the way. She could get horses from them. She could also fish and hunt to provide food. Once, she saved important papers from being lost.

Sacajawea was brave and strong. She got the Indians to help the explorers. She helped to keep peace. In our country, mountains, lakes, and rivers are named for her.

A-7 Testing Yourself

NUMBER RIGHT

1. Sacajawea was an Indian ________________.

2. Sacajawea helped ________________.

Draw a line under the right answer.

3. The story as a whole is about
   a. crossing the mountains.
   b. a Shoshone woman.
   c. buying horses.
   d. fishing and hunting.

4. Sacajawea saved important papers from being lost.
   Yes No Does not say

5. There are many places in our country named for Sacajawea.
   Yes No Does not say

6. What word in line three of the story means **fighting?** ________________

Getting Ready for the Next Story

SAY AND KNOW

seed
feed
food

right
fight

baby
babies

worker
queen
tunnel
soldiers
storeroom

Draw a line under the right word.

1. It begins with the same sound as **feed.** **need** **food** **deep**
2. It rhymes with **right.** **rear** **carry** **fight**
3. It means **more than one baby.** **soldiers** **babies** **queen**
4. **A hole that runs underground** is **a** **river** **tunnel** **trap.**
5. It rhymes with **feed.** **fear** **sand** **seed**
6. What two words put together make **storeroom?**

   ________________ ________________

7. Write the small word in **worker.** ________________

A-8 Not a Minute Lost

Ants live and work together the way people do. They live in ant cities, which they work hard to build. Every ant has its own work to do.

The queen ant lays the eggs. Some ants help by caring for her and bringing her food. Other ants take care of the babies.

Worker ants dig tunnels and build storerooms. They carry seeds and sand. Other ants work as soldiers. They stand watch, ready to fight.

Ants build their cities in many places. Some build in tree tops. Some build in the ground. Some ants even build their cities in pieces of old wood. An ant city is always a busy place.

A-8 Testing Yourself

NUMBER RIGHT 

1. The work of the queen ant is to ______________________.

2. Where do ants store their food underground? ______________

Draw a line under the right answer.

3. The story as a whole is about
   a. builders.
   b. queens.
   c. how ants live.
   d. eggs.

4. Ants are good workers. Yes No Does not say

5. Each ant has its own work to do. Yes No Does not say

6. In line two of the story, what word means **large towns?** ______________

The Ants and the Grasshopper

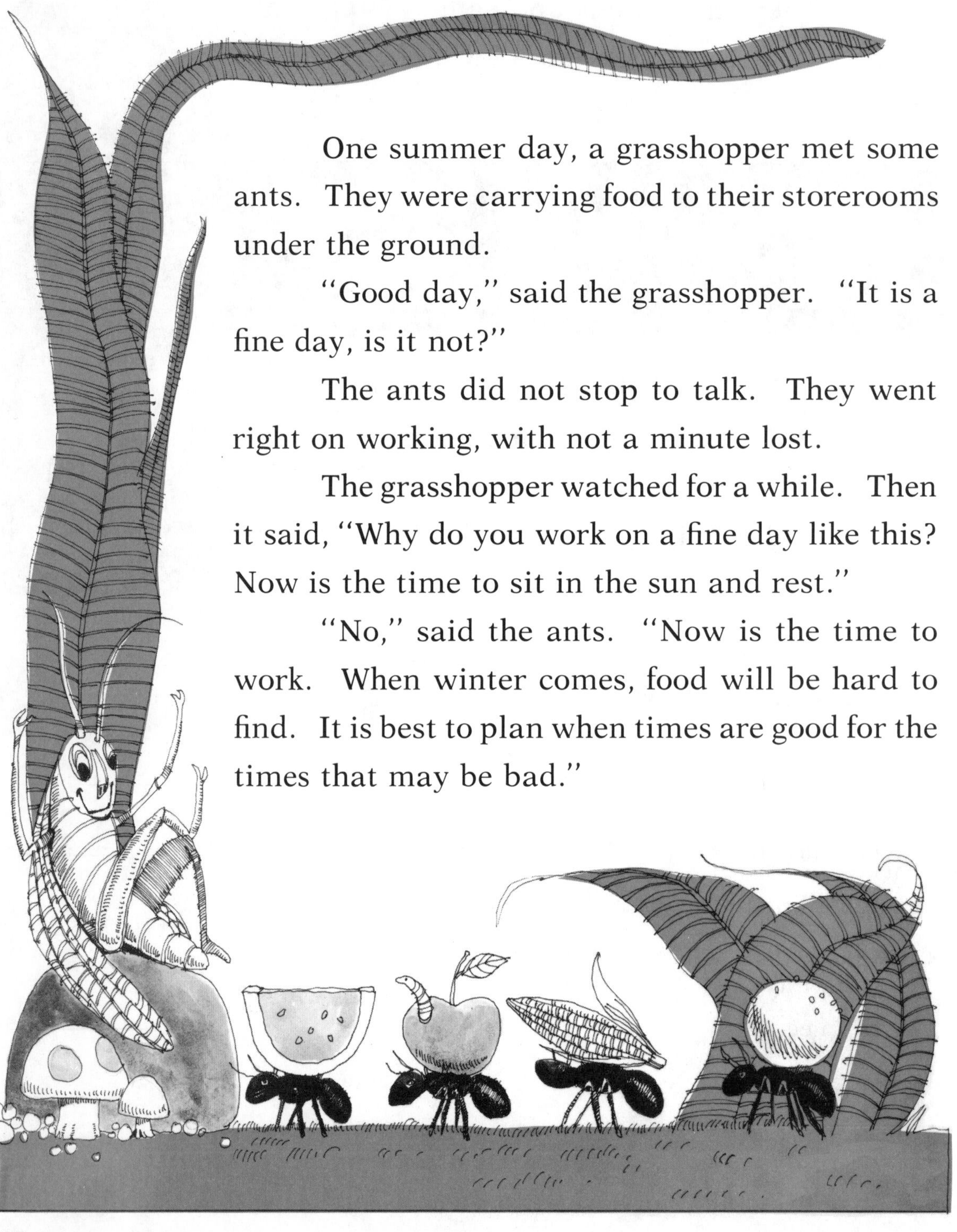

One summer day, a grasshopper met some ants. They were carrying food to their storerooms under the ground.

"Good day," said the grasshopper. "It is a fine day, is it not?"

The ants did not stop to talk. They went right on working, with not a minute lost.

The grasshopper watched for a while. Then it said, "Why do you work on a fine day like this? Now is the time to sit in the sun and rest."

"No," said the ants. "Now is the time to work. When winter comes, food will be hard to find. It is best to plan when times are good for the times that may be bad."

The grasshopper laughed at the ants and went on its way.

Months went by. The days grew cold. The ground was covered with snow.

Under the ground, the ants were warm and happy. They had all the food they needed.

But the grasshopper, above, was thin and hungry. Shaking with cold, it thought of the busy ants. "I should not have laughed at them," it said. "The ants were right. It is best to plan when times are good for the times that may be bad."

Thinking It Over

1. Is this a true story?

2. What did the grasshopper learn?

3. Can people learn anything from a story that is not true?

Getting Ready for the Next Story

SAY AND KNOW

break
snake

slide
slides

surprise
surprising

every
everything

tongue
swallow

Draw a line under the right word.

1. It rhymes with **break.** **eyes** **snake** **slide**
2. It rhymes with **hung.** **can** **tongue** **eat**
3. You do it in your throat. **eyes** **swallow** **skin**
4. It begins with the same sounds as **sleep.** **small** **swallow** **slide**
5. In making the word **surprising** from **surprise,** what letter is dropped? ________
6. Write the last small word in **everything.** ________

B-1 New Skin for Old

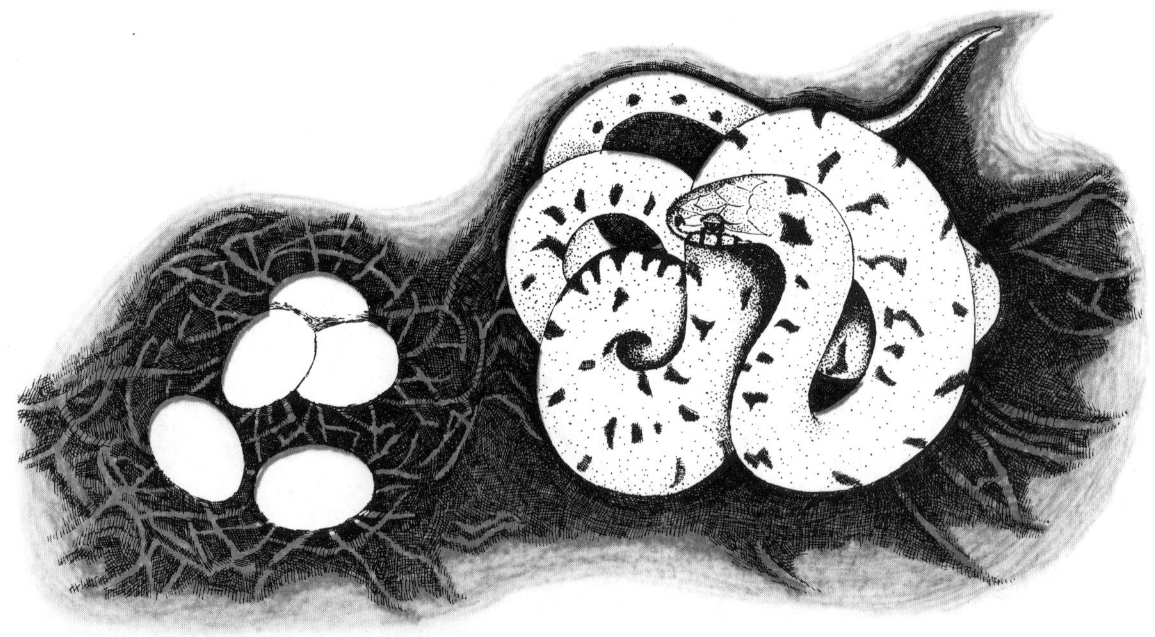

The snake is a very surprising animal. It sleeps with its eyes open. It feels with its tongue. The snake can move very fast.

A snake grows a new skin many times each year. It slides out of its old skin as if it were an old coat.

But here is the most surprising thing of all. A snake swallows things all in one piece. It can swallow animals bigger than itself. Small snakes can swallow birds' eggs and not even break them.

Snakes eat mice. They eat bugs. They can be a big help around a farm. Farmers like the kinds of snakes that eat mice and bugs.

B-1 Testing Yourself

NUMBER RIGHT

1. The snake can move very ____________.

2. What does the snake grow many times each year? ____________

Draw a line under the right answer.

3. The story as a whole is about
- a. having a farm.
- b. a snake skin.
- c. what snakes eat.
- d. surprising things about snakes.

4. The snake can swallow an animal bigger than itself. Yes No Does not say

5. The snake can slide out of its old skin. Yes No Does not say

6. What word in line two of the story is **what we see with?** ____________

Getting Ready for the Next Story

SAY AND KNOW

slow
glow
glowworm

fire
fly
firefly
fireflies

flash

lightning
pretty

Draw a line under the right word.

1. It means **to show a light.** **send** **flash** **cover**
2. It ends with the same sound as **pig.** **give** **bug** **but**
3. It rhymes with **slow.** **sleep** **how** **glow**
4. It begins with the same sound as **flash.** **grass** **if** **fly**
5. Write two letters you do not say in **lightning.** ____ ____
6. Write the two small words in **firefly.**

____________ ____________

B-2 Fly-by-Night

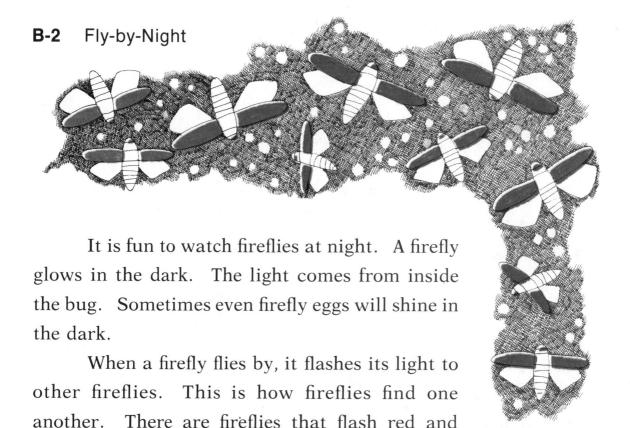

It is fun to watch fireflies at night. A firefly glows in the dark. The light comes from inside the bug. Sometimes even firefly eggs will shine in the dark.

When a firefly flies by, it flashes its light to other fireflies. This is how fireflies find one another. There are fireflies that flash red and

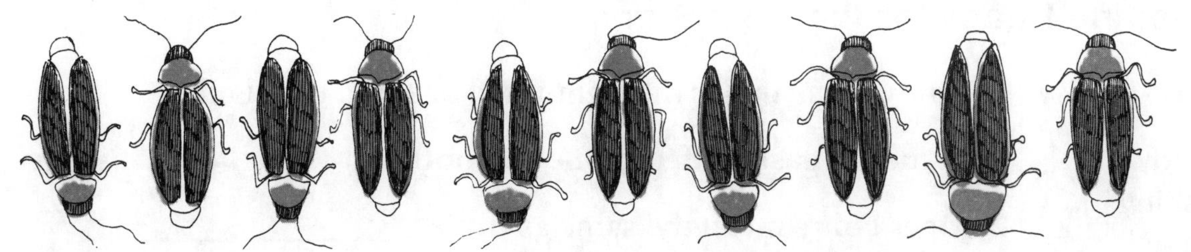

green lights. They are very pretty, and their lights are very bright. Many fireflies together could give enough light to show you your way in the dark.

There are many kinds of fireflies. Those without wings are called glowworms. Others are called lightning bugs. Fireflies are seen most in warm parts of the country.

B-2 Testing Yourself

NUMBER RIGHT 

1. Fireflies glow in the ________________.
2. Where does the firefly's light come from?

____

Draw a line under the right answer.

3. The story as a whole is about
   a. glowworms.
   b. green lights.
   c. insect eggs.
   d. the light of fireflies.
4. All fireflies flash green lights. Yes No Does not say
5. Sometimes eggs shine in the dark. Yes No Does not say
6. What word in line three of the story means the same as **glow?** ____________

Getting Ready for the Next Story

SAY AND KNOW	Draw a line under the right word or fill in the blank.
crow shiny black feathers	1. It means **pass on from one to another.** **run** **corn** **relay** 2. Does **shiny** mean the same as **dull?** ________________ 3. It means **information.** **trouble** **feathers** **messages**
sometimes trouble	4. Do **trouble** and **train** begin with the same sounds? _________ 5. Does **crow** rhyme with **grow?** ________________
groups relay messages	6. Write the two small words in **sometimes.** ________________ ________________

B-3 Very Smart Birds

Crows are birds with shiny black feathers. Some people like them. Other people don't. That is because there are two sides to the story about crows.

Crows are very smart and fast. Sometimes this gets them into trouble with farmers. Crows like to eat corn and other foods that farmers grow. But most times, crows are so smart that they stay away from trouble. Crows live longer than a lot of other birds.

Crows like to stay in groups. They make their nests close together. They work in groups to get food. They relay messages to one another by making some sounds again and again.

Crows are smart in another way. They can learn to talk and make other animal sounds. They can sound like a chicken, a dog, and a cat. Crows are very surprising!

B-3 Testing Yourself

NUMBER RIGHT

1. Crows have shiny black ________________.
2. Crows like to stay in ____________________.

Draw a line under the right answer.

3. The story as a whole is about
   a. how crows fly.
   b. what crows eat.
   c. how crows live.
   d. how smart crows are.
4. Crows live longer than many other birds. Yes No Does not say
5. All birds send messages. Yes No Does not say
6. What word in line one, paragraph three, means **bunches of things**?

____

Getting Ready for the Next Story

SAY AND KNOW

stay
stick
shoot
pull
afraid
quill
touches
porcupine
something

Draw a line under the right word.

1. It begins with the same sound as **stay.** **shoot** **stick** **way**
2. It ends with the same sound as **pull.** **long** **slow** **quill**
3. It is an animal. **quill** **shoot** **porcupine**
4. It means **to feel something.** **pull** **shoot** **touch**
5. It rhymes with **hill.** **animal** **quill** **pull**
6. What two words put together make **something?**

_______________ _______________

B-4 Do Porcupines Shoot Their Quills?

Do porcupines shoot their quills?

The porcupine is covered with long hair. On its back and side are quills. These quills can come right out if something touches them. They can be a big help to the slow-moving porcupine.

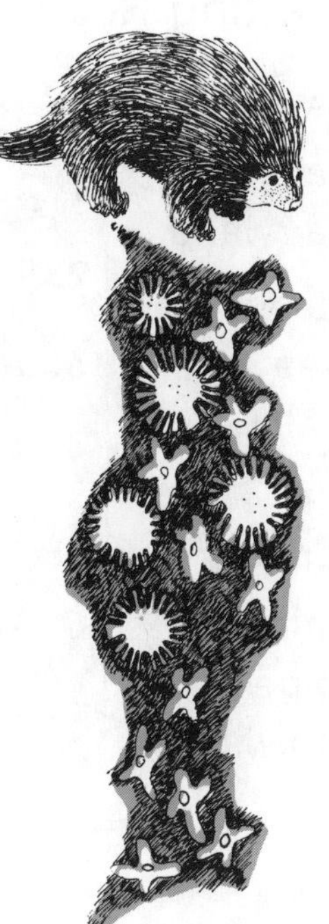

When the porcupine is afraid, it does not try to run away. It makes its quills stand up. If an animal touches the porcupine, it touches the quills first. The quills stick into the animal. When the animal backs away, the quills stay in it. They pull right out of the porcupine.

So you see, the porcupine does not shoot its quills. They come out when they stick into something.

B-4 Testing Yourself

NUMBER RIGHT

1. The porcupine has many ______________.
2. What do the quills do when something touches them?

____

Draw a line under the right answer.

3. The story as a whole is about
   a. how a porcupine lives.
   b. how a porcupine uses its quills.
   c. animals in the woods.
   d. animals on a farm.
4. When something touches the porcupine's quills, the quills stick into it.
   Yes No Does not say
5. The porcupine shoots its quills. Yes No Does not say
6. What word in line nine of the story means **to push into?** ______________

Getting Ready for the Next Story

SAY AND KNOW

fairy
fairyland

deep
sea
salt

dry
dries

mine
pipes
bowl

Draw a line under the right word.

1. It begins with the same sound as **salt.** **come** **sea** **show**
2. It ends with the same sound as **brought.** **water** **salt** **sand**
3. It rhymes with **fly.** **file** **dry** **dig**
4. It means **far under the ground.** **sleep** **deep** **dig**
5. It rhymes with **hole.** **owl** **bowl** **show**
6. What two words put together make **fairyland?**

_______________ _______________

B-5 Underground Fairyland

Most of the salt we use comes from salt mines under the ground. Sometimes people must dig very deep to find it. Salt is white and clean and beautiful. A salt mine looks like a fairyland.

We get salt from salt wells, too. A salt well is much like a deep water well. The salt is brought to the top in pipes.

In some countries, people get salt from the sea. They dig great bowls and fill them with sea water. When the sun dries up the water, the salt is left on the ground.

People need salt. Animals need salt, too. We could not live without it.

B-5 Testing Yourself

NUMBER RIGHT

1. Most of the salt we use comes from salt ______________.

2. In what is salt brought up from a salt well? ______________

Draw a line under the right answer.

3. The story as a whole is about
   a. living in fairyland.
   b. wells and water.
   c. where people get salt.
   d. how people use salt.

4. Animals need salt. Yes No Does not say

5. Some salt comes from the sea. Yes No Does not say

6. What word in line three of the story means **to make a hole?** ______________

Getting Ready for the Next Story

SAY AND KNOW

gum
some

roll
rolled

chew
chewing

sap
juice
sweet
climb

Fill in the blanks.

1. Do **new** and **chew** begin with the same sound? ____________

2. Do **climb** and **gum** end with the same sound? ____________

3. Do **bag** and **sap** rhyme? ____________

4. Is **sap** a kind of juice? ____________

5. Do **gum** and **some** rhyme? ____________

6. What letters do you add to **chew** to make **chewing?** ____________

7. Write the small word in **rolled.** ____________

B-6 Chewing Gum Trees

Did you know that chewing gum comes from trees? It comes from a kind of juice that we call sap. The tree that gives us chewing gum sap grows in hot countries.

To get the sap, a person climbs the tree. The climber ties a bag to the trunk. A cut is made in

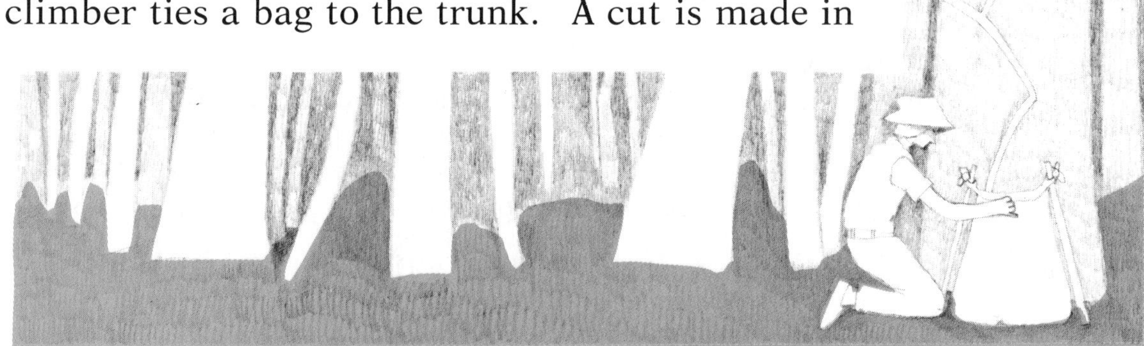

the tree. The cut goes all around the tree. The sap runs down the cut. It runs into the bag. The sap is white, like milk.

After the sap is cooked, it becomes sweet. Then it is rolled out. Last, it is cut into sticks.

Next time you have chewing gum, will you think of all these things?

B-6 Testing Yourself

NUMBER RIGHT

1. Sap comes from a ______________.

2. What is chewing gum made from? ______________

Draw a line under the right answer.

3. The story as a whole is about
   a. how to cook sap.
   b. making candy.
   c. cutting down trees.
   d. how we get chewing gum.

4. Trees that give chewing gum sap grow in a cold country.
   Yes No Does not say

5. Chewing gum comes from the tree in little sticks.
   Yes No Does not say

6. What word in line eleven of the story means about the same as **pieces?**

____

Getting Ready for the Next Story

SAY AND KNOW

all
small

tiny
beautiful

helicopter
teaspoon
feather

hum
humming

bird
hummingbird

Draw a line under the right word.

1. It means **very small.** **tiny** **light** **egg**
2. It can fly straight up and down. **wings** **helicopter** **baby**
3. It rhymes with **bird.** **word** **fly** **light**
4. What three-letter word is in **small?** **bee** **all** **hum**
5. It means **very pretty.** **bright** **humming** **beautiful**
6. It is used to eat with. **egg** **teaspoon** **nest**
7. What two words put together make **hummingbird?**

______________ ______________

B-7 In a Nut Shell

The hummingbird is a tiny bird. It is so light, it can sit on a flower. No other bird is so small.

A hummingbird's nest would fit into one side of a nut shell. It holds two eggs. The eggs are as tiny as bees. Four baby hummingbirds would fill a teaspoon.

A hummingbird has beautiful, bright feathers. Its wings move so fast, it can seem still in the air. Like a helicopter, it can fly straight up. It can fly straight down. It can fly to the back, to the front, or to the side. The wings make humming sounds because they move so fast. That is how the hummingbird got its name.

B-7 Testing Yourself NUMBER RIGHT

1. A hummingbird nest would fit in the shell of a ______________.

2. How many baby hummingbirds will one teaspoon hold? ______________

Draw a line under the right answer.

3. The story as a whole is about
   a. how birds fly.
   b. helicopters.
   c. living in a nut shell.
   d. the tiny hummingbird.

4. The hummingbird is the smallest bird there is.
   Yes No Does not say

5. The hummingbird's nest holds about four eggs.
   Yes No Does not say

6. What word in line two of the story means **not heavy?** ______________

Getting Ready for the Next Story

SAY AND KNOW

hunt
hunting

long
short

dog
rabbit
beagle
favorite
gentle

sad
happy

Draw a line under the right word.

1. It ends with the same sound as **pet.** **top** **tap** **short**
2. It means **not happy.** **gentle** **well liked** **sad**
3. It means **liked the most.** **happy** **favorite** **friend**
4. The favorite pet of many children is a **cow** **dog** **pig.**
5. A pet is a good pet when it is **small** **large** **gentle.**
6. A good family dog likes **hunting** **people** **food.**
7. Some dogs like to hunt **rabbits** **fish** **sheep.**

B-8 Sad-Eyes

The beagle is a favorite dog in our country. It is a good hunting dog. Of all the dogs there are, the beagle is one of the best for hunting rabbits. But that is not why it is so well liked.

The beagle is a good pet. It is gentle. It likes to play with people. But it is a good watchdog, too.

Children have fun with this small hunting dog. They like to pet its hanging ears. They like its smooth white coat with its black and brown spots. The beagle is a long dog, but its legs are short. Short legs are good for running after rabbits.

B-8 Testing Yourself

NUMBER RIGHT

1. The beagle is a good dog for hunting ______________.

2. What kind of legs does the beagle have? ______________

Draw a line under the right answer.

3. The story as a whole is about

a. how a beagle can hunt.
b. why the beagle is a good pet.
c. chasing rabbits.
d. how to play with a pet.

4. The beagle has hanging ears. Yes No Does not say

5. The beagle is the best dog for hunting all kinds of animals.
Yes No Does not say

6. What word in line five of the story means **not rough?** ______________

The Dog and the Rabbit

A farmer and a beagle were walking in a field. All at once, a rabbit came out of a rabbit hole.

The dog saw the rabbit. The rabbit saw the dog. Away ran the rabbit. Away ran the beagle after it, as fast as it could go.

The farmer got up on a fence to watch. Around and around went the rabbit. Around and around went the dog. Up and down and around the field they ran.

The dog ran fast. But so did the rabbit! Then the rabbit headed for the woods and did not come back any more.

The beagle hunted and hunted. But it could not catch the rabbit. Soon the dog came puffing back to the field.

The farmer saw the dog coming and started to laugh. "What a joke!" said the farmer. "A fine hunting dog you turned out to be! You are three times as big as that rabbit. Why did you let it get away?"

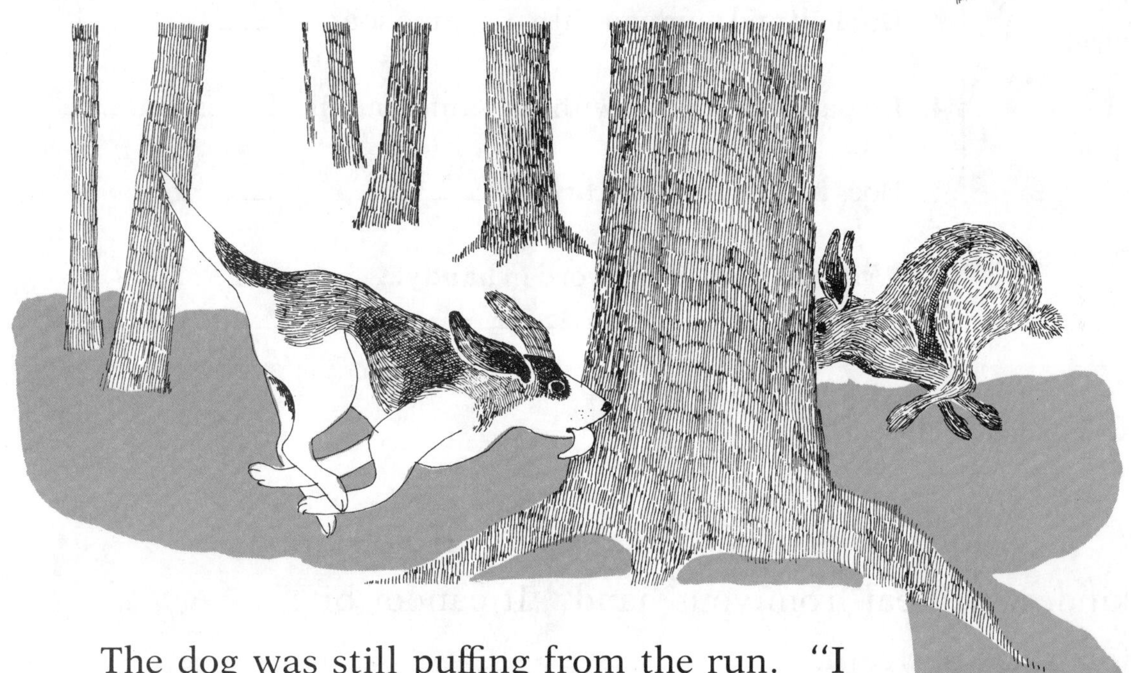

The dog was still puffing from the run. "I know I am bigger than the rabbit," it said. "But that is not all that matters. I was only running for my dinner. The rabbit was running for its life!"

Thinking It Over

1. In a race between animals, does the biggest one always win?
2. In a race between people, does the biggest one always win?
3. When people say, "May the best person win," do they mean the person who is biggest?

Getting Ready for the Next Story

SAY AND KNOW

bright
bite

teeth
pet
afraid

shell
hole

handy
tortoise

Fill in the blanks.

1. Can an animal be afraid? ______________

2. Is a **tortoise** a living thing? ______________

3. Do **shell** and **hole** end with the same sound? ______________

4. Do **pan** and **pet** end with the same sound? ______________

5. Does **bite** rhyme with **bright?** ______________

6. Write the four-letter word in **handy.** ______________

C-1 Part-Time Pet

A tortoise is a good little pet. If you are kind, it will eat from your hand. It cannot bite, for it has no teeth.

The tortoise likes to swim. It likes to lie in the sun. If you find one, dig a hole in the ground for it. Put a pan of water in the hole. This will keep your pet happy.

The tortoise likes to hide. One hiding place that is always handy is part of its own back. When the tortoise is afraid, it can pull its head in, under its hard, round shell.

Before winter comes, let your tortoise go. It will dig its own hole and sleep until spring.

C-1 Testing Yourself **NUMBER RIGHT**

1. A tortoise cannot bite because it has no ______________.

2. What does the tortoise do in the winter? ______________

   Draw a line under the right answer.

3. The story as a whole is about
   a. how to feed a tortoise.
   b. how a tortoise hides.
   c. fun in winter.
   d. a tortoise as a pet.

4. The tortoise likes to tell lies. Yes No Does not say

5. The tortoise will eat from your hand. Yes No Does not say

6. What other word in line two of the story means **good?** ______________

Getting Ready for the Next Story

SAY AND KNOW

bee
hive
beehive

honey
nectar

summer
summertime

hurry
hurries

flowers
music

Draw a line under the right word.

1. It tells where bees live. **house** **hill** **hive**
2. It is something that bees make. **flowers** **honey** **music**
3. It means **to go fast.** **furry** **hurry** **hurt**
4. It ends with the same sound as **bees.** **might** **hurries** **lie**
5. What two words put together make **summertime?**

_______________ _______________

6. Write the two small words in **beehive.**

_______________ _______________

C-2 Busy as a Bee

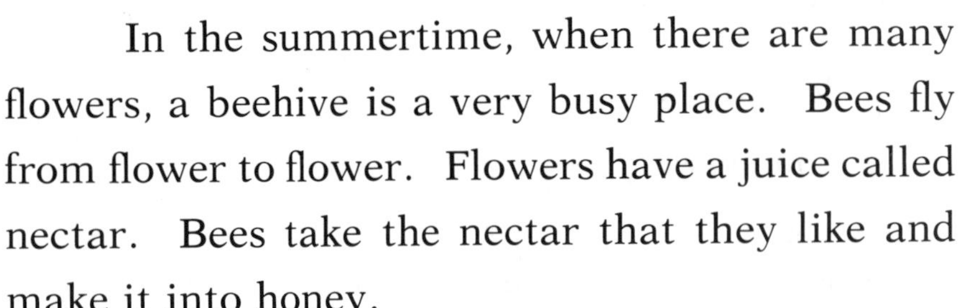

In the summertime, when there are many flowers, a beehive is a very busy place. Bees fly from flower to flower. Flowers have a juice called nectar. Bees take the nectar that they like and make it into honey.

When a bee finds some good nectar, it hurries home. It wants to tell the other bees where the nectar came from. And it does! It tells by doing a dance.

The dance tells which way to fly. It tells how far to go. The bees go back together for more nectar.

Every bee in the beehive is busy. That is why we say that someone who works hard is "busy as a bee."

C-2 Testing Yourself

NUMBER RIGHT 

1. Bees can make ______________.

2. Bees need flowers to get ______________.

Draw a line under the right answer.

3. The story as a whole is about
   a. how bees fly.
   b. how bees get nectar for honey.
   c. how bees dance.
   d. summertime.

4. A bee's dance tells other bees where to go. Yes No Does not say

5. In the summertime, bees play all day long. Yes No Does not say

6. What word in line two of the story means **to move through the air with wings?** ______________

Getting Ready for the Next Story

SAY AND KNOW

scientist
studies
divers
equipment
breathe

dolphins
exciting

explore

Draw a line under each right answer or fill in the blank.

1. It means **spends time to learn things.**
   studies **breathes** **explores**
2. It means **people who go down deep in the water.**
   animals **plants** **divers**
3. It means **tools and other things needed for a job.**
   ways **divers** **equipment**
4. It means **fun and interesting.**
   plants **exciting** **dolphins**
5. In **dolphins,** the **ph** has the sound of ____________.
6. You do this when you go and look for new things.
   swim **explore** **breathe**

C-3 Working Underwater

People go to work every day. They walk. They ride in cars. They ride on buses and on trains. Sylvia Earle gets to her work in another way.

Sylvia Earle swims and dives underwater to get to her job. She is a scientist who studies ocean plants and animals. She is also one of the best underwater divers. She puts on equipment to help her breathe underwater.

In her work, Sylvia has played with dolphins. She has followed whales. She has lived on the ocean floor for two weeks. There she found plants that no one had seen before. Her work is always exciting.

Not many women do what Sylvia does. She hopes that more women and men will want to go underwater. There is always something new to explore.

C-3 Testing Yourself

NUMBER RIGHT

1. Sylvia Earle works ____________________.

2. Sylvia breathes underwater with ____________________.

Draw a line under the right answer.

3. The story as a whole is about
   a. underwater animals.
   b. how Sylvia breathes.
   c. Sylvia getting to work.
   d. Sylvia's underwater job.

4. Many people go to work the way Sylvia does. Yes No Does not say

5. Not many people do the work that Sylvia does. Yes No Does not say

6. What word in line thirteen means **all the time**? ____________________

Getting Ready for the Next Story

SAY AND KNOW	Draw a line under the right word or write the correct answer.
bears zoo favorites tricks clumsy slow fast climb asleep	**1.** They are not house pets. **cats** **bears** **dogs** **2.** It rhymes with **go.** **clumsy** **fast** **slow** **3.** It starts with the same sounds as **train.** **tall** **tell** **trick** **4.** It means **not awake.** **asleep** **clumsy** **fast** **5.** It means **stiff and slow.** **clumsy** **favorite** **big** **6.** When you say **climb**, what letter does not have a sound? ____________ **7.** What word at the side rhymes with **too?** ____________

C-4 Bears In and Out of the Zoo

Of all the animals in the zoo, bears are often the favorites. This is because bears are so big and look scary. But they can do tricks, too.

Bears have short legs. When they walk, they look clumsy and slow. But they can run fast. They can climb, too.

Bears cannot see far. They have small eyes. Their noses tell them where to look for food. Fish and nuts are what they like to eat. And honey! Bears love honey.

When it grows cold, and food is hard to find, wild bears go to sleep and stay asleep all winter. But bears in zoos are warm. They do not sleep all winter. People can visit them all year.

C-4 Testing Yourself

NUMBER RIGHT

1. The legs of bears are ____________________
2. What do wild bears do in the winter? ____________________

Draw a line under the right answer.

3. The story as a whole is about
   a. polar bears.
   b. animals in a zoo.
   c. how fast bears are.
   d. what bears are like.
4. Bears in zoos stay asleep all winter. Yes No Does not say
5. Bears like fish best of all. Yes No Does not say
6. What word in line thirteen names a time when it is cold?

____

Getting Ready for the Next Story

SAY AND KNOW

steam
stop

corn
pop
popped
popcorn

inside
kernel

yellow
circus

Draw a line under the right word.

1. It begins with the same sound as **cat.** **cent** **tent** **kernel**
2. It ends with the same sound as **pop.** **pot** **pat** **stop**
3. It rhymes with **horn.** **home** **come** **corn**
4. It is a kind of sound. **ear** **hear** **pop**
5. It rhymes with **dream.** **circus** **inside** **steam**
6. What two words put together make **popcorn?**

__________ __________

C-5 What Makes It Pop?

Most boys and girls love to eat popcorn. At the circus or the zoo, there are always children with big bags of popcorn.

Have you ever seen popcorn being popped? It is fun to watch it popping. The hard, yellow kernels all seem to pop at once. They fill the pan to the top!

Do you know what makes popcorn pop? Not all kinds of corn will do it.

Inside each popcorn kernel, there is a little bit of water. When the kernel gets hot, the bit of water turns to steam. The steam pushes and pushes. Then POP! goes the kernel. The steam pushes the popcorn inside out.

C-5 Testing Yourself

NUMBER RIGHT 

1. The color of popcorn kernels is __________.

2. What is inside each popcorn kernel? ____________________

Draw a line under the right answer.

3. The story as a whole is about
   - a. how good popcorn is.
   - b. going to the zoo.
   - c. why popcorn pops.
   - d. what children eat.

4. Steam can push popcorn inside out. Yes No Does not say

5. Any corn will pop when heated. Yes No Does not say

6. What word in line twelve of the story tells what water becomes when it is heated? __________.

Getting Ready for the Next Story

SAY AND KNOW

cackle
loudly

attack
Romans

tribes
geese

outside

Draw a line under the right word.

1. It means **squawk.** **cackle** **tribes** **strange**
2. It means **groups of people.** **tribes** **leader** **walls**
3. It means **people who live in Rome.** **tribes** **Romans** **enemy**
4. It rhymes with **crack.** **Romans** **night** **attack**
5. It means **in a loud way.** **cackle** **watch** **loudly**
6. What are the two words in **outside?** ________ ________

C-6 How Geese Saved a City

Geese hear very well. They can hear little noises. They cackle loudly at strange sounds. On a farm they make good watch dogs.

People have many stories about geese. One very old story tells how geese once saved the city of Rome. About A.D. 390, tribes from the north had come down to attack Rome. The tribes had made a camp outside the old city walls.

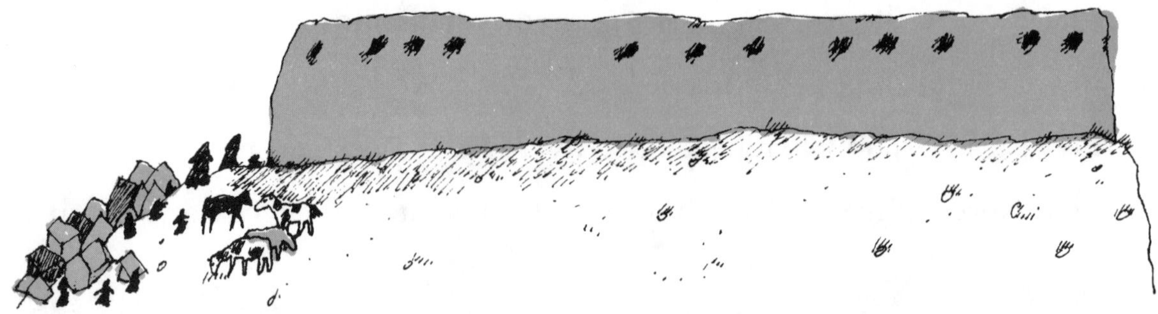

Late one night, the geese of the city began to cackle. They woke the leader of Rome. He rushed out to see what was the matter. The enemy tribes were climbing the walls. The leader shouted. Geese cackled. People yelled. The Romans drove the enemy away from their walls. Thanks to the geese, the city was saved from the enemy tribes.

C-6 Testing Yourself

NUMBER RIGHT 

1. Geese can hear very ____________.

2. What do geese do when they hear strange sounds? ____________

Draw a line under the right answer.

3. The story as a whole is about
   a. geese as pets.
   b. enemy tribes attacking Rome.
   c. geese saving Rome.
   d. watch dogs.

4. One night geese woke up the leader of the Romans.
   Yes No Does not say

5. The Romans lost the battle with the enemy tribes.
   Yes No Does not say

6. What word in line eleven of the story means **hurried?** ____________

Getting Ready for the Next Story

SAY AND KNOW	Draw a line under the right word.
crowded	**1.** It rhymes with **stars.** **clean** **cars** **home**
	2. It means **not easy to do.** **drives** **hard** **this**
hard cars	**3.** Something that belongs to you is your **own** **bus** **work.**
	4. Many people pushed together are ________.
own	**5.** If you have many things to do, you are ________.
busy	**6.** Does **their** sound the same as **there?** Yes No

C-7 Busy City Streets

Rita works in the busy streets of the city. She drives a bus. It is hard work.

Our big cities are very crowded. The streets are filled with cars. Some people don't like this. They say that our air is too dirty. It is not good to breathe this air. They say that the air is not clean because there are too many cars.

Rita has an idea. People don't have to drive their cars to work. They can take her bus to work and back home again. She thinks that the air will be cleaner that way.

Rita used to like to play with toy cars and buses. Now she drives a bus of her own!

C-7 Testing Yourself

NUMBER RIGHT

1. Rita works in the streets of __________ __________.

2. Some people say that our air is __________ __________.

Draw a line under the right answer.

3. The story as a whole is about
   a. hard work.
   b. how to drive a car.
   c. a woman who drives a bus.
   d. playing with cars.

4. Rita's work is very hard. Yes No Does not say

5. Too many cars make our air dirty. Yes No Does not say

6. What words in the next-to-last line of the story show that a person did something once but does not do it anymore? __________ __________

Getting Ready for the Next Story

SAY AND KNOW	Draw a line under each right answer.
nearby healthy	1. It means **to keep safe.** **run** **protect** **move**
harm	2. It means **to hurt.** **clean** **help** **harm**
factories	3. It is the opposite of **sick.** **hope** **sad** **healthy**
garbage polluted	4. It starts like **goose.** **river** **passed** **garbage**
laws	5. They are rules to obey. **clothes** **laws** **fish**
protect	6. It means **unhealthy and dirty.** **river** **passed** **polluted**

C-8 The Story of a River

The Nashua River is in Massachusetts. Long ago the river was clean. Fish lived in the river. Animals made their homes nearby. The land and trees near the river were green and healthy.

The few Native Americans who lived near the river did not harm it. Later, more people moved near the river. They built factories. They put garbage and other things in the river. The river became polluted. The fish died. The animals went away.

One day a woman named Marion Stoddart moved near the Nashua River. She was very sad to see the polluted river. She set up a group to clean it up. The group cleaned up the garbage. The group talked about the river to many people.

At last, all the work and talk helped. Laws were passed to protect the Nashua River. Now it is green and healthy again. The fish and animals are back. And now the people are careful.

C-8 Testing Yourself

NUMBER RIGHT

1. Once the Nashua River was ____________________.

2. The river became ____________________.

Draw a line under the right answer.

3. The story as a whole is about

a. fishing in a river.
b. Native Americans.
c. changes in the Nashua River.
d. Massachusetts.

4. Marion Stoddart did not notice the river was polluted.

Yes No Does not say

5. People will be careful forever about the river. Yes No Does not say

6. What word in line three of the story means **close to something**?

____

The Wise Lark

One spring a lark made a nest in a field of wheat. When the baby larks came, the wheat was short and green. But summer followed spring. And fall followed summer. The wheat grew tall.

One day, the farmer came to the field with his son. "The wheat is ready," the farmer said. "Ask our friends to come tomorrow to help us harvest the wheat."

The little larks were afraid. They wanted to move at once. But their mother said, "Wait. The farmer counts on others to do the work. There will be no harvest tomorrow."

The next day, the farmer's friends did not come. "The wheat must be cut tomorrow," he told his son. "Call the family. We cannot count on our friends."

The little larks were more afraid than ever. But their mother said, "The farmer still counts on others. There will be no harvest tomorrow."

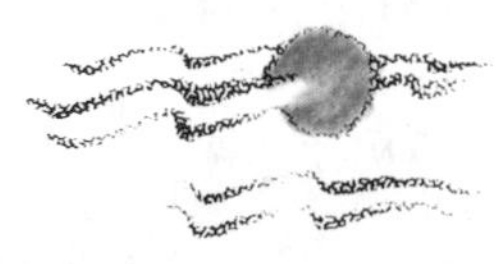

The next day, the aunts and uncles and cousins did not come. "The seeds are falling," the farmer told his son. "We cannot wait for others to help. We will harvest the wheat tomorrow, you and I."

When the lark heard this, she said, "Come, my little ones. The farmer is ready to do his own work. It is time for us to move."

Thinking It Over

1. Did the lark think the farmer would cut the wheat the first time he spoke?
2. Did she think he would cut it the next time?
3. When did she change her mind, and why?

Getting Ready for the Next Story

SAY AND KNOW

star
starfish

tip
two

dry
eye

whole
different

Draw a line under the right word.

1. It has five points. **sea** **star** **arm**
2. It means **a pointed end.** **two** **piece** **tip**
3. It rhymes with **eye.** **dry** **sea** **five**
4. It means **all together.** **part** **piece** **whole**
5. It begins with the same sound as **hole.** **grow** **more** **home**
6. What two words put together make **starfish?**

__________ __________

D-1 Something Different

Starfish are not real fish at all. They are animals that live in the sea.

A starfish looks like a star. Most of them have five arms. Some have even more. At the tip of each arm is an eye. The starfish has as many eyes as it has arms!

In many ways, this animal is different. If an arm is lost, it can grow a new one. If a starfish is cut in two, each piece will grow into a whole new starfish!

Starfish are not good to eat. Dry ones are very pretty. When children find them beside the sea, they like to take them home.

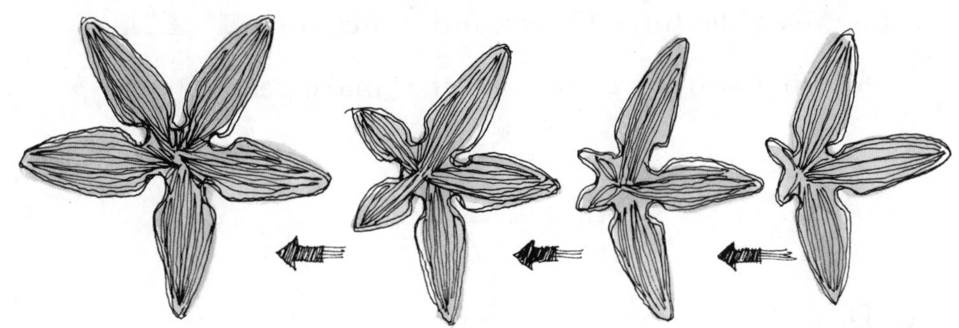

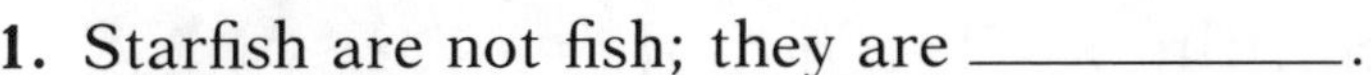

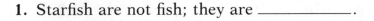

D-1 Testing Yourself

NUMBER RIGHT

1. Starfish are not fish; they are ____________.

2. How many arms do most starfish have? ____________

Draw a line under the right answer.

3. The story as a whole is about
   a. stars.
   b. food from the sea.
   c. fish.
   d. a strange sea animal.

4. Starfish are good to eat. Yes No Does not say

5. A starfish looks like a star. Yes No Does not say

6. What word in line nine of the story means **all of a thing?** ____________

Getting Ready for the Next Story

SAY AND KNOW	Fill in the blanks.
bug beetle	**1.** Do you say **bury** the same as **berry?** ____________
bury burying	**2.** Does **bug** begin with the same sound as **beetle?** ____________
	3. Does **dead** end with the same sound as **hide?** ____________
dead living	**4.** Is **orange** a red-yellow color? ____________
strange peanut	**5.** Write the three-letter word in **beetle.** ____________
black orange	**6.** What two words put together make **peanut?** ____________ ____________

D-2 Dig, Dig, Dig

A very strange beetle is the burying bug. Some beetles eat wood. Some eat fruit and vegetables. Some even eat clothing. But not the burying bug!

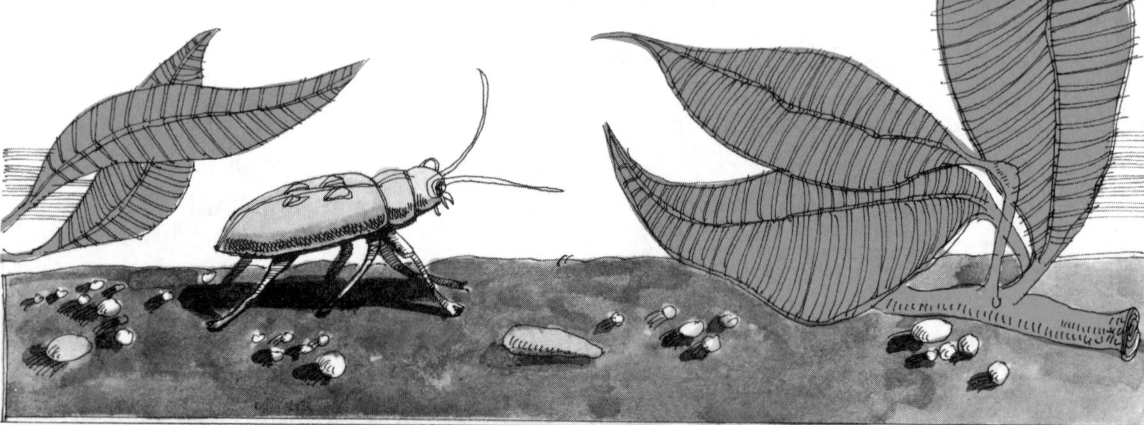

The burying bug is a black and orange beetle as big as a peanut. It sniffs along the ground, looking for little dead birds and animals. When it finds one, it goes to work. It digs until the animal is below the ground. In this hole the beetle lays its eggs. The baby beetles will feed on the dead animal. They will have all the food they need, right there at home! It is a strange place, but a good one, for a nest.

D-2 Testing Yourself

NUMBER RIGHT 

1. The burying beetle is as big as a ____________.

2. How does the burying bug find dead animals? ________________________

   Draw a line under the right answer.

3. The story as a whole is about
   a. beetle eggs.
   b. the burying bug.
   c. a green bug.
   d. a potato bug.

4. The burying beetle lays its eggs in a tree. Yes No Does not say

5. The little beetles feed on the dead animal. Yes No Does not say

6. What word in the last line of the story means **an animal's home?** __________

Getting Ready for the Next Story

SAY AND KNOW	Fill in the blanks.
dry dries wet	**1.** Do **wasp** and **wash** rhyme? ____________
	2. Does **high** rhyme with **dry?** ____________
wing sting	**3.** Does **wing** begin with the same sound as **sting?** ____________
spider wasp	**4.** Does **spider** rhyme with **sting?** ____________
	5. Does **wasp** begin with the same sound as **water?** ____________
ready ball	**6.** Does **wasp** end with the same sound as **paw?** ____________
wash	**7.** Does to be **ready** mean to be **finished?** ____________

D-3 Mud-Ball House

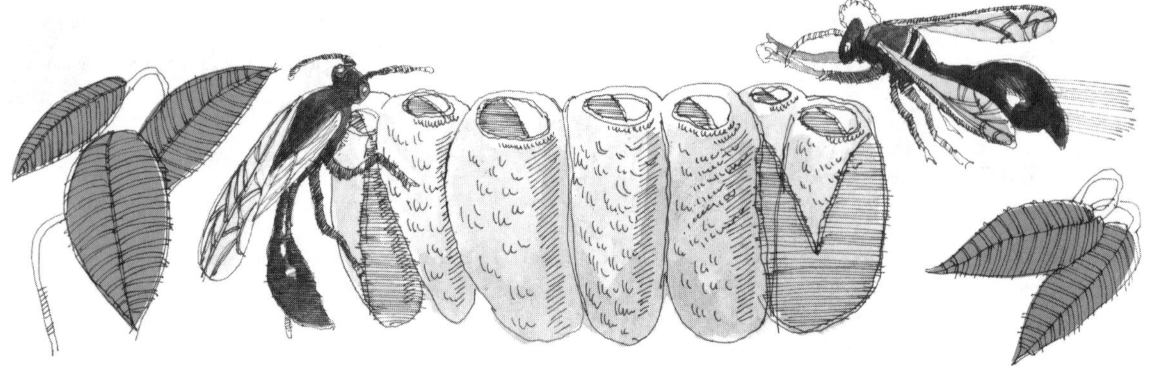

There are many kinds of wasps. One kind uses mud to build its home. It rolls mud into little balls with its legs and mouth. It carries the mud balls to its nesting place. Then it goes back many times for more mud.

When the wet mud dries, it is hard. It is very, very strong. Rain cannot wash it away. Wind cannot break it.

Now the wasp fills its home with food. Spiders are good food to a wasp. The wasp can sting as many spiders as it needs. It carries them home to its new mud house.

Now everything is ready. It is time for the wasp to lay its eggs.

D-3 Testing Yourself

NUMBER RIGHT

1. One kind of wasp builds its house of __________.
2. What does the wasp roll the mud balls with?

____

Draw a line under the right answer.

3. The story as a whole is about
   a. different wasps
   b. how a wasp finds food.
   c. a wasp nest of mud.
   d. rain.
4. Rain can wash the mud house away. Yes No Does not say
5. All wasps build their homes of mud. Yes No Does not say
6. What word in line three of the story means **takes from one place to another?**

____

Getting Ready for the Next Story

SAY AND KNOW

ever
clever

robber
raccoon

hand
band

steal
anything

Draw a line under the right word.

1. It means **to take what is not yours.** **carry** **want** **steal**
2. It means **someone who steals.** **man** **police** **robber**
3. It rhymes with **steal.** **stay** **pay** **feel**
4. It ends with the same sound as **bad.** **can** **bang** **band**
5. It is found in **clever.** **even** **oven** **ever**
6. What two words put together make **anything?**

__________ __________

D-4 A Robber Animal

The raccoon is a very clever animal. It has strong claws, and it can use them well. Across its face, there is a black band. This makes the raccoon look like a robber. And a robber is just what the raccoon is!

Raccoons will steal anything. They steal honey. They steal chickens. They steal eggs from birds' nests. They even steal farmers' corn.

Baby raccoons, like our own babies, need much care. When they cry, they sound like our babies, too. Next time you are in the woods, be on the lookout for Raccoon, the Robber.

D-4 Testing Yourself

NUMBER RIGHT 

1. The raccoon looks like a robber because of the black across its ____________.

2. What does the raccoon have on its paws? ____________

Draw a line under the right answer.

3. The story as a whole is about
   a. raccoons.
   b. animal babies.
   c. chickens.
   d. a walk in the woods.

4. Raccoons like birds' eggs. Yes No Does not say

5. Raccoons are afraid of chickens. Yes No Does not say

6. What word in line two of the story means **sharp nails?** ____________

Getting Ready for the Next Story

SAY AND KNOW	Draw a line under the right word.
corn born	**1.** It begins with the same sound as **both.** **corn** **born** **south**
meet greet	**2.** It ends with the same sound as **greet.** **morning** **night** **green**
	3. It begins the day. **night** **noon** **morning**
south songs	**4.** It sometimes means **to say "hello."** **morning** **greet** **spring**
	5. Write the second little word in **springtime.** ____________
spring springtime	**6.** What time of year comes after winter? ____________
morning night	**7.** Where do many birds fly for the winter? ____________

D-5 The Happy Time

When springtime comes, everything begins to wake up. Many animals in the woods have been asleep all winter. Birds have been away. Under the snow, the ground has been hard and still.

Then, all at once, it is spring! The days begin to grow long. From the south, the birds fly back, ready to build their nests. Animals wake up and start to look for food.

Trees grow new leaves. Plants begin to flower. Baby birds and animals are born. Farmers are busy from morning until night.

In many countries, people greet the spring with songs and dancing. Springtime is a happy time all over the world.

D-5 Testing Yourself

NUMBER RIGHT 

1. When animals wake up from a long winter sleep, they start to look for

__________.

2. What do trees do in the spring?

____

Draw a line under the right answer.

3. The story as a whole is about
 a. living in winter.
 b. birds flying south.
 c. flowers.
 d. springtime.

4. Spring is the time when baby birds and animals are born.
 Yes No Does not say

5. Farmers have little to do in the spring. Yes No Does not say

6. What word in line four of the story means **below?** __________

Getting Ready for the Next Story

SAY AND KNOW	Draw a line under the right word.
go ago	**1.** The word that does not rhyme with **go.** **blow** **roll** **grow**
	2. It begins with the same sound as **fly.** **tumble** **high** **float**
bees seeds	**3.** It has the same vowel sound as **bees.** **buzz** **seeds** **bear**
grow blow	**4.** It means **to roll over and over.** **fall** **fly** **tumble**
	5. It ends with the same sound as **foot.** **too** **float** **grow**
fly float	**6.** It rhymes with **seeds.** **sees** **beads** **freeze**
tumble	**7.** Write the two little words in **ago.** __________ __________

D-6 Going Places

Many plants that grow in our country come from seeds. But not all seeds have come to our country in the same way.

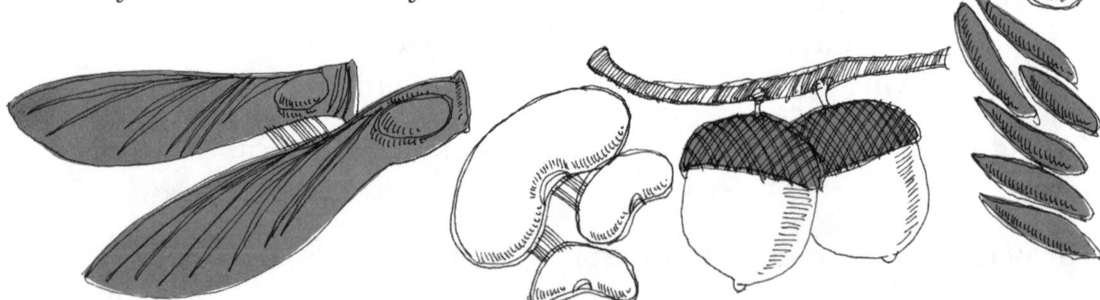

Some seeds were brought by people coming to live here long ago. But most seeds came here alone!

Seeds can fly and float, tumble and roll. Some just hold on to things and ride along. Some seeds ride on the wind. Some ride on the water. Some ride on animals.

The wind blows seeds. Water floats them. Birds and bees carry seeds to other places. You do, too! Seeds stick to your clothes when you walk. Some may fall in a garden. Seeds are always on the go.

D-6 Testing Yourself

NUMBER RIGHT

1. Many plants that grow come from __________.
2. What do birds do to seeds?

____

Draw a line under the right answer.

3. The story as a whole is about
   a. how seeds travel.
   b. how plants grow.
   c. the wind.
   d. riding on water.
4. People carry seeds on their clothes. Yes No Does not say
5. Seeds can move by water. Yes No Does not say
6. What word in the next-to-last line of the story means a **place where you grow flowers?** __________

Getting Ready for the Next Story

SAY AND KNOW	Draw a line under the right word.
soft low	**1.** It means **not hard.** **soft** **high** **talk**
wonder world	**2.** It rhymes with **no.** **wonder** **voice** **low**
same tame	**3.** It begins with the same sound as **world.** **low** **blow** **wind**
teach talk mynah	**4.** It rhymes with **same.** **sand** **like** **tame**
	5. It means **to show how.** **wonder** **teach** **tame**
	6. It is the **name of a bird.** **world** **mynah** **talk**

D-7 Talking Back

One of the wonder birds of the world is the mynah bird. The mynah bird can talk. It can say the same words as you and I.

When you say, "Hello!" the mynah bird will say, "Hello!" too. Say the word in a high voice. The mynah bird will talk in a high voice. Say it soft and low. The mynah bird will, too.

The mynah bird comes from lands far away. Like most birds, it eats bugs and worms.

The mynah bird is not hard to tame. It likes to be with people. That is why mynah birds are good pets. It is fun to teach them words.

D-7 Testing Yourself

NUMBER RIGHT 

1. A bird that can talk is the ____________.

2. What do mynah birds eat? ____

Draw a line under the right answer.

3. The story as a whole is about
a. different birds.
b. how to train a bird.
c. the mynah bird.
d. many kinds of pets.

4. The mynah bird eats bugs and worms. Yes No Does not say

5. The mynah bird is hard to tame. Yes No Does not say

6. What word in line ten of the story means **to make gentle?** ____________

Getting Ready for the Next Story

SAY AND KNOW	Fill in the blanks.
fluffs feathers	1. Does **fluff** end with the same sound as **mouth?** ____________
hot cool	2. Does **warm** rhyme with **form?** ____________
warm cold	3. Does **there** rhyme with **hair?** ____________
tongue mouth	4. Does **tongue** rhyme with **sung?** ____________
hair summer	5. Does **hot** mean the same as **cool?** ____________

D-8 Cover Story

If you want to keep warm on a cold day, you put on more clothes. But what about animals? How do they keep warm?

Their clothes are the hair or feathers that they wear all the time.

A bird fluffs its feathers when it is cold. This holds the warm air in. Dogs and other animals grow more hair in winter. In summer, their hair thins out.

When a dog is very warm, it sticks its tongue out. Cool air comes into its mouth. This cools the dog off.

So you see, animals do not need our kind of clothes. Each has its own way of keeping warm or cool.

D-8 Testing Yourself

NUMBER RIGHT

1. Animals' clothes are ____________ or ________________________.

2. When a bird is cold, what does it do?

____

Draw a line under the right answer.

3. The story as a whole is about
   a. why a dog pants.
   b. winter clothes.
   c. how animals keep warm or cool.
   d. summertime.

4. Animals need our kind of clothes. Yes No Does not say

5. All animals keep warm or cool the same way. Yes No Does not say

6. What word in line three of the story means **not cool?** ____________

The Trader and the Camel

There once was a trader who had a greedy camel.

One cold night, the trader heard a noise inside the tent. There was the camel, looking in!

"Please," said the camel, "it is very cold out here. May I just hold my head inside your tent? You have a fire to keep you warm. I have not."

"You have a coat of hair to keep you warm," said the trader. "I have not. But you may hold your head inside."

Soon the camel said, "The rest of me is cold. May I bring my front legs inside?"

The trader moved over to make room for the camel's front legs.

For a minute, all was quiet. Then, "Please," said the camel, "my back legs are cold. If you moved into the corner, I could get them inside."

So the trader moved, and the camel came in.

Now there was no room to turn. "There is not room for us both," said the camel. "I am bigger than you. You should go outside."

"I should have guessed this would happen," said the trader, as the camel pushed him out into the cold. "Someone who is greedy never has enough."

Thinking It Over

1. Was it right for the trader to let the camel come in?

2. Was it right for the camel to make the trader go out?

Getting Ready for the Next Story

SAY AND KNOW	Draw a line under the right word.
butter butterfly	1. It has a hole at both ends, like a straw. **thin** **tube** **toy**
	2. It begins with the same sounds as **street.** **seat** **straw** **tree**
sweet	3. It means **a pleasant taste or smell.** **bitter** **sweet** **salt**
smell straw	4. An insect with big, colored wings. **ant** **firefly** **butterfly**
sip	5. **The sweet juice of flowers.** **water** **milk** **nectar**
tube nectar	6. What two words put together make **butterfly?** __________ __________

E-1 The Straw That Travels

Butterflies move from flower to flower looking for food. Sweet-smelling flowers are full of nectar. When bees find nectar, they carry it home. They use it to make honey. But butterflies do not take nectar away. They drink it then and there! Butterflies love nectar.

A butterfly sips nectar the way you sip with a straw. Its mouth is a long tube. When this tube is out, it is like a straw. The butterfly sticks it down into the nectar. After it drinks, it pulls up its mouth and goes on its way!

When the butterfly is not eating, it keeps its drinking tube rolled up under its head.

E-1 Testing Yourself

NUMBER RIGHT ____

1. What do butterflies like to drink? ____________

2. What do bees make with their nectar? ____________

Draw a line under the right answer.

3. The story as a whole is about

a. drinking nectar through a straw.
b. the colors of butterflies.
c. making honey.
d. bees.

4. The butterfly's tube is under its wing. Yes No Does not say

5. The butterfly can roll its tube up under its head.
Yes No Does not say

6. What word in line six of the story means **to like very much?** ____________

Getting Ready for the Next Story

SAY AND KNOW	Draw a line under the right word.
too igloo	**1.** It begins and ends with the same sounds as **black.** **house** **igloo** **block**
block black	**2.** It has a large rounded roof. **block** **tepee** **igloo** **3.** It means **a person who hunts.** **winter** **igloo** **hunter**
hunt hunter	**4.** It is one kind of Eskimo house. **black** **too** **igloo**
winter wintertime	**5.** They live near snow and ice. ____________
Eskimo dome	**6.** Write the second word in **wintertime.** ____________ **7.** What are two small words in **meat?** ____________ ____________

E-2 House of Ice

Many Eskimos used to live in igloos. Igloos were houses of ice. They were made in the wintertime, when everything was covered with ice and snow.

To build the igloo, the Eskimos cut out large blocks of ice. They made a dome of the blocks. In this dome, they cut a low doorway. There were no windows at all.

The igloo was a warm place for the Eskimo family to live. Inside, clothes could be dried over the fire. Meat could be cooked.

In the summertime, the Eskimos left the igloos. They lived in tents.

This was all in times gone by. Now most Eskimos live in houses much like ours.

E-2 Testing Yourself

NUMBER RIGHT

1. An igloo is made of blocks of __________.

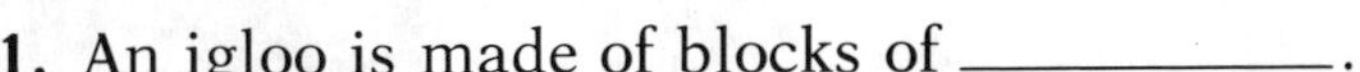

2. What people make igloos? __________

Draw a line under the right answer.

3. The story as a whole is about
   a. cooking outdoors.
   b. igloos.
   c. making ice cubes.
   d. going hunting.

4. There was a high doorway in the igloo. Yes No Does not say

5. Eskimos lived in tents in the winter. Yes No Does not say

6. What word in line six of the story means **pieces of something?** __________

Getting Ready for the Next Story

SAY AND KNOW

clown
claws

hid
hide
hiding

opossum
kangaroo

pouch
dead
pretend

Draw a line under the right word.

1. It is a **kind of animal.** **knee** **oak** **kangaroo**
2. Some animals use it like a hand. **heat** **arm** **claw**
3. Are **teeth** the same as **claws?** **yes** **no** **sometimes**
4. It begins with the same sounds as **clown.** **down** **cow** **claw**
5. It is a small animal. **kangaroo** **elephant** **opossum**
6. It rhymes with **lid.** **hide** **ride** **hid**
7. It means the same as **bag** or **pocket.** **hid** **dead** **pouch**
8. It means **to make believe.** **pretend** **hide** **opossum**

E-3 Playing 'Possum

The opossum is a small animal about as big as a cat. It has a pouch like a kangaroo. It carries its babies in this pouch, as kangaroo mothers do.

At first, opossum babies are no bigger than bees. But they grow fast. Soon they can ride along on their mothers' backs. They also learn to swing by their tails from a tree.

The opossum likes to hunt at night. It has strong claws. It has strong teeth, too. Often, it breaks into chicken houses.

When the opossum is afraid, it tries to hide by playing dead. People often say someone is "playing 'possum" when the person is pretending to sleep.

E-3 Testing Yourself

NUMBER RIGHT 

1. The opossum has a pouch like a ___________ has.
2. What does the opossum carry in its pouch? ___________

   Draw a line under the right answer.
3. The story as a whole is about
   a. kangaroos.
   b. hunting at night.
   c. pretending to sleep.
   d. the opossum.
4. The opossum has strong claws. Yes No Does not say
5. When the opossum is afraid, it runs away. Yes No Does not say
6. What word in line two of the story means **a kind of bag** or **pocket?**

   ____

Getting Ready for the Next Story

SAY AND KNOW

warm
cold

hollow
holes

have
cave

roll
heavy
color
coat
wood

Fill in the blanks.

1. Does **hollow** rhyme with **hole?** ____________
2. Do **cold** and **hole** have the same vowel sound? ____________
3. Does **warm** begin with the same sound as **winter?** ____________
4. Do **roll** and **coat** have the same vowel sound? ____________
5. Does **have** end with the same sound as **cave?** ____________
6. If a log is **hollow,** can it still be full of **wood?** ____________
7. Does **heavy** mean the same as **light?** ____________

E-4 When Winter Comes

When winter comes, birds fly away. Most birds cannot live where it is cold. They cannot find food when the ground is hard and covered with snow. They fly where it is warm.

But animals cannot fly away. What do they do when winter comes?

Many animals sleep all winter. They roll up in hollow logs, in holes in the ground, or in caves. Then they go to sleep. Animals who do not go to sleep grow heavy winter coats to keep them warm.

Some animals change their color. The wild rabbit turns from summer brown to winter white. Then hungry animals cannot see it in the snow.

E-4 Testing Yourself

NUMBER RIGHT

1. In winter, birds cannot find __________.
2. Why do birds fly south in the winter?

____

Draw a line under the right answer.

3. The story as a whole is about
   a. flying south for winter. c. rabbits.
   b. how animals live in winter. d. bears.
4. Some animals grow heavy coats for winter. Yes No Does not say
5. The rabbit turns brown in winter. Yes No Does not say
6. What word in line eight of the story means **empty inside?** __________

Getting Ready for the Next Story

SAY AND KNOW

American
Mexican

workers
migrant

English

different
parents

Vietnam

Draw a line under the right word.

1. It means **one who moves around.**

   parents **Vietnam** **migrant**

2. Does **different** mean **alike?** ____________

3. It means **from America.** ____________

4. What is the basic word in **workers?** ____________

5. Are mothers and fathers **parents?** ____________

6. What do we call the language in this book?

   English **Mexican** **migrant**

E-5 New Friends from Other Places

There are many children in American schools. The children may come from the same street. They may come from far away. But they can all be friends. Today there are children like Kim and Todd from Vietnam. Their old home is far away. They are learning to read English.

There are children like Billie and Pete. Their parents are migrant workers. They move around the country to help on different farms.

These children may go to many different schools each year.

Maria and Tony are Mexican children. They know games and songs which are great fun. They can tell their class about many new things.

Do all the children in your class come from your street? Where do the others come from? What can they tell you?

E-5 Testing Yourself

NUMBER RIGHT

1. There are many children from other countries in American ________.

2. Kim and Todd are learning to read ________.

   Draw a line under the right answer.

3. The story as a whole is about
   a. children from the same street.
   b. Mexican games and songs.
   c. migrant workers.
   d. children who come from far away.

4. Migrant children may go to many schools in a year.
   Yes No Does not say

5. Children from other countries can tell their classes many new things.
   Yes No Does not say

6. What word in line four of the story means **this day?** ________

Getting Ready for the Next Story

SAY AND KNOW	Draw a line under each right answer or fill in the blank.
goldfish pets	1. Fish live in it. **think** **food** **tank** 2. Which word means **trees** or **grass** or **bushes?** **shade** **plants** **goldfish**
gold	3. It begins with the same sounds as **cry.** **call** **crumbs** **bread**
tank plants shade	4. It is a place where you are out of the sun. **small** **stay** **shade**
once crumbs	5. It means **one time.** **first** **last** **once** 6. What two words put together make **goldfish?** ____________ ____________

E-6 What about Goldfish?

Many people have fish as pets. Fish are pretty. Fish are fun to watch. They swim around all the time. Fish are easy to keep.

One kind of fish that people like is the goldfish. You would think that all goldfish are gold. But they are not. Goldfish are red, gold, orange, brown, gray, black, and white!

You can start out with a few goldfish in a small tank. The water you put in must not be too cold. The water must also be clean. You can put in some plants to make the tank look pretty. Do not put the tank in the sun. Goldfish must be in the shade.

You need to feed the goldfish once a day. They eat worms, bread crumbs, and plants. Pet stores also sell fish food. If you take good care of your goldfish, they will stay around a long time.

E-6 Testing Yourself

NUMBER RIGHT

1. Many people like to have fish as ________________.

2. You keep fish in a ________________.

Draw a line under the right answer.

3. The story as a whole is about
   a. all pets.
   b. the colors of fish.
   c. plants.
   d. goldfish as pets.

4. Fish swim around all the time. Yes No Does not say

5. All fish need to be in the shade. Yes No Does not say

6. What word in line two of the story means **to look at**? ________________

Getting Ready for the Next Story

SAY AND KNOW

smell
tell

nose
clothes

ears
years

if
sniff
no
not
note

Fill in the blanks.

1. Does **sniff** mean the same as **smell?** ________
2. Does **tell** rhyme with **smell?** ________
3. Does **clothes** end with the same sound as **nose?** ________
4. Does **ears** begin with the same sound as **years?** ________
5. Does **note** rhyme with **nose?** ________
6. Do **not** and **note** sound alike? ________
7. Write the little word in **sniff.** ________

E-7 The Nose Knows

A dog's nose tells it more than its eyes do. The dog sniffs at its food before it eats. It sniffs at people to tell who they are. When it looks for something, a dog sniffs to find it.

A dog's nose helps not only the dog. It can help people, too. Dogs have helped the police find people who are lost. A dog cannot see as well as it can smell.

Dogs can hear well, too. They can hear sounds that are far away. They can hear sounds that we cannot hear. Every noise seems loud to them. Very high notes that people cannot hear will often hurt a dog's ears.

E-7 Testing Yourself

NUMBER RIGHT

1. A dog cannot see as well as it can ____________________

2. What helps a dog to find what it is looking for? ____________________

Draw a line under the right answer.

3. The story as a whole is about
   a. feeding a dog.
   b. hunting.
   c. training a dog.
   d. how dogs smell and hear.

4. Dogs can hear sounds we cannot hear. Yes No Does not say

5. Dogs like very high sounds. Yes No Does not say

6. What word in line ten means **not near**? ____________________

Getting Ready for the Next Story

SAY AND KNOW	Draw a line under the right word.
whale	**1.** It sounds the same as **see.** **scene** **seat** **sea**
hammerhead	**2.** Does **shark** rhyme with **garbage?** ______
angel	**3.** It is **a kind of shark.** **angel** **garbage** **attack**
attack	**4.** It means **to go after something.** **hammerhead** **attack** **whale**
shark	**5.** Does **whale** begin with the same sound as **wheel?** ______
garbage	**6.** What are the words in **hammerhead?** ______ ______

E-8 News about Sharks

We hear many frightening stories about sharks. Some of the stories are true. Some are not. There are hundreds of kinds of sharks.

There are whale sharks. These sharks may weigh two times as much as an elephant. There are little sharks only four inches (about ten centimeters) long. There are hammerhead sharks. There are angel sharks, and monk fish sharks, and many more.

Sharks are meat eaters. They eat dying fish. They eat garbage. They can be fierce hunters. They swim fast. Sharks can smell and hear for great distances. Some sharks will attack people.

If you swim in waters where sharks live, you must be careful. There are rules to follow to stay safe.

E-8 Testing Yourself

NUMBER RIGHT

1. There are many kinds of ____________.

2. How long are the smallest sharks? ____________ ____________

   Draw a line under the right answer.

3. The story as a whole is about
   - a. garbage.
   - b. whales.
   - c. sharks.
   - d. elephants.

4. Sharks can hear noises from far away. Yes No Does not say

5. Sharks are plant eaters. Yes No Does not say

6. What word in line eleven of the story means **wild** or **violent?** ____________

Why Hawks Kill Chickens

Once all the animals could talk to each other.

One day a hen borrowed a wembe* from the hawk.

"Be very careful with my wembe," the hawk said. "If you lose it, you will pay!"

The hen was busy that day. She dropped the wembe. It fell on the ground. The poor hen looked for it. She scratched and scratched in the dirt. She made sad little noises. She could not find the wembe.

She was afraid of what the hawk would do. All the other hens came to help. They scratched too. But they could not find the wembe.

The hawk flew down. "I came for my wembe," it said.

The hen had to tell her story. She had lost the wembe.

The hawk was angry.

"That's bad!" it cried. "You will pay for this! From this day on, all hawks will hunt chickens from the sky. We will eat chickens until the day you give back my wembe!"

So hawks eat chickens. That is not all. Chickens always scratch in the dirt. They sing a sad little song. The day the hens find the wembe, the hawks will stop eating chickens.

*wembe—a small tool used for cutting (Swahili)

Thinking It Over

1. Is this a true story?
2. How can you tell?
3. Why do you think hawks kill chickens?

Getting Ready for the Next Story

SAY AND KNOW	Draw a line under the right word.
upright curl	**1.** It means **to come out of an egg.** **hatch** **hide** **swim**
hat hatch	**2.** It is **a place where fish are kept.** **pencil** **aquarium** **wet**
pony horse	**3.** It begins with the same sound as **sweep.** **swim** **hat** **pony**
swim swimming	**4.** It has the same vowel sound as **hold.** **pot** **pig** **pony**
seaweed aquarium	**5.** It rhymes with **girl.** **curl** **upright** **curly**
	6. What two words put together make **seaweed?** __________ __________

F-1 The Sea Horse

A pretty fish you may never have seen is the sea horse. It is very small. Its head looks like the head of a little pony.

When it swims, the sea horse stands upright. When it wants to stay still, it curls its tail around seaweed. Then it holds on.

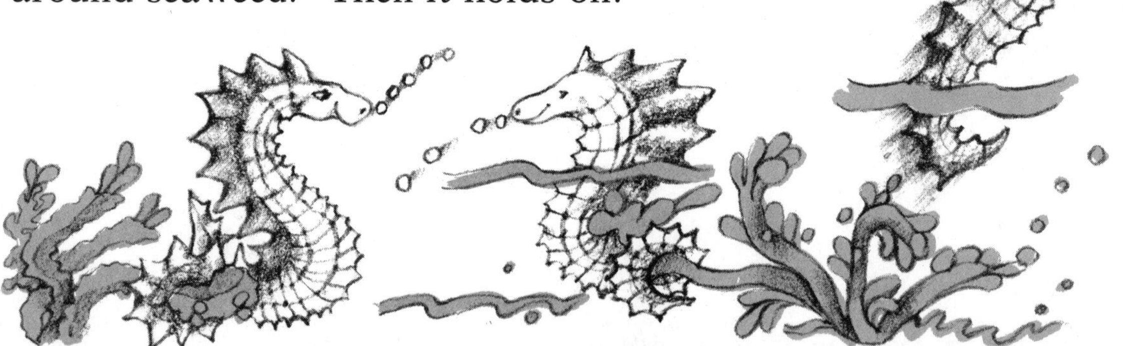

The sea horse keeps its babies in a pocket. The pocket is on the father! The mother lays the eggs in the father's pocket. The father cares for them. He keeps them until they hatch.

If you go to an aquarium, ask if there are any sea horses. It is fun to see these little fish swimming in the water.

F-1 Testing Yourself

NUMBER RIGHT 

1. The sea horse is not a horse; it is a __________.

2. What does the head of the sea horse look like?

____

Draw a line under the right answer.

3. The story as a whole is about
   a. ponies.
   b. fish eggs.
   c. riding horses.
   d. the sea horse.

4. A sea horse mother lays its eggs in the father's pocket.
   Yes No Does not say

5. The mother takes care of the eggs. Yes No Does not say

6. What word in line four of the story means **moves through water?** ________

Getting Ready for the Next Story

SAY AND KNOW	Draw a line under the right word.
thread said web	1. It is something spiders make. **weed** **web** **bed**
	2. It begins with the same sounds as **splash.** **hide** **side** **spider**
high fly	3. It ends with the same sound as **trick.** **try** **fly** **stick**
	4. It does not have the same vowel sound as **said.** **thread** **web** **maid**
stick sticky	5. It rhymes with **sky.** **food** **fly** **right**
spider catch	6. It rhymes with **hatch.** **stick** **high** **catch**
away	7. Write the two words that make **away.** ________ ________

F-2 The Spider and the Fly

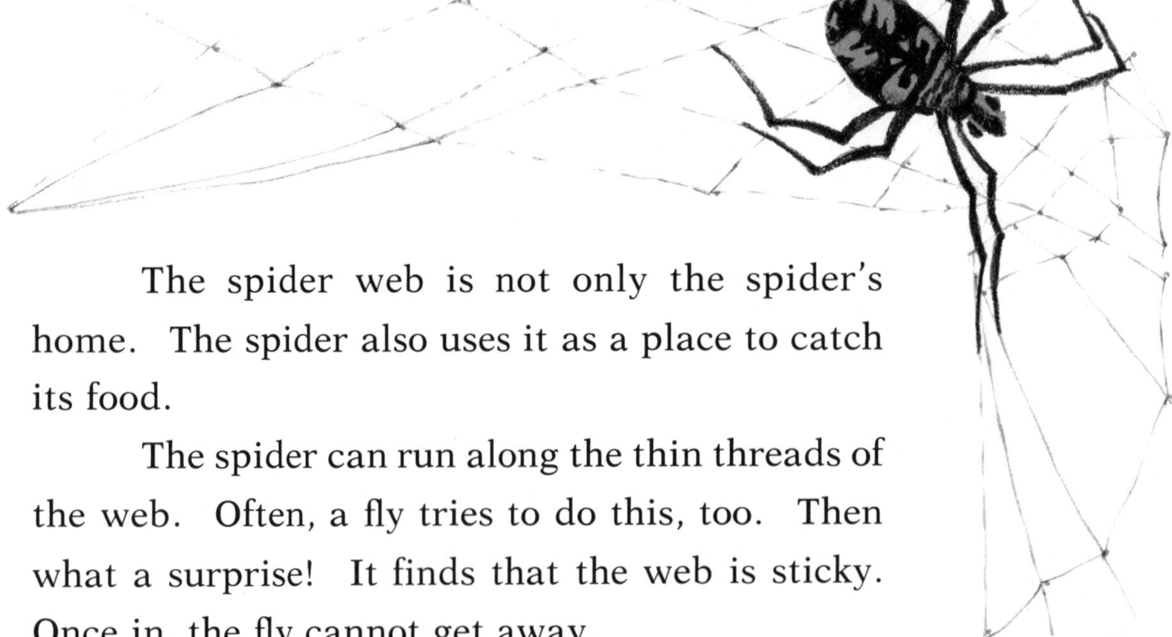

The spider web is not only the spider's home. The spider also uses it as a place to catch its food.

The spider can run along the thin threads of the web. Often, a fly tries to do this, too. Then what a surprise! It finds that the web is sticky. Once in, the fly cannot get away.

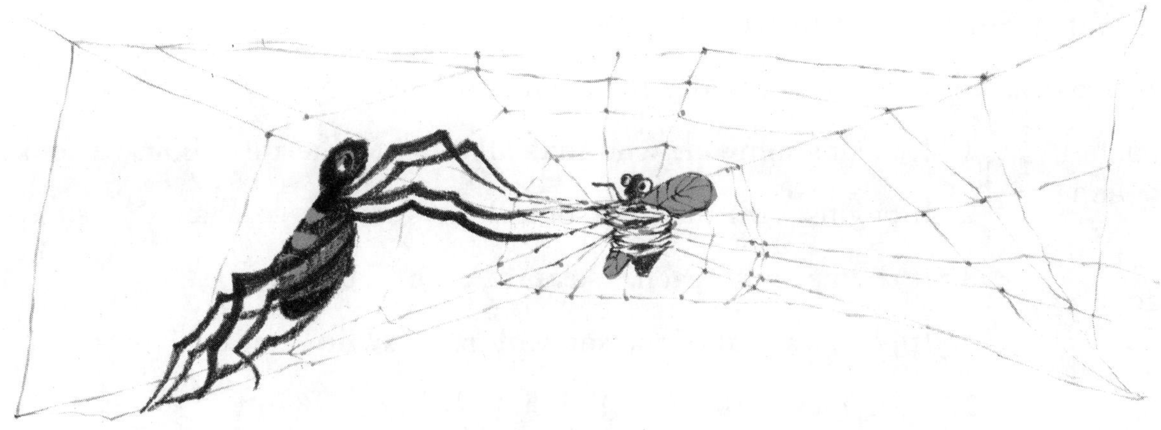

The spider sees the fly. It comes running out. And it does not come to help!

Around and around the fly the spider goes. It winds more sticky threads. It covers the fly all around. Soon the fly cannot move at all!

This is how the spider catches its food.

F-2 Testing Yourself

NUMBER RIGHT 

1. The spider's web is its ____________.

2. What else does the spider use its web for? ________________________

Draw a line under the right answer.

3. The story as a whole is about
   a. how a spider gets its food.
   b. different kinds of spiders.
   c. flies.
   d. a spider's nest.

4. The threads of the spider web are sticky. Yes No Does not say

5. The spider sticks to its web. Yes No Does not say

6. What word in line four of the story means **not thick?** ____________

Getting Ready for the Next Story

SAY AND KNOW	Draw a line under the right word.
each beach	**1.** It means **someone who lives all alone.** **hermit** **house** **book**
tail snail	**2.** It begins with the same sounds as **snow.** **so** **snail** **sun**
it fit	**3.** It rhymes with **each.** **eats** **crab** **beach**
live living	**4.** It is an animal of the sea. **bird** **swim** **crab**
out outside	**5.** It rhymes with **sit.** **if** **fit** **big**
hermit crab	**6.** In forming **living** from **live,** the **e** is **doubled** **kept** **dropped.**
	7. It begins with the same sounds as **crash.** **beach** **crab** **each**
	8. Write the two small words in **outside.** __________ __________

F-3 Moving Day at the Beach

The hermit crab does not build a house. It finds one on the beach. If another crab is living there, it pulls the other out. If the house belongs to a snail, the crab eats the snail. Then it moves in.

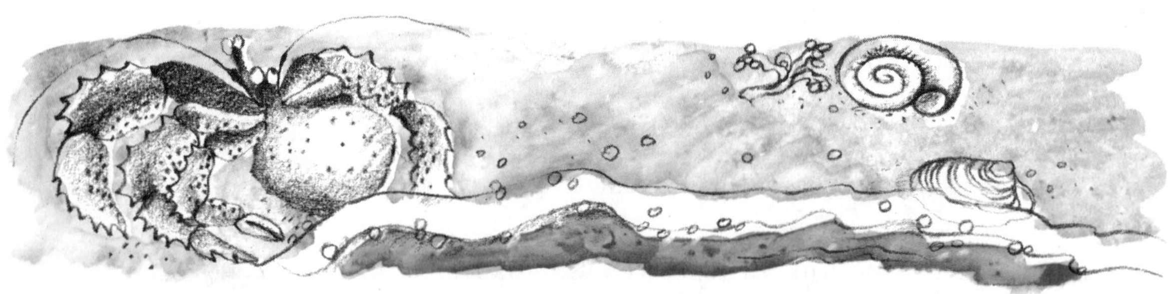

The back parts of the crab are soft. It moves its back end into its new house first of all. If it fits, the crab stays. Only its claws are left outside. It uses its claws for a door.

The hermit crab lives there until it grows too big for this house. Then it moves out. You can see it will not be hard to find another house!

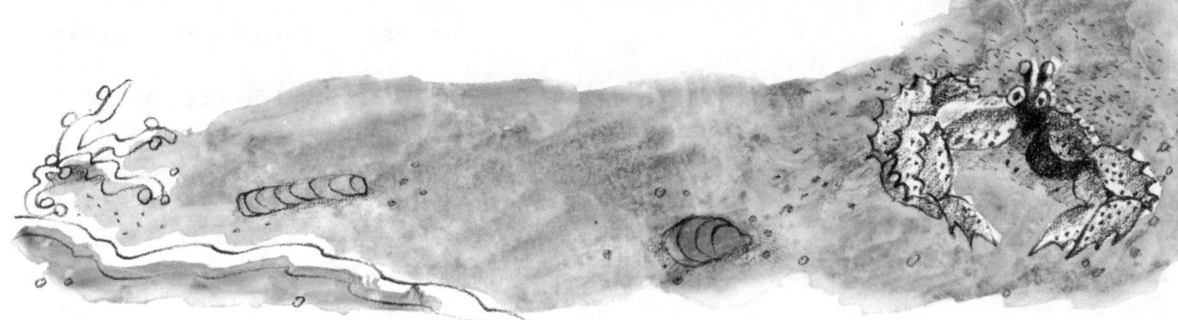

F-3 Testing Yourself **NUMBER RIGHT** 

1. The hermit crab does not build its own __________.

2. Where does the hermit crab find a house? ____________________

Draw a line under the right answer.

3. The story as a whole is about
   a. snails.
   b. eating crabs.
   c. building houses.
   d. a house for the hermit crab.

4. The hermit crab tries on its house to see if it fits.
   Yes No Does not say

5. The hermit crab keeps its claws inside its house.
   Yes No Does not say

6. What word in line six of the story means **not hard?** __________

Getting Ready for the Next Story

SAY AND KNOW

Earth
garbage

planet
materials
recycling
aluminum
plastic

melted

collect
neighborhood

Draw a line under each right answer.

1. Some cans are made of **garbage** **aluminum** **recycling.**
2. It means **gather.** **use** **throw** **collect**
3. It begins with the same sounds as **play.** **put** **plastic** **people**
4. A word for **what things are made of** is **many** **materials** **make.**
5. It means **using materials again.** **are** **red** **recycling**
6. Ice cream **made soft by heat** has **recycled** **melted** **collected.**

F-4 Use It Again—and Again

People used to throw away everything. Then people learned that this was bad for the Earth. Too many good things in the Earth were getting used up. Too much garbage was going into the Earth.

People have learned to take better care of planet Earth. One way is to use materials again. This is called recycling. People are recycling aluminum cans. They are recycling glass bottles. They are recycling things made of paper and plastic.

How is the recycling done? The materials are melted down. Old aluminum is used to make new cans and other things. Old glass is used to make new bottles and other glass things. The same thing happens with old paper and plastic.

Many places collect materials for recycling. Do you know where to go in your neighborhood?

F-4 Testing Yourself

NUMBER RIGHT

1. Using materials again is called ____________________.

2. People are recycling aluminum ____________________.

   Draw a line under the right answer.

3. The story as a whole is about
   a. cleaning up the streets.
   b. recycling materials.
   c. cleaning up your room.
   d. throwing away garbage.

4. All cities collect materials for recycling. Yes No Does not say

5. Old materials are melted to make new things. Yes No Does not say

6. What two words in line six name **the place where we live**?

   ____________________ ____________________

Getting Ready for the Next Story

SAY AND KNOW

drop
falls
flakes

trees
freeze
freezing

know
snow
snowflakes

cover
blanket

Fill in the blanks.

1. Does **falls** rhyme with **flakes?** ____________

2. Does **freeze** rhyme with **trees?** ____________

3. Does a **blanket** keep you warm? ____________

4. Is **snow** cold? ____________

5. Does **snow** rhyme with **now?** ____________

6. What two words put together make **snowflakes?**

____________ ____________

7. Write the word from which **freezing** is made. ____________

F-5 Water, Water Everywhere

In many parts of the world, snow falls every winter. It falls on trees and houses. It covers the ground like a great, white blanket. Like a blanket, too, it keeps things in the ground from freezing.

Snowflakes are made from water in the air. Bits of water are in the air all the time. The little bits get together. They make drops. The drops keep getting bigger. When they are too heavy to stay up any more, they fall. If the air is not very cold, they fall as rain. If the air is freezing, the drops of water freeze as they fall. Then they fall as snow.

F-5 Testing Yourself

NUMBER RIGHT 

1. Snow keeps things in the ground from __________.

2. Snow comes at what time of year? __________

Draw a line under the right answer.

3. The story as a whole is about
   - a. rain.
   - b. winter.
   - c. snow.
   - d. cold weather.

4. When the air is not very cold, water falls as rain. Yes No Does not say

5. Snow falls only when the air is freezing. Yes No Does not say

6. What word in line one of the story means the same as **drops?** __________

Getting Ready for the Next Story

SAY AND KNOW	Draw a line under the right word.
trees forests	1. They grow in forests. **park** **wood** **trees**
	2. It means **to take care of something.** **man** **guard** **belong**
nation national	3. It begins with the same sound as **fire.** **rest** **best** **forest**
	4. It has an **sh** sound, like **push.** **national** **open** **writing**
be belong	5. It rhymes with **should.** **smoke** **smell** **wood**
guard woods	6. It means **a person who guards a forest.** **nation** **ranger** **woods**
ranger people	7. What two words put together make **belong?** ______ ________

F-6 On Guard

There are many forests in our country. In some, no trees may be cut. People may not go hunting. They may not build houses. These are our national forests, or national parks. Such forests belong to everybody.

Forest rangers guard our national forests. They help people who visit the park. They tell people to be careful about making fires.

Rangers must be on guard for signs of smoke. In the woods, a small fire can grow very fast.

Many fires are started each year by people who are not careful. When you are in the woods, be sure your cooking fire is out before you go away.

F-6 Testing Yourself

NUMBER RIGHT

1. In the national forests, people may not build ____________.

2. To whom do our national forests belong? ____________

Draw a line under the right answer.

3. The story as a whole is about
   a. guarding our national forests.
   b. planting trees.
   c. houses in the woods.
   d. cooking in the forest.

4. The ranger watches for signs of smoke. Yes No Does not say

5. Careful people leave only little fires. Yes No Does not say

6. What words in line nine of the story mean **watching for?** ____________

Getting Ready for the Next Story

SAY AND KNOW

life
living

train
trained

hide
guide

owner
blind
care

family
puppy

Draw a line under the right word.

1. It begins with the same sound as **good.** **wood** **guide** **hide**
2. It means **a very young dog.** **pony** **colt** **puppy**
3. It ends with the same sound as **if.** **five** **eye** **life**
4. It rhymes with **air.** **bake** **care** **aid**
5. It is the person who owns a dog. **puppy** **catcher** **owner**
6. It is **the name for people who can not see.** **blink** **blind** **bill**
7. What letters are silent in **guide?** ___ and ___

F-7 Eyes for the Blind

Many blind people have guide dogs that help them. The dog lets its owner know when to cross streets. It shows the blind person where to go when there is something in the way. Guide dogs must know many things.

A guide dog is picked when it is a puppy. For its first year, the dog lives with a family. Its life is like the life of any other dog. The dog must be well cared for. It must be used to people.

After that year, the dog is ready to go to school. There it is trained. It learns to "see" for its owner. That is why some guide dogs are called "seeing-eye" dogs.

F-7 Testing Yourself

NUMBER RIGHT 

1. Guide dogs help people who are __________.

2. When is a guide dog picked? ______________________________

Draw a line under the right answer.

3. The story as a whole is about
  a. blind people.
  b. training a puppy.
  c. sheep dogs.
  d. "seeing-eye" dogs.

4. The first thing a guide dog must learn is to live with a family.
Yes No Does not say

5. A guide dog goes to school. Yes No Does not say

6. What word in line one of the story means **showing the way?** __________

Getting Ready for the Next Story

SAY AND KNOW

many
many-colored

pretty
beautiful
handsome

female
male

woman
women
peahen
peacock

Draw a line under the right word.

1. It means **very pretty.** **feathers** **beautiful** **color**
2. It is a bird. **bee** **fly** **peacock**
3. It rhymes with **tail.** **mate** **male** **late**
4. It ends with the same sound as **male.** **tall** **female** **mate**
5. It means **more than a few.** **two** **any** **many**
6. The last half of **peacock** rhymes with **coke** **lock** **cot.**
7. What two words put together make **handsome**?

__________ __________

F-8 Show-Off

In the world of people, both women and men wear bright clothes. Most people like to dress up! But in the world of birds, the male is the one who wears the bright feathers.

The peacock is a many-colored bird. His feathers are beautiful to see. The peacock knows it, too. He holds his tail feathers high. He opens them like a fan. How handsome he looks! Even his neck has a splash of color.

The female, called a peahen, is brown all over. There is almost no color on her feathers at all.

This is so with all birds. When you see the one with the brightest feathers, you know it is a male.

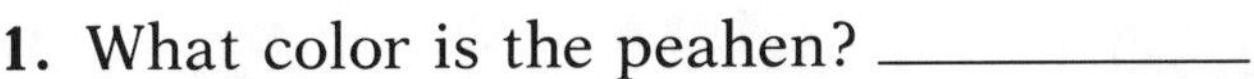

F-8 Testing Yourself

NUMBER RIGHT

1. What color is the peahen? ____________

2. When the peacock opens his tail, what does it look like? ____________

Draw a line under the right answer.

3. The story as a whole is about

a. a fan.
b. a plain bird.
c. a parakeet.
d. a many-colored bird.

4. The peacock is brown. Yes No Does not say

5. In the world of birds, the males are always the brightest ones.
Yes No Does not say

6. What word in line eight of the story means **good-looking?** ____________

The Jay and the Peacock

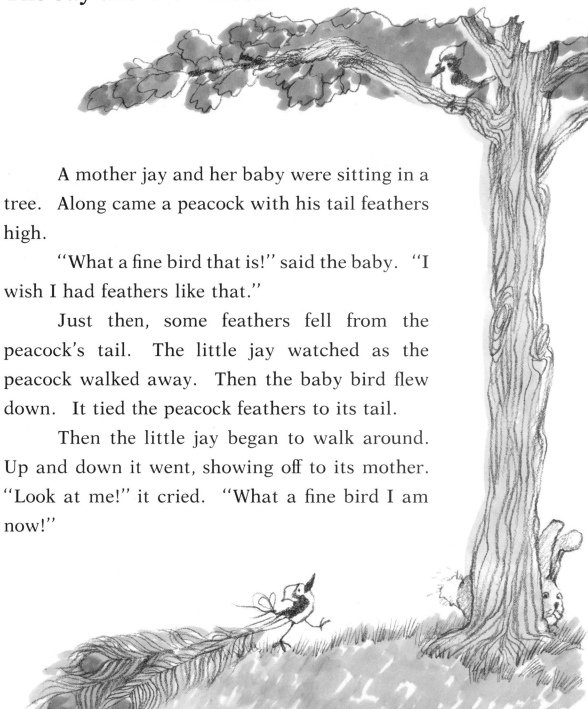

A mother jay and her baby were sitting in a tree. Along came a peacock with his tail feathers high.

"What a fine bird that is!" said the baby. "I wish I had feathers like that."

Just then, some feathers fell from the peacock's tail. The little jay watched as the peacock walked away. Then the baby bird flew down. It tied the peacock feathers to its tail.

Then the little jay began to walk around. Up and down it went, showing off to its mother. "Look at me!" it cried. "What a fine bird I am now!"

The peacock heard the little jay and came flying back. "Those are my feathers!" said the peacock. And he started to pull them out.

"Stop! You are hurting me!" cried the little jay. But the peacock picked and pulled until all the feathers were out. Then he marched away with his beautiful tail held high.

"What a cross old thing that peacock is!" said the little jay. "He is not a fine bird at all!"

"What about you?" said the mother. "You think that wearing peacock feathers makes a peacock out of you. But it takes more than fine feathers to make a fine bird."

Thinking It Over

1. Was the peacock a fine bird?
2. Was the peacock a fine-looking bird?
3. Is a fine-looking person always a fine person?
4. Can a person who is not fine-looking be a fine person?

Getting Ready for the Next Story

SAY AND KNOW

silver
dollar
holes
rows
bones
skeleton
live
die

Draw a line under the right word.

1. It means the part that is all **bones.** **dog** **dollar** **skeleton**
2. It has the same vowel sound as **holes.** **rows** **cow** **found**
3. It rhymes with **knows.** **bones** **rows** **cows**
4. It rhymes with **give.** **gave** **live** **die**
5. It is a piece of money. **sand** **buy** **dollar**
6. It is a shiny, white metal. **hole** **silver** **gold**

G-1 Skeleton of the Sea

Have you ever seen a silver dollar? If so, you can guess where the sand dollar gets its name.

Sand dollars live on the bottom of the sea, in the sand. They are covered with little hairs.

There are rows of holes on their undersides. There are holes on their top sides, too. Out of these holes, the sand dollar sticks its feet.

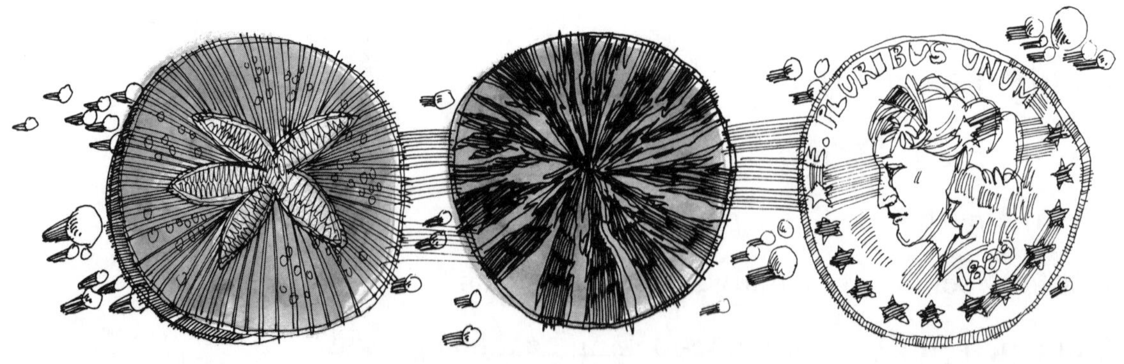

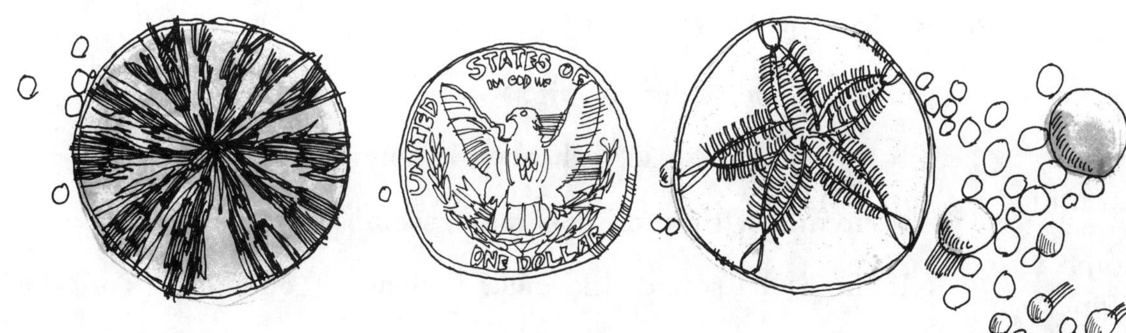

Sometimes the sand dollar gets turned upside-down. Then it sticks out its feet on that side. It turns right over again!

When sand dollars die, they wash up out of the water. It is only a skeleton you find when you pick one up by the sea.

G-1 Testing Yourself

NUMBER RIGHT

1. Sand dollars live at the bottom of the ____________.
2. What does the sand dollar stick its feet out of?

____

Draw a line under the right answer.

3. The story as a whole is about
   a. a sand dollar.
   b. a silver dollar.
   c. finding money.
   d. bones.
4. The sand dollar has many feet. Yes No Does not say
5. The sand dollars sell for one dollar each. Yes No Does not say
6. What word in lines five and six of the story means the same as **bottoms?**

____

Getting Ready for the Next Story

SAY AND KNOW	Draw a line under the right word.
sound ground	1. It is a kind of noise. **hear** **listen** **hum**
	2. It rhymes with **hum.** **same** **seem** **some**
some hum	3. Its first part sounds like **sick.** **cicada** **chicken** **cork**
	4. It rhymes with **rugs.** **rows** **bugs** **ruts**
born cicada summer	5. It is **an insect.** **cicada** **chicken** **hum**
	6. It rhymes with **ground.** **some** **summer** **sound**
bugs insects	7. Write the name of the insect in the word **plants.** ________________

G-2 Ho-Hum

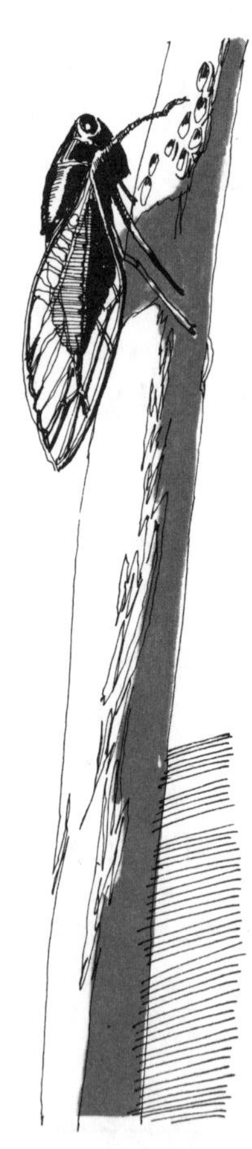

On hot summer days, you will often hear insects humming in the trees. One insect you may hear is the cicada (sə kā′ də).

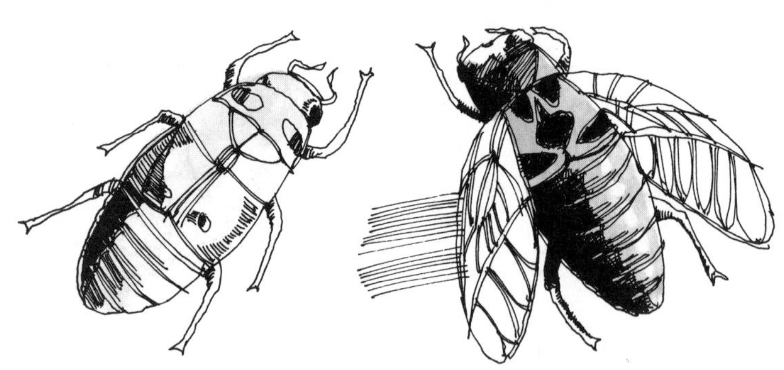

Cicadas lay their eggs in twigs. They cut little holes in the wood. Then they put their eggs in them.

Soon the baby cicadas are born. They fall to the ground. They get their food from roots and plants near the tree.

When they grow up, they fly into trees to make their nests. It is the father cicada who makes the humming noise. He hums when it is time to start a family.

Cicadas are not insects that we like. The holes they make will often hurt a tree.

G-2 Testing Yourself

NUMBER RIGHT 

1. The cicada is an ___________.

2. Where do cicadas lay their eggs? ___________

Draw a line under the right answer.

3. The story as a whole is about
   a. helpful insects.
   b. a winter bug.
   c. a noisy insect.
   d. roots and plants.

4. Cicada babies eat roots and plants. Yes No Does not say

5. Cicadas are good for trees. Yes No Does not say

6. What word in line two of the story means the same as **bugs?** ___________

Getting Ready for the Next Story

SAY AND KNOW

caterpillar

milk
silk

spider
spring

safe
tent

branch
world

Draw a line under the right word.

1. It is **an insect.** **bird** **caterpillar** **cat**
2. It rhymes with **milk.** **sun** **caterpillar** **silk**
3. It begins with the same sounds as **spring.** **side** **spider** **sing**
4. It has the same vowel sound as **baby.** **bug** **big** **safe**
5. It is part of a tree. **tent** **silk** **branch**
6. It ends with the same sounds as **world.** **word** **whirl** **curled**
7. Write the two little words in **inside.** ________ ________
8. Write the first little word in **caterpillar.** ________

G-3 House of Silk

In springtime, trees are full of caterpillars. Caterpillars live in a large family. It takes many leaves to feed all the caterpillars. Sometimes they eat all the leaves on a branch! They may kill a tree.

Tent caterpillars make their house of silk. The silk comes from inside the caterpillars. When a caterpillar makes silk, it moves its head from

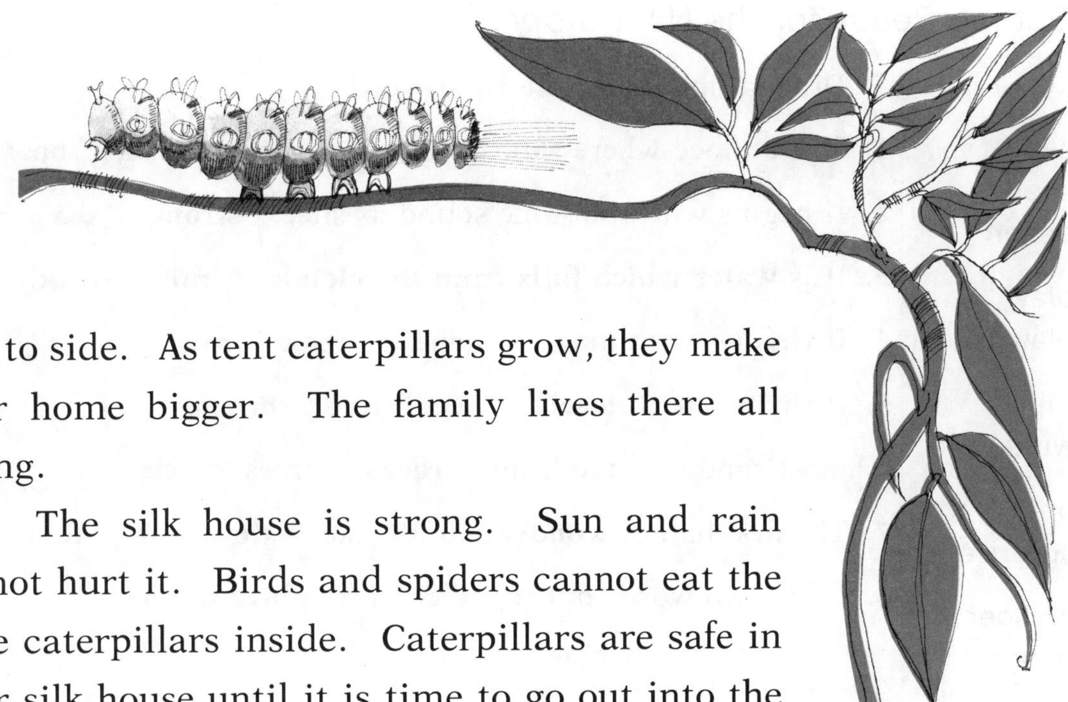

side to side. As tent caterpillars grow, they make their home bigger. The family lives there all spring.

The silk house is strong. Sun and rain cannot hurt it. Birds and spiders cannot eat the little caterpillars inside. Caterpillars are safe in their silk house until it is time to go out into the world.

G-3 Testing Yourself

NUMBER RIGHT 

1. Caterpillars eat ____________.

2. What does the tent caterpillar make its nest of? ____________

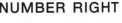

Draw a line under the right answer.

3. The story as a whole is about
- a. tent caterpillars.
- b. making silk.
- c. birds and spiders.
- d. many kinds of insects.

4. The silk house is very strong. Yes No Does not say

5. Caterpillars live in the silk house all their lives.
Yes No Does not say

6. What word in line six of the story means the same as **home?** ____________

Getting Ready for the Next Story

SAY AND KNOW

sand
shell
beach

play
playground

rain
wind

break
surprise

wonder
rock

Draw a line under the right word.

1. It is a place where sand is found. **bed** **beach** **boat**
2. It begins with the same sound as **she.** **strong** **sea** **shell**
3. It is **water which falls from the clouds.** **rain** **wind** **salt**
4. It rhymes with **make.** **rope** **break** **row**
5. It rhymes with **teach.** **bee** **tree** **beach**
6. Most sand is made from **rocks** **trees** **bees.**
7. The first half of **wonder** sounds like **tin** **one** **tone.**
8. What two words put together make **playground?**

__________ __________

G-4 Sand

It is fun to play with sand. We play with it at home in sandboxes. We play with it at the beach. We play with it at parks and playgrounds, too. All your life, you have played with sand. But did you ever stop to wonder where it comes from?

Most sand comes from rocks. Rocks wear away and make sand. They wear away in many ways. Strong waves roll over rocks and break them up. Rain, wind, and ice break rocks, too. Some sand is made of bits of shells, all ground up.

Isn't it surprising that long ago something as soft as sand was part of a hard, hard rock?

G-4 Testing Yourself **NUMBER RIGHT** 

1. Most children like to play with __________.

2. What can rain and wind and ice do to rocks? ____________________

Draw a line under the right answer.

3. The story as a whole is about
   a. playgrounds.
   b. storms.
   c. how rocks were made.
   d. how sand came to be.

4. When rocks break up, sand is made. Yes No Does not say

5. All rocks break up in the same way. Yes No Does not say

6. What word in line three of the story means **the shore of a sea or a lake?**

____

Getting Ready for the Next Story

SAY AND KNOW

poison
ivy
woods

branch
bright
orange
itch

soap
hope

careful
cover

Draw a line under the right word.

1. It is something that can hurt you. **grass** **food** **poison**
2. It is the name of a plant. **animal** **ivy** **seed**
3. It ends with the same sound as **catch.** **cat** **itch** **that**
4. It has the same vowel sound as **dive.** **ivy** **fill** **skin**
5. It rhymes with **hope.** **hurt** **top** **soap**
6. Write the four-letter word in **careful.** ____________
7. Write a word from the list to rhyme with **tight.** ____________

G-5 Be on the Lookout

When you go walking in the woods, be on the lookout! Watch out for poison ivy. Poison ivy is a plant that hurts people. It can make your skin itch for a long, long time.

Poison ivy has green leaves. They shine. Each one branches out to make three small

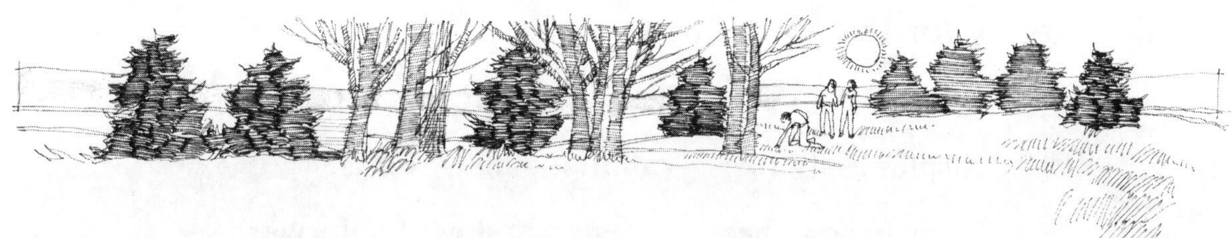

leaves. In the fall, they turn bright red or orange. People often pick the leaves because they are so pretty!

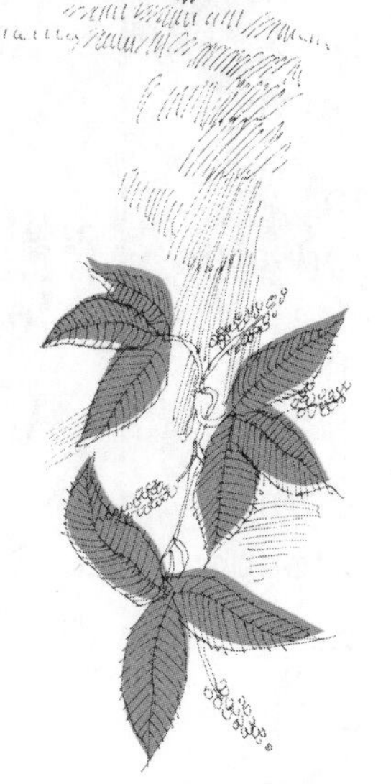

Find out if poison ivy grows where you live. If it does, be careful! Cover your arms and legs when you go into the woods. When you come home, wash your skin with strong soap. Don't let poison ivy poison you!

G-5 Testing Yourself

NUMBER RIGHT ______

1. Poison ivy can hurt your __________.

2. What color are poison ivy leaves in summer? __________

Draw a line under the right answer.

3. The story as a whole is about
   a. helpful plants.
   b. a walk in the woods.
   c. poison ivy.
   d. a pretty leaf.

4. If you go where there is poison ivy, it is good to wash with soap when you come home. Yes No Does not say

5. Poison ivy leaves branch into five small leaves from each big one. Yes No Does not say

6. What word in the last line of the story means **able to kill or harm?**

____

Getting Ready for the Next Story

SAY AND KNOW	
slow slowly for forward fast faster strong stronger air airplane	Draw a line under the right word. 1. Airplanes fly like **rabbits** **air** **birds.** 2. It means **on ahead.** **faster** **slowly** **forward** 3. It rhymes with **last.** **slow** **fast** **strong** 4. It has the same vowel sound as **low.** **top** **slow** **slide** 5. Write the first small word in **forward.** ________ 6. **Stronger** is made by adding what to **strong?** ________ 7. What four-letter word is in **slowly?** ________

G-6 High in the Sky

Birds can fly far. They can fly fast. They can fly for a long, long time. People have watched birds fly. That is how they learned to make airplanes.

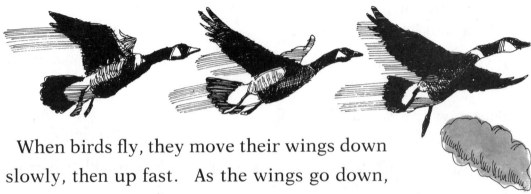

When birds fly, they move their wings down very slowly, then up fast. As the wings go down, the bird moves forward.

When the wings move down, the feathers are together. Air moves fast over the top of them. It moves faster than the air below. But the air just under the wing is stronger than the faster moving air on top. It is strong enough to push the bird up. It keeps the bird in the air. This is how birds stay up and fly.

G-6 Testing Yourself

NUMBER RIGHT

1. People watched birds fly to learn how to make ___________.
2. Which way does the bird move when the wings go down?

____

Draw a line under the right answer.

3. The story as a whole is about
   a. airplanes.
   b. the wind.
   c. the sky.
   d. how birds fly.
4. When the wings go down, the feathers are together.
   Yes No Does not say
5. The air moves fast over the wings when they go down.
   Yes No Does not say
6. What word in line one of the story means **to move through the air?** ________

Getting Ready for the Next Story

SAY AND KNOW

stay
obey

manners

out
outside

young

some
come

Draw a line under the right word.

1. If you say **please** and **thank you,** you have good
friends **manners** **hands.**

2. It rhymes with **some.** **told** **mind** **come**

3. It begins with the same sounds as **stop.** **pats** **has** **stay**

4. It means **not old.** **out** **kind** **young**

5. Write the three-letter word in **outside.** ___________

G-7 "Come, Sit, Stay"

Does your dog have good manners?

A dog with good manners will obey. It will not jump on people. It will sit when told. When you call, the dog will come. If you tell it to, it will stay. A dog with good manners will wait outside the door and not bark.

It is not hard to teach your dog good manners. But you should begin when it is young. First, teach the puppy to obey when you say, "Come" or "Sit." Then teach the dog "Stop," "Down," and "No."

Your dog wants to please you. Your dog wants you to like it. Your voice will tell it when it has done something well.

G-7 Testing Yourself

NUMBER RIGHT 

1. A dog can be trained to have good ________.

2. You should start to train a dog when it is ________.

Draw a line under the right answer.

3. The story as a whole is about
- a. how dogs bark.
- b. good manners for dogs.
- c. stop signs.
- d. feeding your pet.

4. A dog can learn to do only two or three tricks.
Yes No Does not say

5. It is hard to train dogs because they do not like to learn.
Yes No Does not say

6. What word in line two of the story means **to do as you are told?** ________

Getting Ready for the Next Story

SAY AND KNOW	Draw a line under the right word.
mate wolves den	**1.** It is **a place where wild animals live.** **tag** **herds** **den** **2.** They are a pair. **pups** **leader** **mates**
tug-of-war tag	**3.** What is the basic word in **leader?** __________ **4.** It is **a pulling game.** **tug-of-war** **tag** **attack**
leader attack	**5.** It means **more than one wolf.** **wolfs** **wolves** **herds**
herds	**6.** Does **attack** mean the same as **leader?** __________

G-8 The Gray King and Queen

King and Queen are large gray wolves. They are mates. This pair will stay together all of their lives.

King and Queen have four wolf pups. When the pups are little, they stay in their den home. The mother and father bring them small animals and fish to eat.

The pups play together like children. They box and play tug-of-war. They play tag. They chase each other.

King is the leader of the wolf pack. He will train the best pup to be the leader some day.

People are only beginning to learn about wolves. They do not attack people. Wolves kill sick animals. By killing the old and weak, they help many animal herds stay strong.

G-8 Testing Yourself

NUMBER RIGHT ____

1. Wolf mates stay together all of their ____________.

2. Baby wolves eat small animals and ____________.

   Draw a line under the right answer.

3. The story as a whole is about
   a. how a wolf family lives.
   b. how wolves kill animals.
   c. having a wolf for a pet.
   d. wolf pups playing together.

4. All wolves live where there are hills and trees. Yes No Does not say

5. Wolf pups play together like children. Yes No Does not say

6. What word in line eleven of the story means **the one that leads?** ____________

The Boy Who Cried Wolf

A farmer brought a new boy to the fields to care for the sheep.

"If a wolf comes, call as loud as you can," said the farmer, "and I will come running."

The boy soon found he did not like being all alone. One morning he thought of a way to have some fun. He put his hands to his mouth. He called, "The wolf! The wolf!"

The farmer came running. "Where is the wolf?" the farmer asked.

"It was only a joke," said the boy. "The wolf was not here."

"Let us have no more jokes," said the farmer.

The next day, the boy again grew tired of being alone and he called, "Wolf! Wolf!" Again the farmer came. Again there was no wolf.

The next day, a wolf did come. The boy called for help as loud as he could.

The farmer heard but did not come. The farmer thought it was just another joke.

With no one to stop him, the wolf killed two of the sheep. When the farmer found out, the boy lost his job.

"If you tell lies," said the farmer, "no one will ever believe you. Not even when you are telling the truth!"

Thinking It Over

1. If you tell lies sometimes, will people believe anything you say?
2. Will they believe everything you say?
3. If you do not tell lies, will people believe everything you say?

Getting Ready for the Next Story

SAY AND KNOW

sea
seashell

soon
moon

round
snail
native
wampum

Draw a line under the right word.

1. They are **the first people to live in a place.**
   natives **traders** **snails**
2. It rhymes with **spoon.** **soon** **shell** **bones**
3. It begins with the same sound as **warm.**
   money **moon** **wampum**
4. It rhymes with **tale.** **bean** **snail** **laugh**
5. What two words put together make **seashell?**

   __________ __________

H-1 By the Sea

Have you ever looked for seashells by the sea? The shells you find along the sand have nothing in them. But once they did! Once they were the coverings of living animals.

There are many kinds of animals that live in shells. Snails are one kind. They carry their shells on their backs. Another kind of animal has two sides to its shell. Some can go in and out of their shells whenever they want to.

Some shells are round, like moons. Some shells are long, like teeth. Most shells shine and have very pretty colors.

Long ago, both the settlers and the Native Americans used strings of shells as money. They called this shell money "wampum."

H-1 Testing Yourself **NUMBER RIGHT** 

1. Shells come from animals that live in the __________.

2. What is one kind of animal that lives in a shell? __________

Draw a line under the right answer.

3. The story as a whole is about
   a. snails. c. life in the sea.
   b. seashells. d. shell money.

4. Seashells are always round. Yes No Does not say

5. Long ago, some people used shells for money. Yes No Does not say

6. What word in line ten of the story means **not straight at all?** __________

Getting Ready for the Next Story

SAY AND KNOW

long
strong

grass
hop
grasshopper

air
pair

rub
rubbing

wing

Fill in the blanks.

1. Does **long** begin with the same sound as **strong?** ____________

2. Does **air** rhyme with **pair?** ____________

3. Does **pair** mean **two of a kind?** ____________

4. Are two wings a **pair** of wings? ____________

5. What must be doubled to make **rub** into **rubbing?** ____________

6. What two words put together make **grasshopper?**

____________ ____________

H-2 Hop, Jump, Fly

A grasshopper has long, strong legs. It can jump and hop very high. Many people are surprised to find that a grasshopper flies, too. Not only does it fly, but it has two pairs of wings.

Under its wings, it has ears. But it has no voice. No voice at all!

The grasshopper makes a sound by rubbing its top wings together. The sound comes from rubbing a leg and a wing together, too.

Grasshoppers live in the grass. Most of them are green. Their color helps them to hide in the grass. When they want to get away fast, they hop. Can you tell why they are called grass-hoppers?

H-2 Testing Yourself

NUMBER RIGHT

1. A grasshopper's legs are long and ________.

2. How many pairs of wings has a grasshopper? ________

Draw a line under the right answer.

3. The story as a whole is about
   a. flies.
   b. a singing bug.
   c. the grasshopper.
   d. a red insect.

4. The grasshopper has ears under its wings. Yes No Does not say

5. The grasshopper makes sounds with its voice. Yes No Does not say

6. What word in line two of the story means **not low?** ________

Getting Ready for the Next Story

SAY AND KNOW

box
wax

home
comb
honey
honeycomb

dive
hive

to
together

Draw a line under the right word.

1. It is **a place where bees live.** **together** **hive** **family**
2. It is **something bees make.** **flowers** **honey** **candy**
3. It rhymes with **dome.** **goat** **most** **comb**
4. It ends with the same sound as **box.** **bee** **we** **wax**
5. It sounds like **two.** **snow** **to** **took**
6. What two words put together make **honeycomb?**

   __________ __________

7. What letter is silent in **comb?** __________

H-3 Home, Sweet Home

Honeybees make their homes of wax. They build their homes in all sorts of places. Hollow trees and rocks are the kinds of places they like. They will also build a home in a box.

The bees' home is called a hive. It takes many bees to build a hive. They live and work together as one big family.

In the beehive, or "house," are many little "rooms." The bees make these "rooms" from wax. The wax comes from inside the bees. In these "rooms," the bees store their honey. The little wax rooms, all together, are called honeycombs.

Honeycombs are very good to eat. Try one sometime and see!

H-3 Testing Yourself

NUMBER RIGHT

1. What do honeybees make their homes of? ____________

2. What is a bee's home called? ____________

Draw a line under the right answer.

3. The story as a whole is about

a. animal houses.
b. bread and honey.
c. a wasp.
d. the homes of honeybees.

4. The rooms filled with honey are called honeycombs.

Yes No Does not say

5. A honeycomb is good to eat. Yes No Does not say

6. What word in line two of the story means **kinds?** ____________

Getting Ready for the Next Story

SAY AND KNOW	Draw a line under the right word.
friend friendly	**1.** It is a small animal. **bear** **squirrel** **gray**
	2. It has the same vowel sound as **far.** **boat** **sharp** **soon**
park sharp	**3.** It has the same vowel sound as **fly.** **lit** **feel** **bite**
	4. It ends with the same sound as **trunk.** **tree** **park** **remember**
bite right	**5.** It has the same vowel sound as **fur.** **squirrel** **sharp** **share**
remember	**6. To remember** is **not to** **learn** **forget** **bite.**
squirrel	**7.** It rhymes with **lend.** **plan** **friend** **tin**

H-4 A Funny Kind of Thanks

Gray squirrels are friendly little animals. You will often see them in a park. They are quick to learn that people like them. They will come up to your house for food. Sometimes they will come to open windows.

It is easy to make friends with gray squirrels. They will come right up and take food from your hand. But watch out! It is all right to put out food for squirrels. But never, never feed them from your hand. Squirrels have sharp teeth. And they bite! They may bite the hand that feeds them.

So, remember! When you give food to a squirrel, put it on the ground.

H-4 Testing Yourself

NUMBER RIGHT 

1. Gray squirrels are friendly ______________.

2. What is one place where you will often see squirrels? __________

Draw a line under the right answer.

3. The story as a whole is about
   a. feeding squirrels.
   b. walking in the park.
   c. peanuts.
   d. an unfriendly animal.

4. You should feed squirrels from your hand. Yes No Does not say

5. Squirrels have sharp teeth. Yes No Does not say

6. What word in the next-to-last line of the story means **to think about something again?** __________

Getting Ready for the Next Story

SAY AND KNOW

dead
without
vegetables
animals
earth
soil
bits
mix
together
ground

Draw a line under the right word.

1. It is what all of us live on. **sky** **water** **earth**
2. It has the same vowel sound as **boy.** **low** **animal** **soil**
3. It has four syllables. **without** **animals** **vegetables**
4. It rhymes with **fix.** **this** **sick** **mix**
5. To beat eggs and milk together is to **plant** **soil** **mix.**
6. Write the four-letter word in **without.** ____________

H-5 Good Earth

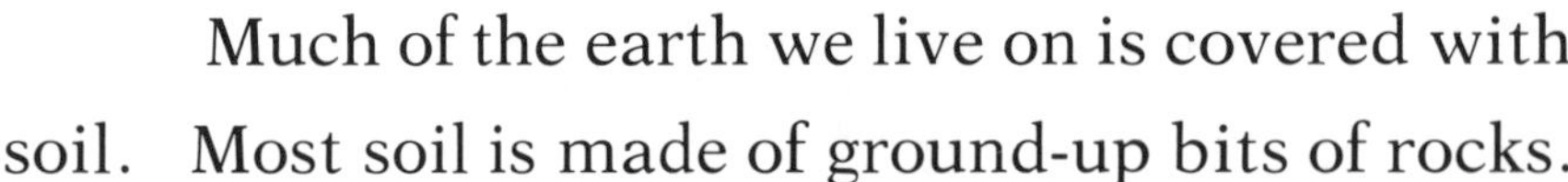

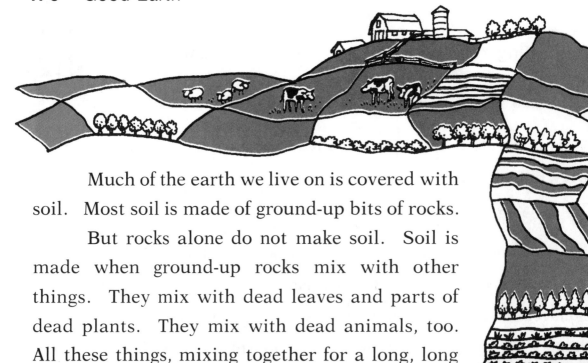

Much of the earth we live on is covered with soil. Most soil is made of ground-up bits of rocks.

But rocks alone do not make soil. Soil is made when ground-up rocks mix with other things. They mix with dead leaves and parts of dead plants. They mix with dead animals, too. All these things, mixing together for a long, long time, make soil.

Most of the food we eat grows in soil. Our vegetables grow in soil. Our fruits do, too. The grasses which our animals eat must have soil to grow in. Without soil, we could not grow anything to eat. We could not live without soil.

H-5 Testing Yourself

NUMBER RIGHT 

1. Much of our earth is covered with ___________.
2. What makes up much of our soil?

____

Draw a line under the right answer.

3. The story as a whole is about
   a. growing vegetables.
   b. rocks.
   c. how soil came to be.
   d. dead leaves.
4. Fruits grow in soil, but vegetables grow in water.
   Yes No Does not say
5. Without soil, we would have to grow our food on the grass.
   Yes No Does not say
6. What word in line five of the story means **beat** or **shake all together?**

____

Getting Ready for the Next Story

SAY AND KNOW

pine
pineapple
points
middle
juicy
fruit
cover
covering
grow
ground

Draw a line under the right word.

1. It is a kind of fruit. **eat** **vegetable** **pineapple**
2. It begins with the same sound as **jump.** **put** **keep** **juicy**
3. It has the same vowel sound as **oil.** **fruit** **point** **pick**
4. It has the same vowel sound as **cup.** **cover** **move** **grow**
5. It has the long sound of **o.** **ground** **grow** **point**
6. What two words put together make **pineapple?**

__________ __________

H-6 Sweet to Eat

Pineapple is a sweet fruit that grows only in hot countries. It does not grow on trees, as some fruit does. It grows up from the ground. The tops may be cut off and planted. The pineapple plant grows about two feet (about 60 centimeters) high.

The pineapple looks like a large pine cone. It has a hard, brown covering. Its leaves have points. Inside it is yellow and juicy. The middle part is hard, and is not used for canning. But the middle part is sweet! Next time you have fresh pineapple, try a piece of the hard middle part.

Canned or fresh, the pineapple is a good fruit to eat.

H-6 Testing Yourself

NUMBER RIGHT 

1. Pineapple is a kind of ________.
2. In what kind of countries do pineapples grow?

____

Draw a line under the right answer.

3. The story as a whole is about
   a. a sweet fruit.
   b. the fruit of a tree.
   c. a pine cone.
   d. a vegetable.
4. You can eat pineapple canned but not fresh. Yes No Does not say
5. The pineapple plant grows about ten feet high. Yes No Does not say
6. What word in line two of the story means **to get bigger and bigger?** ________

Getting Ready for the Next Story

SAY AND KNOW

marathon
Olympics
especially
barefoot
Ethiopia
Africa
train
runners

Draw a line under the right word.

1. It is a long race. **many** **run** **marathon**
2. To **get ready to do something** is to **believe** **run** **train.**
3. It is a country in Africa. **Olympics** **Abebe** **Ethiopia**
4. It means **without shoes or socks.** **buy** **barefoot** **marathon**
5. It has many games and sporting events. **marathon** **Olympics** **runners**
6. **People who race on foot** are **runners** **ran** **won.**

H-7 The Long Run

A marathon is a very long running race. There is always a marathon in the Olympics.

It is very hard to run a marathon. It is especially hard to run a marathon barefoot. But that is what Abebe Bikila (ah-BEE-bee bih-KEE-lah) did in 1960.

Abebe was used to running. He lived in a mountain town in Ethiopia, Africa. He got from one place to another by running. When he was ready, he began to train for the marathon.

Abebe had wanted to buy new running shoes. But none of the shoes fit him well. So Abebe ran barefoot. And he won! He ran the fastest time ever in the Olympics marathon.

Abebe was the first black man from Africa to win the marathon. After him, many others from Africa went on to be the best runners.

Abebe won another Olympics marathon, too. He ran faster than his first time. But this time he had his shoes on!

H-7 Testing Yourself

NUMBER RIGHT

1. The marathon is a long ____________________.

2. Abebe Bikila won his first marathon ____________________.

Draw a line under the right answer.

3. The story as a whole is about
   a. one marathon.
   b. all the Olympics.
   c. living in Ethiopia, Africa.
   d. Abebe and his marathons.

4. Abebe was the fastest of all in two marathons. Yes No Does not say

5. No one has run faster than Abebe Bikila. Yes No Does not say

6. What word in line four of the story means **in a special way**?

____

Getting Ready for the Next Story

SAY AND KNOW

husky
Inuit
huskies

snowshoes

bark
howl

trained
lead

Draw a line under each right answer or fill in the blank.

1. It is a person who lives in the cold lands of the North. **people** **Inuit** **bark**
2. It is a loud noise. **hole** **howl** **high**
3. It means **to show the way.** **last** **first** **lead**
4. It is a **dog that lives in cold places.** **bark** **husky** **Inuit**
5. This word rhymes with **dark.** **howl** **lead** **bark**
6. Write the second four-letter word in **snowshoe.** ____________
7. What word in the list rhymes with **owl?** ____________

H-8 Snow Dog

Husky dogs are strong and they have heavy coats. This is because they live with the Inuit people in very cold places. Huskies work for the Inuit, pulling their sleds over snow and ice.

Huskies have large feet. Their feet are covered with long, heavy hair. These hair-covered feet are like snowshoes. They help the dog to stay on top when the snow is deep and soft.

Many of these dogs do not bark. They put back their heads and howl.

Huskies are trained to pull long sleds. Many dogs work together. The first dog is called a lead dog. It shows the other dogs what to do.

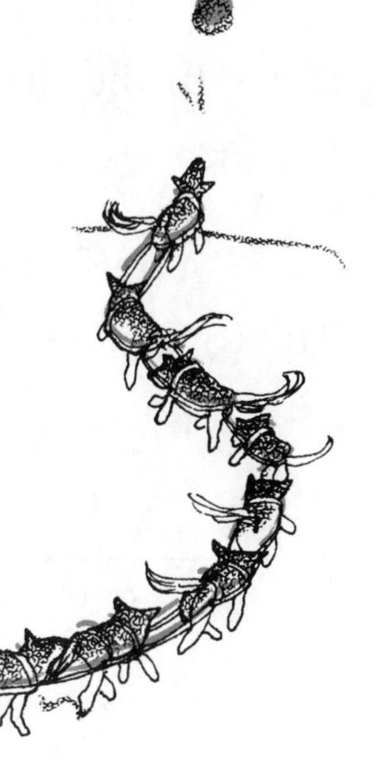

H-8 Testing Yourself **NUMBER RIGHT**

1. Husky dogs have heavy coats to protect them from the ________________.

2. Their hair-covered feet are like ____________________.

Draw a line under the right answer.

3. The story as a whole is about
   a. a house pet.
   b. huskies.
   c. sleds.
   d. snowshoes.

4. The husky is trained to pull long sleds. Yes No Does not say

5. Huskies have short, thin hair. Yes No Does not say

6. What word in the next-to-last line of the story means **to be in front**?

____

Keeping Track of the Number Right

1. The first chart can be filled in after each test. In the first square, write the total right for the first test in Unit A.

A perfect total score for Unit A would be 48. The total possible for all tests would be 384.

Tests	A	B	C	Units D	E	F	G	H	
1									
2									
3									
4									
5									
6									
7									
8									Total
Total									

2. To begin the second chart, look back over the test pages for Unit A. Count the number of times Question 1 was answered right. Put that number in the first square. Continue for each question in each unit.

These figures tell you what you need to know to fill in the graphs on the next page.

A perfect score for all tests in each unit would be 48.

	Units								
Questions	A	B	C	D	E	F	G	H	Total
1									
2									
3									
4									
5									
6									
Total									

Keeping Track of Growth

Study this sample graph. To record the score for Unit A, put a dot on the line beside the number which tells how often Question 4 was answered right. Do the same for Units B, C, and so on. Draw a line to join the dots. The line will show how this reading skill is growing.

Notice that each graph records the progress made on one question. See how this reader improved in answering Question 4 in each unit except Unit E.

Diagnostic Progress Records

Sample

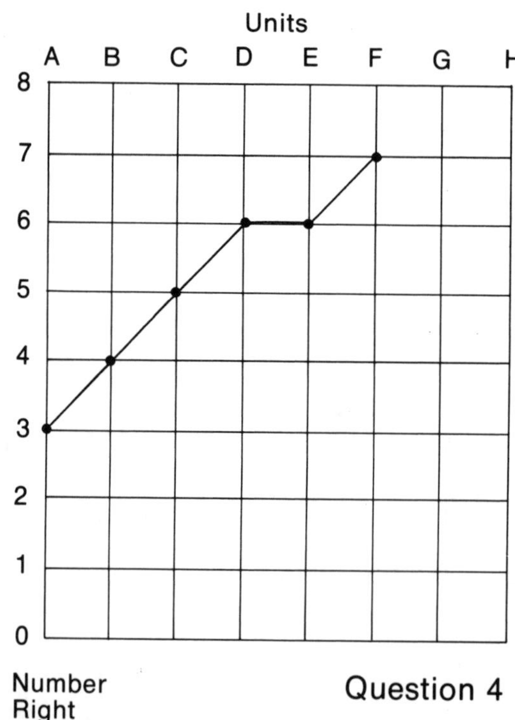

Giving Details

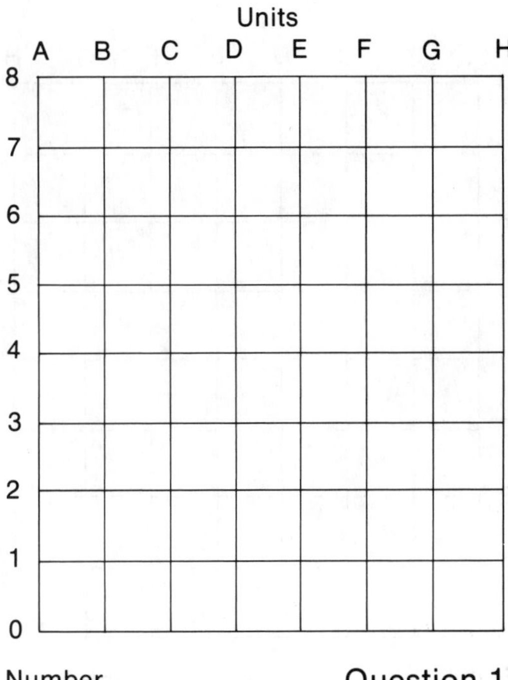

Question 1

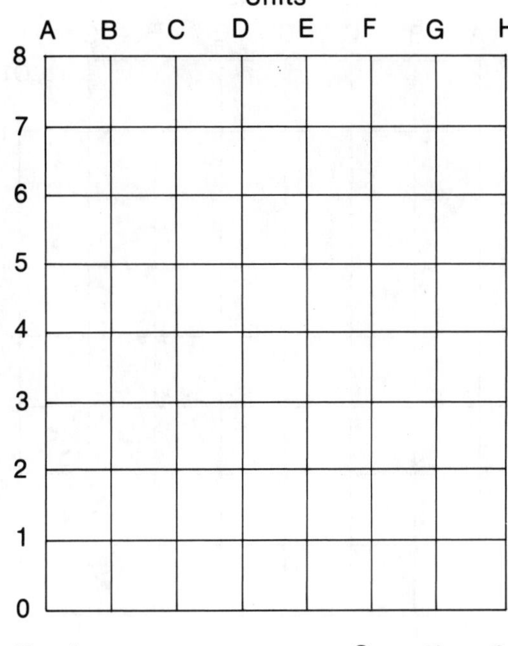

Question 2

Seeing the Meaning of the Whole

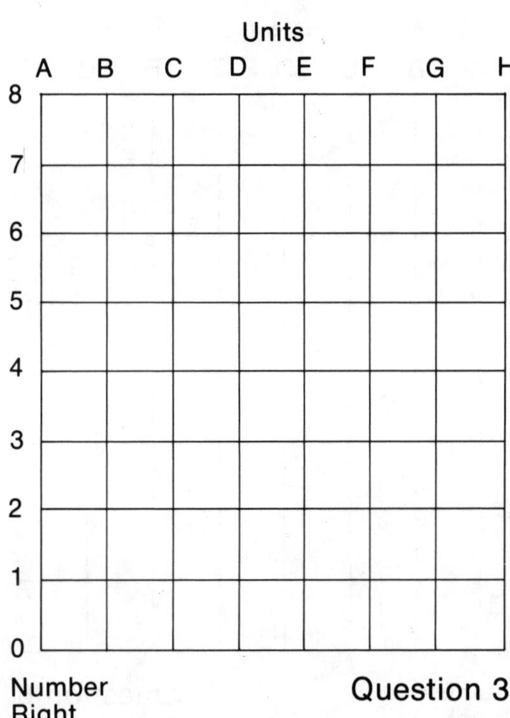

Question 3

Checking on Ideas

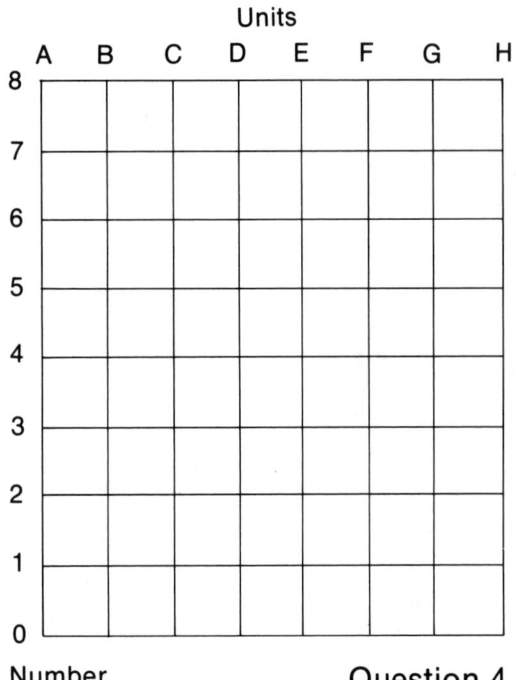

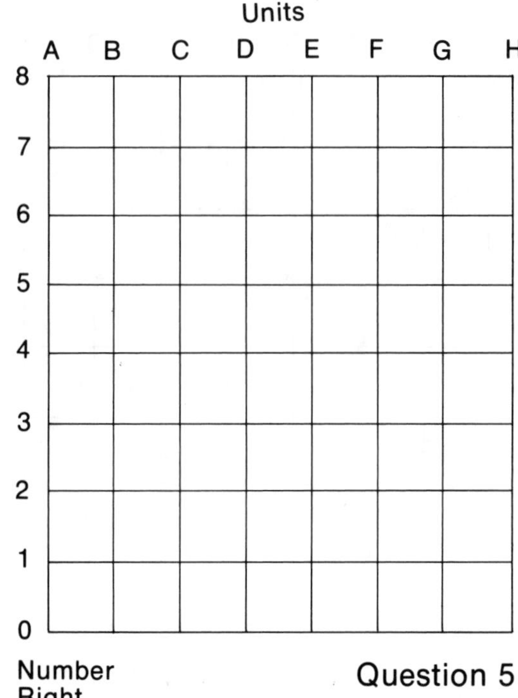

Understanding Words

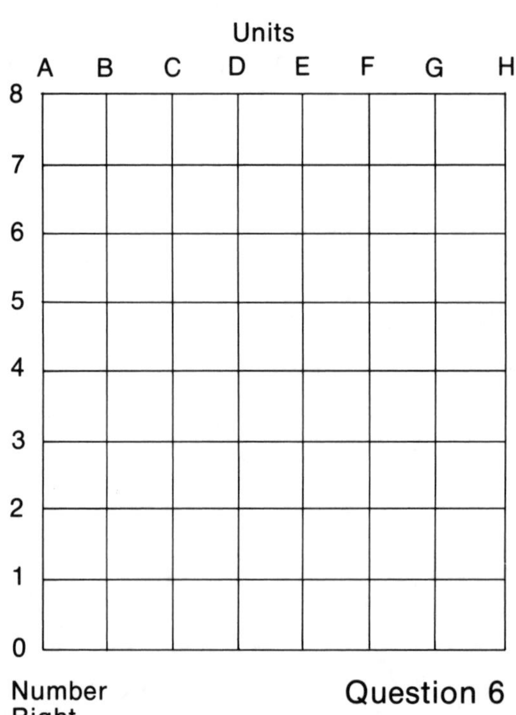

Selling Online with Drupal e-Commerce

Walk through the creation of an online store with Drupal's e-Commerce module

Michael Peacock

BIRMINGHAM - MUMBAI

Selling Online with Drupal e-Commerce

First published: March 2008

Production Reference: 1180308

Published by Packt Publishing Ltd.
32 Lincoln Road
Olton
Birmingham, B27 6PA, UK.

ISBN 978-1-847194-06-0

`www.packtpub.com`

Cover Image by Nilesh R. Mohite (`nilpreet2000@yahoo.co.in`)

Credits

Author

Michael Peacock

Reviewers

Bruno Massa

Gordon Heydon

Greg Holsclaw

Senior Acquisition Editor

Douglas Paterson

Development Editor

Nikhil Bangera

Technical Editor

Dhiraj Chandiramani

Editorial Team Leader

Mithil Kulkarni

Project Manager

Abhijeet Deobhakta

Project Coordinator

Abhijeet Deobhakta

Indexer

Hemangini Bari

Proofreader

Chris Smith

Production Coordinator

Aparna Bhagat

Cover Work

Aparna Bhagat

About the Author

Michael Peacock is a web developer and senior partner of Peacock, Carter & Associates (`http://www.peacockcarter.co.uk`) a web design and development business. Michael loves building websites and web applications, and when he isn't, likes to read, watch films, and occasionally take part in amateur dramatics.

I would like to thank everyone at Packt Publishing for making this book possible, in particular Douglas Patterson for the idea of the book, and helping me define a structure for it. Patricia Weir, Abhijeet Deobhakta, and Nikhil Bangera for keeping me on track, and Dhiraj Chandiramani for preparing the book for publication. My thanks also goes to the reviewers (Greg Holsclaw, Bruno Massa, and Gordon Heydon) who helped improve the quality of the book, and made sure everything was in check.

I'd also like to thank my fiancée Emma for her support while working on the book, and my business partner Richard for keeping the business running during the times when I was writing about websites as opposed to building them.

A special mention, and thanks is due to Martin Baker of Merrill Valley Photography (`http://www.merrillvalleyphotography.co.uk/`) for his contributions to the photography section in Chapter 3.

Finally, I'd like to thank you, the reader; I hope that you enjoy this book and end up with a fantastic website and store!

About the Reviewers

Bruno Massa is one of the three authors and maintainers of the e-Commerce module for Drupal. Graduated in Business, he is founder and president of Titan Atlas, a Brazilian dotcom company. Massa is a national expert in e-business and open-source software applications in Brazil.

Greg Holsclaw holds a Bachelor's Degree in Computational Mathematics and has been developing intranet and internet web applications for the past five years. After developing ASP applications for a large engineering division for a number of years, Greg became acquainted with PHP and Drupal, first to develop personal projects, which then led to a full time Drupal development position at a self-funded startup.

Table of Contents

Preface

This book takes Drupal, a powerful and extendable Content Management System, and uses it to set up and manage an online store using the available e-Commerce modules. By integrating the store directly into the website, customers are provided with a consistent experience with the other areas of the site.

Many aspects of Drupal and e-commerce are covered as well as the e-Commerce modules to create not only a great online store, but also a great website.

What This Book Covers

Chapter 1 introduces you to Drupal, e-commerce, and the advantages of using Drupal e-Commerce rather than regular online shopping carts before going through the installation process and performing some basic configurations.

Chapter 2 looks at how to use Drupal and many of its Content Management features to create a website.

Chapter 3 goes through steps involved in planning an online shop including legal issues, the shop's structure, product details, and how to take great photographs of products for the store.

Chapter 4 takes our planning from Chapter 3 to show you how to create an online product catalog.

Chapter 5 shows you how to manage users, roles, and permissions within Drupal, particularly to create and manage customers to use the store, and staff members to help manage the store.

Chapter 6 takes a look at branding the website and the store to provide a website that reflects your business.

Chapter 7 lets you start making money from your store by looking through and customizing the checkout process as well as taking payments from customers.

Chapter 8 helps you to create an even better selling experience for customers by looking at additional modules and features that can make the website and the overall selling experience even better. This looks at adding images to product listings, enabling search options and different ways of offering discount or incentive to customers including bulk purchasing discounts.

Chapter 9 takes a detailed look at taxes, payment, and shipping options allowing you to accept as many different forms of payment as possible, as well as dealing with taxation issues and calculating shipping prices based on the items ordered or the location of the customer.

Chapter 10 takes your new site, secures it, and deploys it onto the Internet ready for use to generate business, as well as explaining how to maintain the shop.

Chapter 11 looks at generating invoices and a more advanced way to manage your customers, by installing a Customer Relationship Manager into Drupal to help manage customer support, appointments, and even telephone calls.

Chapter 12 gives you the knowledge you need to help promote and market your business online by looking at optimizing the store for search engines, advertising your site, and helping to bring back visitors to your site as well as some important tips and advice when advertising, promoting, and marketing on the Web!

What You Need for This Book

Drupal is a free and open-source modular web application framework and content management system (CMS) written in PHP that can run in many environments, including Windows, Mac OS X, Linux, and FreeBSD. You just need to have a development environment set up on your computer, e.g. WAMP, or XAMP.

Conventions

In this book, you will find a number of styles of text that distinguish between different kinds of information. Here are some examples of these styles, and an explanation of their meaning.

There are three styles for code. Code words in text are shown as follows: "Support for friendly or clean URLs requires `mod_rewrite` and the ability to use `.htaccess` files."

A block of code will be set as follows:

```
<img src='http://www.dougsdinos.com/drupal-
          5.7/files/garland_logo_0.png'
     style='float:left; padding: 5px;' alt='PRODUCT NAME' />
```

When we wish to draw your attention to a particular part of a code block, the relevant lines or items will be made bold:

```
<title>
  <?php print $head_title; ?>
</title>
```

New terms and **important words** are introduced in a bold-type font. Words that you see on the screen, in menus or dialog boxes for example, appear in our text like this: "clicking the **Next** button moves you to the next screen".

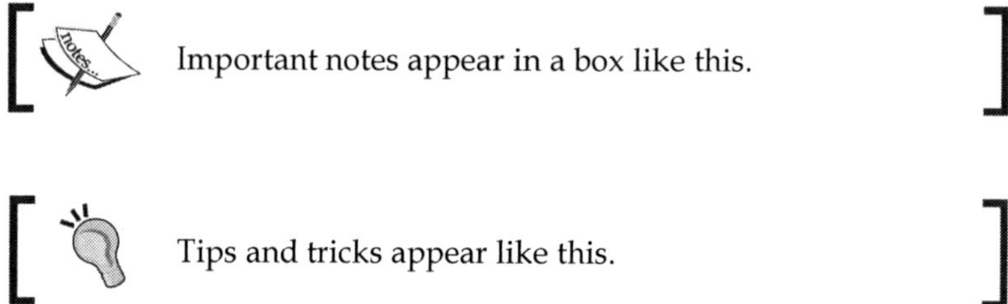

Important notes appear in a box like this.
Tips and tricks appear like this.

Reader Feedback

Feedback from our readers is always welcome. Let us know what you think about this book, what you liked or may have disliked. Reader feedback is important for us to develop titles that you really get the most out of.

To send us general feedback, simply drop an email to feedback@packtpub.com, making sure to mention the book title in the subject of your message.

If there is a book that you need and would like to see us publish, please send us a note in the **SUGGEST A TITLE** form on www.packtpub.com or email suggest@packtpub.com.

If there is a topic that you have expertise in and you are interested in either writing or contributing to a book, see our author guide on www.packtpub.com/authors.

Customer Support

Now that you are the proud owner of a Packt book, we have a number of things to help you to get the most from your purchase.

Downloading the Example Code for the Book

Visit `http://www.packtpub.com/files/code/4060_Code.zip` to directly download the example code.

The downloadable files contain instructions on how to use them.

Errata

Although we have taken every care to ensure the accuracy of our contents, mistakes do happen. If you find a mistake in one of our books—maybe a mistake in text or code—we would be grateful if you would report this to us. By doing this you can save other readers from frustration, and help to improve subsequent versions of this book. If you find any errata, report them by visiting `http://www.packtpub.com/support`, selecting your book, clicking on the **let us know** link, and entering the details of your errata. Once your errata have been verified, your submission will be accepted and the errata will be added to the list of existing errata. The existing errata can be viewed by selecting your title from `http://www.packtpub.com/support`.

Questions

You can contact us at `questions@packtpub.com` if you are having a problem with some aspect of the book, and we will do our best to address it.

1
Introduction and Installation

Welcome to Drupal e-Commerce! During the course of this book we are going to look at how to use a **content management system** in particular Drupal as well as its **e-Commerce** module to set up and manage an online shop. We will install the software, have a look at its features, plan our shop, create our shop, look at customer management, create a design for our shop, and cover security, taxes, shipping, and even marketing our business.

In this chapter, you will learn:

- What a Content Management System is, and What's Drupal
- What e-commerce is and what it can do for us
- What Drupal e-Commerce is, and why it is better than a regular online shopping cart system
- How to install Drupal, perform some basic configurations, and install its e-Commerce module
- How Drupal and its e-Commerce module work

We will also take a look at the store we will create during the course of this book, Doug's Dinos.

What is a CMS and What is Drupal?

Content Management Systems are one of the common methods for creating and managing content on the Internet and on intranets, particularly in environments where there is more than one person working on the content, or where there is a lot of content involved.

These systems generally have the ability for users to:

- Create content
- Edit, delete, and generally manage content
- Manage, provide, and restrict access to view and edit the content
- Have a separate layer for design
- Collaborate effectively
- Manage versions of content

With a CMS, content and design are kept separate, which means that the design of a website can completely change, and this will have no impact on the content of the website. This is quite an important feature as it means that the design need only be changed once, and not across each page of the website, making it easy for websites of any size to easily and quickly change design, and it protects the design, as content editors do not need to integrate design into their content—which could cause problems.

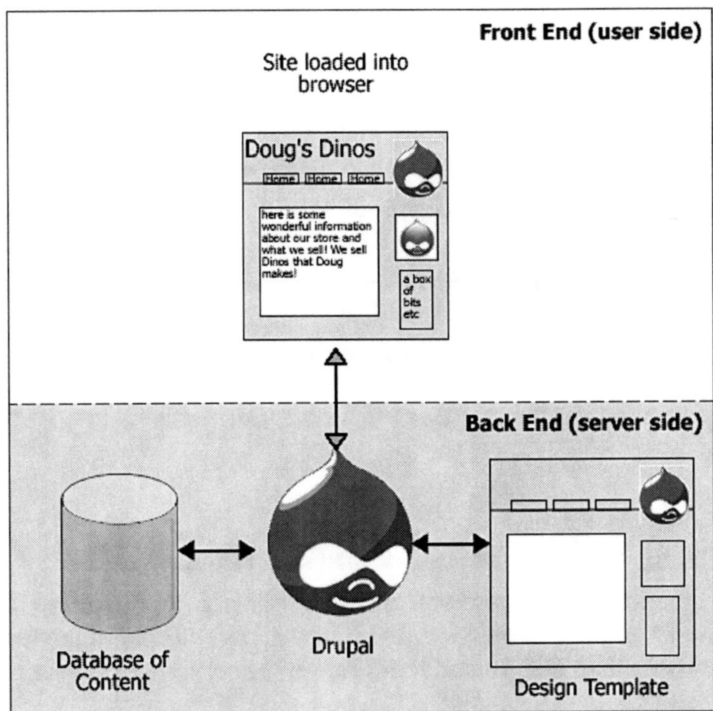

The diagram opposite illustrates the separation of these layers and how they are brought together when the page loads into the visitors' web browsers.

Drupal is a free, open-source content management system, which allows individuals or a community of users to easily publish, manage, and organize a wide variety of content on a website. The Drupal website, containing lots of information on Drupal, its history, and its features is `http://drupal.org/`.

What is E-Commerce and What can it do for Us?

E-Commerce is the process of conducting business, by means of the sale and purchase of goods and services as well as the transfer of funds, over networks and through computers. We will create an online shop that will enable us to do business electronically over networks (the Internet) allowing us to sell goods as well as receive payments electronically, although it can also cater for the option for manual payments by cheque or money order.

E-Commerce can help us reach new potential with our business, making our products and services available to a wider audience. It can of course do more for us; it's just a case of where we want it to end! It can also:

- Manage stock control
- Implement a better workflow of the sales process
- Enable us to accept business from new locations
- Enable us to process payments from customers who would have otherwise been unable to purchase from us
- Help generate new business by offering more than just a shop—if we also have a website with which our online shop is interconnected, then visitors to our website will also be attracted to our online shop.

What is Drupal e-Commerce?

...and why is it better than a regular online shopping cart?

Drupal e-Commerce is the combination of Drupal, the content management system, and the e-Commerce module, which can be plugged into it, bringing a wealth of e-commerce functionality to the software.

If we consider websites that are purely shops, they provide the customer with one thing—the opportunity to buy some products or services. Websites that are not at all shops, generally provide information on a subject, and sometimes offer visitors additional features or access to online communities. Drupal e-Commerce helps us bridge the gap in a seamless fashion. Traditionally, if someone wanted a website that had an online shop as well as a website, the two would be bolted together similar to a garage being joined to a house. With Drupal e-Commerce we are not bolting the two together, we are extending one into the other, similar to a new extension being added to a house.

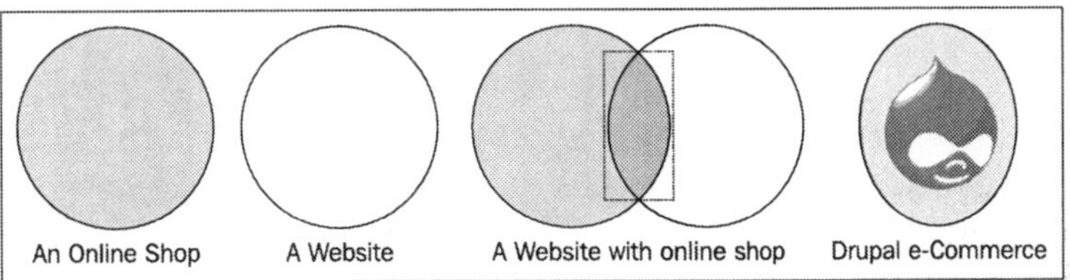

The figure above illustrates these different types of websites and shows that with Drupal e-Commerce the shop and website are the same and interlinked, as opposed to two separate entities.

With separate shopping carts bolted onto a website, they generally loose the consistent theme of the website, and provide an added bonus for the visitor. We will create an online shop and an online resource where each complements the other. As e-Commerce is embedded into Drupal it allows us to make the most of a very powerful CMS to improve the presentation of our products.

Our Site

Doug is an avid dinosaur and model enthusiast, and runs his own shop and museum selling model dinosaurs and offering information and facts on various dinosaurs. He only has one property, and it's based a few miles outside the center of Newcastle, a large city in the UK. Because his store isn't based in the center, he doesn't get as much business from tourists and visitors to the city as he would like, and his main customer base is school children in the local area; occasionally local schools make a few bulk orders from him and bring a few large groups to see the museum.

Because Doug's business has been slowly declining for the past few years, he wants to set up a website to advertise his store and museum but also to sell models online. He hopes that this will increase his sales as he will be able to serve customers across the globe, and also as tourists and visitors to the city will be more likely to find out about his museum and realize it is only a short bus journey from the center, he may get more customers for the museum too.

Throughout the course of this book, we are going to create an e-commerce website for Doug and his business.

Installation

Now that we know what Drupal and e-Commerce are, and we have a website and shop to build, it is time to download and install the software. This section contains some detailed technical information regarding requirements and installation steps.

> This assumes that you have a development environment set up on your own computer, e.g. WAMP, or XAMP. See Appendix A for details on installing a development environment. We will deploy our shop onto the web once it is ready in Chapter 10—*Securing, Deploying, and Maintaining Your Shop*.

If you already have a development environment set up which differs from the one detailed in Appendix A, you need to be aware of the requirements for both Drupal and the e-Commerce module to ensure your development environment supports the software.

- PHP 4.3.3 and greater or PHP 5; PHP 5.2 and above is recommended
- Either MySQL (version 4.1 or greater is recommended) or PostgreSQL
- Apache web server and MySQL (recommended; these are assumed throughout the course of this book)
- Other web servers and database combinations have not been as extensively tested
- To utilize XML-based services you may need PHP's XML extension; for the e-Commerce module this may not be needed (optional)
- Support for friendly or clean URLs requires `mod_rewrite` and the ability to use `.htaccess` files (optional)

More details on Drupal requirements are available in the Drupal handbook, `http://drupal.org/requirements`. There are also some guidelines on setting up your own development server environment on the Drupal website at `http://drupal.org/node/260`.

We need to:

- Download Drupal
- Install Drupal
- Download e-Commerce Module and other dependencies such as the Token module
- Install the dependencies
- Install the e-Commerce Module

Downloading Drupal

We can download a copy of Drupal from the download page on the Drupal website `http://drupal.org/download`; this page is for the **Drupal project** (there are other downloads available from the **downloads** link on the website's menu); the version we want to download is one of the 5.x range, (Drupal e-Commerce requires at least version 5.2) which at the time of writing was 5.4

Installing Drupal

Once we have downloaded Drupal, we should use an unzipping program (such as WinZip, Power archiver, or Windows' built-in "compressed folders" system) to unzip the archive and place it in our development environment's web folder (see Appendix A for more information).

More technical installation details are available in the `INSTALL.txt` file in the folder we have just unzipped.

We now need to create a database, which Drupal will utilize; to do this we need to visit our phpMyAdmin page within our development environment (see Appendix A for more information); typically this will be located at `http://localhost/phpmyadmin/`. On the page that loads there is a textbox for creating a new database; let's call our new database **drupalecom** and then click **Create** to create the new database.

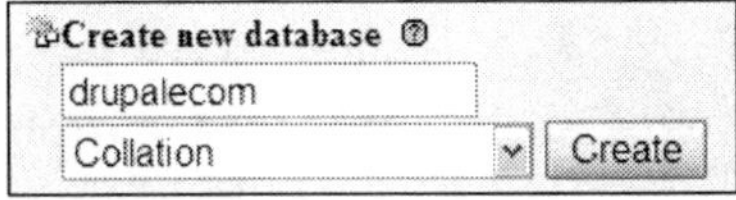

Now that we have our database, we can run the Drupal install script; we will need to have our database username and password to hand (see Appendix A if you used that method to create a development environment). For most development environment software such as WAMP and XAMP, the username and password is typically 'root' with no password.

The Drupal installer can be accessed by visiting the Drupal directory in our development environment, which is `http://localhost/drupal-5.7/`; when we visit this page Drupal detects that it has not yet been installed and will take us to the installer page.

Here we need to enter our **Database name**, **username**, and our **Database password**, so Drupal can connect to the database and install the default data. The two database types we have are **mysql** and **mysqli**. **mysqli** is an improved `mysql` driver (hence the i) but is not available on all installations; if you are in doubt, just choose **mysql**.

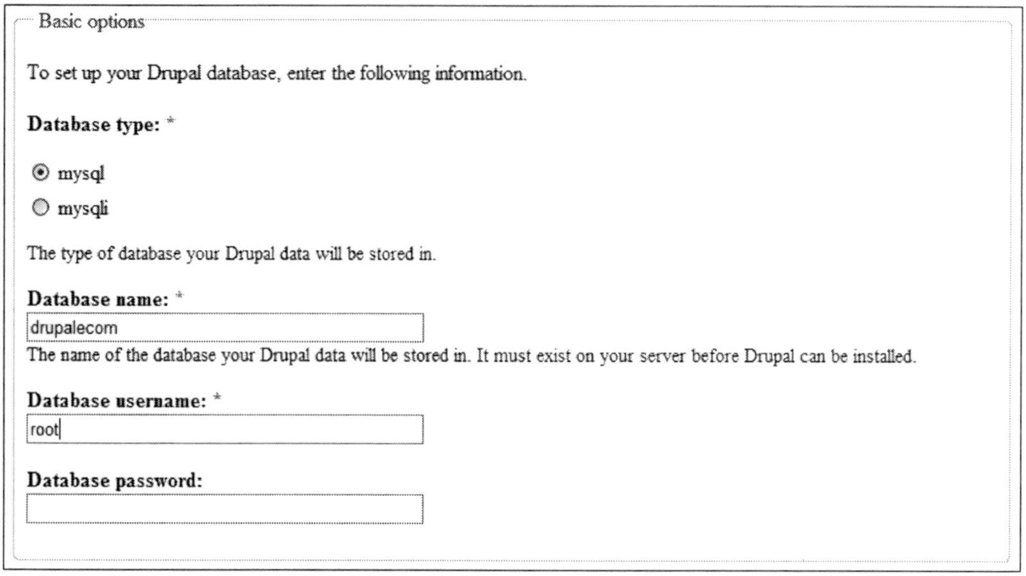

Basic options

To set up your Drupal database, enter the following information.

Database type: *

(•) mysql

( ) mysqli

The type of database your Drupal data will be stored in.

Database name: *

[drupalecom]

The name of the database your Drupal data will be stored in. It must exist on your server before Drupal can be installed.

Database username: *

[root]

Database password:

[ ]

Once we have entered that information, we can click the **Save configuration** button. If all goes well, we should now see a screen saying Drupal installation is complete; if not we will be taken back to the page shown above and informed of what information was incorrect so we can adjust it.

If we now proceed back to our main Drupal directory, `http://localhost/drupal-5.7/`, we can see that Drupal has indeed been installed and we are asked to **create the first account**, which will be given full administrator privileges.

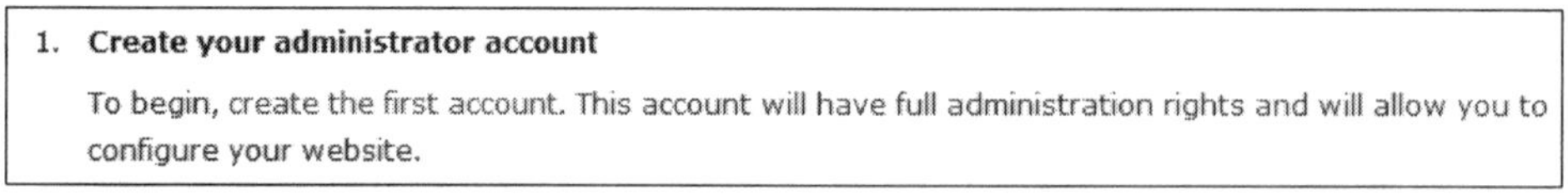

1. **Create your administrator account**

   To begin, create the first account. This account will have full administration rights and will allow you to configure your website.

To create this account we only need to enter a username and an email address and then click **Create new account**.

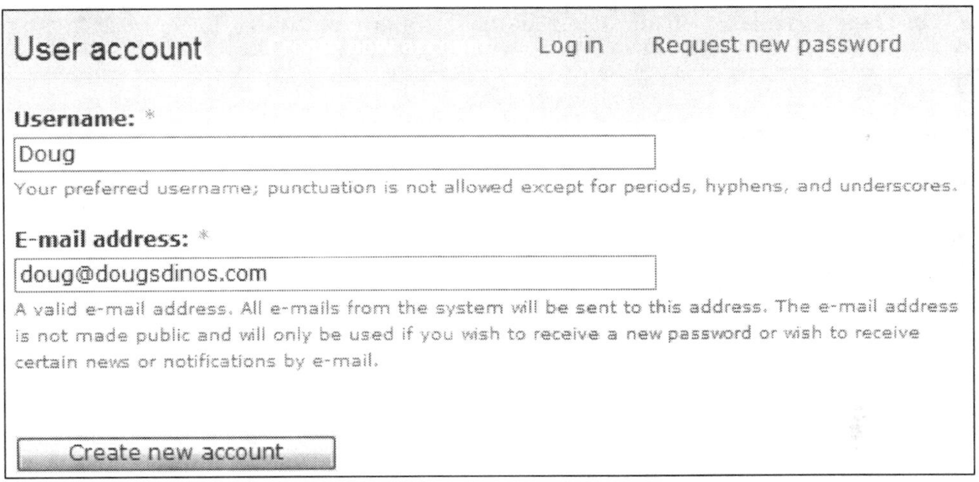

You may see an error message on the next page, something along the lines of:

Warning: mail() [function.mail]: Failed to connect to mailserver at "localhost" port 25, verify your "SMTP" and "smtp_port" setting in php.ini or use ini_set() in C:\wamp\www\drupal-5.7\includes\common.inc on line 1979.

We don't need to worry about this error; it is just telling us that it failed to email the administrator account password to us, which is understandable since we don't have a mail server configured within our development environment. When we put the website online in a live hosting environment we shouldn't have these problems.

The password that Drupal has generated for us is shown on the page with the error message; we need to take a note of the password.

Welcome to Drupal. You are user #1, which gives you full and immediate access. All future registrants will receive their passwords via e-mail, so please make sure your website e-mail address is set properly under the general settings on the site information settings page.

Your password is *dtKwS4gGTk*. You may change your password below.

We also have an option of changing our account password on this page, and making other changes to our account, including setting our time zone, and setting a signature for our posts and messages.

That's all there is to installing Drupal! Before we move on to the e-commerce module, let's take a look at the basic settings available to tweak and change.

Configuring Drupal

We can get to the configuration settings from the links that are on the front page of our Drupal installation.

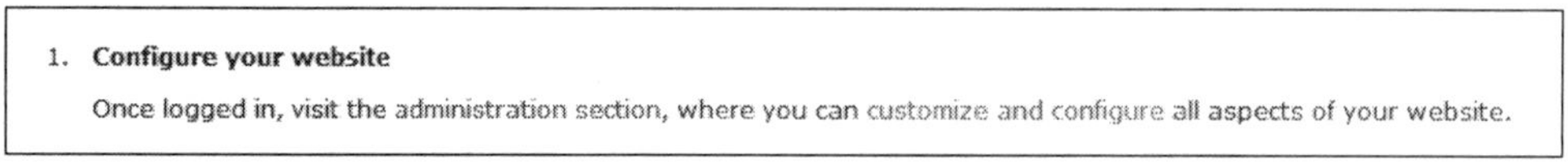

1. **Configure your website**

   Once logged in, visit the administration section, where you can customize and configure all aspects of your website.

The **customize and configure** link then takes us to the **Site Configuration** page, which contains a range of different configuration sections:

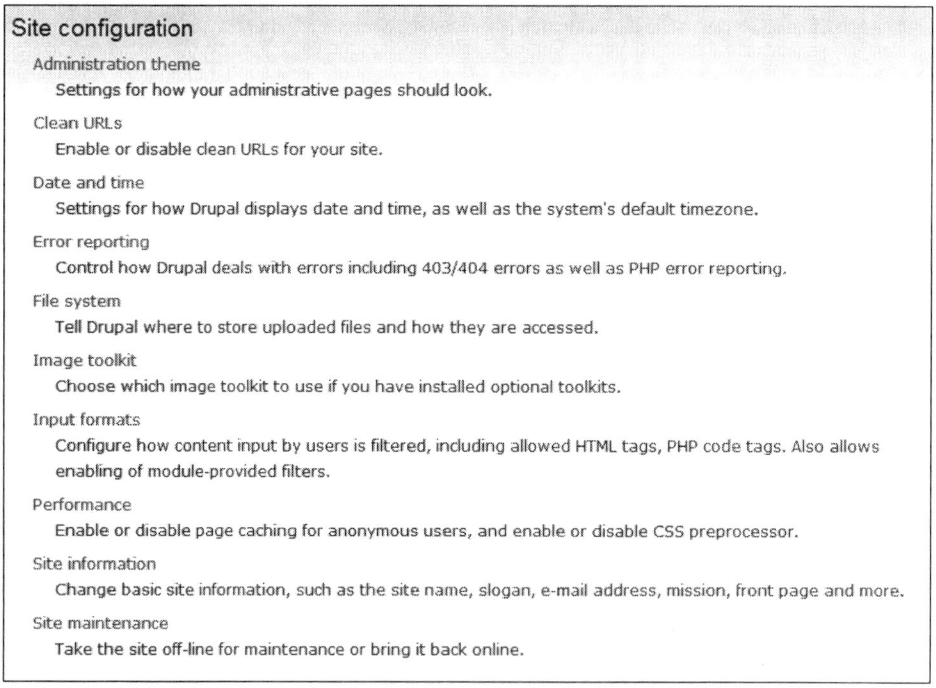

Site configuration

Administration theme
Settings for how your administrative pages should look.

Clean URLs
Enable or disable clean URLs for your site.

Date and time
Settings for how Drupal displays date and time, as well as the system's default timezone.

Error reporting
Control how Drupal deals with errors including 403/404 errors as well as PHP error reporting.

File system
Tell Drupal where to store uploaded files and how they are accessed.

Image toolkit
Choose which image toolkit to use if you have installed optional toolkits.

Input formats
Configure how content input by users is filtered, including allowed HTML tags, PHP code tags. Also allows enabling of module-provided filters.

Performance
Enable or disable page caching for anonymous users, and enable or disable CSS preprocessor.

Site information
Change basic site information, such as the site name, slogan, e-mail address, mission, front page and more.

Site maintenance
Take the site off-line for maintenance or bring it back online.

Administration Theme

The **Administration theme** allows us to change the theme and style of the administrative section of Drupal, which isn't that important right now—it's more of a personal preference for administrators.

Clean URLs

The `mod_rewrite` Apache module can allow us to enable clean URLs within Drupal; this would change links from things like `http://www.example.com/?q=node/83` to something that looks more presentable to the end user, such as `http://www.example.com/node/83`. It provides no additional features or functions, but it does make things easier for the user, allowing them to remember URLs more easily. Let's click the **Clean URLs** link and enable the feature. If you don't have the `mod_rewrite` module installed, the **handbook page on Clean URLs** link provides more information on setting this up.

Within this page we only have the option to enable or disable the feature, but there are a couple of useful links in there too.

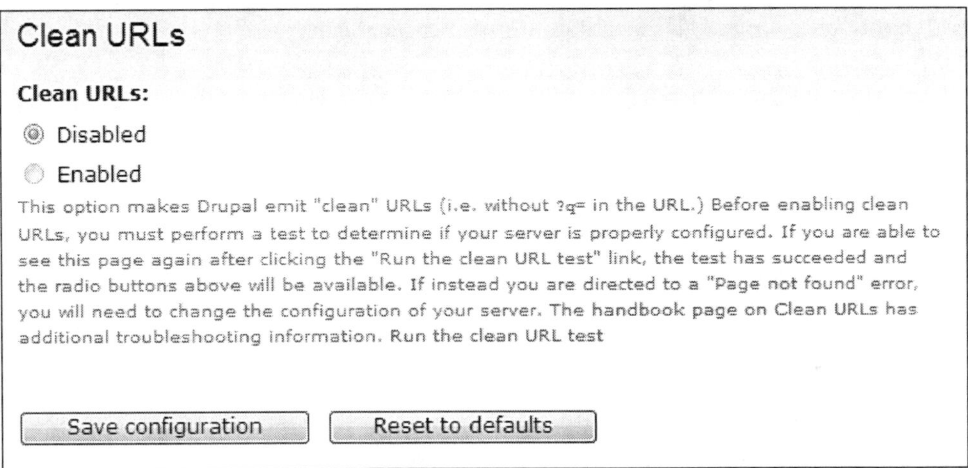

The first link leads to some more technical details on the Clean URLs feature and the second is a test to see if the feature can be enabled on our installation. Provided we are running an Apache web server, and have the `mod_rewrite` module enabled (if you followed Appendix A, that is the case) the feature should work, so let's click the test link. If all goes well, we should be sent back to the same page, but without the links at the bottom. Doug doesn't like websites with "un-clean" URLs and wants them to be clean. To enable this feature, we just need to click the **Enabled** option and then click the **Save configuration** button.

Date and Time

The **Date and time** settings allow us to set the default time zone. We will have to enable it if we want users to be able to set their own time zones and the format in which dates will be shown on our site.

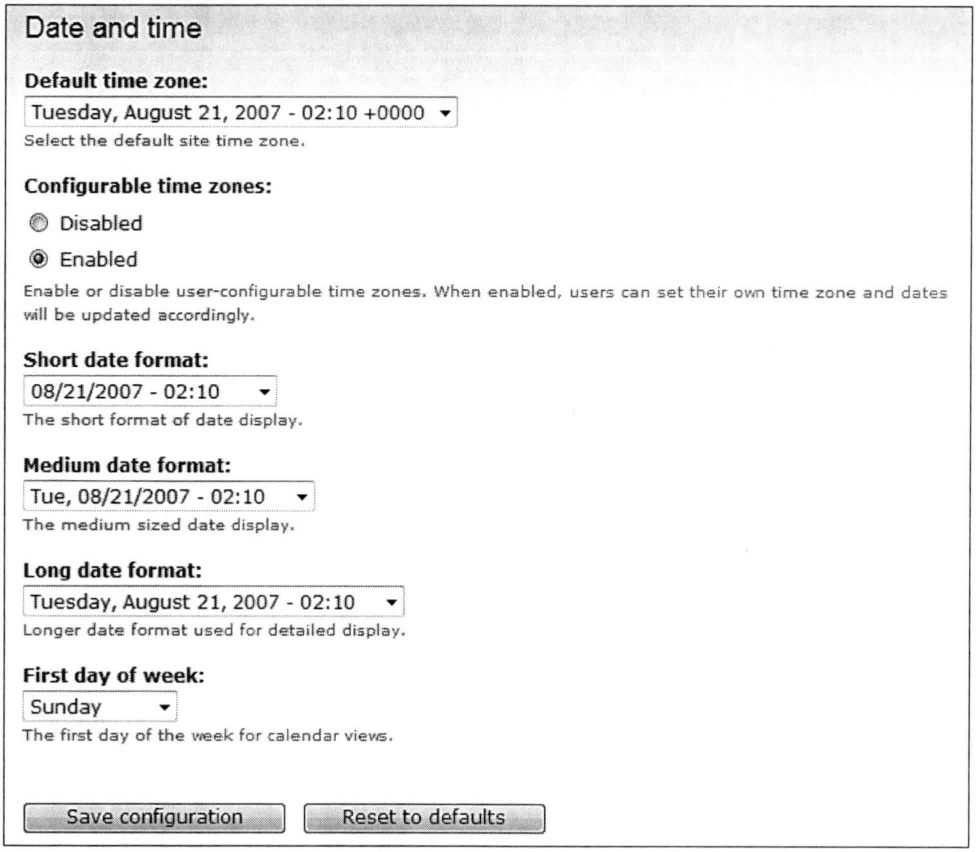

Date and time
Default time zone:
Tuesday, August 21, 2007 - 02:10 +0000
Select the default site time zone.
Configurable time zones:
Disabled
Enabled
Enable or disable user-configurable time zones. When enabled, users can set their own time zone and dates will be updated accordingly.
Short date format:
08/21/2007 - 02:10
The short format of date display.
Medium date format:
Tue, 08/21/2007 - 02:10
The medium sized date display.
Long date format:
Tuesday, August 21, 2007 - 02:10
Longer date format used for detailed display.
First day of week:
Sunday
The first day of the week for calendar views.
Save configuration
Reset to defaults

Although Doug's store is based in the UK, he is hoping to target users in other countries too, and sees a larger potential with the US market, so he wants the default time zone set accordingly to the US. Because there will be customers from the UK and other countries, Doug also wants users to be able to set their own time zone, so we need to ensure that feature is enabled. Let's leave the short and medium date formats, as they are by default set to American style (mm/dd/yyyy).

Default time zone:
Monday, August 20, 2007 - 21:10 -0500
Select the default site time zone.
Configurable time zones:
Disabled
Enabled

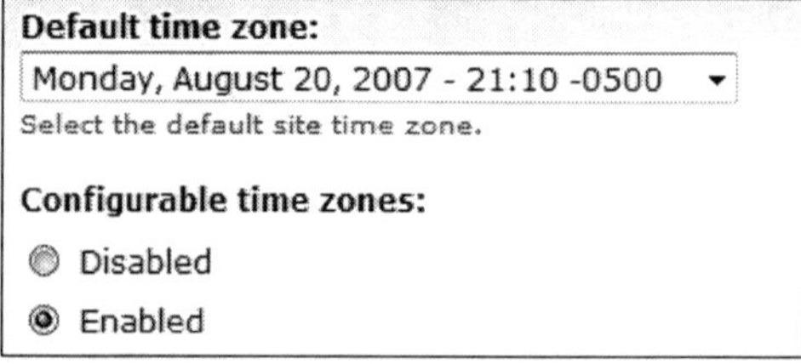

With these changes made, we just click **Save configuration** to apply the changes.

For future reference, we may wish to install the auto time zone module at some point, to automatically adjust time zones with the user's time zone.

Error Reporting

The **Error reporting** settings are for two main purposes:

- Which pages to display if a page does not exist or the user is not permitted access to the page
- How to handle technical (Drupal, PHP and MySQL) error messages

The error page settings are shown:

Default 403 (access denied) page:

http://mkpeacock.dyndns.org/drupal-5.7/

This page is displayed when the requested document is denied to the current user. If unsure, specify nothing.

Default 404 (not found) page:

http://mkpeacock.dyndns.org/drupal-5.7/

This page is displayed when no other content matches the requested document. If unsure, specify nothing.

If a user is not authorized to view a page, or a page does not exist, then these default pages will be shown to the user instead of the pages that they cannot access. As we don't have any content in our site, we also don't have any pages to use as error pages so we will leave these settings and return to them in Chapter 2—*Getting Started with Drupal*.

The error reporting settings, however, deal with how Drupal should act if it encounters an internal error, such as a missing file, a PHP error, or a MySQL error.

Error reporting:

Write errors to the log and to the screen

Where Drupal, PHP and SQL errors are logged. On a production server it is recommended that errors are only written to the error log. On a test server it can be helpful to write logs to the screen.

Discard log entries older than:

1 week

The time log entries should be kept. Older entries will be automatically discarded. Requires crontab.

Right now, as we are working in a development environment, we want to be informed of all errors so we can fix them. However, when we put our site online, we will have to come back to these settings as we don't really want to present our customers with technical jargon and details.

We will cover these again in Chapter 10—*Securing, Deploying, and Maintaining Your Shop.*

File System

The **File system** settings below determine where uploaded files will be stored and how files are downloaded. When we first open this setting, there is a message in a green box informing us that **The directory *files* has been created** [*sic*]. This is because the folder was not created on installation, and the file system page detected that the folder did not exist, so it created it for us.

The directory *files* has been created.

File system path:

files

A file system path where the files will be stored. This directory has to exist and be writable by Drupal. If the download method is set to public this directory has to be relative to the Drupal installation directory, and be accessible over the web. When download method is set to private this directory should not be accessible over the web. Changing this location after the site has been in use will cause problems so only change this setting on an existing site if you know what you are doing.

Temporary directory:

c:/wamp/tmp

Location where uploaded files will be kept during previews. Relative paths will be resolved relative to the Drupal installation directory.

Download method:

(•) Public - files are available using HTTP directly.

( ) Private - files are transferred by Drupal.

If you want any sort of access control on the downloading of files, this needs to be set to *private*. You can change this at any time, however all download URLs will change and there may be unexpected problems so it is not recommended.

It isn't advisable to move the file system path later when we have a live site running from our installation, so if we do wish to move it, now is the time. The **Temporary directory** is a folder used by the web server to temporarily store files that are used or generated during the running of the website, for instance when users upload files they go to the temporary folder before being moved to the appropriate place. We don't need to change this setting as it should auto-detect the correct setting for us.

The download methods allow files to be more secure. If we have files in our website that we only want registered users to see, we can restrict access to them. If an authorised user requests access, Drupal grabs the file and moves it to a temporary location for the user to download. Doug's site will only have images or resource papers to download, and these will be visible to anyone, so we don't need to change that either.

Image Toolkit

The **Image toolkit** allows us to control the quality of images that are generated on the fly. One of the most common methods for image generation is GD2, which we should have installed on our development environment. Drupal detects the available image toolkit and provides us with the option to change the quality of the images.

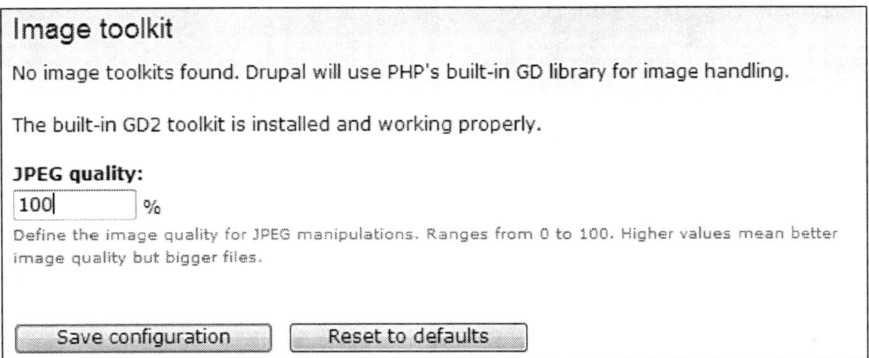

Doug wants the highest quality possible of images and photographs, so let's ensure that's set to **100%** for him.

> **Imagemagick library**
>
> There is the option to use the imagemagick library (although this may require additional configurations on the server), this is faster than GD and can handle images better. The `image.imagick.inc` file within the image module folder contains more information and settings for this.

Input Formats

When we enter content into Drupal the default setting is to process the input as if it is HTML, so if we later created a page with content like:

```
This <strong>massive</strong> offer is only available for a short
while <a href="order">Order <strong>NOW!</strong></a>
```

Drupal would process the HTML from the input so the words *massive* and *now* were bold, and the words *order now* were a link to the order page. The **Input formats** section allows us to control who can enter input in different formats.

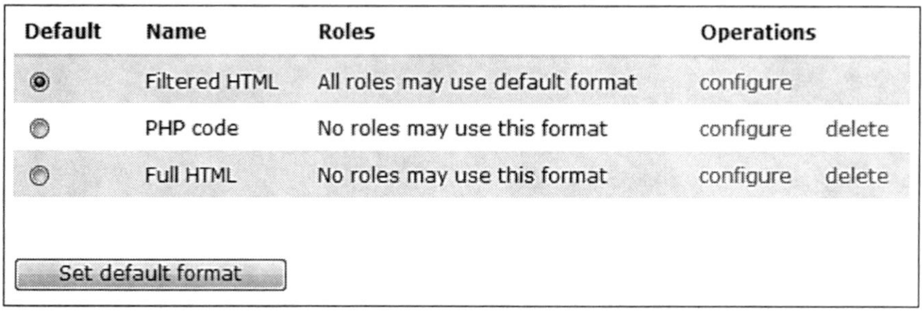

Default	Name	Roles	Operations	
◉	Filtered HTML	All roles may use default format	configure	
○	PHP code	No roles may use this format	configure	delete
○	Full HTML	No roles may use this format	configure	delete

Set default format

The options available are:

- Filtered HTML
- PHP code
- Full HTML

With **Filtered HTML** only certain bits of HTML are processed, with **PHP code** any PHP code added will be processed and with **Full HTML** the HTML will be processed as is, with no filtering of potentially malicious entities.

Generally users should not have access to **PHP code** as it is very dangerous. Only a select few administrators should be given the option to use this. To allow other users to do this, we need to configure **roles** within Drupal, which indicate which users can do what. We will discuss these roles in detail in Chapter 2—*Getting Started with Drupal*.

Performance

The **Performance** settings allow us to optimize the performance of our Drupal installation, which is particularly useful when we have lots of visitors to our website.

For now, let's set **Page cache** to **Normal** as this is recommended.

Page cache

Enabling the cache will offer a significant performance boost. Drupal can store and send compressed cached pages requested by *anonymous* users. By caching a web page, Drupal does not have to construct the page each time someone wants to view it.

Caching mode:

- Disabled
- Normal (recommended, no side effects)
- Aggressive (experts only, possible side effects)

The normal cache mode is suitable for most sites and does not cause any side effects. The aggressive cache mode causes Drupal to skip the loading (init) and unloading (exit) of enabled modules when serving a cached page. This results in an additional performance boost but can cause unwanted side effects.

Currently, all enabled modules are compatible with the aggressive caching policy. Please note, if you use aggressive caching and enable new modules, you will need to check this page again to ensure compatibility.

Minimum cache lifetime:

none

On high-traffic sites it can become necessary to enforce a minimum cache lifetime. The minimum cache lifetime is the minimum amount of time that will go by before the cache is emptied and recreated. A larger minimum cache lifetime offers better performance, but users will not see new content for a longer period of time.

Page caching prevents Drupal from loading and processing pages every time they are requested, instead, it stores a copy of a processed page (known as a cached version) and when anonymous users visit the site, who are less likely to use dynamic elements that require processing, Drupal serves the cached page. With websites under lots of strain, caching is very useful to reduce unnecessary load on the server from many visits. The **Minimum cache lifetime** prevents Drupal from processing the page too frequently, ensuring a cache is used for at least a specific amount of time before a new, more up-to-date copy, is processed. This setting is more suited for very busy sites.

Every time a user visits our site data is transferred from our web server to the user; this data transfer is commonly within a specific bandwidth set by hosting companies or service providers. Very busy sites can use lots of bandwidth, which can in turn cost the website owners money. Drupal has some basic **Bandwidth optimizations** available for us.

Bandwidth optimizations

These options can help reduce both the size and number of requests made to your website. This can reduce the server load, the bandwidth used, and the average page loading time for your visitors.

Aggregate and compress CSS files:

- (•) Disabled
- ( ) Enabled

Some Drupal modules include their own CSS files. When these modules are enabled, each module's CSS file adds an additional HTTP request to the page, which can increase the load time of each page. These HTTP requests can also slightly increase server load. It is recommended to only turn this option on when your site is in production, as it can interfere with theme development. This option is disabled if you have not set up your files directory, or if your download method is set to private.

These optimizations compress the style information of our website (CSS) using less bandwidth on each page request. For Doug's site, he does not anticipate a massive use of his website, so we will leave that **Disabled** for now; we can always keep an eye on our bandwidth usage and if needed enable it later.

Site Information

Information on the website is set in the **Site information** section, which includes:

- Website Name
- Contact E-Mail Address
- Slogan
- Website Mission
- Footer Message
- Anonymous User
- Default Front Page

Let's complete this information for Doug's site:

Name: *

Doug's Dinos!

The name of this web site.

E-mail address: *

doug@dougsdinos.com

A valid e-mail address to be used as the "From" address by the auto-mailer during registration, new password requests, notifications, etc. To lessen the likelihood of e-mail being marked as spam, this e-mail address should use the same domain as the website.

Slogan:

T-Riffic! A wide range of fantasic dinosaurs.

The slogan of this website. Some themes display a slogan when available.

We will call the site **Doug's Dinos!** Add Doug's email address as the contact email address, and add Doug's cheesy slogan to the settings.

The website mission is just for the purpose of the website, and the footer message is something appended to the bottom of this page, I've added a copyright notice, so all of Doug's customers realize the website is copyrighted material.

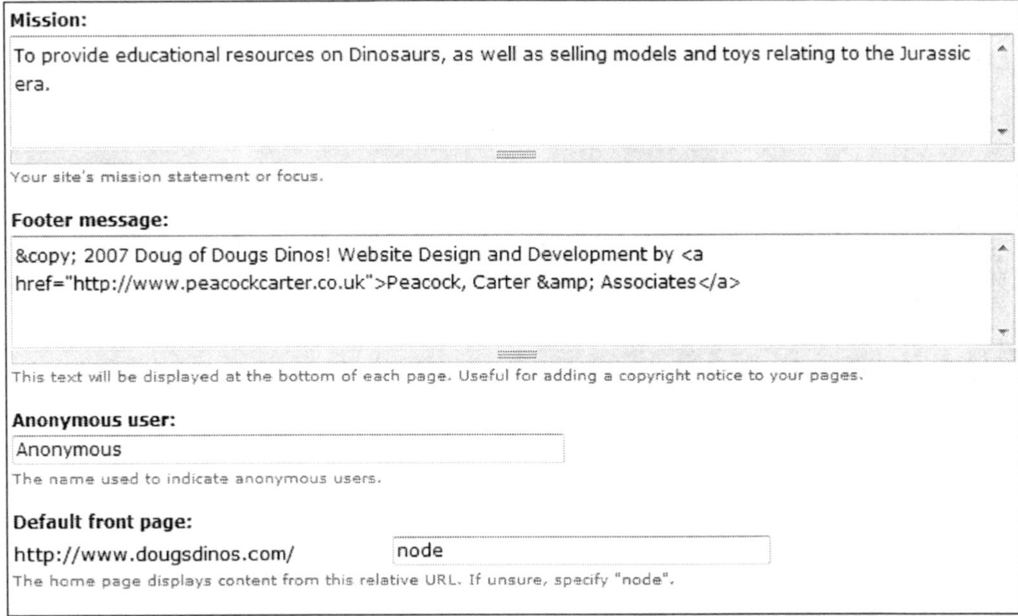

The **Anonymous user** is the user name used to indicate anonymous users and finally there is the **Default front page,** which tells Drupal which page in our site should be classed as the front page. We will leave this as it is for now, and once we have some content on our site, we shall return to it in Chapter 2—*Getting Started with Drupal*.

Site Maintenance

The final section of settings is **Site maintenance**, which contains an option to turn our website offline and display a message to the user.

Site maintenance

Site status:

◉ Online

○ Off-line

When set to "Online", all visitors will be able to browse your site normally. When set to "Off-line", only users with the "administer site configuration" permission will be able to access your site to perform maintenance; all other visitors will see the site off-line message configured below. Authorized users can log in during "Off-line" mode directly via the user login page.

Site off-line message:

Doug's Dinos! is currently under maintenance. We should be back shortly. Thank you for your patience.

Message to show visitors when the site is in off-line mode.

At the moment, our site is in a development environment so we don't need to turn it **Off-line**; however, if we were working on a live site, it would be best to turn it **Off-line** while making major changes to it, to avoid confusing the website visitors!

The Drupal e-Commerce Module

E-Commerce functionality is not included with Drupal "out of the box", so we need to download and install the e-Commerce module. Let's do that now!

Downloading the Module

The e-Commerce module's website is located at `http://drupal.org/project/ecommerce` and the download link for the module is near the bottom of the page. We want to download the file for **5.x-3.3** or a newer version if available.

Releases

Official releases	Date	Size	Links
5.x-3.3	2007-Aug-01	1.25 MB	Download · Release notes
4.7.x-3.3	2007-Aug-01	1.16 MB	Download · Release notes
Development snapshots	**Date**	**Size**	**Links**
5.x-3.x-dev	2007-Aug-10	1.25 MB	Download · Release notes
4.7.x-3.x-dev	2007-Aug-10	1.16 MB	Download · Release notes

We also need another module, called the **Token** module. The e-Commerce module depends upon this module, so let's download that from its project page `http://drupal.org/project/token`. We want the version for Drupal 5.x, which is version 1.8 (or newer; version 1.9 has subsequently been released) of the token module.

Releases			
Official releases	**Date**	**Size**	**Links**
5.x-1.8	2007-Aug-13	19.03 KB	Download · Release notes
4.7.x-1.4	2007-Jan-20	11.03 KB	Download · Release notes

The purpose of the token module is to provide an API (Application Programming Interface—the ability for programmers to easily link their code into the software) for text substitution and replacement within Drupal.

Installing the Modules

We need to open the module files we have just downloaded and unzip their contents into the **modules** folder within our Drupal installation, **C:\wamp\www\drupal-5.7\sites\default\modules**, so that we now have two folders within our modules folder. The modules folder may need to be created as it is not there by default.

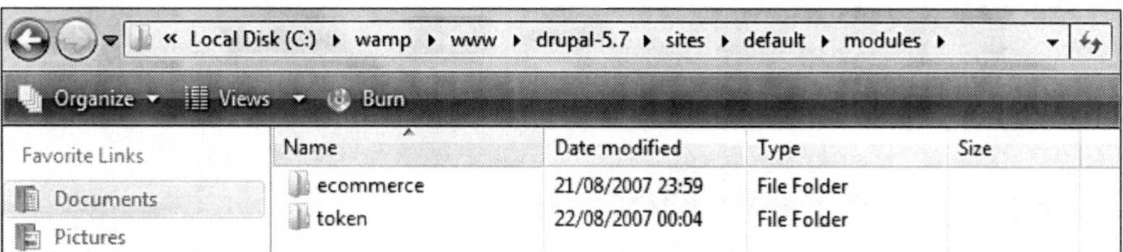

Now that the module files are in the correct location, we can go and enable the modules in the Drupal administration section. This section is under **Site building** and then **Modules** from the **Administer** menu.

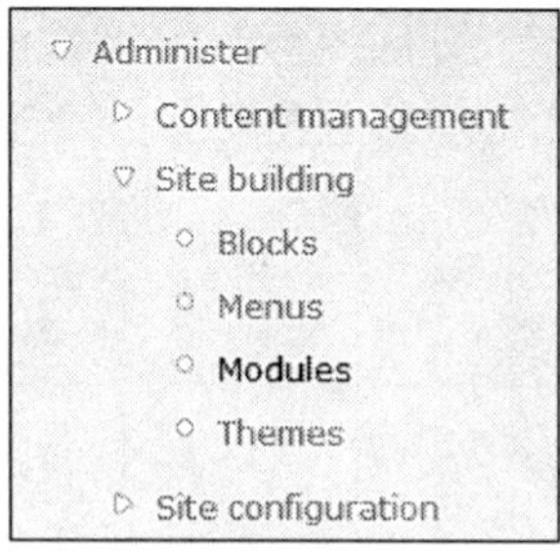

The **modules** page contains a very long list of module components contained within categories; the new modules' categories that should be listed are:

- E-Commerce core
- E-Commerce customer interface
- E-Commerce payment methods
- E-Commerce product types
- E-Commerce uncategorized
- Other

The **Token** module is listed under **Other**, and as the **Store** module under **E-Commerce Core** depends on it, let's enable the module by ticking the check box and clicking the **Save configuration** button at the bottom of the page.

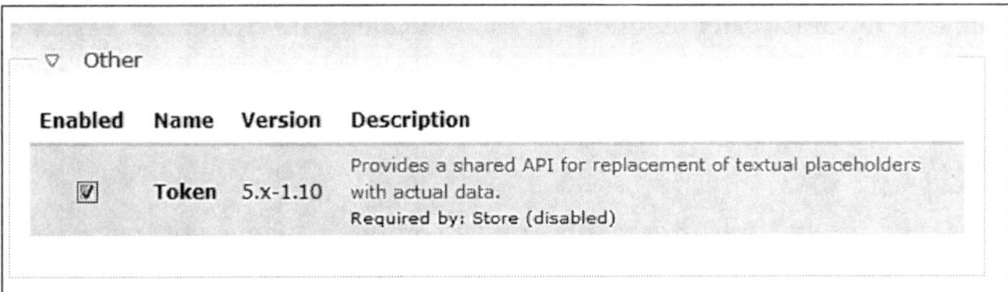

The only other module that we should install for any e-commerce functionality is the **Store** module under **E-Commerce Core**; all of the other modules are required for a fully functioning store; however, we will look at these individually later, along with the functionality they provide and modules for which they are required.

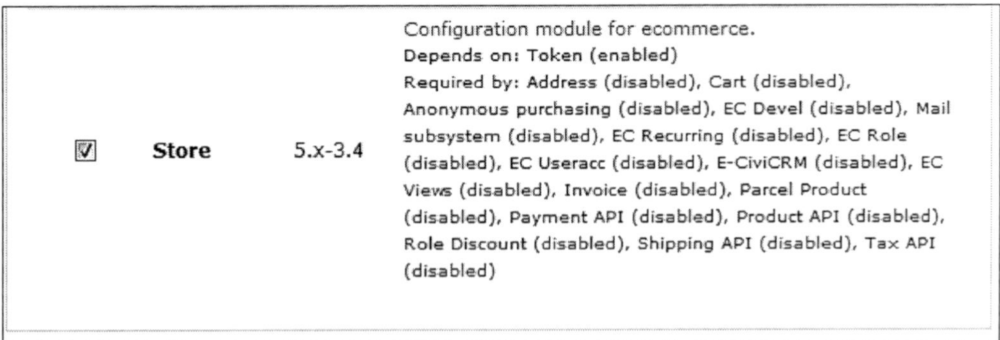

If we then click on **Save configuration** we will have our store module installed along with a few other modules that it installs for us at the same time.

Playing Together

We have installed Drupal and its e-Commerce module; now let's discuss what these modules are and how they work together with Drupal.

On its own, Drupal is a CMS, that is, it is designed for managing website content. Other than that, it does not do much. Additional features, which may not be needed by most users and are not included in the main release, are written by the Drupal community (or anyone really, who wants to write one) as modules which "plug in" to our Drupal installation.

Modules can effortlessly be plugged into the system, and then removed from it later, making it really easy to extend the basic system, and in our case, we are converting a powerful content management system into a powerful e-commerce website.

The module developer's guide (`http://drupal.org/node/508`) contains advanced information on the structure of modules, and information on how to write your own modules.

Summary

In this chapter, we had a brief look into what a content management system is, what Drupal is, what it can do for us, and how it works in relation to the e-commerce module.

We also installed and configured the Drupal content management system and installed the token module and the e-Commerce module, and we are now ready to enable some e-Commerce features in our website for Doug's Dinos.

2

Getting Started with Drupal

Drupal has a wealth of features available for managing content, so now that we have installed Drupal, let's take a look at some of these features and how they work. Drupal's features could fill a separate book in their own right and in fact they do—*Drupal: Creating Blogs, Forums, Portals, and Community Websites* by David Mercer, ISBN 978-1-904811-80-0 published by Packt Publishing, `http://www.packtpub.com/drupal/book`. Since this book primarily focuses on the e-commerce features, we will quickly look through these features in this chapter; if you want more information check out the other Drupal book from Packt. If you remember from Chapter 1, Doug wants his website to be twofold:

- An online store of products
- A wealth of information on Dinosaurs

In this chapter, we will focus on the information side of Doug's website and also his business. Most of the content will be added using the built-in features of Drupal; however, Doug wants a few extra content-focused features such as a contact form and a blog, so we will create those too.

Preparing the Content

Before we can start adding content to the site, we need to know what Doug wants on his site, and then we can think about how to best implement the content into the site:

- A home page
- A contact page
- A dinosaurs section
    - Containing sub-pages on individual dinosaurs

- A museum section
    - Containing sub-pages on his museum
- A blog (Doug has heard how blogs can help businesses, so he wants a blog on his site.)

Let's take an in-depth look at the various contents to be added to the site:

Home Page

The home page will contain a short introduction to Doug's business and to the website, which he had prepared:

> **Hello, and welcome to Doug's Dinos! We are the county's number one model dinosaur store and educational resource on the Jurassic era. We are based just a short journey outside the center of Newcastle and have a fantastic range of model dinosaurs. Our newest range includes high tech remote-controlled programmable robots perfect for guarding rooms, scaring family and friends, or just for fun. Our museum is open weekdays until 6pm and weekends until 4pm; see our museum section for more information.**

Contact Page

Doug wants his contact page to serve two purposes; he wants the contact information for his business, along with a contact form to allow customers to directly contact Doug via the website.

Doug provided us the following content to go on the contact page:

> **Doug's Dinos Limited**
>
> **17 High Street**
>
> **Outskirts**
>
> **Newcastle upon Tyne**
>
> **NE9 9ZZ**
>
> **Directions from Google Maps**
>
> **Telephone: 0191 123 456 Fax: 0191 123 457**
>
> **Email us: doug@dougsdinos.com (general) sales@dougsdinos.com (sales related) support@dougsdinos.com (regarding your support plan)**

Opening Times:

- ○ **Monday to Friday: 9am - 6pm**
- ○ **Saturday: 9am - 4pm**
- ○ **Sunday: 9am - 4pm**
- ○ **Bank Holidays: Closed (museum open by request of advanced group booking)**

He also wants all enquiries sent through an online form to be sent to `doug@dougsdinos.com`.

Dinosaur Section

Within this section Doug has requested a structure listing each type of dinosaur to have a separate page; a snippet of this structure is illustrated below:

- **Dinosaurs** (general information on the eras when Dinosaurs existed)
    - **T-Rex**
    - **Pterodactyl**
    - **Triceratops**
    - **Stegosaurus**

Museum Section

Similar to the dinosaur section, we have the following structure for the museum section of the site.

- **Our Museum**
    - **Tickets, Costs, and Opening Times**
        - **Special group offers**
    - **Photo Gallery**
    - **Testimonials**

Content Management

In order to create this content on the site we need to explore a number of different features within Drupal, including:

- Creating content
- Menu management
- Default homepage

Creating Content

Creating content in Drupal is really straightforward. Once logged in, there is an option on the main menu to **Create content** as shown:

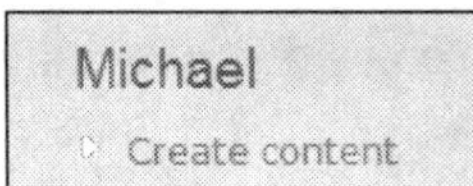

The **Create content** screen lists all of the different types of content that we can create; the list is dynamically based on the installed modules. By default we only have the **Page** and **Story** options available; however as we have installed the e-Commerce module in Chapter 1 we also have the option to add products.

Future version notice: This has been changed in e-Commerce version 4, which at time of writing is still under development; the **Product** node type has been replaced with a new defined node, which can have product types connected with it.

Create content
Choose the appropriate item from the list:

Page
If you want to add a static page, like a contact page or an about page, use a page.

Product
A product is a good or service that you wish to sell on your site.

Story
Stories are articles in their simplest form: they have a title, a teaser and a body, but can be extended by other modules. The teaser is part of the body too. Stories may be used as a personal blog or for news articles.

The figure above shows the content types available in the **Create content** menu. Later on in this chapter, we will look into some of the other types of content that can be created, by installing additional modules.

Pages and stories are similar in terms of the information submitted to create them; however, stories post author information and the time the story was created onto the site whereas, this is not posted with pages. If enabled under theme configuration, pages can also be made to post this information; this is just the default behavior.

We will look at creating content again in Chapter 4 when we create our product catalogue; however, let's have a brief look at it now so that we can create content.

Title and Body

The first two options when creating a **Page** are title and body as shown:

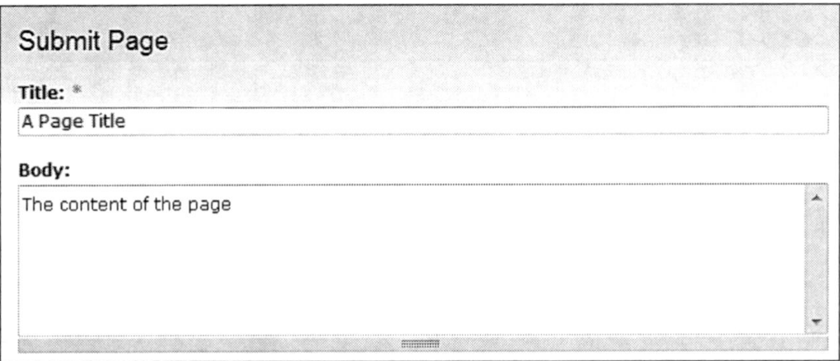

The **Title** is the title of the page, and the **Body** field is the main content for the page.

Input, Product, and Log

Next we have **Input format**, **Product**, and **Log message** as shown below:

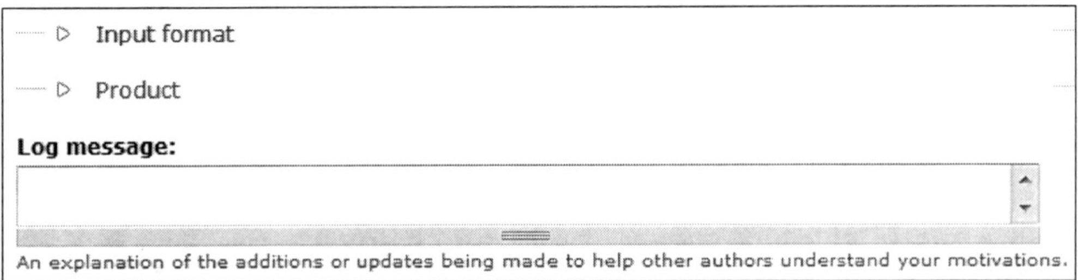

The **Input format** defines how Drupal will process the content in the **Body** field (i.e. process as **HTML**, **PHP code**, or **Filtered HTML**); for now the default will do; in Chapter 4 we will explore these options in more detail. The **Product** option specifies if the page will be handled as a product and if so which type of product. At the moment we are just looking at content management and Drupal's general features, and are not concerned with the e-commerce features just yet, so we can leave the default for that option (the default is to not handle as a product). The **Log message** option allows us to leave a note to other authors or administrators of our Drupal installation, so they can see why we created the page or performed a particular operation.

Final Page Options

The final options are:

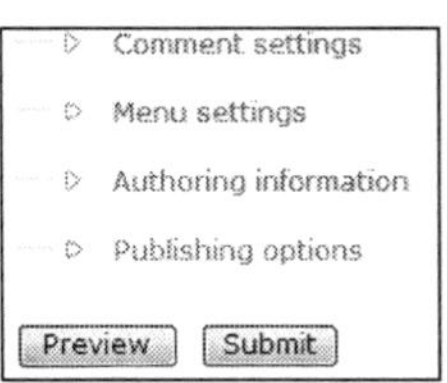

The **Comment settings** allow us to decide if we want users to be able to comment on the page; the options within available are: **Disabled**, **Read only**, and **Read/Write**. **Disabled** disables the comments system for that particular page, **Read only** prevents new comments being added to a page, and **Read/Write** allows new comments to be added as well as all comments to be read. The defaults for these can be set under the **Content types** management screen. Because we are talking about content in the context of a page, Doug does not want comments on pages; however, this may be useful for products, to encourage reviews and discussion on products.

The **Menu settings** define how the page should be handled in the various menus available to us; within here we should enter a title of the page to be displayed in the menu.

Authoring information records the author of the page, and the time the page was saved; this is mainly used by stories and not pages.

Finally we have **Publishing options**, which allows us to define—if a page is published or not, if we promote the page to the front page, if it is displayed at the tops of lists (i.e. sticky), or if it is a new revision. Because we are only taking an overview of the content management features, we will only be concerned with content that is set to be published.

Now that we know how to create pages, let us look into menus and setting pages as the home page, before moving on to create the content in our site.

Menu Management

Menus make it easy and convenient to navigate between the sections of a website, so it is important to be able to use our menus effectively. By default we have two menus:

- Primary links
- Navigation

With the default theme, primary links are displayed along the top of the page and navigation links are displayed down the left-hand side of the page.

The image below shows the primary links menu on the default theme in our site.

The image below shows the navigation menu of the default theme in our site:

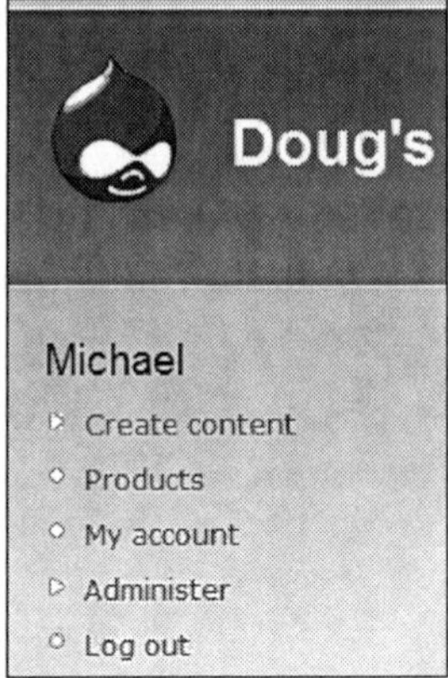

When pages are created, they appear in the navigation menu by default, although we can change this later. Let us now look at managing these menus.

In the navigation menu under **Administer | Site building** there is the **Menus** link, which takes us to the menu manager. The navigation menu is as shown:

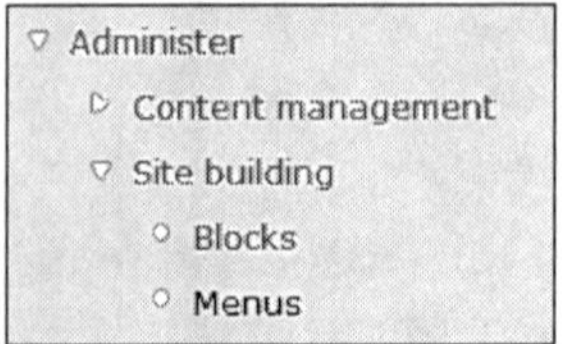

This then takes us to the menu management page:

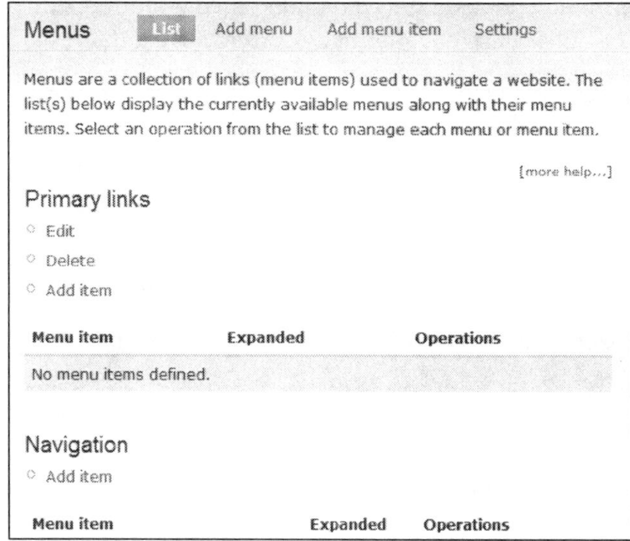

From here we can see the menus available, and the menu items within each. We can create new menus using the **Add menu** option, and add new items using the **Add menu item** option. Items can easily be reordered by editing the menu item and then using the drop-down list to select where the item appears in the list. The menu item edit screen is as shown:

Changing menu item position just involves selecting the item's parent item in the menu, and altering the weight. The parent item defines where the item appears in the hierarchy of the menu, and the weight defines in which order the item appears compared to other items in the same level of the menu.

Default Homepage

The page that acts as the default homepage within our site is set in the **Site information** options, which can be found in the **Site configuration** section of the **Administer** menu:

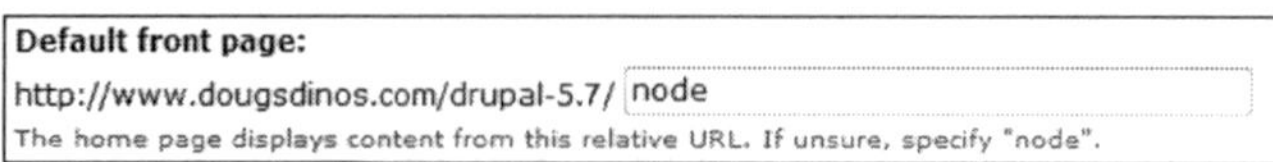
Default front page:
http://www.dougsdinos.com/drupal-5.7/ node
The home page displays content from this relative URL. If unsure, specify "node".

Creating the Content

Now that we know how to create content with Drupal, we can begin adding the content we prepared earlier to our website!

Home Page

The homepage involves two tasks:

- Creating the homepage
- Setting the page as the default page

Creating the page itself is straightforward; we looked at creating pages earlier, the only difference to what we covered there is that we should not list the page in the menu (it will be the homepage after all).

Once we have created the page, we will be taken to that page. We then need to take note of the page URL, so we can set it as the homepage. The page URL is as shown:

http://www.dougsdinos.com/drupal-5.7/node/16

We need to take note of the section: **node/16** from the URL, and put that into the **Default front page** option in the **Site information** section.

We now have a homepage as shown:

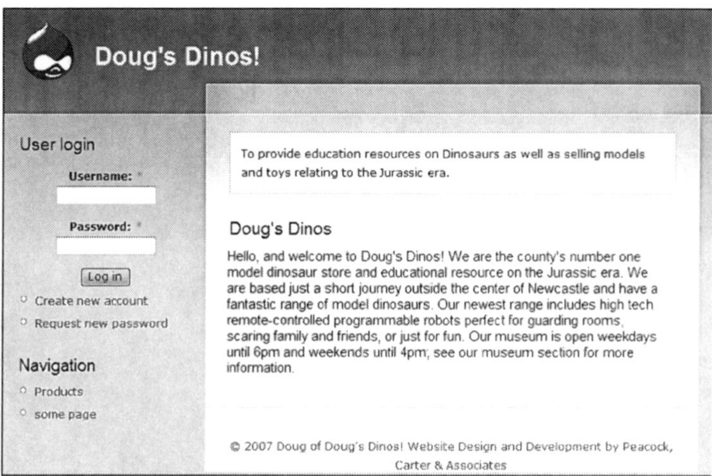

Contact Page

Content can be created similar to the homepage, although when it comes to the menu, we want the link to be the first one in the menu. To do this we select the **Parent item** as **Navigation**, and then give the item a light weighting. I've selected **-10** as the **Weight**, in case we decide to add a lot more menu items later. The menu setting for the contact page is as shown:

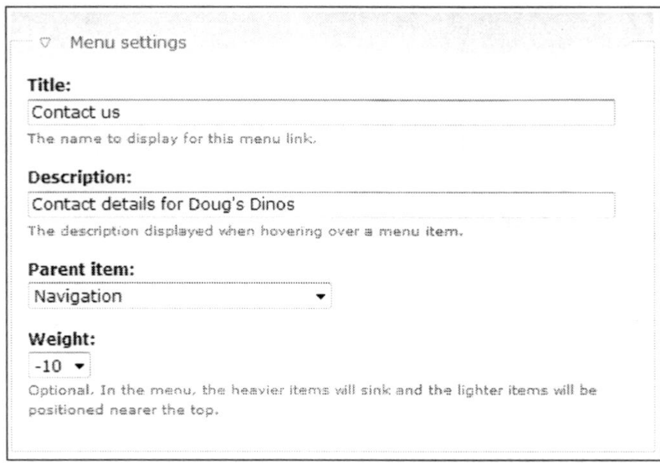

The contact page would also be appropriate on the primary links menu so we should add it to that too. The **Menu settings** to add a contact page in the primary link is as shown below:

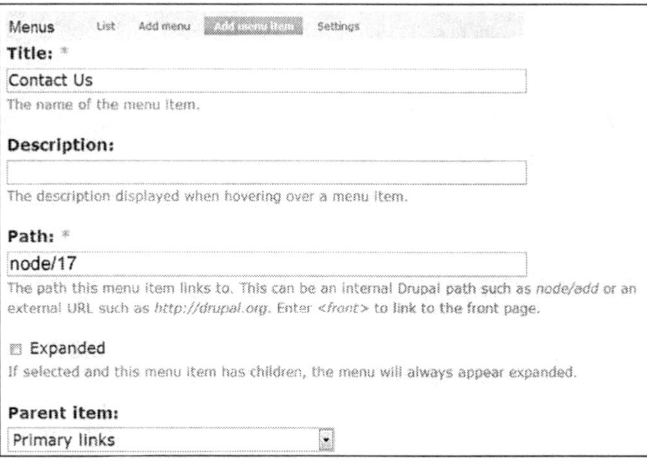

Already our site is starting to take shape with something in our primary menu and a second page to our site! We now have a contact page as shown:

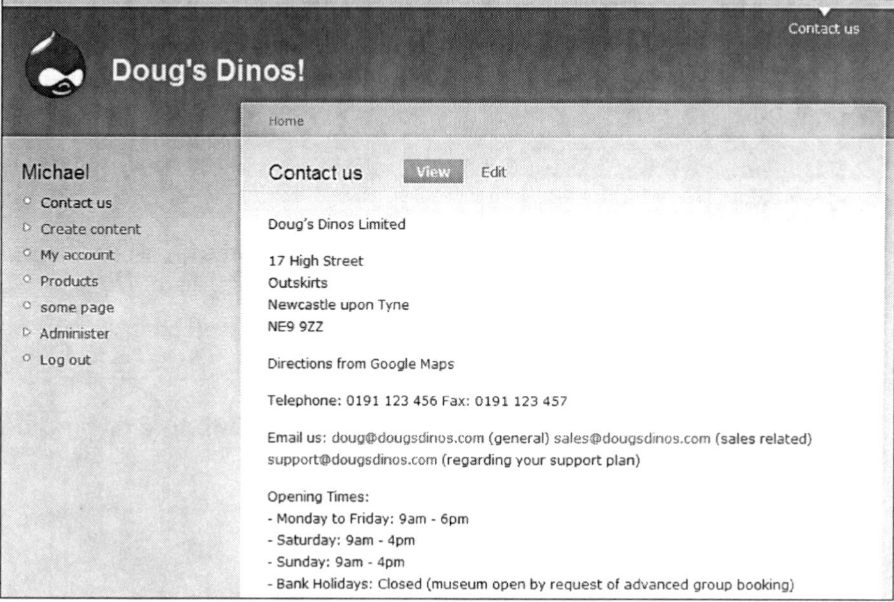

Dinosaur and Museum Sections

These sections just involve more of the same creating content as before, although we need to structure our menu a little differently to get the sub-pages to display properly in the menu.

The Dinosaurs section has the potential to expand to contain lots of pages; however, the museum page probably won't expand very much. Because of this it may be a good idea to set the museum section to always be expanded, and the dinosaurs section to only expand when we open that section. This should give us a menu similar to the one shown below:

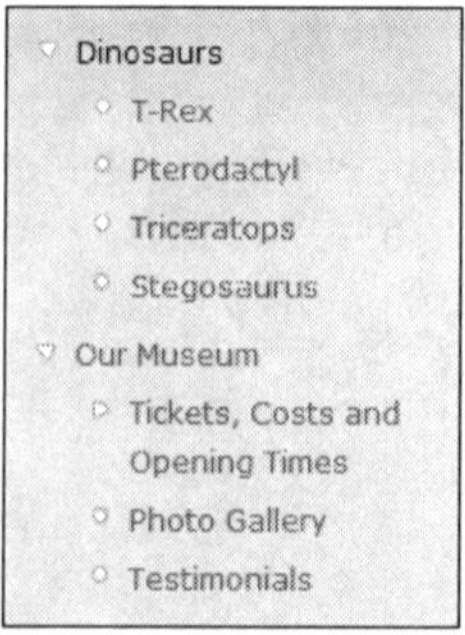

Other Content Modules

In order to have a contact form, blog, and photo gallery on the site, we need to install or enable some other modules. The contact form and blog modules are preinstalled, and just require enabling from within the **Administer** section of our Drupal installation, whereas for the photo gallery we will have to find, download, and install a separate module.

Contact Form

First, let us enable the module; this can be done from the **Modules** section from the **Site building** area of the **Administer** section as shown:

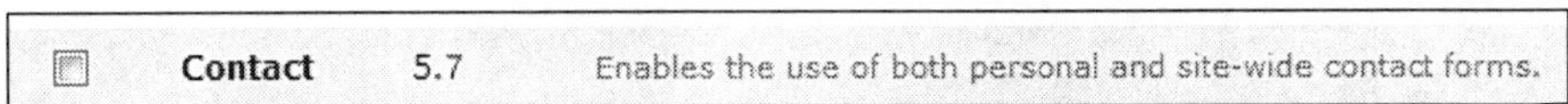

Once we have this enabled, we have a new item in the **Site building** menu called **Contact form**:

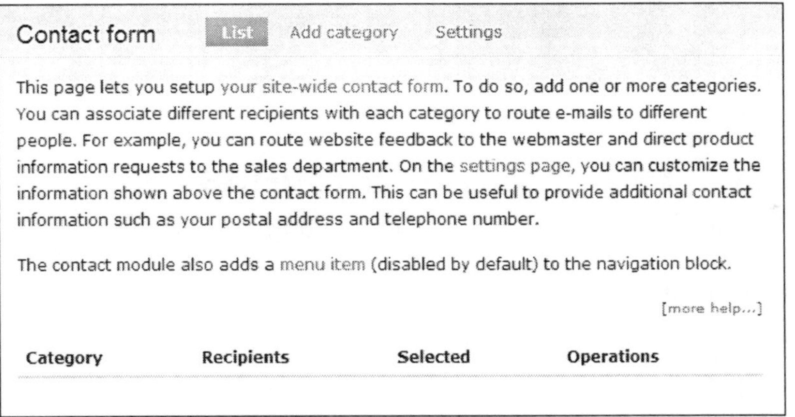

From this section we can set up a contact form for our site, although it requires some further configuration first. To set up the form we need to have at least one category. The categories allow emails to be sent to different groups of people. Although Doug only wanted the form to send things to `doug@dougsdinos.com` he did list a number of other email addresses on the contact page. Because the contact form supports categories, we can in fact incorporate all of these contacts into the contact form. Let us add the categories from the **Add category** link.

Categories have the following settings:

- **Category**—Name of the category.
- **Recipients**—Email addresses of the recipients.
- **Auto-reply**—We have the option to automatically send a reply to those who use the contact form. This could be useful to send a quick note of thanks, along with a message about how long it would take to receive a response.
- **Weight**—It allows us to set where the category appears in the list of categories.
- **Selected**—The final option sets if the category is the default.

We should create the following setup for the contact form.

Category	Recipients	Auto-reply	Weight	Selected
General	doug@	Yes	0	Yes
Sales	sales@	Yes	1	No
Support	support@	Yes	2	No

When this is set up correctly we should have settings that resemble the following:

Category	Recipients	Selected	Operations	
General Enquiries	doug@dougsdinos.com	Yes	edit	delete
Sales and Billing Issues	sales@dougsdinos.com	No	edit	delete
Support Issues	support@dougsdinos.com	No	edit	delete

By default, users who are not logged in cannot access the contact form. This is relatively simple to change, and just requires us to alter the role of anonymous users. We do this from the **Roles** area within the **User management** section. This page lists the different roles available; we need to click the **edit permissions** link next to the **anonymous user** role. We need to enable the **access site-wide contact form** from the **contact module** as shown:

With that done, we now have a fully functional contact form, which all users can use; it should automatically appear in our menu:

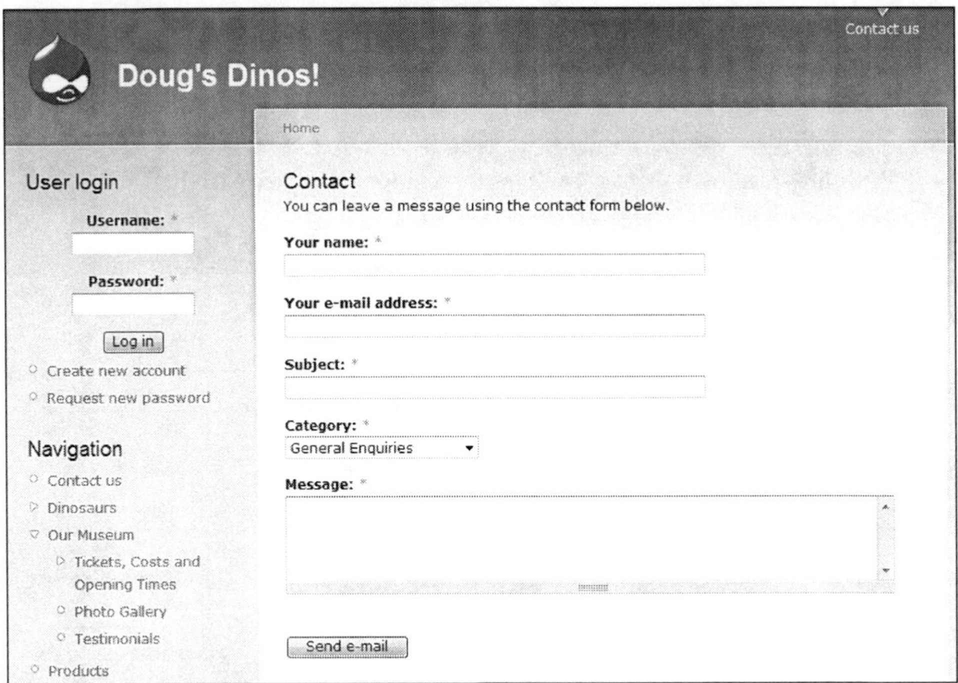

Blog

The **Blog** module is a lot less involved than the contact form. Once the module is enabled (the same way we enabled the contact form module), content can be added from the **Create content** section. Within here there is a new option for **Blog entry**, which appears exactly the same as a page or a story (they just get processed differently).

I've set up a blog to use, and all of the other users, including Doug should be able to set up their own with very little effort!

There are other settings and options available for blogs, such as RSS feeds, comments, permissions, and so on, but we will leave those for you to figure out on your own if you wish to use the blog module.

Photo Gallery

Adding a blog was really simple; unfortunately to add a photo gallery, which Doug wants for his museum, is more complicated. This is because there are so many different modules available including:

- **Flickr Gallery**—integrates with your Flickr album
- **Gallery**—integrates with your gallery installation on the website
- **Lightbox**—can be used to create a Lightbox gallery

We can also create complicated galleries using views, Image Field, and Content Construction Kit modules.

Doug is not sure how he wants his gallery to work, and is going to think about this. We'll come back to it later, once we have looked into enhancing our store and adding images to products.

Summary

In this chapter, you have learned:

- How to create content in Drupal
- How to manage menus in Drupal
- How to define our homepage
- How to create a contact form and a blog using additional modules

Now that we have looked into Drupal's fundamental features, let's move on to planning our e-Commerce store, and looking into our product catalog in Chapter 3—*Planning Your Shop*.

3
Planning Your Shop

We now have Drupal with the e-Commerce module installed, and we have a basic understanding of how Drupal works, so let's start planning our shop. As well as discussing some general planning advice, we will also plan our online shop, Doug's Dinos.

In this chapter we will cover:

- Things to think about when planning to sell online
- Legal issues that we need to consider
- The structure of the shop
- Things we need to convey about our products
- Ways to take photographs of our products to show them off to our potential customers

Planning to Sell Online

Selling online is similar in many ways to physical selling, both aim to sell products or services to customers; however, online selling has a number of crucial differences compared to physical selling.

With online transactions it is easier for someone to use a stolen card (no risk of CCTV cameras catching them unlike in a physical shop) so we are at greater risk of fraud, which could potentially result in more chargeback requests from purchases, which introduce additional costs.

A brief example of how this can be a problem, even with a genuine transaction—I received a number of emails recently thanking me for ordering products from various websites. The person ordering the products was not me, but shared my initials, and must have entered the wrong email address. As it was my email address, I could cancel the order, and in some cases log in to an account page of the company to view the order. From here I could have potentially made more orders, since card details may have been stored on file, or changed the shipping address. As for the consumer, they would either have more than they bought or their items would not arrive, and the seller would face charge backs and have an upset customer.

Our errors can cause great problems to our store. If we were to make a mistake with a product description, we could get an increased number of returns, whereas with a physical sale the customer would see the product for themselves and not need to read a description (other than what may be provided on the packaging).

With selling any product or service, the customer is entitled to purchase the product or service at whatever price is advertised, regardless of any mistakes in price. With physical selling this is less of a problem:

- It may just be on one product whereas with an online store, a price mistake carries through to every single one of those products, even if there are hundreds in stock.
- In a store, a customer could easily ask if the price is correct for an overpriced item, whereas an online buyer would be more likely to just abandon the site!
- We would be more likely to notice these issues while we are walking around a shop we are working in, but with the website, we may only check it now and again, or only check the administration areas.

Besides the software that we have already downloaded and installed, there are other things that we will need to get our online store up and running. The other technical requirements will be discussed later in Chapter 10—*Securing, Deploying, and Maintaining Your Shop.*

Legal Issues

As with most things in business, and in life, there are a number of legal issues we need to be aware of and consider:

- The Americans with Disabilities Act of 1990, Disability Discrimination Act 1995 (UK), and general Accessibility guidelines
- The Distance Selling Act (UK)
- The Companies Act (UK)

- Trade Descriptions
- Spam Laws (most countries)
- Data Protection (many countries) and privacy policy

Nothing mentioned here should be considered as legal advice, if you are uncertain about any of this information, or for full details about the laws applicable to your business you should seek professional legal advice.

Disability Discrimination

A number of countries have legislation in place to prevent discrimination against those with disabilities (for the UK this is the Disability Discrimination Act 1995, and for the USA the Americans with Disabilities Act of 1990). These are in place to ensure a wide range of rights for those who have disabilities (such as equality in employment) but also to ensure access to facilities, premises, and information. In the same way that provisions should be in place to allow visitors with disabilities to access our store, this affects visitors to our website. Blind or visually impaired users may use screen readers to hear the content of websites. We need to ensure our website is standards compliant (so it can be interpreted by as many web browsers as possible, including screen readers) so that the information is properly displayed. Websites that use frames cannot be interpreted by some browsers and screen readers, and with table-based layouts sometimes the content is read in the wrong order.

Distance Selling

Many countries have regulations in place to govern distance selling, for instance in the UK the Distance Selling Regulations govern the sale of goods or services to consumers over the Internet, digital TV, mail order, telephone, and fax. These laws state that the seller must provide certain information to the consumer and also allow for cooling off periods. For more specific information you should look up or seek advice on the law in your country or region.

Companies Act and Trust

With recent changes to the Companies Act in the UK, websites must clearly state information such as company number, VAT number, and registered office on websites and emails. Even if this is not a legal requirement for your business, it is strongly advised to provide this information to your customers about your business, including its status as a legal entity and also any contact details. At the very least, this conveys an open message to consumers, so they feel more secure in dealing with your business.

Trade Descriptions

I mentioned earlier about the issues arising with incorrectly pricing and describing goods. Many countries have trade description laws to ensure product information is accurate, and what the consumers' rights are with respect to incorrect descriptions and pricing. You may already be aware of such laws if you have a physical store; these laws are important and you should look into them in more detail.

Spam Laws

Because our store will be online, we will most likely be taking our customers' email address when they order online, and using this to send emails—be these emails regarding their order, or promotional marketing. Because of the overwhelming amount of spam emails being sent, many countries have imposed laws regarding emails that can be considered spam. Generally, you can only email individual marketing promotions to those individuals who have agreed to receive them and they should have the option to opt-out (businesses are often a different case), although many websites still send spam even when they are a reputable company. In 2003, the US introduced the CAN-SPAM Act to regulate the sending of spam, email content, and methods to allow recipients to unsubscribe.

Privacy Policies and Data Protection

It is important that we tell our customers exactly what data we will be collecting from them and what we will be doing with it. This should be in the form of a privacy policy; templates of these can normally be purchased from legal sites for a nominal fee, or directly from solicitors or lawyers. Some countries also impose data protection laws, which govern what data you can collect and what you can do with it. In the UK for instance, there is the Data Protection Act, which even defines that data can only be used for the intention it was initially collected for, and recommends various security procedures for safeguarding the data collected; there is even a registration process to register as a data controller.

General Planning

We have looked briefly at the legal issues and one or two other issues; now let's start planning the shop itself. The shop we will be creating throughout the course of this book, as discussed in Chapter 1, is Doug's Dinos—a shop selling model dinosaurs and also providing information on dinosaurs through the rest of the website.

Product Types

There are three main types of product that are sellable using Drupal e-Commerce:

- Apparel—clothing e.g. T-Rex T-Shirts
- Shippable goods e.g. model dinosaurs
- Non-shippable goods e.g.
    - Services—Dinosaur repair and repaint
    - Media—Downloadable booklets on dinosaurs for teachers to use in lessons
    - Privileges—Customers could pay to access other areas of the website

As our shop is mainly concerned with model dinosaurs we will be mainly selling shippable goods and creating those types of products; however, we will also look into the other types, so we can see how to use them if the Doug's Dinos online store wishes to offer repairs, services, or premium content at a later time.

Although apparel is intended for clothing, it provides an additional feature to standard shippable products, and that is **sub-products** or **variations**. These allow us create variations of the same product, but with different attributes, such as color, or size, and set a surcharge for these sub-products.

When going through the product lines of your own shop, it is important to work out which types of products you want to offer, and also if you can offer products in one or more types. For instance, if we were to sell downloadable booklets or books, we may also wish to sell tangible, hard copies of them to our customers. We will go through the product lineup for Doug's Dinos later in the chapter.

Product Groupings

As well as the type of product we can offer, we also need to think about grouping products together into categories. Drupal's provisions for categories describe them as vocabulary, terms for describing the piece of content (the product listing).

When trying to relate our product lineup to our shop, we need to consider the best ways to categorize our products, but also alternative ways of categorizing our products. With a physical store, you would generally have a particular product in a particular area of the store, for instance at a supermarket milk would be in the dairy section, however with an online store this is not a limitation! What if we also wanted milk next to breakfast cereals? This is not a problem with online shops!

It is worth thinking of the product's primary category, the section of the store where it will get the most attention, and also the secondary categories, where it may not get as much attention, but where it may be considered supplemental to other products within that category.

Product Information

Our website will need information on the products themselves; the standard details available for all product types in Drupal e-Commerce are:

- Product
- Product description
- Price
- Anonymous purchasing policy—Do we want it so that only registered users can buy the product?
- Stock Keeping Unit (SKU)—This is an ID number for the product from another system. For instance, if we had our online shop tied into a central system with our physical shop, we would use the product ID from the main system (e.g. a stock control product) as the SKU.
- Add to cart link visibility—Do we want the link for adding the item to the shopping cart hidden or visible?

For Apparel and Shippable goods we also need the following information:

- Inventory control—Do we want to show the stock levels on the site, and allow items to be sold out? If yes, we need to set a stock level.
- Availability estimate—General time frame for the item to leave the fulfillment centre once the order has been placed.

With product variations for apparel products we can create additional attributes; for example, we could create options for different sizes, colors, or materials. We can then specify any weight difference or surcharges that apply to the product variation.

Planning Our Shop

Now that we know the information that needs to be collected we should investigate our own product line and the best ways to promote our products. In Chapter 4—*Creating Your Product Catalog*, we will put the catalog we have prepared in this chapter onto our store!

Product Lineup

For our store we will mainly be selling model dinosaurs, so let's start with those, and prepare and collect the appropriate information. Here we are going to describe just a few sample products; you should think up a few of your own, and collate them in a spreadsheet for later when we start adding products to the shop! If we have them prepared in advance, then when the shop is ready, we will know what to add to it.

Sample Product—Shippable Goods

For our sample shippable product, let's take a model T-Rex. We want to keep our product name short, yet descriptive, so something like "**T-Rex with sound effects (1m)**" would suffice. We don't want to overload the customer with information in the name, yet we want to leave it so the customer will want to read more on the product.

For the description we don't want to say something such as "1m T-Rex dinosaur, Red, with sound effects and motion sensors allowing it to roar whenever someone enters a room". That description is very dull, and only describes the bare minimum, and reading it makes it seem like even we don't know much about the product!

Something like this would be more appropriate:

"**Our 1 meter scale model of T-Rex (model: TR15) is bound to scare anyone, especially with its new motion sensor, which sets off a lifelike 'Roar'. This model is a must-have for any model dinosaur lover; it is made of durable, shock resistant plastic complete with fantastic hand-painted detail. This model requires two AA size batteries (not included) and comes with a 6-month guarantee; we think you will love this product—but if for whatever reason it falls below the standards you expect, we are happy to offer a no-fuss 30-day money back guarantee. Any questions just call us on 555-0135.**

Emma from Newcastle said 'This dinosaur was fantastic! I bought one for my brother and he just loves it, especially when an unsuspecting visitor to his room gets a nasty shock!' "

With that description you can see that not only is the product described in detail, but also technical aspects (such as battery needs) are described. This could link into a page offering low cost batteries for sale. We also mention about our refund and guarantee policies, which can be linked to directly from the description.

There isn't much to say about the price really! For this product, we will have a price of **$94.99**. (We will add the product, and a few others to our store later in the book!)

The **Anonymous purchases** policy can be a little tricky to decide upon, as both restricting and not restricting purchases have advantages. If the user needs to register, then they may be put off by the process, but alternatively they will have signed up to the website, and will most likely be able to receive an e-newsletter. For products where there is no real need for them to be a user on the website, it is best to allow anonymous users to make a purchase.

For the **SKU** we could use the reference number, a reference number for a stock control system for the main shop, or just leave it blank. Its main use is when the system is tied in with another system, so we don't really need to think about these at this time.

If this product is not yet available, i.e. something we expect to get soon (but potentially may not get) then we would want to hide the **'Add to cart'** link. This dinosaur is one of our star products, so we should leave a note not to hide the link.

If we wish to show these products are in stock, we can enable **Inventory control** – so we would put a note in that column in our spreadsheet (where we are collating this information) if it is **Enabled**; we also need to enter the amount that we have in stock.

There are also a number of options available for how long we estimate the product will ship, these include: within 24 hours, 2-3 days, 1-2 weeks, 4-6 weeks. Since these models are one of our star products, and we have loads ready in stock to ship, we would say within 24 hours.

Sample Product—Non-Shippable Goods

Out of the box provisions for non-shippable goods are similar to the other two products without variations, stock control, and availability.

A sample product could be repairs on damaged products. "**3-year repair plan on Model T-Rex**" described as: "**If your model becomes damaged during the next three years, we will repair the model back to its original condition if you have purchased this plan. This is subject to our acceptable damage policy, and the customer must pay shipping costs to the repair center.**"

With this product we may actually want it to only be available to members, i.e. people who have already made purchases, or signed up to access our pages with help and support for the products. It is also worth noting that this type of service could be grouped with the models themselves.

Sample Product—Apparel

For our sample apparel product, let's have a T-Shirt with a picture of a T-Rex on it. As before we want a short and snappy name, which is also descriptive, so something like "**Children's T-Rex T-Shirt**" would suffice. Although we will specify sizes separately, as variations—I've described this as a child's shirt as we may have some shirts intended only for adults or children.

We need a useful, description for the shirt, but we don't need to go into as much detail as with the model dinosaur. I'm going to use:

"**Our high quality 100% cotton T-Shirt sports a detailed T-Rex on it, along with a witty slogan on the back 'T-Rex T-Shirt'. It is machine washable and available in a range of colors and sizes.**" I have purposely omitted the actual sizes and colors from the description as when we create variations of this product, they will share the same description.

Cost: $**18.95**

As before, we have no real need for anonymous users to be restricted from purchasing, and we also don't really need the SKU value, and the add to cart link visibility should depend on if we have the product or if its something we hope to add to our lineup in the future. Stock control and availability estimate are the same as with shippable products (as apparel is also shippable!).

We can create variations on these products; the variations have weight and surcharge provided, and provisions to add any attributes we wish. So we could have:

Colors: Red, Black, Brown and Sizes: S, M, L, XL, XXL. These would probably be the same cost (so no surcharge) and similar weight. Additionally we could have a variation that glows in the dark, which would then incur a surcharge.

Getting the Message Across

The description of our product is very important; it should make the product appealing to potential customers and also cover technical details. It may be useful to look into professional copy-writing services to get the most out of your product description. Below are some useful tips and suggestions for professional content.

- **Be honest, truthful, and accurate**—This not only helps building trust with customers if they know you are honest with your products (particularly useful for returning customers) but it is also the law in many countries. (See *Trade Descriptions* earlier in this chapter.)
- **Keep the content plain and simple**—We don't want a description that confuses the potential customer!

- **Provide additional information**—If your product has specific specifications, such as computer software or technical equipment, make sure you mention as much of that as possible, in addition to the more friendly descriptions.
- **Visualize your customers**—Imagine your average potential customer, and write as if you were describing it directly to them.

Here are a few websites you may find useful on the subject:

Business Link—Fair trading, trade descriptions, and Trading Standards: `http://www.businesslink.gov.uk/bdotg/action/detail?type=RESOURCES&itemId=1073792290`

The Federal Trade Commission has resources for businesses including how to comply with the "made in USA" rules when marketing products as being made in the US, as well as labeling requirements for clothing and other useful information for US-based businesses: `http://www.ftc.gov/bcp/menus/business/resources.shtm`.

Bill Fryer Copywriting Tips, `http://www.billfryer.com/info/info4.html`.

A Picture Says a Thousand Words

Further down the line we will add photographs to our product listings. Here are some advice and tips to consider when taking photographs, which will help take great pictures for your store.

These tips were provided courtesy of award-winning photographer Martin Baker who has a website dedicated to photography and image engineering: `www.merrillvalleyphotography.co.uk`.

Equipment

The camera and support equipment we use are very important.

Camera

We don't particularly need an expensive camera, but the following features really will be helpful:

- A camera with a resolution of 3 Megapixel will be sufficient, especially if you are able to fill most of the image with the product. A higher resolution camera will allow you to compose more freely, cropping the image later to size.

- An optical zoom helps you compose your shots. Ignore quoted values for "digital zoom" as these settings operate by using a relatively small area of the sensor, which you can do more easily and to a higher quality, in post production.
- The ability to adjust such settings as aperture, ISO, and white balance will make a big difference. Such adjustments are now available on many compact digital cameras.
- Finally, your camera should have a remote control release so you can fire it without touching the camera. If this is not possible you can use the delay timer (which can usually be set to either 2 or 10 seconds delay).

Support Equipment

While it is possible to take good product shots with the camera handheld it is more convenient to have some sort of support for the camera. A small tripod is perfect. Failing that, rest your camera on a sturdy table or with a pile of books so that it cannot move between shots. Use the remote control release (if available) or the delay timer to fire the shutter so you do not move the camera as you are taking the photograph.

Camera Settings

Cameras often have lots of settings available; these are optimal settings which should be used:

File Format

Higher-end cameras may offer a number of file formats in which to save the photographs (e.g. RAW, TIFF, JPEG). RAW can offer more flexibility in post processing the images but for most purposes choose JPEG.

File Size and Resolution

Choose the largest resolution available on the camera as this uses the full recording capability of the sensor.

Quality

Set the highest quality available on the camera. Lower settings throw away some of the information recorded by the sensor.

Sharpening

Choose the lowest degree of sharpness available. It is much more effective to apply sharpening in post production. If you are not planning to do any post processing, you may want to use a slightly higher setting.

White Balance

This setting is used to match the predominant lighting in the photograph. If there is an "auto" setting you can try that but you will get more reproducible results if you use one of the "preset" values (Daylight if you are using daylight; Tungsten if you are using one or more table lamps to light your product).

ISO

This setting is equivalent to "film speed" in film cameras. Use the lowest value available. This will mean you need a slower shutter speed but as your product is (probably!) not moving and your camera is on a tripod or other firm support, this will not be a problem.

Program Settings

If your camera offers a "close-up" or "macro" option try that, though you may need to move the camera close to the product for it to focus correctly.

Focus

Sharp focus is critical in product shots. Take care to focus carefully, and if your camera has an aperture (f-stop) setting, set it to a high value (e.g. f/8, f/11 or higher) as most of the depth of the photographs will be in sharp focus.

Remote Control or Delay Timer

Set the camera to use the remote control (if available), or the delay timer to fire the shutter, so you do not move the camera as you are taking the shot.

Setup

In addition to the camera and the settings on it, the environment can make a big difference to the quality of the photographs.

Lighting

Do not be tempted to use the camera's own (onboard) flash as it is likely to be far too powerful at close range and will cast ugly shadows.

Either using daylight by setting the product up near a window or using normal adjustable table lamps, preferably one either side of the product to reduce shadows would work. Note that you will need to set the camera's white balance (see above) depending on the source of light you are using; otherwise the colors of the product will not be reproduced faithfully.

Reflector

If you are using just one light source (a window or just one table lamp) then use a reflector (piece of white card or aluminum foil) to reflect some of the light onto the shadow side of the product to reduce the harshness of the shadows.

Background

The simplest background is probably a white or plain colored wall. For a more professional look, use a long sheet or roll of paper. Stand the product on the paper and lift the back of the sheet so that there is a curve of paper behind the product.

Light Tent

If you are going to take a lot of product photographs it will be worth investing in (or making) a light tent. This is a box or frame structure with the sides made of thin, light-diffusing material. With the product inside the box and the lights set up outside (shining through the sides) you should be able to get very high quality shots with well-controlled shadows.

Post Processing

This covers anything you do to the image from the moment you take the photograph. Some cameras offer limited options in-camera but post processing is usually something you do to the image after you have uploaded the file to your computer.

Many cameras come bundled with image editing software or there is a wide range of free or shareware software available on the Internet. Commercial packages such as Adobe Photoshop, Adobe Elements or Paint Shop Pro are also available.

- You may need to adjust the exposure (brightness) of the image. This is especially likely if your camera has automatic metering and you are using a white or light-colored background. In this case the image may require brightening a little. If this happens repeatedly, see if your camera has an exposure compensation setting. If so, set it to +1/2 or +1 to force the camera to overexpose the image.
- A low level of sharpening will probably improve your image but take care not to apply it too strongly. Look carefully at the edges in your image after applying sharpening. If you can see a distinct "halo" around your subject you have sharpened the image too strongly.

- The final stage is to crop or resize the image to the size you need for your website. Think about what versions of the image you need: perhaps a small, "thumbnail" image of 60x80 pixels, a medium size of 300x400 pixels and a large size of 600x800 pixels. Save the file you have been working on, then using the software resize the image down to the largest of the sizes you need (600x800 pixels in this example). Save the file in JPEG format with a different filename from the original file from your camera. Resize down to the next size (300x400 pixels) and save as a new JPEG file. Repeat again for the smallest file (60x80 pixels).

How Not to Advertise a Product?

Quite a lot of small businesses with online shops don't put much effort into their website and store—with many of these sites the amount of effort they put into their site is apparent; however, a good amount of time in initial preparations should mean that we only have to put in minimal maintenance time in the future, and still have a fantastic store for our customers. These examples are ones that I have found on real websites, but have been recreated to ensure anonymity.

Example One—Detail

The following example illustrates a completely useless product description and listing:

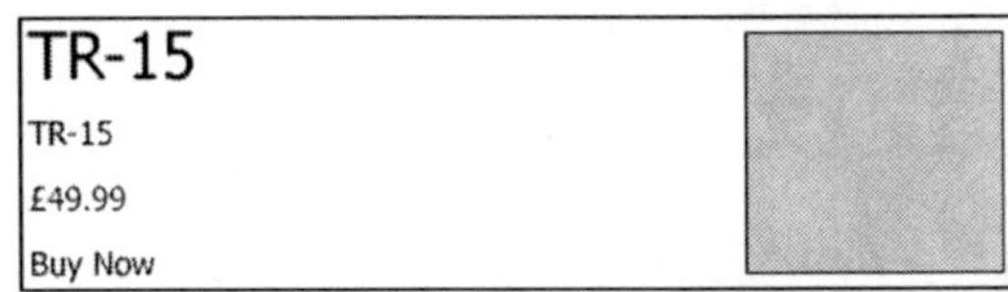

The product name and description are both the reference number for the product, probably taken from the manufacturer's own catalog. The gray box would be a photograph of the product—but it doesn't really add to the quality of the listing!

Example Two—No Photo

Photos are really important—if you can go through the trouble to describe the product—photograph it! Otherwise it looks like you are describing it in detail and not showing the photo because the description is incorrect.

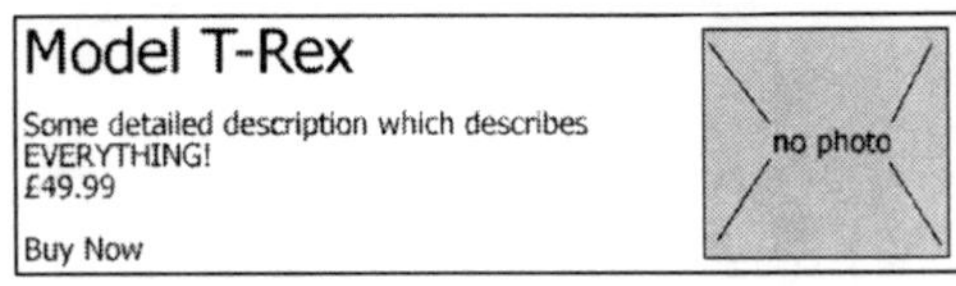

Example Three—Spot the Difference?

Some shops list every model of product—which is fine, but what many don't do is differentiate the models. They use the same photograph, the same name, and write the different model number next to it, leaving the customer wondering why there is a price difference.

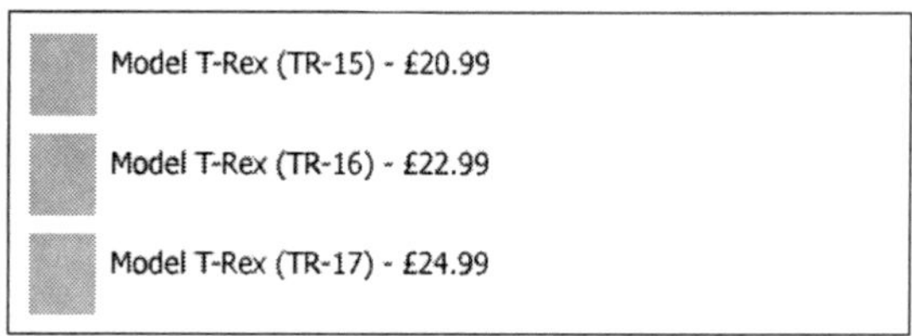

Can you spot the difference in terms of product advantages? You would need to actually read the full information page on each product—which would turn off any customer! If at a glance they could see one had flashing eyes, whereas another had motorized legs, it would be much easier!

Customer Service

One of the most important aspects of any business is **customer service**; this is even more important with online stores where the customer does not feel reassured by physical contact and immediate response to questions i.e. they have to wait for a reply to an email rather than asking an assistant at a physical store.

Without a proper customer service systems in place, an online business will quickly crumble, because:

- Poor customer service leads customers with bad experiences not returning.
- It leads to a bad reputation for the business.
- Essentially losing money!

So, let's look at the best ways to ensure quality customer service:

- Be clear about guarantees, refund policies, and replacement policies.
- Be flexible with these policies; if a customer who has used our store many times wishes to return an item, which would normally not be allowed, it may be more viable to accept the return (causing a small loss) to ensure the customer has a positive overall experience, and is encouraged to continue coming back.

- Have as many contact methods available as possible, and make sure it is easy to get those details from the website. If a customer wants to know more about a product and they can't even get your contact number, they may abandon their shopping cart (which could contain a number of items) and go elsewhere. If a phone number is on every page of the site with a message like, **Have a question? Just give us a call on 555-0135**, the customer immediately sees how they can get their questions answered there and then so that they may proceed with their order.
- Payment Options: Make it clear which payment methods are accepted.
- After-purchase care: Offering support for products once they have been purchased.
- Communication: The user needs to be clear at every stage of the website how they are progressing through the shop, how they can cancel their order, and they ideally should be contacted at least by email once their order has been placed and dispatched.

Another important part of customer service is dealing with complaints—it is important to show the customer that you have a system in place for dealing with complaints; this could just be the main business phone number but with a mention that it's used also for complaints, or a dedicated email address. This shows the customer that you are happy to listen to complaints, and use the complaints to help improve the business, and shows that you care for the customer, valuing their input!

These policies and procedures should be carefully planned out before your store goes online, so that as soon as it does go online, the systems are in place ready for excellent customer service and a professional, trustworthy service is ready for customers immediately.

Summary

In this chapter, we have looked at a wide range of issues involved with creating an online shop, and doing business online. We have discussed some legal and professional issues, how to promote our products, how to photograph them to get the most from them, and taken a look at some sample products. We have also looked at some examples of how not to advertise a product online—to ensure we avoid some common problems. With this knowledge, we should be able to prepare our business policies, consider the legal issues in more detail, and collate the details of our own catalogs so as to know exactly what we will be selling.

4
Creating Your Product Catalog

Now that we have planned our Drupal e-Commerce store, let's create our online product catalog.

In this chapter, we will cover:

- Creating pages for products
- Creating packages of products
- The shopping process for our users

Further e-Commerce Configuration

In Chapter 1, we installed the Drupal e-Commerce module, and enabled the **Store** module. This is essentially the minimum to classify the module as installed. We now need to enable more of the e-commerce modules in order to give us the features we need for our store.

The modules that we need to install are the **E-Commerce Product Types** modules, which allow us to create a range of different product types. The available product type modules are:

- **Apparel**
- **Auction**
- **Donate**
- **EC Media**
- **File Product**
- **Generic Product**
- **Parcel Product**
- **Tangible Product**

Of those modules we only need to install the following:

- **Apparel**
- **File Product**
- **Generic Product**
- **Parcel Product**
- **Tangible Product**

To install them, we need to go to the **Administer** menu in our Drupal installation, select **Site building** and then choose **Modules**. From here we can then tick the appropriate check boxes for the modules before installing them by clicking **Save configuration**:

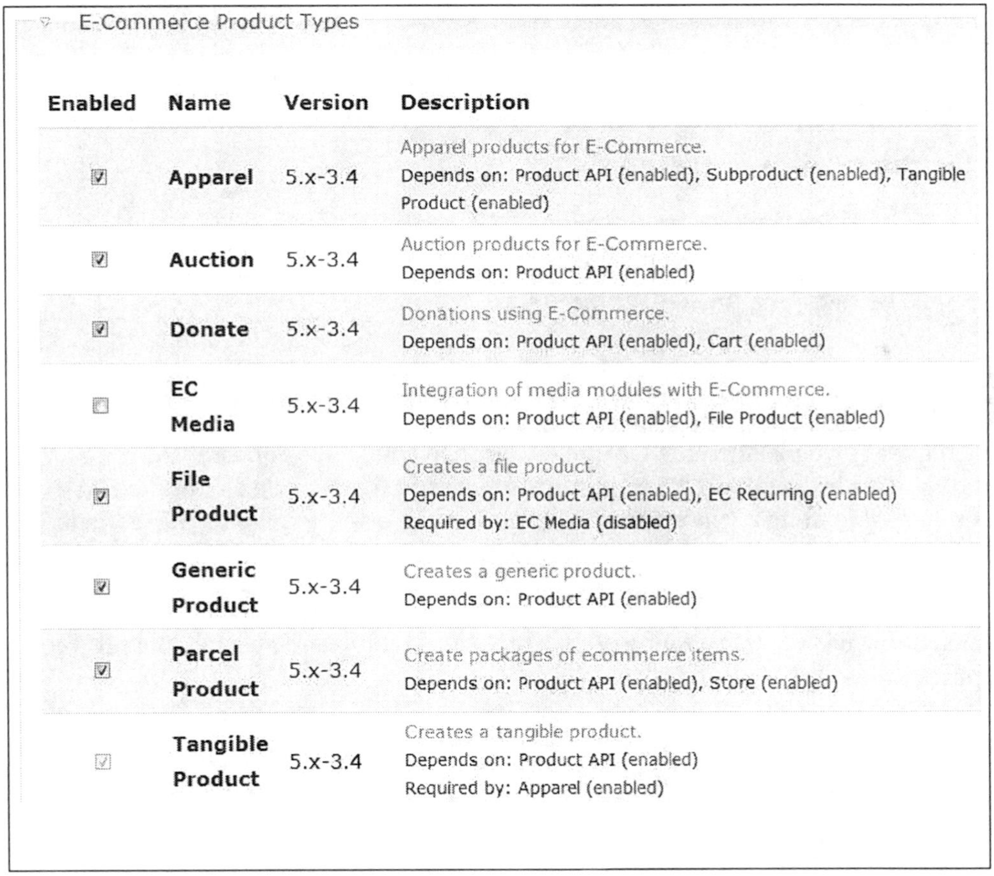

E-Commerce Product Types

Enabled	Name	Version	Description
☑	**Apparel**	5.x-3.4	Apparel products for E-Commerce. Depends on: Product API (enabled), Subproduct (enabled), Tangible Product (enabled)
☑	**Auction**	5.x-3.4	Auction products for E-Commerce. Depends on: Product API (enabled)
☑	**Donate**	5.x-3.4	Donations using E-Commerce. Depends on: Product API (enabled), Cart (enabled)
☐	**EC Media**	5.x-3.4	Integration of media modules with E-Commerce. Depends on: Product API (enabled), File Product (enabled)
☑	**File Product**	5.x-3.4	Creates a file product. Depends on: Product API (enabled), EC Recurring (enabled) Required by: EC Media (disabled)
☑	**Generic Product**	5.x-3.4	Creates a generic product. Depends on: Product API (enabled)
☑	**Parcel Product**	5.x-3.4	Create packages of ecommerce items. Depends on: Product API (enabled), Store (enabled)
☑	**Tangible Product**	5.x-3.4	Creates a tangible product. Depends on: Product API (enabled) Required by: Apparel (enabled)

While installing these modules, we may be prompted to install some additional sub-modules, which these depend upon:

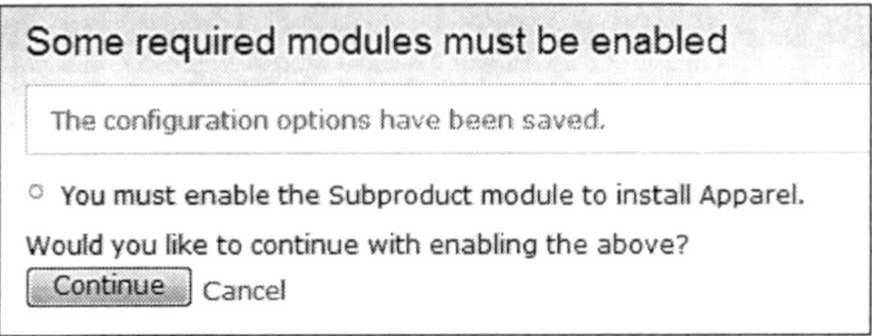

To proceed we click on the **Continue** button.

Creating Products

Now that we have the appropriate modules and sub-modules enabled, and we also have a list of products to add to our store as discussed in Chapter 3—Planning Your Shop we can start to add these to our Drupal e-Commerce installation.

A product for our site is just another form of content, and can be created from the **Create content** section of our Drupal menu; from here we can create a **Page**, **Story**, or a **Product**:

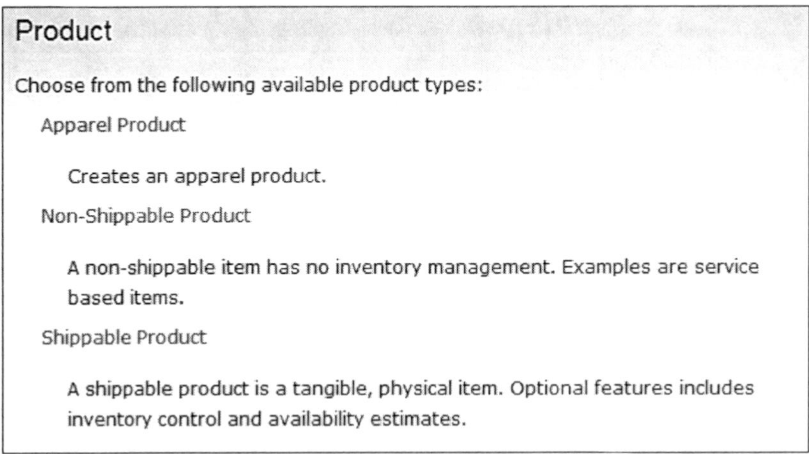

Let's start by adding our Dinosaurs! These are shippable products.

Creating a Shippable Product

The sample **Shippable Product** we discussed in Chapter 3—*Planning Your Shop* was a T-Rex model, so let's add it to our store!

We should start by typing in the products **Name** and **Description** (both of which are mandatory fields):

Name: *

T-Rex with sound effects(1m)

Description: *

Our 1 meter scale model of T-Rex (model: TR15) is bound to scare anyone, especially with its new motion sensor, which sets off a lifelike 'Roar'.

<!--break-->

This model is a must-have for any model dinosaur lover; it is made of durable, shock resistant plastic complete with fantastic hand-painted detail. This model requires two AA sizes batteries (not included) and comes with a 6-month guarantee, we think you will love this product—but if for whatever reason it falls below the standards you expect, we are happy to offer a no-fuss 30-day money back guarantee. Any questions just call us on 555-0135.

Emma from Newcastle said 'This dinosaur was fantastic! I bought one for my brother and he just loves it, especially when an unsuspecting visitor to his room gets a nasty shock!'

Provide the product details to display on the page.

After the first sentence of the description I have typed the line <!--break-->. This allows the text to split depending on the page we are on. If we are on a list of products, we will only see the first sentence, but if we view a page containing information on the product, we will see the entire description.

If we enable or install one of the rich-text editors that can be used in Drupal (such as TinyMCE, WYMEditor, or FCKEditor), the break function will not work. If you have these modules installed and wish to use the break function, you will need to turn off the rich text editor.

By default, only certain HTML tags can be used in product descriptions in the **Filtered HTML** option, if we wish to use more HTML tags later then we need to select the **Full HTML** format from the **Input format** section of the form.

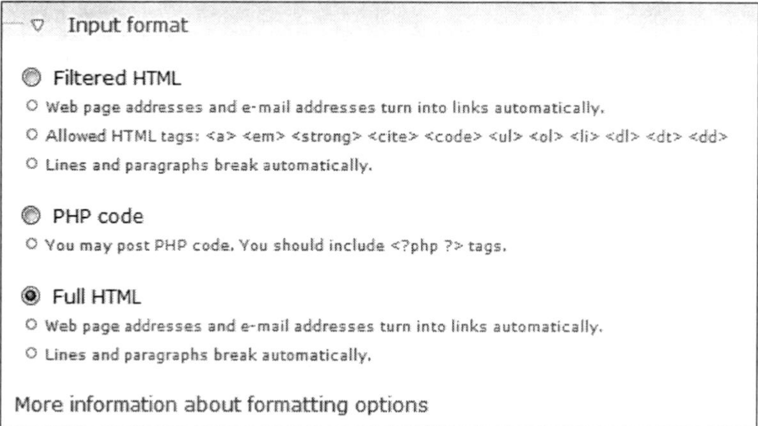

Next we can type in the **Price** of the product and select a **Renewal schedule**:

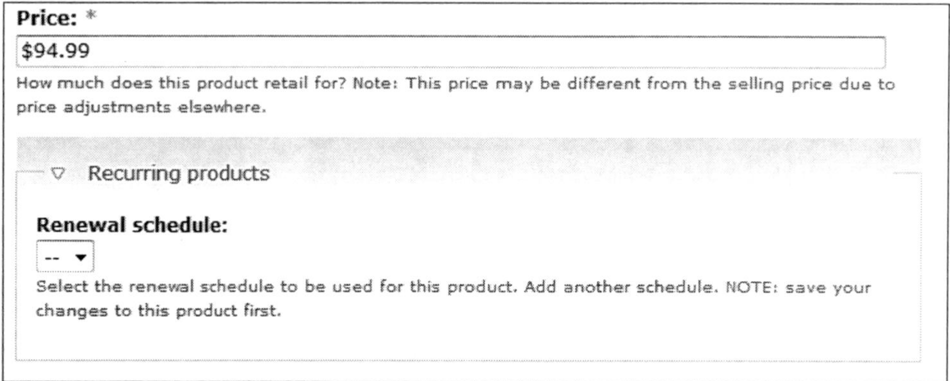

There are no renewal schedules in the list, as we have not defined any. A **renewal schedule** defines how often stock should be renewed for a product.

As this product is available to anyone and not just someone who has a user account with Doug's Dinos (i.e. like repair services) we should set **Anonymous purchasing policy for this product** to be **Flexible**, which states that: **Customers can choose to register, login or checkout anonymously**.

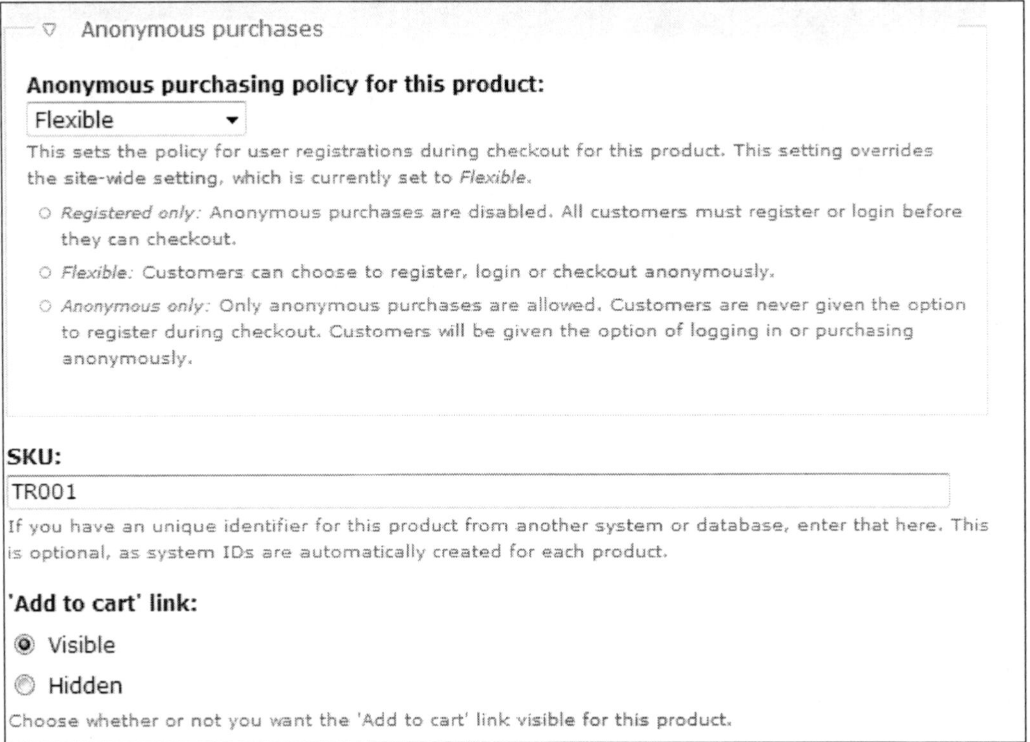

The catalog number for the T-Rex in Doug's supplier's catalog is **TR001**, so we should enter that as the **SKU**. It is not important, but it may make things easier if we were to integrate additional systems with our e-Commerce store at a later time. We also want visitors to be able to buy this product so we should have the '**Add to cart' link** set to visible.

If we are always going to have a surplus in stock, then there is little point in enabling the **Inventory control** feature; however, Doug only has a small amount of stock, and would like to be able to keep tabs on his stock. So let's enable it and set the initial number in stock as **25**.

Inventory control

Inventory management for this item:

Disabled

Enabled

When enabled, the number in stock will be decremented whenever an order of this item is made. When stock reaches zero, the 'Add to cart' will be replaced with 'Sold out'.

Number in stock:

25

Number of products in inventory.

Availability estimate:

Usually ships in 24 hours.

How long it will take this item to leave the fulfillment center once the order has been placed?

As Doug has a fair amount in stock, and does not expect overwhelming demand, he will be able to ship the product within 24 hours, so let's use that option!

The final option on the page is a **Log message**; this is just a tab to leave notes for other administrators of our Drupal installation to say what we have done. Let's just write a note to say **We have added a T-Rex product**, and then click the **Submit** button.

The Finished Product

If we look at the front end of our Drupal installation we can see the finished product!

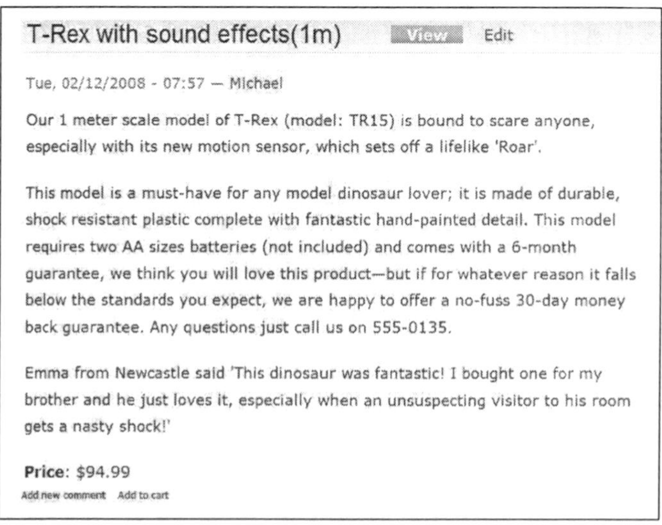

T-Rex with sound effects(1m)
View
Edit
Tue, 02/12/2008 - 07:57 — Michael
Our 1 meter scale model of T-Rex (model: TR15) is bound to scare anyone, especially with its new motion sensor, which sets off a lifelike 'Roar'.
This model is a must-have for any model dinosaur lover; it is made of durable, shock resistant plastic complete with fantastic hand-painted detail. This model requires two AA sizes batteries (not included) and comes with a 6-month guarantee, we think you will love this product—but if for whatever reason it falls below the standards you expect, we are happy to offer a no-fuss 30-day money back guarantee. Any questions just call us on 555-0135.
Emma from Newcastle said 'This dinosaur was fantastic! I bought one for my brother and he just loves it, especially when an unsuspecting visitor to his room gets a nasty shock!'
Price: $94.99
Add new comment
Add to cart

Creating a Non-Shippable Product

In this section let's make two types of non-shippable products:

- Repair service—For repairs on damage to models.
- Education information sheets—Information booklets, which can be downloaded on purchase. This requires a few extra modules to be installed.

Repair Service

The repair service product is just a standard **Non-Shippable Product** from the list of product types. The options available for a **Non-Shippable Product** are nearly identical to those in a **Shippable Product** with the following exceptions:

- No inventory management options
- No availability estimate

Creating the Product

Let's start with the **Name** and a brief **Description** of the product, and its **Price**:

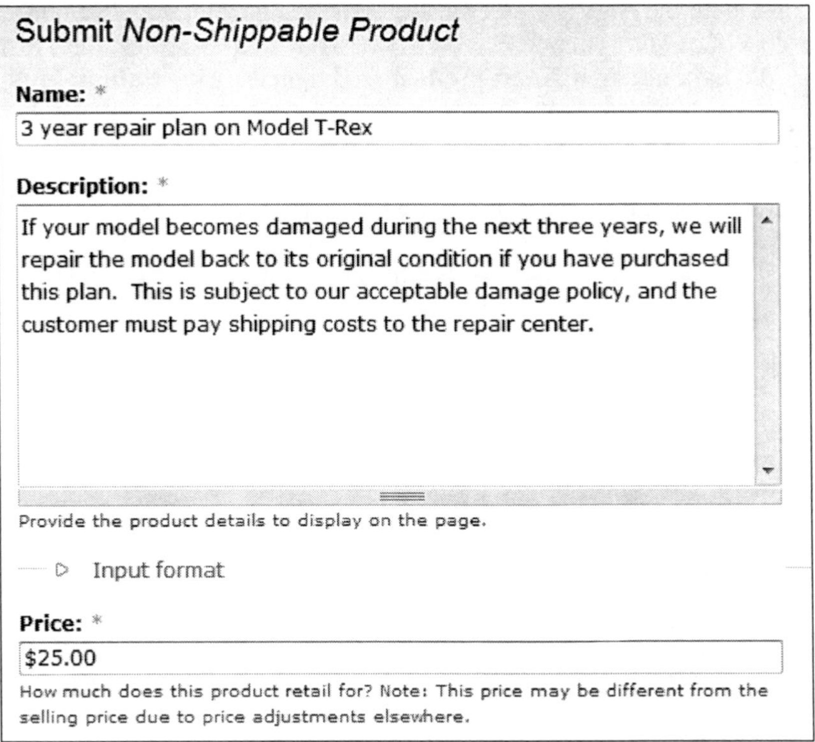

Out of the remaining options the only one that may need altering is the **Anonymous purchasing policy for this product**. This is because visitors who purchase this service should already have purchased a dinosaur from Doug's Dinos and so should ideally be a registered user. We should set that to **Registered only**, before clicking the **Submit** button.

The End Product

The end result of this product looks like this:

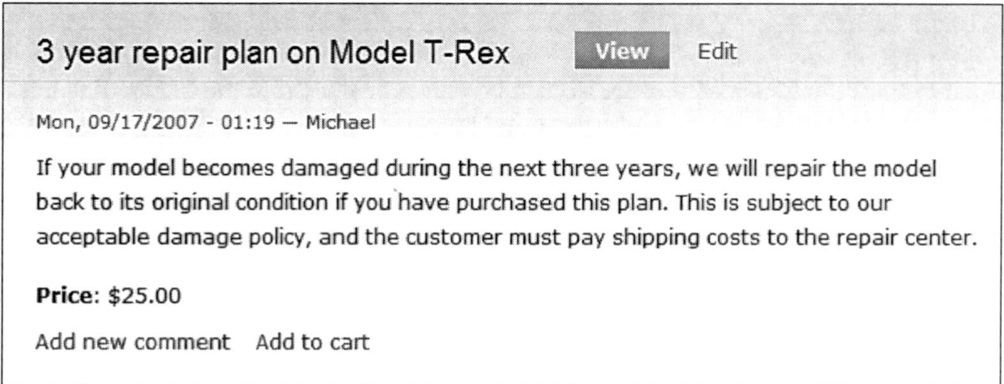

Education Information Sheets

Although educational information sheets are non-shippable products, we may wish for the end product to be a file for the user, which they can download. This unfortunately is not within the default **Non-Shippable Product** option; however, we installed the **File Product** module, so we will create it using that.

Creating the Product

Files used by the **File Product** types are stored in the default files directory for Drupal, which is set in **Administer | Site Configuration | File system** in the main menu. The file that we want to include needs to be uploaded into this folder, which by default is called `files`. It is often advisable to set this folder to be outside of the Drupal installation folder, to prevent any unauthorised access to the files stored within. We should upload our file to this location using an FTP program such as Filezilla (`http://sourceforge.net/projects/filezilla/`).

Similarly for standard non-shippable products, inventory management and availability estimate settings are not available for **File Products**, but there is a new option for setting the file we wish to use.

Doug wants one of his products to be an "info sheet" on the T-REX, so we should upload that using an FTP program and then link it to the product here:

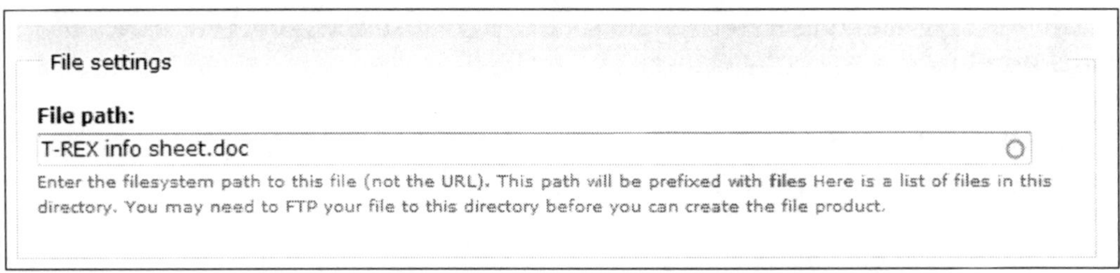

A list of files that have been uploaded can be viewed by clicking the **list of files** link under the **File path** text box. Unfortunately there are no provisions for selecting the file and it populating the box; we have to type (or copy) the name into the box manually.

The Final Product

This is what the end product looks like; let's also see what it is like to purchase one of these products.

T-Rex Educational Information Sheet

Mon, 09/17/2007 - 01:44 — Michael

Our T-Rex educational booklet is suitable for classes of children aged 7 - 10 years, and contains lesson plans for upto two lessons, a homework exercise and other activities for students including coloring in and word searches. These can be photocopied for upto 30 children as per license.

Price: $7.98

Add new comment Add to cart

Once this has been purchased and the order subsequently approved, the file is listed for us to download in the **My Files** option from the navigation menu:

Michael's files

Some files may not be available until your transactions has finished being processed.

Click here to view your expired files.

filename	size	expires	operations
T-Rex Educational Information Sheet	50 KB	0 sec	download

Creating Apparel

The major difference with an **Apparel Product** compared to other product types is that we can create variations of a single product, be they different color, size, material, pattern detail, or any other attribute we decide.

The product we are creating is a **Children's T-Rex T-Shirt**.

Creating the Product

Creating the product itself is just the same as creating a normal **Shippable Product**; all of the options are exactly the same. So let's create the product using the information we discussed in Chapter 3—*Planning Your Shop*:

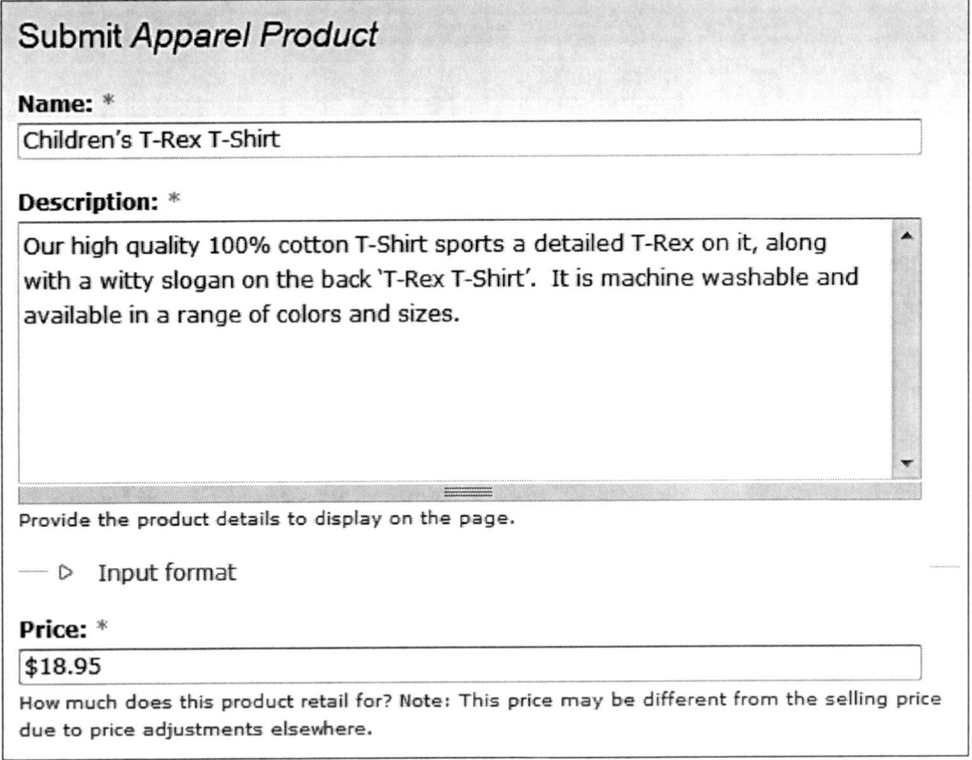

This then creates the standard product for us, which is a product in its own right:

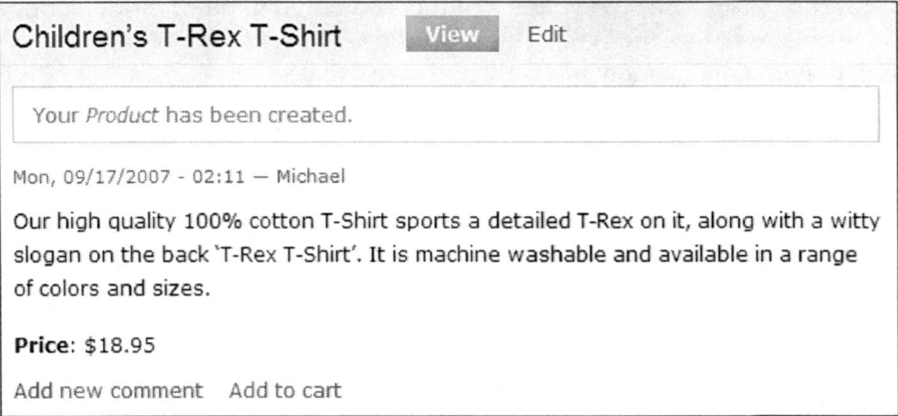

Now we need to create the variations on the product.

Creating Variations

The **Product variations** option is in the **Administer** menu under **E-Commerce configuration:**

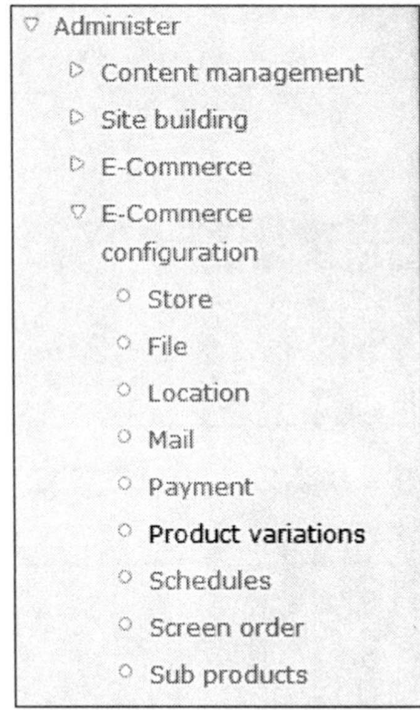

We have no variations at the moment, so to add the variation we need to select the product type, which is **Apparel Product**:

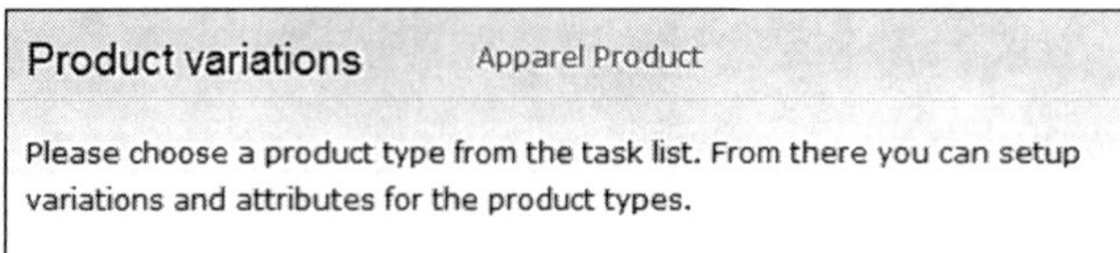

This page then lists all of the variations for **Apparel** products, but since we don't have any variations yet we need to click the **Add variation** link to create a new variant:

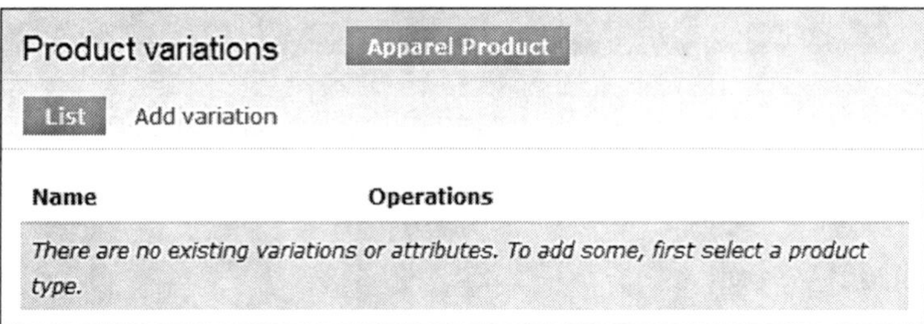

A variation only has two options: a **Variation name** and a **Weight**. Let's create a variation of **Color** (and later a variation of size); the **Weight** option isn't actually related to the physical weight of the product but its weight in any menu or list within Drupal.

Items with a higher weight sink lower in menus and lists and items with lower numbers float up nearer the top of the menus and lists.

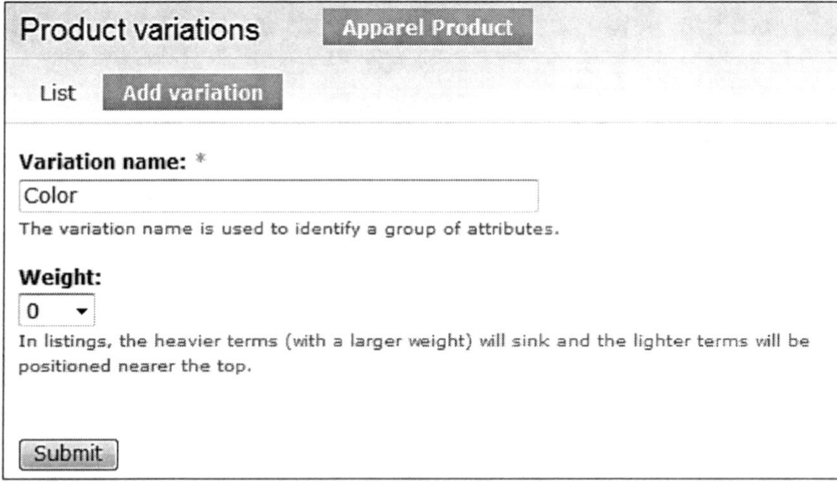

Now that we have the variation, we can create and assign a number of attributes to the variation. We do this by clicking the **Add attribute** option, which has now appeared since we have a variation:

For the **Color** variation we should create attributes for all of the colors in which the T-Shirt is available:

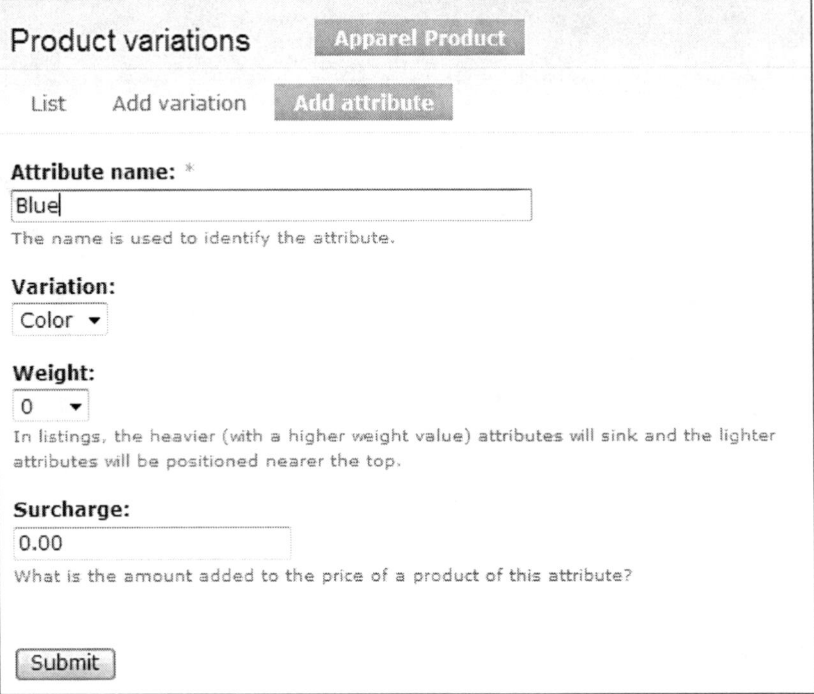

In addition to being able to set an **Attribute name** and **Weight** as with the **Variation** itself, we can also include a **Surcharge**. This may be useful for sizes of T-Shirts, if we have an uncommon size such as extra large, we may wish to add a surcharge for extra production costs incurred.

We should create a number of **Color** attributes, and also a variation for **Size**, complete with a number of appropriate attributes for it:

Name	Operations
Color	edit variation | delete variation
-- Blue	edit attribute | delete attribute
-- Red	edit attribute | delete attribute
Size	edit variation | delete variation
-- Large	edit attribute | delete attribute
-- Medium	edit attribute | delete attribute
-- Small	edit attribute | delete attribute
-- XL	edit attribute | delete attribute

Although we have created these attributes and variations, we need to assign these variations to the products themselves, as some variations and surcharges may not apply to all apparel items.

We need to go to the **Products** page (from the products item in the navigation menu) and click the **Subproducts** link on the details page.

From here, we can click the **Add** link, which allows us to generate the appropriate attributes for the product.

Children's T-Rex T-Shirt: select default values for each of the following variations.

On this page you can select which parameters to use for generating subproducts, and also set stock counts.

Settings you put here for stock will be *summed* to give a default stock amount for each subproduct.

	Parameter	Surcharge	# in stock
		Color	
☑	Blue	0.00	5
☑	Red	0.00	5
		Size	
☑	Large	0.00	5
☑	Medium	0.00	5
☑	Small	0.00	5
☑	XL	1.00	5

Here we enter the number of each of the items that are in **Stock**, tick the boxes of the items that we wish to generate and then click on **Review options** at the bottom of the page.

Children's T-Rex T-Shirt: refine settings for each subproduct.

Here is the full list of subproducts. You can select which ones you wish to create and adjust their settings before generating.

	Color	Size	Price	Stock
☑	Blue	Large	18.95	10
☑	Blue	Medium	18.95	10
☑	Blue	Small	18.95	10
☑	Blue	XL	19.95	10
☑	Red	Large	18.95	10
☑	Red	Medium	18.95	10
☑	Red	Small	18.95	10
☑	Red	XL	19.95	10

Finally we can review the generated list, to ensure the combinations of variations and stock numbers are correct before clicking the **Generate** button.

The **Apparel Product** is now complete!

The Finished Product

The product page now has two drop-down lists, one for **Color** and one for **Size**, the data for which is taken from what we just generated:

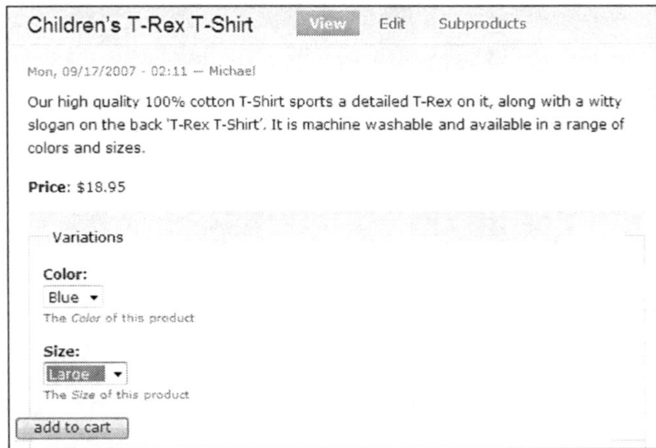

Grouping Products

Products are grouped into what Drupal e-Commerce refers to as parcels. A parcel can be purchased by a user, which may give the user a discount for purchasing these products all at once, or just the convenience of purchasing a group of products at once. This is in itself a product type for which we installed the module at the start of the chapter.

Grouping the Products

Doug wants to have a special offer on his T-Rex model and also its service plan with a $15 saving on buying both together.

To create the parcel, go to the **Create content** menu, select **Products** and then **Collection of Products**. The options on this screen are almost the same as a **Non-Shippable Product** (no inventory control or availability estimates because they depend upon the individual products within the package) but it has a field for the **list of all products**. The ID numbers are the ID numbers assigned by Drupal to the product not the product SKUs that we can set our self. The list of created products can be viewed by clicking the **list of all products** link under the **Product IDs** text box:

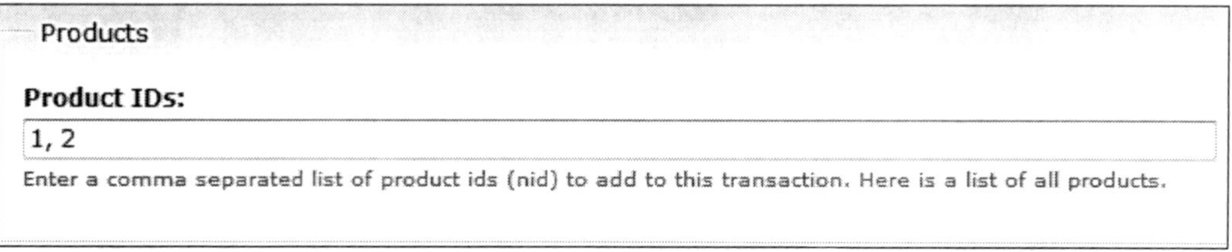

Once this is created we have a product that looks just like a normal product. It may be an idea to include links to the individual products in the description; otherwise it does not contain much information like the one shown below:

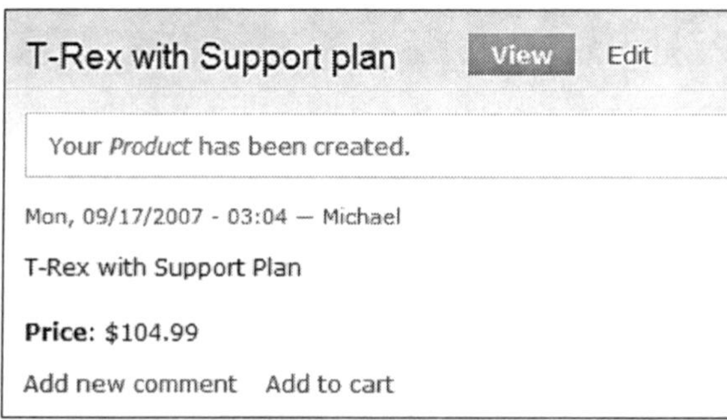

Our Store

Let's take a look at our store, as it stands, in action!

Product Listings

The products are all displayed on the **Products** page (`http://localhost/drupal-5.7/products`):

Products

T-Rex with Support plan	Children's T-Rex T-Shirt	T-Rex Educational Information Sheet
T-Rex with Support Plan	Our high quality 100% cotton T-Shirt sports a detailed T-Rex on it, along with a witty slogan on the back 'T-Rex T-Shirt'. It is machine washable and available in a range of colors and sizes.	Our T-Rex educational booklet is suitable for classes of children aged 7 - 10 years, and contains lesson plans for up to two lessons, a homework exercise and other activities for students including coloring in and word searches. These can be photocopied for up to 30 children as per license.

Product Information

The product information page contains more information on the product (as defined by our use of the `<!--break-->` line in our description); additionally we can add the product to our shopping cart from this page.

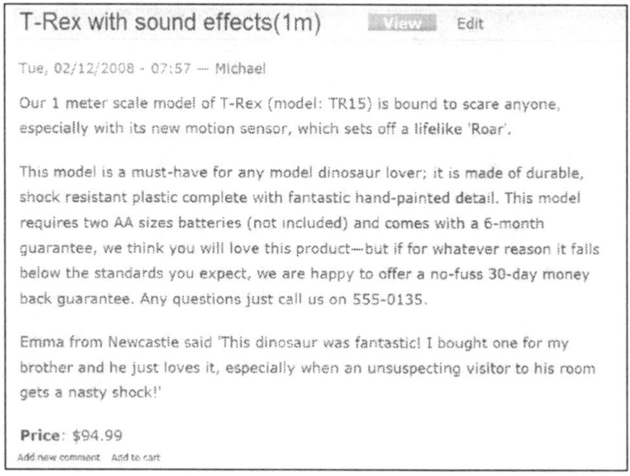

T-Rex with sound effects(1m)
View
Edit
Tue, 02/12/2008 - 07:57 — Michael
Our 1 meter scale model of T-Rex (model: TR15) is bound to scare anyone, especially with its new motion sensor, which sets off a lifelike 'Roar'.
This model is a must-have for any model dinosaur lover; it is made of durable, shock resistant plastic complete with fantastic hand-painted detail. This model requires two AA sizes batteries (not included) and comes with a 6-month guarantee, we think you will love this product—but if for whatever reason it falls below the standards you expect, we are happy to offer a no-fuss 30-day money back guarantee. Any questions just call us on 555-0135.
Emma from Newcastle said 'This dinosaur was fantastic! I bought one for my brother and he just loves it, especially when an unsuspecting visitor to his room gets a nasty shock!'
Price: $94.99
Add new comment Add to cart

Adding to the Cart

We can add the product to our cart, which also provides us with a link to the shopping cart:

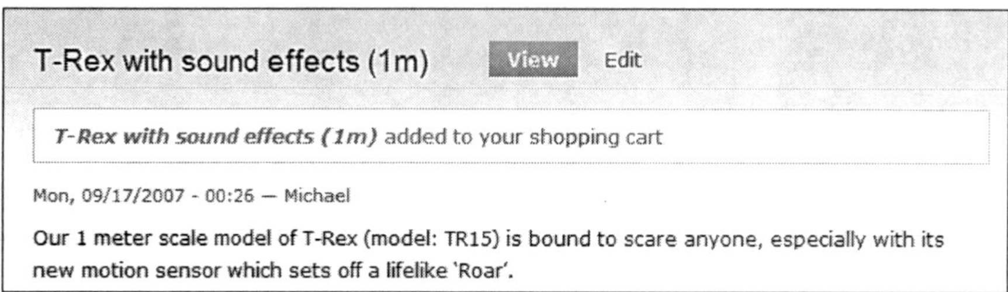

The Shopping Cart

The **Shopping cart** lists the products we have requested to purchase; we can adjust the quantity (**Qty**) of the products and **Remove** them, and also check out the products within.

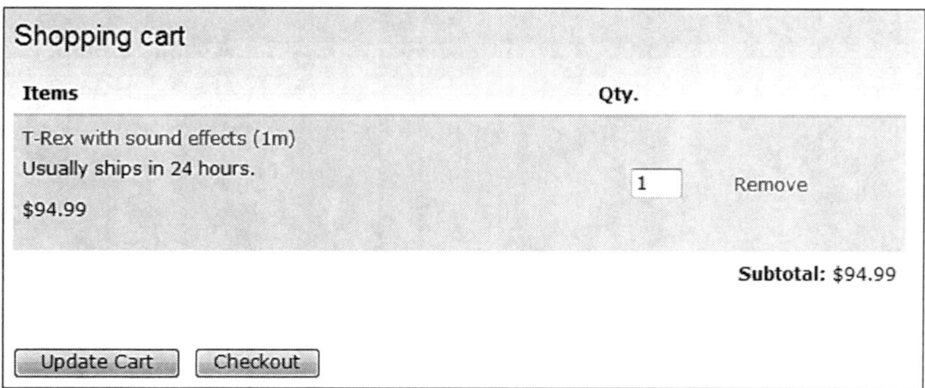

We need to work on our store more before our visitors can fully **Checkout** and place orders, but essentially we only need to enable payment options to start making money with our store!

Summary

In this chapter, we looked at the products and product types we discussed in Chapter 3—*Planning Your Shop*, and added them to our store in the form of a product catalog; we also created some new products including a downloadable file and a parcel of multiple products.

With our catalog set up, users can:

- View products
- View more information on the product
- Add the product to their shopping cart
- View their shopping cart
- Check out their cart

They can't however:

- Make payment
- Receive tax or shipping information

Now it is time to move on to look at our customers, and how we handle them in our store.

5

Customers and Staff

There would be no point in running an online store without customers, so let's take a look at our customers and how they are managed using Drupal.

We will also take a look at staff members, who are also users within Drupal. Doug only has a small workforce; however, he wants them all to be able to help him out with his online store!

Within this chapter we need to take a look at the two sides of users in our store:

- Users, roles, and permissions—After all, customers who register for our site become users and staff members who manage the store will also be users.
- Customer and staff management—How to plan, set up, and manage these users, and managing customers who are not registered users.

Users, Roles, and Permissions

Firstly, let's take a look at how users, roles, and permissions work in Drupal; then we will use this knowledge to set up our website for customers and staff members. These settings can be found in the **Administer** section of Drupal, listed under **User management**:

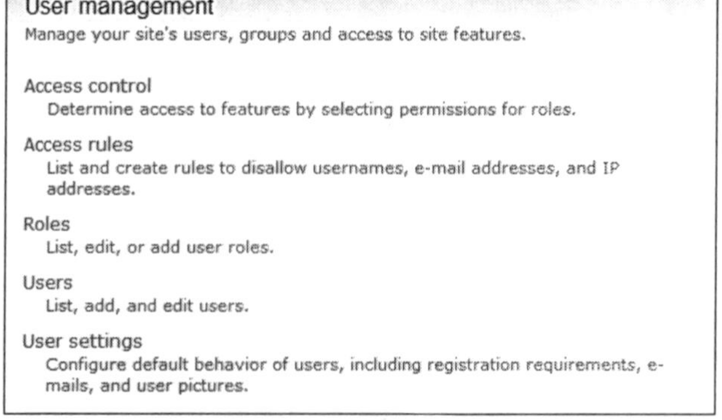

User management
Manage your site's users, groups and access to site features.

Access control
Determine access to features by selecting permissions for roles.

Access rules
List and create rules to disallow usernames, e-mail addresses, and IP addresses.

Roles
List, edit, or add user roles.

Users
List, add, and edit users.

User settings
Configure default behavior of users, including registration requirements, e-mails, and user pictures.

Roles and Permissions

On their own, users have no permissions; instead permissions are grouped into **Roles,** which are then assigned to users. All registered users who log in, automatically receive permissions from the authenticated user role (which is available by default) combined with additional roles that we decide to assign to them; users who are not logged in or are first time users are considered anonymous. The two default roles available are:

- Anonymous users
- Authenticated users

These roles can be edited but they cannot be renamed nor can they be deleted because they are used automatically by Drupal; that is why the operations column in the table below is **locked**:

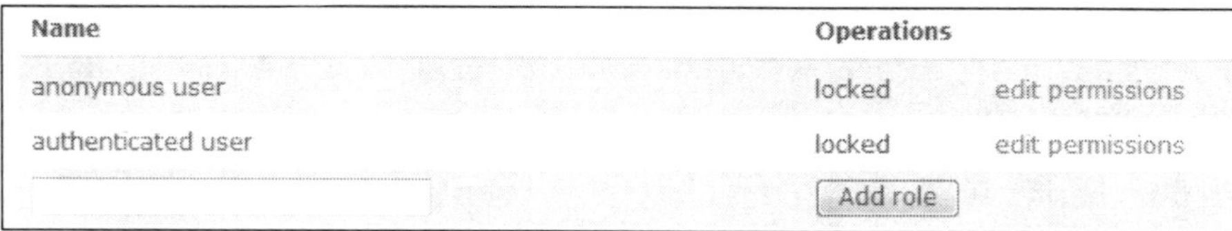

Name	Operations	
anonymous user	locked	edit permissions
authenticated user	locked	edit permissions
	Add role	

The permissions primarily relate to users being able to manage and administer individual modules or sub-modules within Drupal.

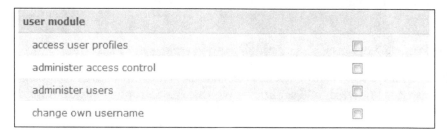

There are four main types of access control used in various permissions:

- **Access**—This allows a user to use a module but not change how it functions.
- **Administer**—This allows the user to change the function of a module and should only be given to trusted users, and certainly never to anonymous users.
- **Create**—This allows the user to create specific types of content, but not edit the content they create. Particularly useful if we were to have a user purely for creating products.
- **Edit own**—This provides the user with the ability to modify content they have created, for instance being able to edit products the user has added.

Settings and Rules

We have a number of **User settings** available for managing. These are:

- **User registration settings**—This allows us to decide who can create user accounts and who must approve the user accounts.
- **User e-mail settings**—This allows us to customize the content of emails sent to users when they register, request a new password, or have an account created for them.
- **Picture settings**—This allows us to decide whether users can upload a picture in their profile.

These settings are found under **User management | User settings**:

User settings
Configure default behavior of users, including registration requirements, e-mails, and user pictures.

User Registration Settings

Let's take a look at them in a little more detail. Firstly, we have the **User registration settings** to define how new accounts are created and approved:

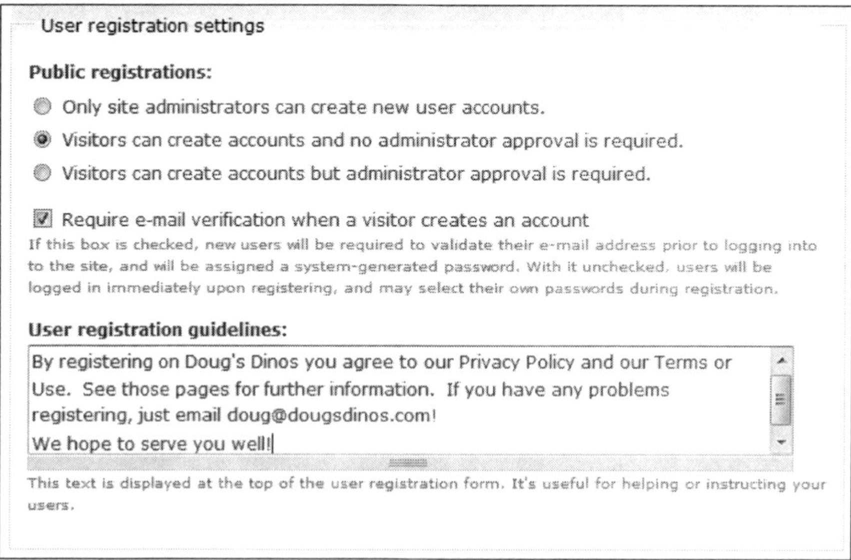

The settings selected in the preceding screenshot specify that visitors can create their own accounts and they don't require administrator approval. For Doug's site, this is the option I would recommend. If we had set the first option, then we would have to create user accounts for customers who wanted their own username, which would make it very difficult for customers to become users in our site. The final option allows visitors to create accounts but requires an administrator approval on the account. In an e-commerce situation this is certainly not recommended; if we have a user ready to pay we would not want to tell them to wait until someone approves their account.

Underneath those three options is a check box that states **Require e-mail verification when a visitor creates an account**. This option will require that the user validates their email address before they can log in for the very first time. With this option we can reduce the number of fraudulent user accounts created, ensuring they are all tied to a valid and active email address.

User E-Mail Settings

Emails are automatically sent when:

- A user signs up
- An administrator creates a username
- A user signs up but their account needs an administrator approval
- A user requests a change in password

The content of these emails can be changed from the **User e-mail settings**. There are a number of variables used in these emails, including ones that become the users' username, their password or the log-in page of the website. These variables are described beneath each individual email, and are prefixed with an exclamation mark.

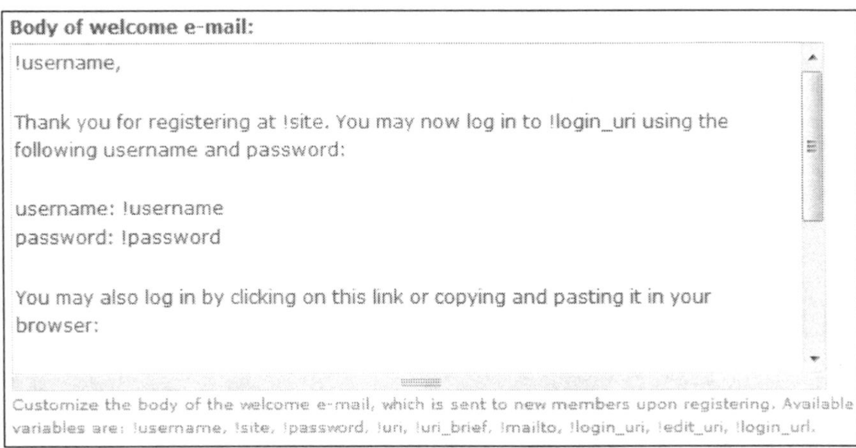

When a user signs up, these variables are replaced with their user details and sent to them as an email, which is shown below:

michaelpeacock,

Thank you for registering at Doug's Dinos!. You may now log in to http://www.dougsdinos.com/drupal-5.7/user using the following username and password:

username: michaelpeacock
password: qajbjUHqww

You may also log in by clicking on this link or copying and pasting it in your browser:

http://www.dougsdinos.com/drupal-5.7/user/reset/2
/1192405596/52b6879965ac9a4c3adf4bceccc5b746

Picture Settings

If we enable **Picture support** then users can upload photographs to be linked to their user account. The settings related to **Pictures** include:

- **Picture support**—This is used for enabling or disabling picture support.
- **Picture image path**—This is the subdirectory in the uploads directory where we will store pictures.
- **Default picture**—This is the URL for a picture to be used if a user has not uploaded any picture.
- **Picture maximum dimensions**—This is the maximum size in pixels for pictures.
- **Picture maximum file size**—This is the maximum size in kilobytes for pictures.
- **Picture guidelines**—This is a notice displayed on the upload form; this would be useful for us to provide instructions to users or a disclaimer, regarding the copyright of images uploaded.

Pictures could be useful in particular for staff members; we could give them special pictures to indicate they are all members of the staff. A default picture that indicates the user is a customer would prove useful when new users sign up. These would work particularly well in conjunction with a forum that displays the user's picture.

Permissions and Taxonomy Access Control

The default permissions that can be applied to roles are quite limited in the overall context of a website, and focus primarily on access control features of the site, whereas when it comes to customers we may prefer to provide them access to special areas of the site. To do this we need **Taxonomy Access Control**.

Taxonomy Access Control is not available by default, so we would need to install the **Taxonomy Access Control** module, which can be downloaded from: `http://drupal.org/project/taxonomy_access`. Once downloaded and uploaded to our site, it can be installed from the **Modules** section within **Site building**:

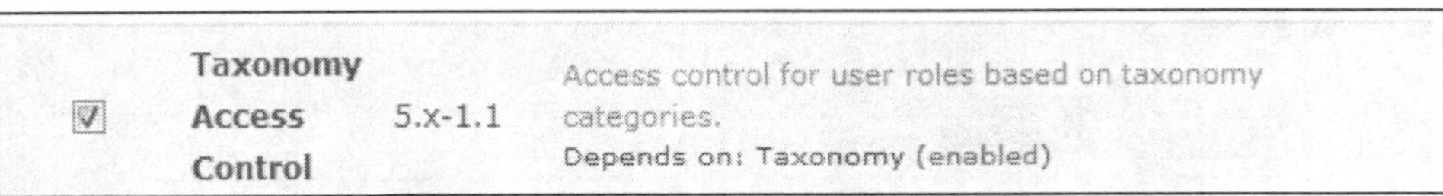

What is Taxonomy?

Drupal's taxonomy module allows us to tag content into categories and sub-categories with terms (like using custom labels). A long description of the details of taxonomy within Drupal is found on the Drupal website: `http://drupal.org/node/22274`. For our application, we can think of Drupal's taxonomy purely as a way to group content into categories.

Creating Categories

Within the **Content management** section of the **Administer** menu there is a **Categories** section, which allows us to create vocabularies and terms to categorize our content.

Categories
Create vocabularies and terms to categorize your content.

Within here there is a link to **Add vocabulary**; this allows us to create the category:

Vocabulary name: *
Registered Only Content
The name for this vocabulary. Example: "Topic".

We can also select the content types we want to associate with this vocabulary (or category as we are concerned):

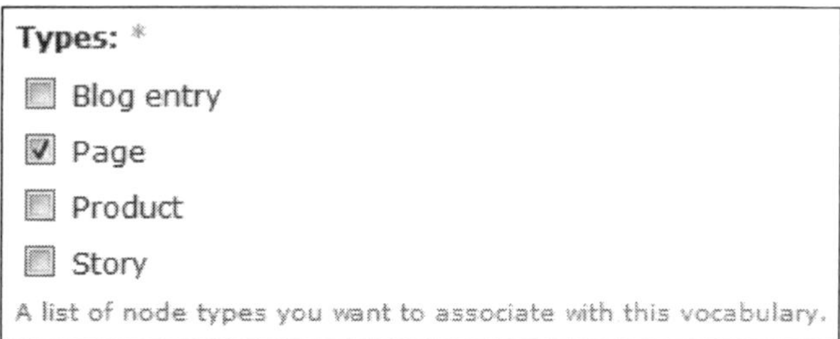

Once we have our vocabulary created we need to **add terms** to it:

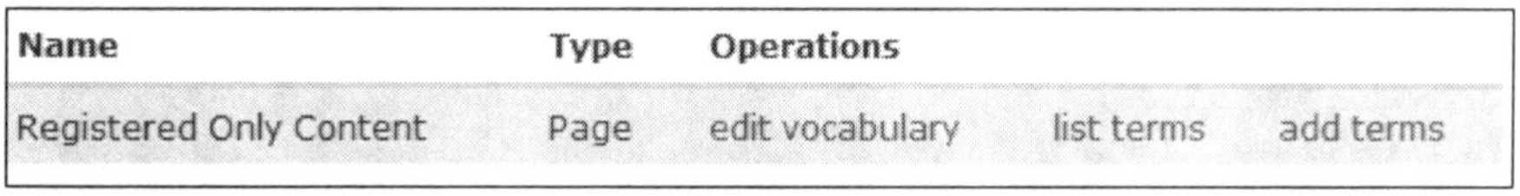

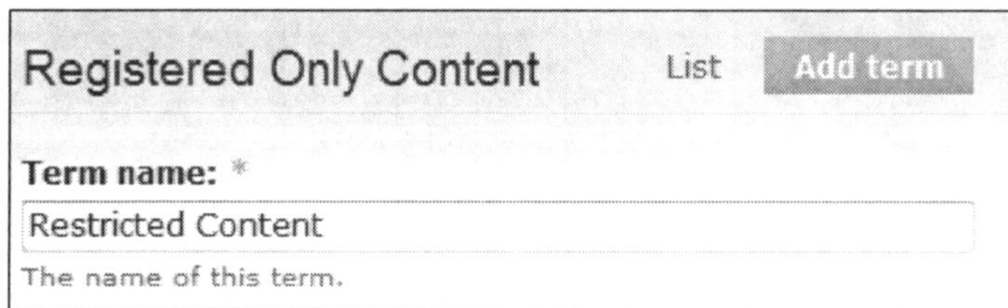

There are other options when creating terms, but we are only concerned with the **Term name** for our usage of taxonomy:

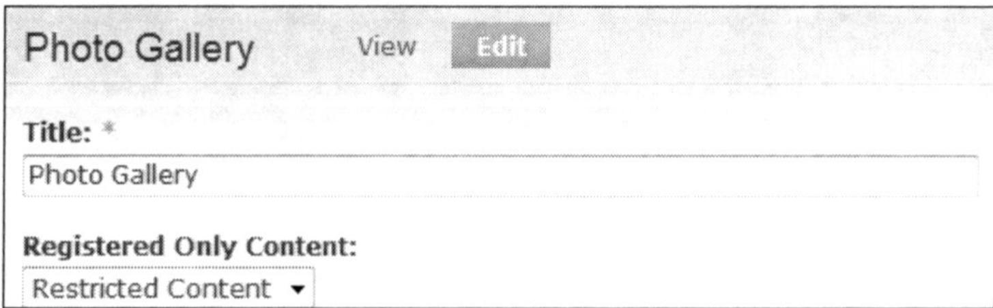

Categorizing Content

Once categories have been created we need to categorize the content; different vocabularies are listed in the **Edit** section of the **Page** content along with the terms associated with them.

We can select the term and then save the page.

Restricting Access Based on Taxonomy Access Control

Under **User management** we have an option called **Taxonomy Access: Permissions**, which allows us to set the taxonomy access permissions for a particular role.

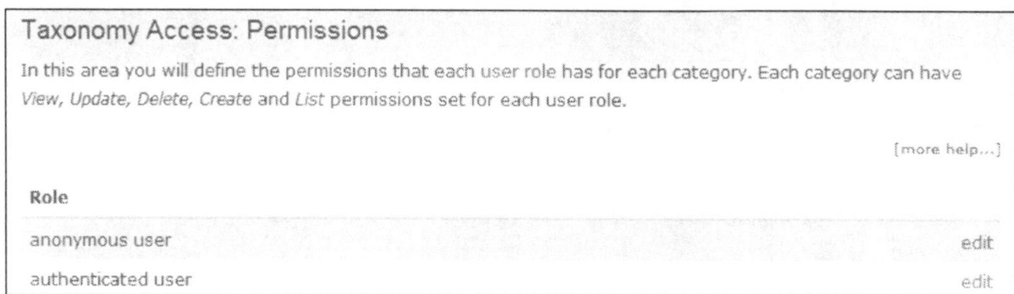

The settings available for these roles provide permissions for:

- Viewing content (**View**)
- Editing content (**Update**)
- Deleting content (**Delete**)
- Tagging content with a term (**Create**)
- Listing the categories within the content (**List**)

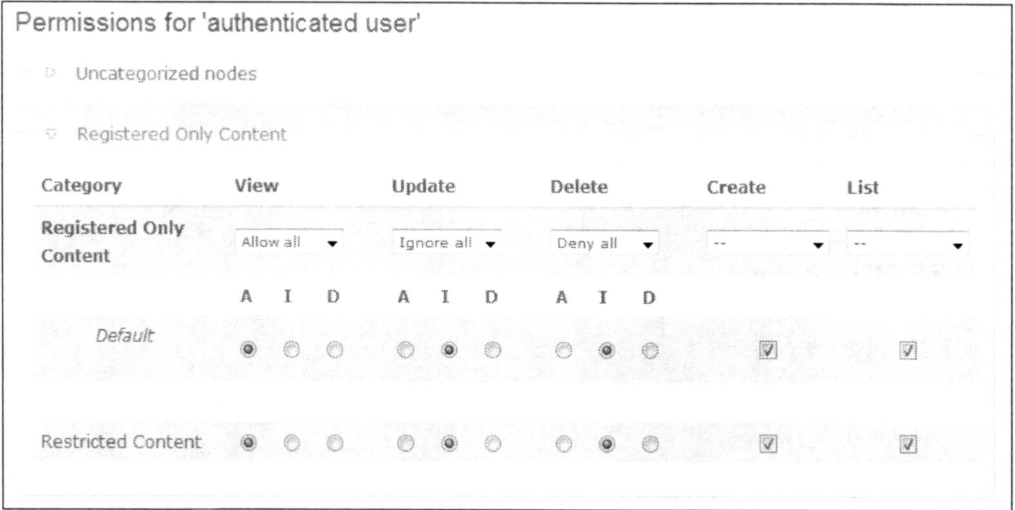

For the **View**, **Update**, and **Delete** settings we can set the following permissions:

- **Allow all**—Grants the appropriate permission to the user.
- **Ignore all**—Denies the appropriate permission to the user, but can be overridden by other allow permissions.
- **Deny all**—Denies the appropriate permission to the user.

The drop-down list at the top of each group can be used to set all of the permissions below it to the same setting.

Customers

Now that we know how Drupal's users, roles, and access permission features work, we can create our customer groups, and look into customer-related settings that may be of use to us, as well as some basic customer management.

Customer Roles

Doug wants a couple of different roles for his customers:

- All customers
- Support plan customers

The general roles won't provide any real extra features, but will be used to classify customers. However, customers can purchase a special support plan, which provides them access to additional areas of the site.

The support plan customer role will allow users to see a number of extra pages and features, which other users will not be able to see. This is a support resource that Doug wants to provide to customers:

- Support section—Provides generic support information.
    - Support contact—Provides special contact information for support plans.
    - Support forums
    - Home maintenance guides—Contains information on user serviceable items.

Once we have this set up, we should have a new section in our menu that looks like this:

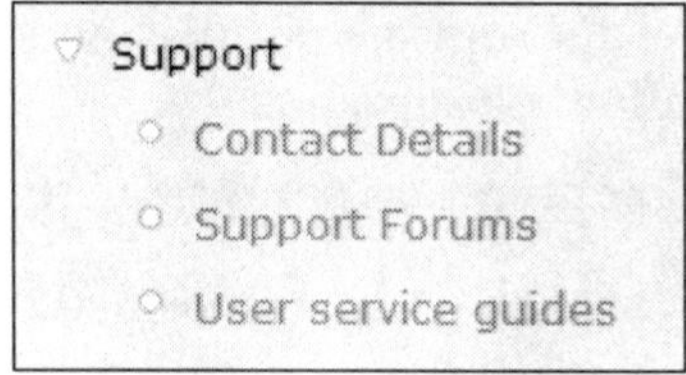

> **Hierarchical Page Structures**
>
> This hierarchical page structure within the menu is created by setting each page's (apart from the **Support** page) **Parent item** as the **Support** page, under the **Menu settings**.

The permissions for this should be set only to be shown to support plan customers. With our customer roles set up correctly we should now have the following roles created and set up with correct taxonomy and feature permissions.

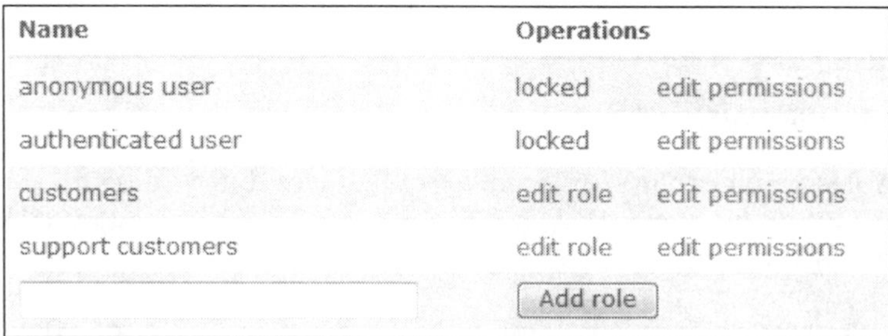

Name	Operations	
anonymous user	locked	edit permissions
authenticated user	locked	edit permissions
customers	edit role	edit permissions
support customers	edit role	edit permissions
	Add role	

Role Assignments

Now that we have:

- Created customer roles
- Set up appropriate permissions on these roles
- Set up pages and content for these specific roles

We need to set up our products to update our customers' role depending on their purchase, i.e. support plans will enable support customer roles, whereas all other products enable the customers role.

EC Role is a part of a module that comes included with the e-commerce package but is disabled by default.

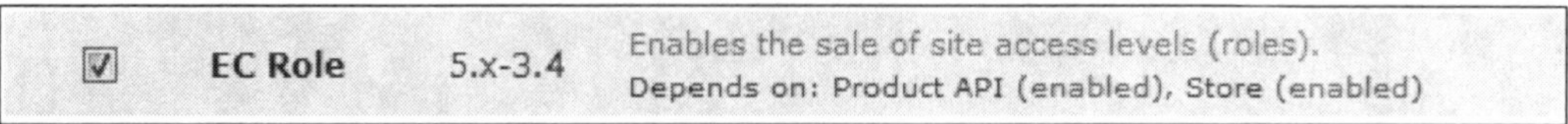

EC Role
5.x-3.4
Enables the sale of site access levels (roles).
Depends on: Product API (enabled), Store (enabled)

Once this module has been installed we have a new group of settings in the product listing called **Role assignments**, which have provisions for:

- Assigning roles when the customer makes a purchase
- Removing roles when the customer makes a purchase
- Removing roles when the product expires (this requires the product to be a recurring purchase)
- Assigning roles when the product expires

This could allow us to fully restore a customer's role to what it initially was once the product expires.

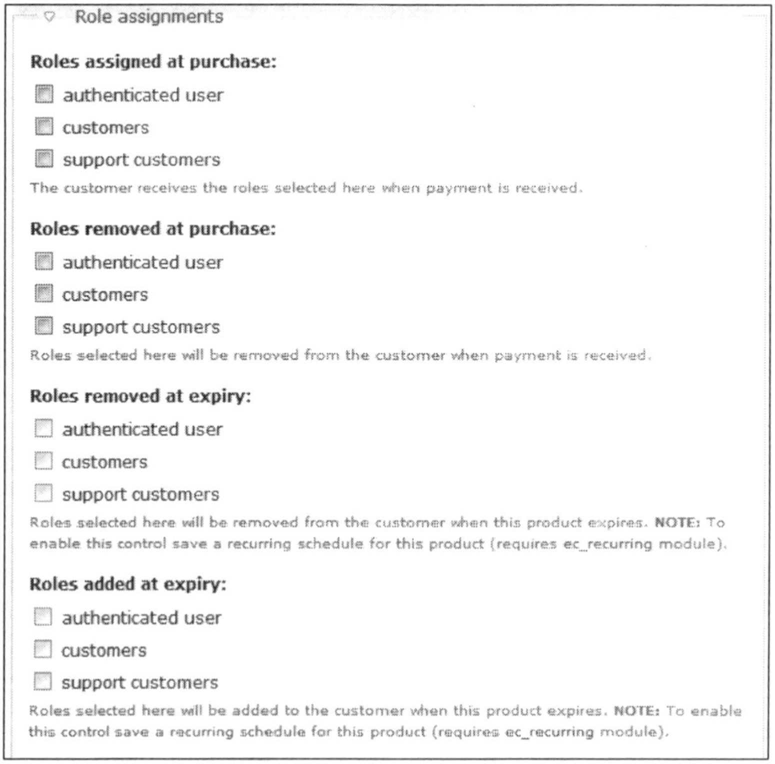

Role assignments

Roles assigned at purchase:

- [ ] authenticated user
- [ ] customers
- [ ] support customers

The customer receives the roles selected here when payment is received.

Roles removed at purchase:

- [ ] authenticated user
- [ ] customers
- [ ] support customers

Roles selected here will be removed from the customer when payment is received.

Roles removed at expiry:

- [ ] authenticated user
- [ ] customers
- [ ] support customers

Roles selected here will be removed from the customer when this product expires. **NOTE:** To enable this control save a recurring schedule for this product (requires ec_recurring module).

Roles added at expiry:

- [ ] authenticated user
- [ ] customers
- [ ] support customers

Roles selected here will be added to the customer when this product expires. **NOTE:** To enable this control save a recurring schedule for this product (requires ec_recurring module).

For the non-support plan products we only want to assign the customer role; however, for the support plan products we want to add both the customer role and the support customers role, and also set it to remove the support customer role once the product expires.

Reminder: Forcing Customers to be Users

If you remember from Chapter 4—*Creating Your Product Catalog*, one of the options for the product listings is the **Anonymous purchasing policy**. This policy defines who can purchase the product.

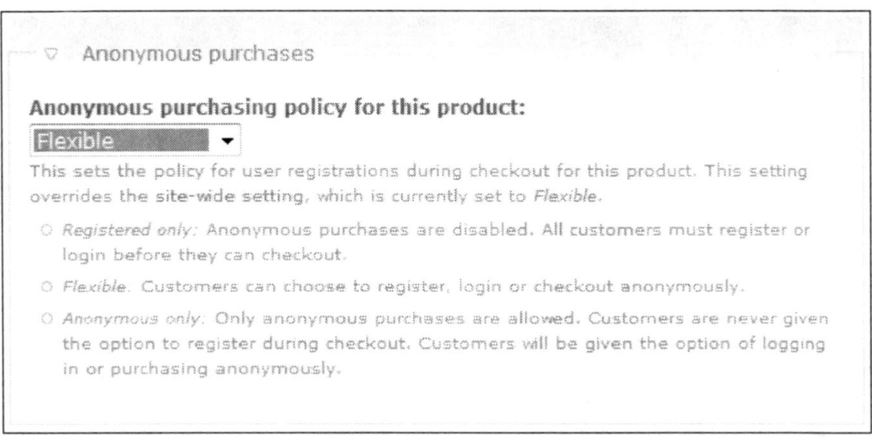

There are three options for the policy:

- **Registered only**—Before this product can be checked out all customers must either register or log in.
- **Flexible**—Customers can choose to register or log in, but they can also check out anonymously.
- **Anonymous only**—This won't give customers the option of registering during the checkout process, but they will be given the option of logging in or making the purchase anonymously.

If we wanted to ensure all our customers are registered users, we would set this to be **Registered only** to disable anonymous purchases.

This option can also be set globally, as opposed to for each individual product; it can be found under the **Store** section of **E-Commerce configuration** within the **Administer** area.

Customer Management

There are no built-in customer management features as such; however, we can manage our user accounts. There are some customer management features we can enable including the **E-CiviCRM** module and the **Address** module; the first allows integration with CiviCRM a third-party customer relationship manager, which we will look at in more detail in Chapter 11—*Invoices and CRM*. The **Address** module enables an address book for users, which we can use to take shipping and billing addresses when the user checks out.

We will also discuss the **Address** module later, in Chapters 8 and 9 – *Creating a Better Selling Experience* and *Taxes, Payment, and Shipping*.

The **Users** section of **User management** does have some features that are useful when related to customer management. Firstly, we can filter our list of users by **role**, so we could see only **customers**, or **support customers**.

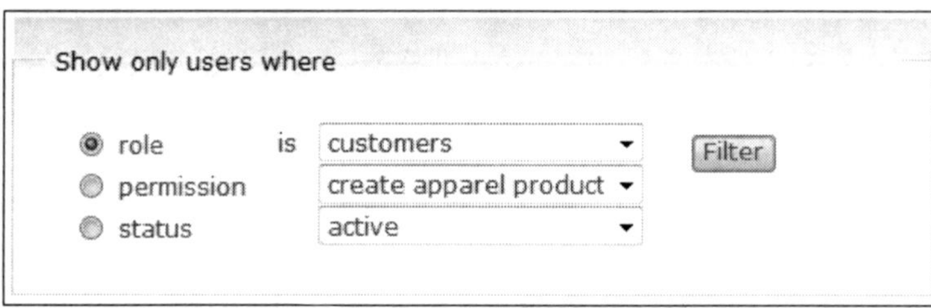

The user list shows us some basic information on the users, including:

- Their **Username**
- Their **Status**, which indicates if they are blocked or unblocked
- **Roles** assigned to them (currently all customers, and any support customers would be listed, as we set to make all customers part of the customer role, with the support customers being an additional role for some of them)
- The length of time they have been a **Member for** and the time they last logged in (i.e. their **Last access** time)

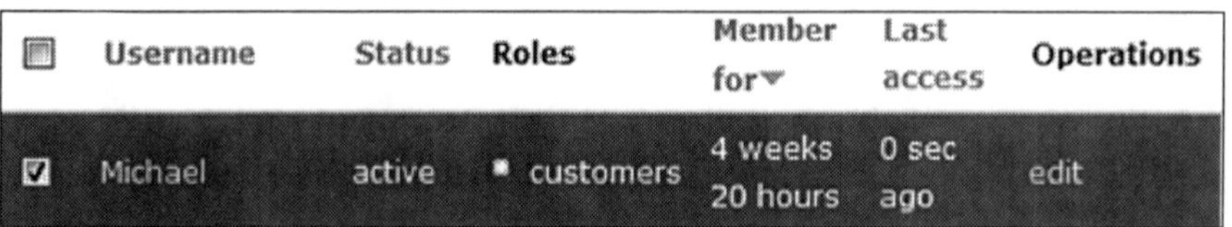

Username
Status
Roles
Member for
Last access
Operations
Michael
active
customers
4 weeks 20 hours
0 sec ago
edit

The **edit** link allows us to edit all of the user's settings. The check box is linked to a drop-down box of user **Update options** that we can perform, including adding or removing roles, blocking, unblocking, and deleting the selected accounts.

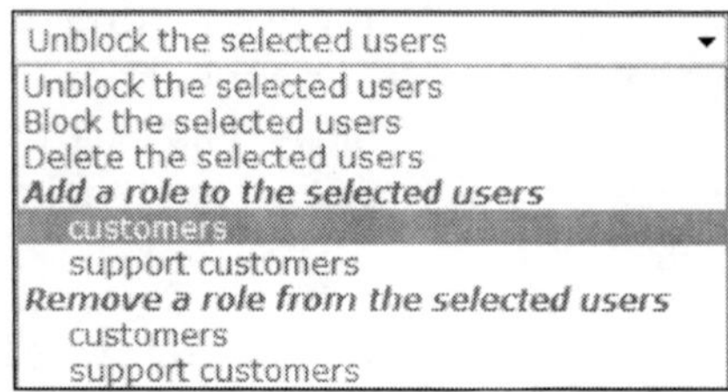

With regards to customers, we can use this to update users to customer status if an existing customer creates a user account and wishes to have customer access to the website.

Obviously this can be done automatically with the e-Commerce **Roles** module, but here we have used it to assign the role to a user who just registered for the site, but was already a customer before that, so their user account now reflects their status as a customer.

User Order History

We can search transactions for a number of different criteria, including username. The **Search** option is in the **Administer** section under **E-Commerce**.

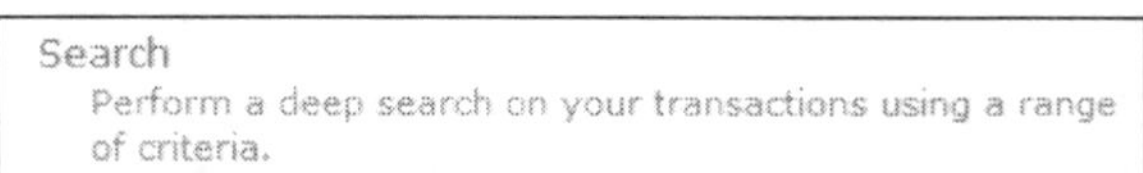

In the **Search** page, we need to select the **Advanced search** option and enter the username we want to search for. I'm going to try searching for **Michael**.

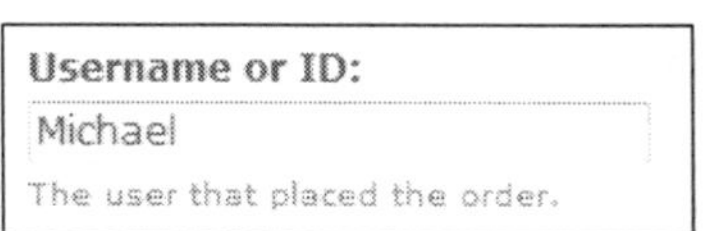

The list of transactions related to that user is then displayed:

txnid	user	payment status	workflow	gross	created	changed	duedate	items ordered	operations
1	Michael	completed	completed	$7.98	17/09/2007 - 01:45	17/09/2007 - 01:50		1 item	edit addresses items

The information contained in the table is explained by the headings in the table; however, the meaning of workflow requires a little explanation.

The **workflow** is how far through the order process the transaction is; if we click the workflow we then have options to perform some other operations including printing invoices and canceling the transactions.

Contacting a User

When we click on a username in our site, in places such as the user management areas, we see the user's profile, and have options for editing the contact and contacting them.

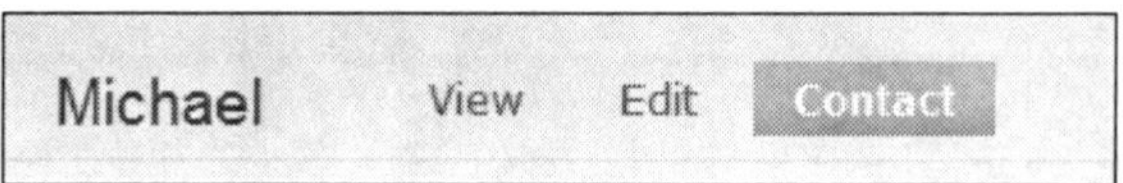

The **Contact** section brings up a **Contact form** as we have installed the **Contact** form module in an earlier chapter. Here we enter a subject, a message, and can opt to have a copy of the email sent to ourselves.

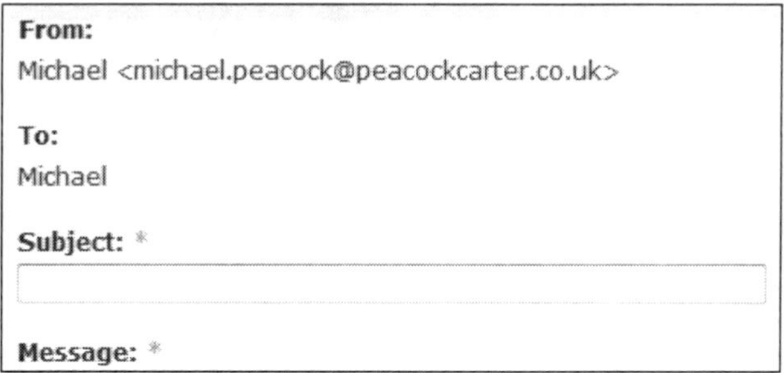
From:
Michael <michael.peacock@peacockcarter.co.uk>

To:
Michael

Subject: *

Message: *

Staff

If you remember, at the start of the chapter, Doug wanted his staff members to be able to use the website, and help him out with things like adding and managing products and helping with some other tasks such as processing orders. Now that we have looked into users, roles, and permissions and we have created our customers, it is time to look into creating user accounts for our staff members.

Planning

Doug has the following members of staff in his team that he wants to help manage and administer the website:

- Himself
- Stock assistant
- Store checkout manager

Doug has the first account, which is an administrator and requires no further configuration. The stock assistant needs to be able to add new products, and edit and manage existing products on the website. His store checkout manager needs to be able to manage users and transactions.

Creating Roles

In order to accommodate these needs we need to create two roles; one for the stock assistant, and one for the checkout manager. Roles are created on the **Roles** page, `http://localhost/drupal-5.7/admin/user/roles`.

Stock Assistant

We start by creating the role with the name **Stock Assistant**:

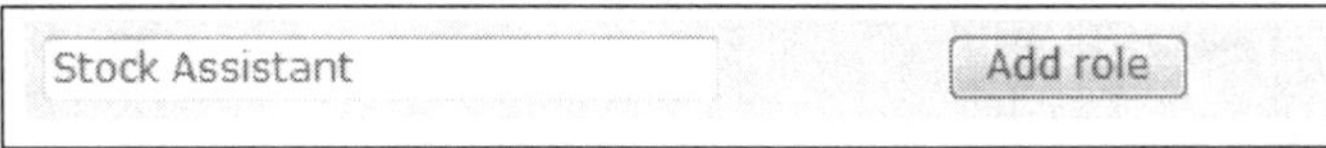

Once it is created, we then click the **edit permissions** link next to the newly created role and select which modules the user can access; this should include:

- Apparel
- Products
- Tangible goods

The **apparel module** should be selected so that the user can create items of clothing to sell on the store.

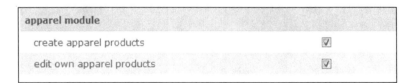

We also want the user to be able to edit, delete, and manage existing products so we will also select the **administer products** module.

Finally, the **tangible module** allows the user to create and edit shippable products.

Now we have our role for the **Stock Assistant** ready.

Checkout Manager

Permissions are not as detailed for the checkout manager because they are not available for the individual processes of managing transactions, so we can only enable the **administer store** permission. This is done via the **edit permissions** link next to the newly created role.

Now, we have our role for the **Checkout manager** ready.

Creating the users

Now we create the users, and assign the appropriate roles to the user account from the list of roles. Don't forget the **authenticated user** role is automatically combined with any roles we add. To add new users we can simply click the **Add user** tab at the top of the **users** management page.

Roles:

- [x] Checkout Manager
- [ ] customers
- [ ] Stock Assistant
- [ ] support customers

The user receives the combined permissions of the *authenticated user* role, and all roles selected here.

We now have our staff members ready to help Doug manage the store reducing his workload, which he is very pleased about!

Summary

In this chapter, we have learned:

- How to create and manage user accounts
- What roles are and how they work with user accounts
- How to restrict access to specific areas of our site based on roles
- How to use users and roles when creating and managing customers and staff members

In the next chapter we will look into branding our site, before moving on to making money with our store!

6
Branding Your Site

Doug is really happy with how his website and store are coming along; his product catalog is online and he has set up customer and staff users on the site; his only complaint so far is how the website looks. He likes the default design, but does not think it is appropriate for his site or his store; he wants something more tailored to his business. In this chapter, we will learn:

- What themes are and which ones are the default Drupal themes
- How to install themes
- How to manage themes
- How to customize the default theme
- How to create themes

Ideally, Doug wants a custom design for his site, but there is no harm in having a look at some of the other ones available in case they are more suitable for him.

Themes

Within Drupal a theme is a collection of images, templates, and style sheets that can make up the design of our Drupal installation. Different themes provide a different type of look and feel to the site. A number of different themes come pre-installed with Drupal, so let's look at those.

Before we can look at the different themes, we need to enable them so that we can change our theme in our user settings. To enable these themes we need to go to the **Themes** section of Drupal's **Administer** area.

Themes
Change which theme your site uses or allows users to set.

All the themes are listed within this area; to enable them we just need to tick the box in the **Enabled** column and then click the **Save configuration** button.

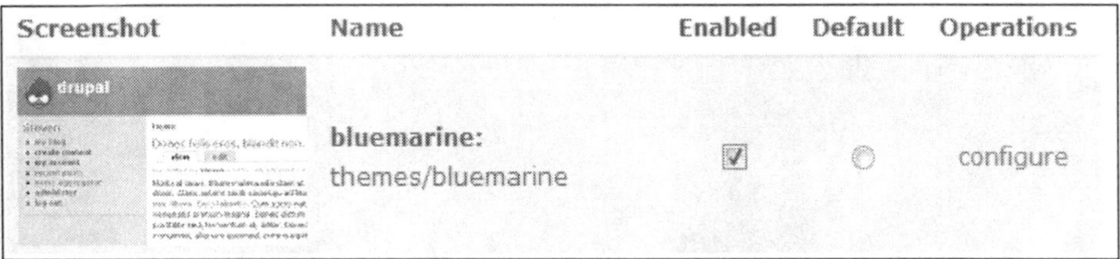

Now that we have enabled these themes we can swap between them from the **Edit** section of **My Account**; this page contains a section entitled **Theme Configuration** from where we can select the theme we would like to use. Let's now go through these themes in turn and see what they are like.

Minnelli

This theme is very similar to the default theme with the exception that it has a fixed width and will not expand depending on the screen size.

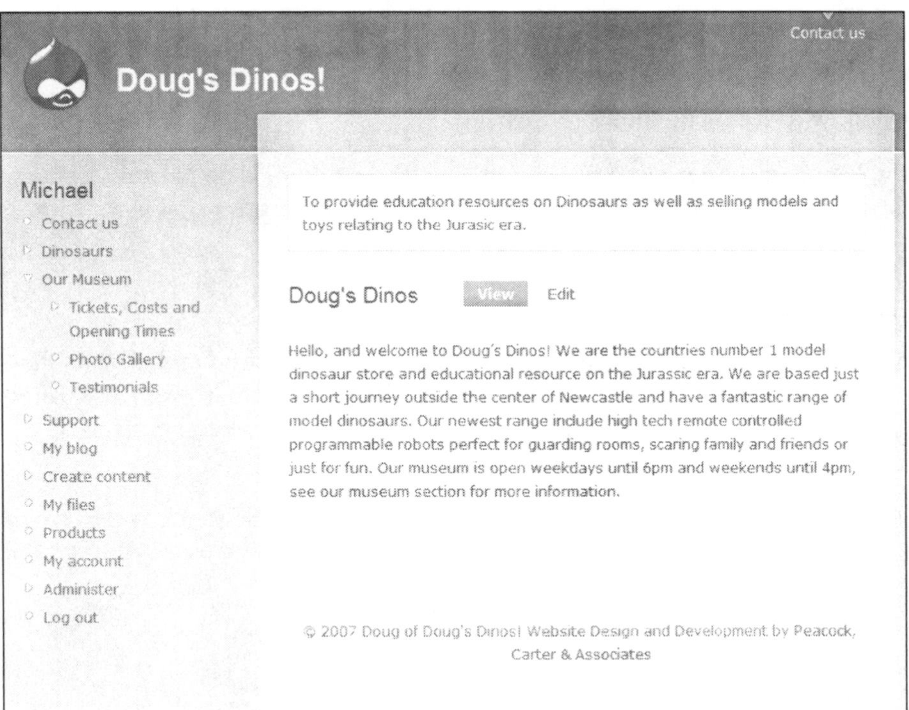

Marvin

Unlike **Minnelli**, the **Marvin** theme is not particularly refreshing; however, it has a more corporate feel to it using less vibrant colors and a simpler design.

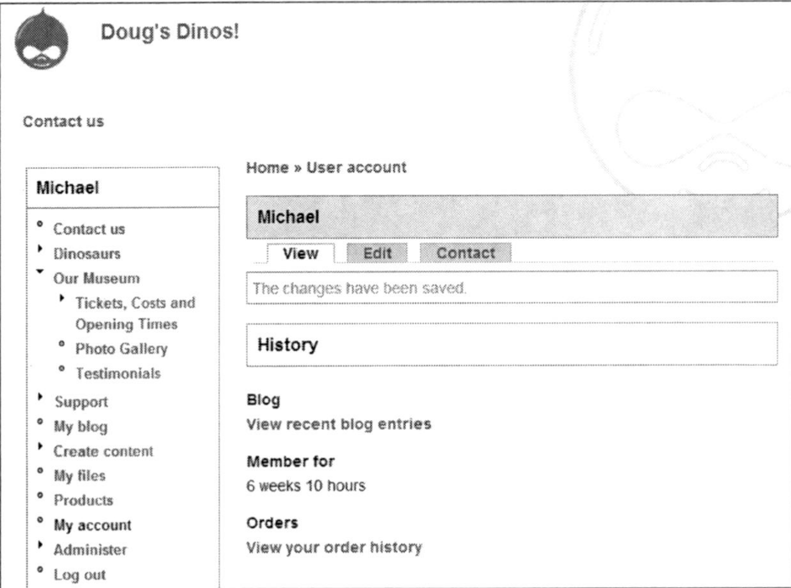

In particular this could be useful in a business site; however, additional modification to the skin would make it look much better.

Bluemarine

Again, this theme is less vibrant than **Minnelli** and the default theme, **Garland**; however, it is more corporate than them, although less so than the **Marvin** theme.

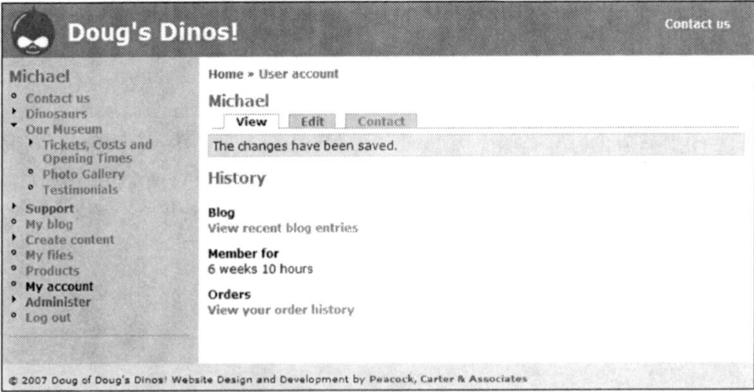

The style is also less smooth and more block-based with a very rigid header and menu.

Pushbutton

With the **Pushbutton** theme, we are given quite a different look. In particular, the typography has been designed with the visually impaired in mind with larger text size and more spacing between text.

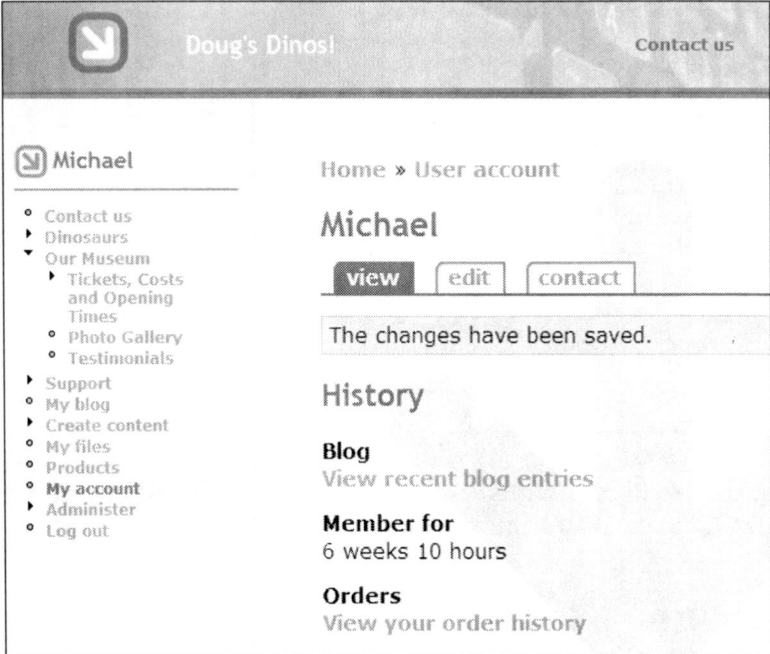

The design is also a little less block-based than some of the other themes and tries to maintain a more professional approach.

Garland

Garland is the default theme, and its only difference with the **Minnelli** theme is that it is a fluid-width theme, so if we are viewing the site on a computer with a smaller or larger screen than Minnelli's default width, the design will shrink or expand to accommodate the screen size.

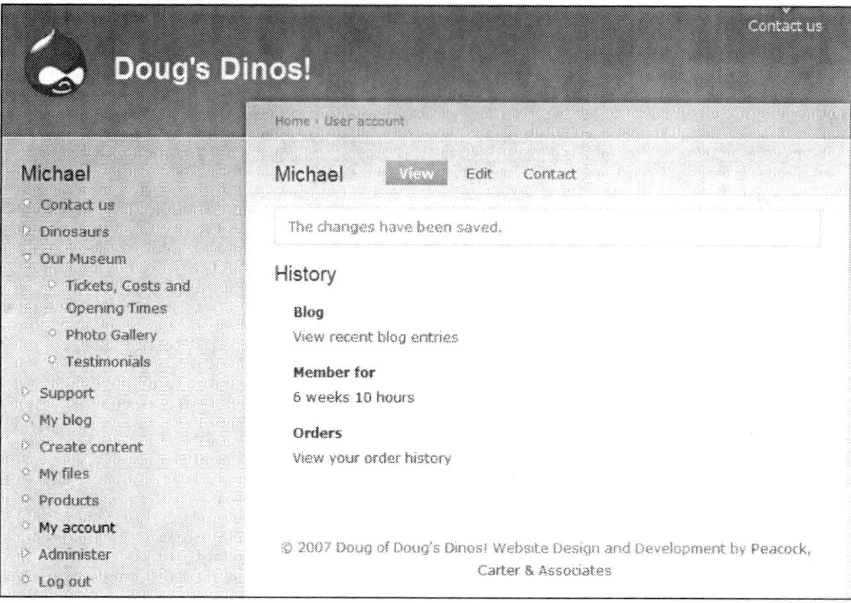

This theme reflects the style many websites are now using, including the gradient color schemes in the menu and the header, a glass style logo, and a nice refreshing color scheme.

Chameleon

A more simplistic approach is taken with this theme, with the entire background being white with a small bar at the top of the page to add something extra to the page.

This design would probably work better on older computers with poor color schemes or even mobile devices.

Customizing the Default Theme

Each of these themes that we have just looked at can be customized beyond its default look. Let's look at the default theme (**garland**) and customize it.

We can customize the following features:

- Color scheme, either based on a color set, or by changing the individual colors
- If certain elements, such as the logo, are displayed
- The logo
- The favicon

Back in the **Themes** section of the **Administer** area, there is a **configure** link next to each theme; if we click this we are taken to the theme's configuration page.

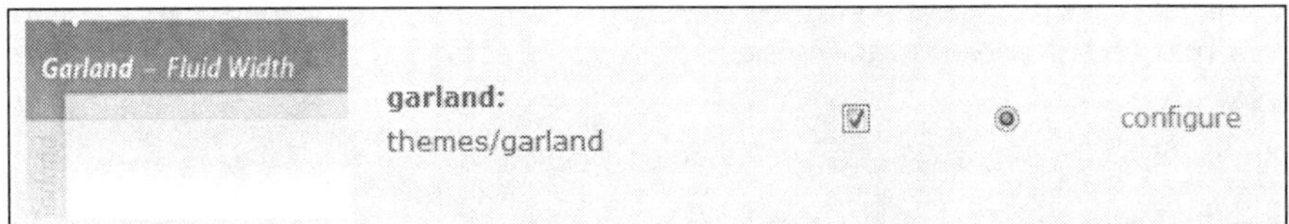

Although Doug ideally wants a new theme that is unique to his website, he also wants to have a look at a few different options for the default theme. In particular, he wants to add his company's logo to the website and try a number of red color schemes as those are his corporate colors.

Color Scheme

The color scheme settings are quite intuitive and easy to change. We can either:

- Select a color set
- Change each color by entering the hexadecimal colour codes (the # followed by 6 characters)

- Select the colors from the color wheel

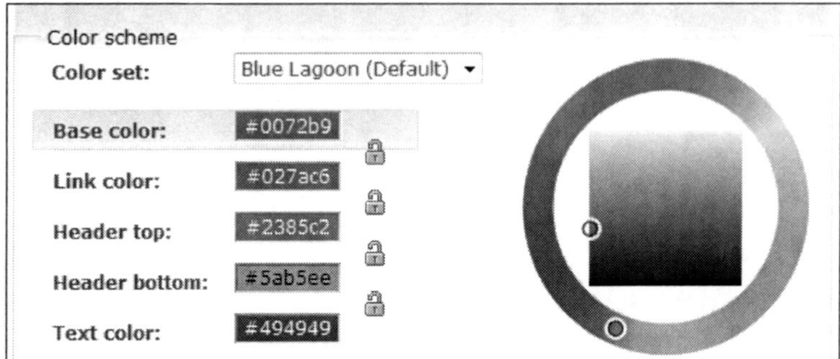

To change a color using the color wheel, we need to click on the color type (base color, link color, etc.) to select it and then chose the general color from the wheel and the shade of the color from the square within.

When we change the colors or color set, the preview window below the settings automatically updates to reflect the color change.

The following color sets are available:

- Blue Lagoon (the default set)
- Ash
- Aquamarine
- Belgian Chocolate
- Bluemarine
- Citrus Blast
- Cold Day
- Greenbeam
- Meditarrano
- Mercury
- Nocturnal
- Olivia
- Pink Plastic
- Shiny Tomato
- Teal Top
- Custom

Quite a number of these are red-based color schemes, let's look into them, they are:

- Belgian Chocolate
- Meditarrano
- Shiny Tomato

Belgian Chocolate Color Set

The Belgian Chocolate color set uses a dark red header with a gradient starting with black flowing into a dark red color. The page's background is a cream color and the main content area has a white background as illustrated by the picture below:

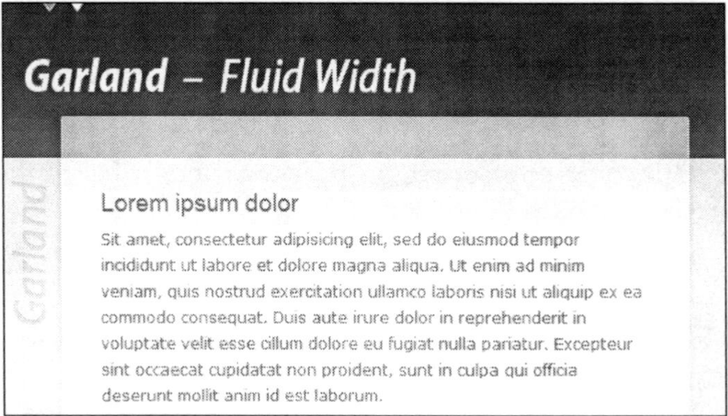

Mediterrano Color Set

The Mediterrano color set uses a lighter red color where the gradient in the header starts with a light orange color which then flows into a light red color. Similar to the Belgian Chocolate color scheme the background is cream in color with a white background for the content area.

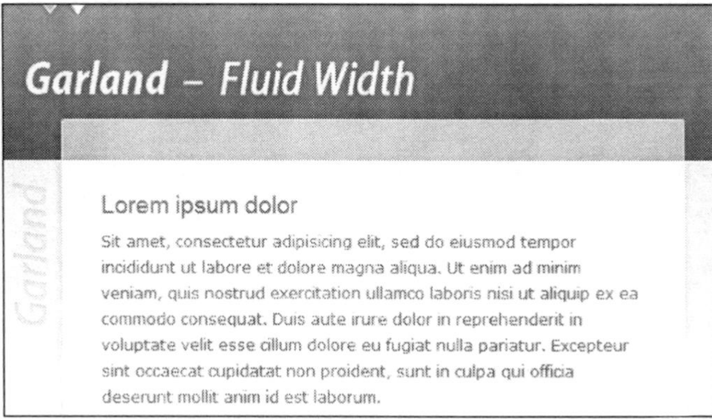

Shiny Tomato Color Set

The Shiny Tomato color set has a gradient header that starts with deep red and flows into a bright red color. The page's background is light grey with white background for the main content area, reflecting a professional image.

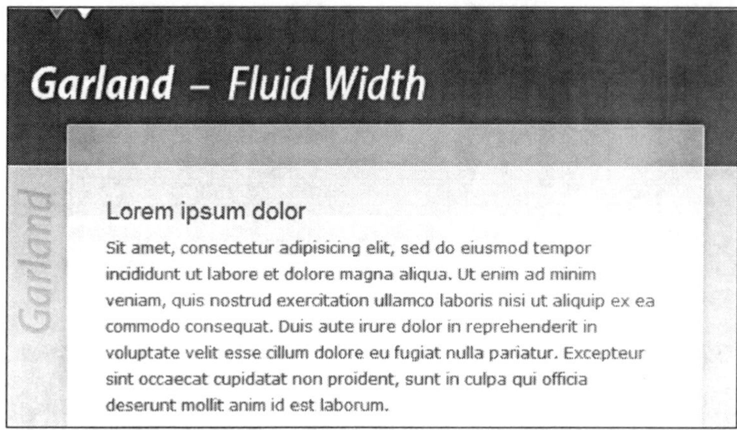

The Shiny Tomato color set uses a red scheme which is in Doug's logo and he feels this set is the most professional of the three and wants us to use that.

Toggle Display

With the toggle display options, we can select the elements we wish to display on our site, these include:

- Logo
- Site name
- Site slogan
- Mission statement
- User pictures in posts
- User pictures in comments
- Search box
- Shortcut icon

By default **Site Slogan**, **User pictures in posts**, **User pictures in comments**, and **Search box** are disabled, the rest are already enabled. Unfortunately with this theme we can only enable the **Site Slogan**; the other three options cannot be enabled with our choice of theme.

Doug initially wanted the slogan to be enabled; however, because of the length of his slogan, users with a small screen would not see the website name or the slogan:

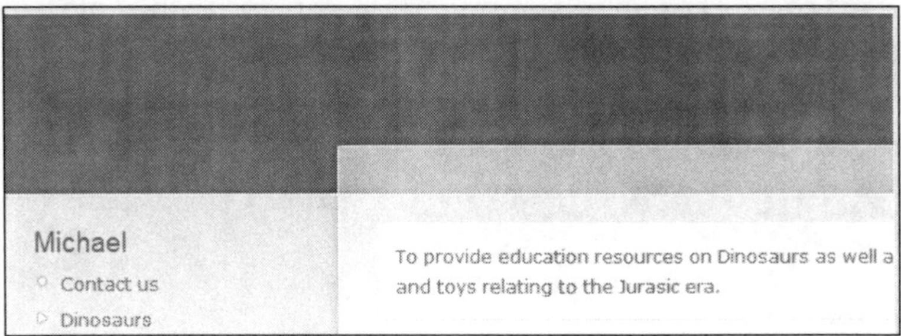

The slogan and site name will only be displayed if we have a larger screen as illustrated below:

Because of this problem, Doug decided it was not worth leaving the option enabled!

Logo Image Settings

As Doug also wants his logo to go into the website, we need to uncheck the option for using the default logo and select the logo file to upload.

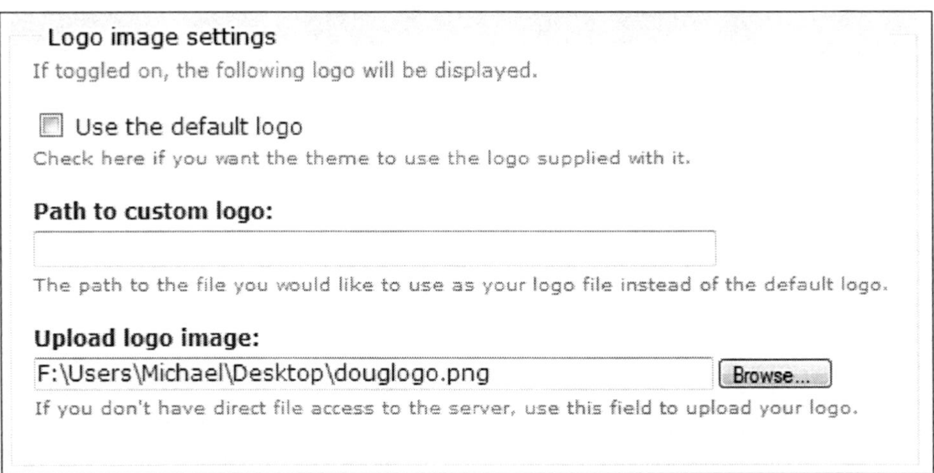

Once the logo has been uploaded, the website's header immediately updates to include the logo we have just uploaded, as shown below:

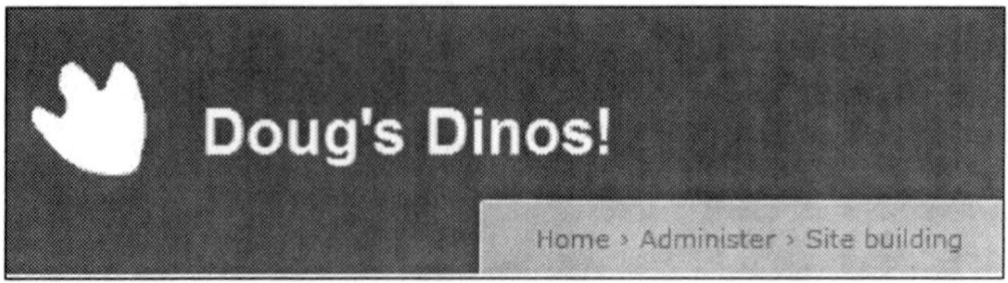

Shortcut Icon Settings

The final option for customizing the sites theme is the **Shortcut icon** settings. The shortcut icon is the favicon displayed in the address bar of our browser next to the web address. By default, this is a small version of the Drupal logo.

Let's customize this to a small version of Doug's logo. Graphics editing programs have little provisions for creating icon files, so let's use a web-based tool to turn the logo into a favicon. We can use `http://www.htmlkit.com/services/favicon/`, which is a popular online favicon generator.

On this website we can upload our logo:

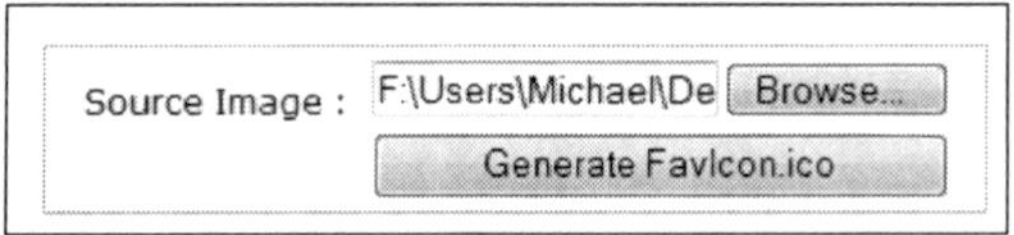

Once the image has been uploaded, a preview of the icon is displayed on the site and we can download a copy of it.

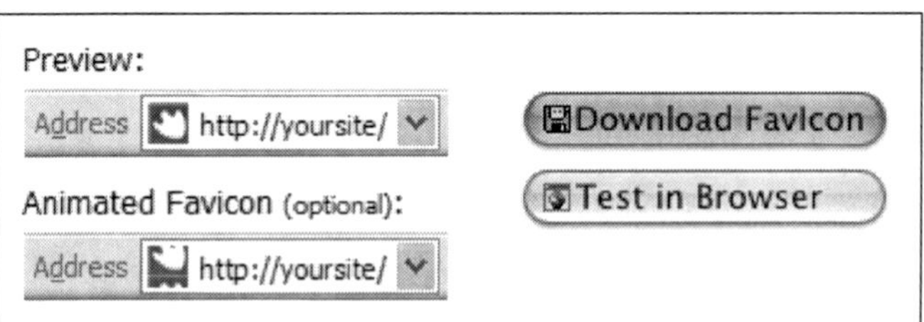

Now that we have our favicon generated and downloaded, we can upload it to our website:

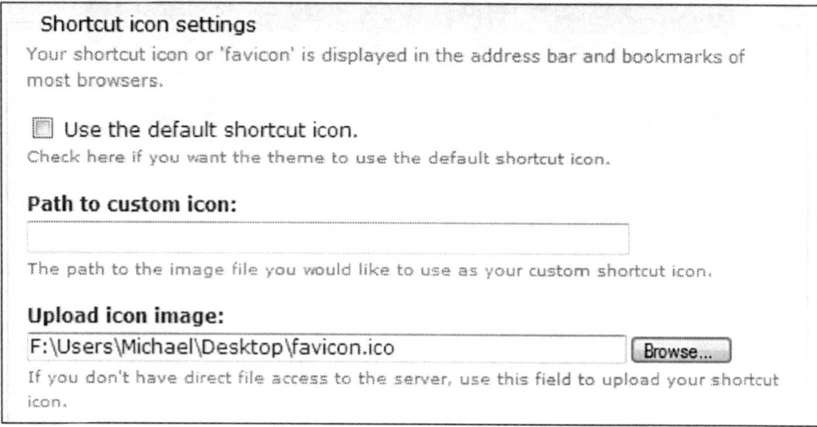

Once this is uploaded our favicon updates automatically, as shown below:

The Customized Skin

These changes leave us with a skin that looks like this:

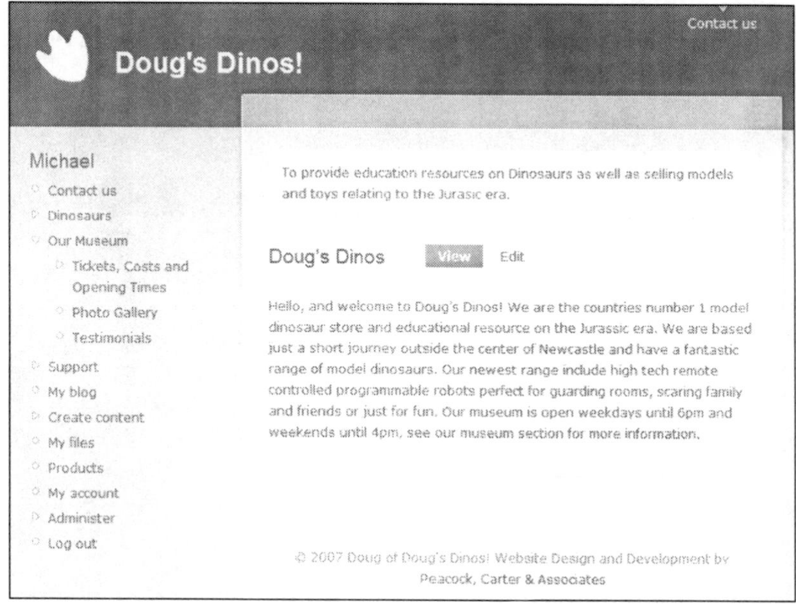

Doug is really pleased with these changes, and thinks it is a massive improvement on the default theme; however, he still wants to have a look at having a new theme created for his site. The customized site really impressed him though, so he may stick with it.

Installing and Managing Themes

In addition to the themes that come with Drupal we can also download new themes and install them in our site. Let's take a look at some of these themes that we can download and install. We will also look into managing these themes and deleting unnecessary themes.

Installing Themes

We can download themes from the themes section on the Drupal website, `http://drupal.org/project/Themes`.

After a brief look through the directory of themes, Doug found one that he quite liked and wanted to try out. The theme that he likes is **Barron**, so let's download it for him and install it to see what it is like.

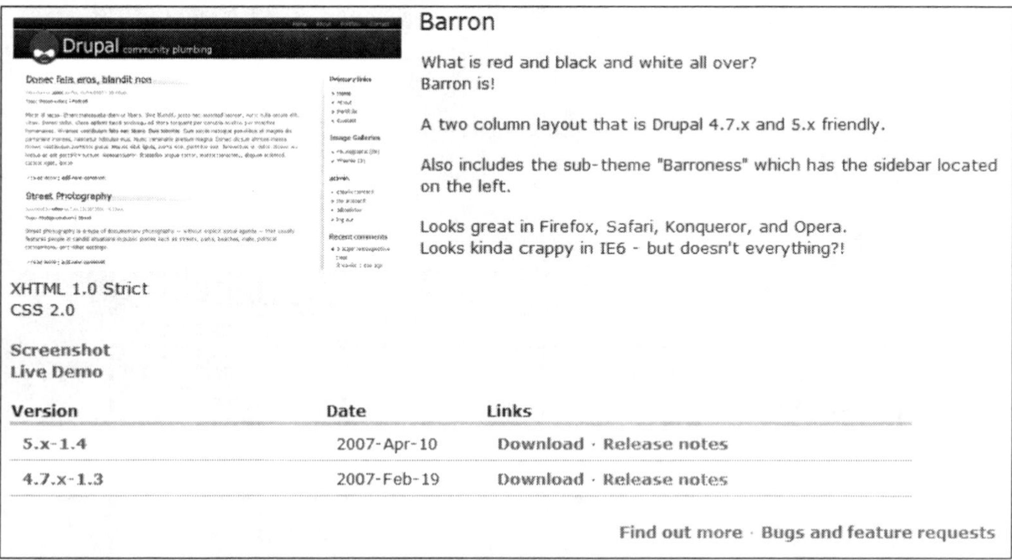

The version we want to download is the **5.x-1.4** version since we are using one of the 5.x versions of Drupal.

To install the theme, we need to uncompress the file we have just downloaded and then upload it to the `themes` directory on our website. Once it is installed, we just need to enable it and then select it as the theme we want to use:

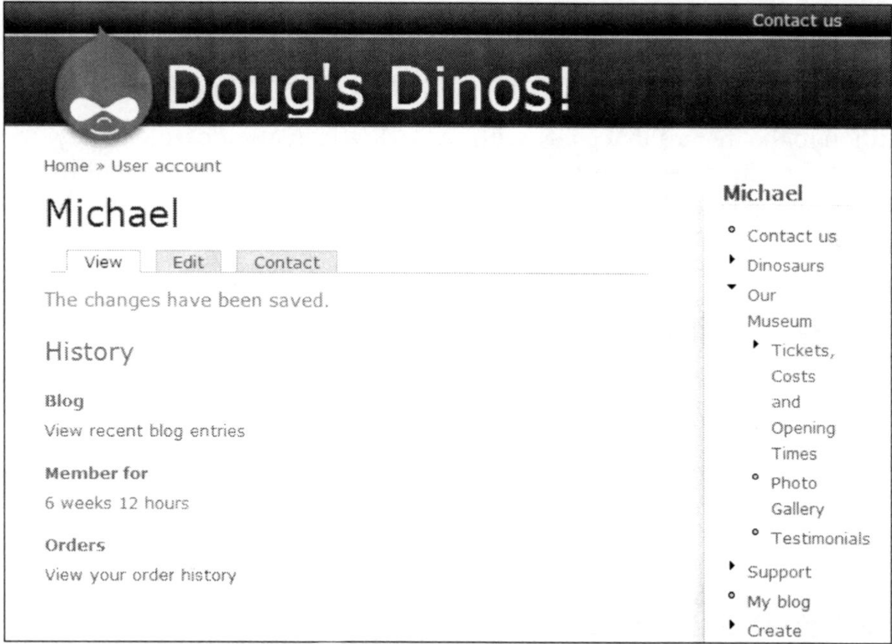

This theme does not promote the image Doug was hoping for in a site, so he has decided not to use it.

Managing Themes

Back into the main theme page we have a number of management options.

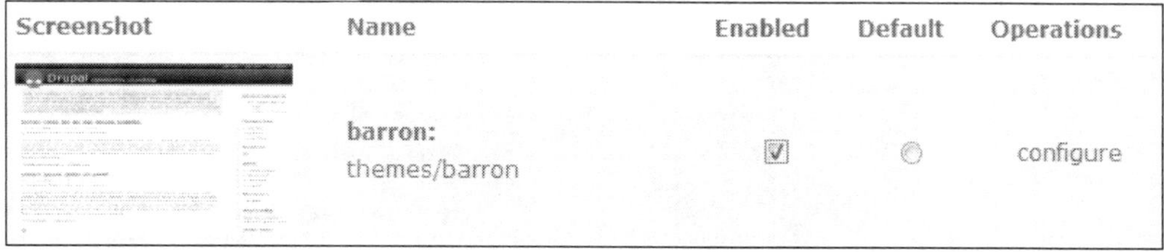

From here we can:

- Enable a theme
- Set a theme as the site's default theme
- View configuration options

To actually delete a theme, we just need to delete its folder from the `themes` directory in our website.

Creating a Theme

A comprehensive guide to themes and theme development can be found on the Drupal website at `http://drupal.org/node/509`. Themes generally consist of three layers:

- A PHP template engine
- An xHTML template
- Styles in the form of CSS

It is recommended to start creating our theme from an existing Drupal theme; the themes that are recommended to use are Zen or Bluebreeze. The theme that we are going to create is only a simple one-page theme, which will use default styling provided by each module.

> *Drupal 5 Themes* by Ric Shreves, **ISBN 978-1-84719-182-3 published by Packt Publishing**, it is a book published specifically for creating themes with Drupal 5; you may wish to try this book if you wish to create more detailed, and complex themes. (See `http://www.packtpub.com/drupal-5-themes/book`.)

Personally, I find it easier to create a webpage template as a working HTML file and then move this across to the theme's template files. Below is the template we have for Doug's Dinos, which we need to turn into a theme:

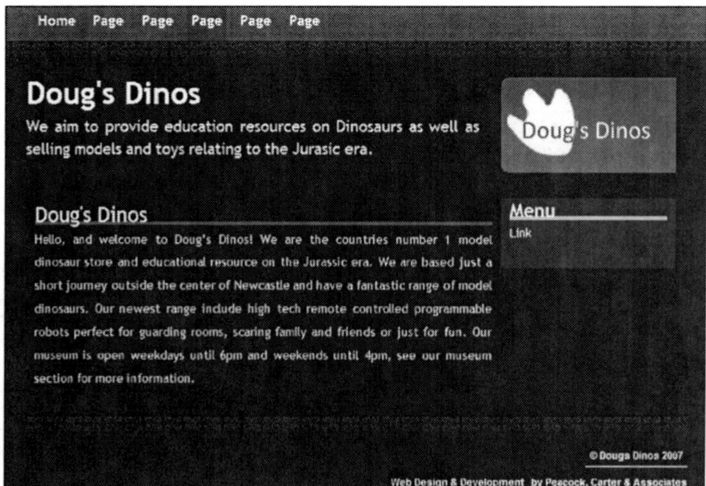

Template Files

These are the default template files with a theme:

- Page theme (`page.tpl.php`)
- Block within a sidebar (`block.tpl.php`)
- Generic container for the main area of the site (`box.tpl.php`)
- Comment theme (`comment.tpl.php`)
- Node theme (`node.tpl.php`)

These files can then be edited with our favorite text editor and we can import our design into the template files.

We now need to examine each of these files and transfer our HTML template to these, and replace the CSS file with the one from our template.

If we start with the `page.tpl.php` file we can get a basic design up and running to see what it is like, then we can concern ourselves with sections such as comments and nodes. The key to doing this is keeping the sections of the template code which are encapsulated within `<?php ?>` tags in the new template but ensuring they are placed correctly within the file.

The code for Doug's `page.tpl.php` file is:

```
<!DOCTYPE html PUBLIC "-//W3C//DTD XHTML 1.0 Strict//EN"
  "http://www.w3.org/TR/xhtml1/DTD/xhtml1-strict.dtd">
<html xmlns="http://www.w3.org/1999/xhtml" xml:lang="en" lang="en">
 <head>
    <title>
          <?php print $head_title; ?>
    </title>
    <meta http-equiv="content-type" content="text/html;
                                        charset=iso-8859-1" />
    <meta name="description" content="Doug's dinos aim to
          provide education resources on Dinosaurs as well as
          selling models and   toys relating to the Jurassic era." />
    <meta name="keywords" content="dougs dinos" />
    <meta name="author" content="Juniper Productions" />
    <meta name="copyright" content="© Peacock, Carter and
                                        Associates/Dougs Dinos" />
    <style type="text/css" title="Default page style"
     media="screen">@import "http://www.dougsdinos.com/drupal-
          5.7/themes/darkjuniper/juniperstyle.css";</style>
    <link rel="icon" href="favicon.ico" type="image/x-icon" />
    <link rel="shortcut icon" href="favicon.ico" type="image/x-icon"
/>
 </head>
```

```
<body>
<div id="orbis">
<ul>
<?php if (isset($primary_links)) : ?>
   <?php print theme('links', $primary_links, array('class' => 'links
     primary-links')); ?>
<?php endif; ?>
<?php if (isset($secondary_links)) : ?>
    <?php print theme('links', $secondary_links, array('class' =>
   'links secondary-links')); ?>
<?php endif; ?>
</ul>
</div><!--end orbis-->
<div id="wrapper">
<div id="header">
   <a href="#" title="Dougs Dinos Home">
   <img src="http://www.dougsdinos.com/drupal-    5.7/themes/
            darkjuniper/images/logo.png" alt="Dougs Dinos logo" />
   </a>
   <h1>Doug's Dinos</h1>
   <?php if ($mission) : print '<p>'. $mission .'</div>';
                                             endif; ?></p>
<div id="content">
  <?php print $content; ?>
</div><!--end content-->
<?php if ($sidebar_left): ?>
   <div id="column">
     <?php if ($search_box): ?>
      <div class="block block-theme"><?php print $search_box; ?>
     </div><?php endif ?>
   <?php print $sidebar_left; ?>
</div><?php endif; ?
<?php print $closure ?>
<div id="footer">
   <ul>
   <li><a href="copyright/" title="Copyright Statement &bull;
                Dougs Dinos">&copy; Dougs Dinos 2007</a></li>
   <li><a href="http://www.peacockcarter.co.uk/" title="Web Design
                &bull; Newcastle, Durham &amp; Leicester">Web Design
                &amp; Development</a> by Peacock, Carter
                &amp; Associates</li>
   </ul>
</div><!--end footer-->
</div><!--end wrapper-->
</body>
</html>
```

If we try this theme out, Doug's site looks like this:

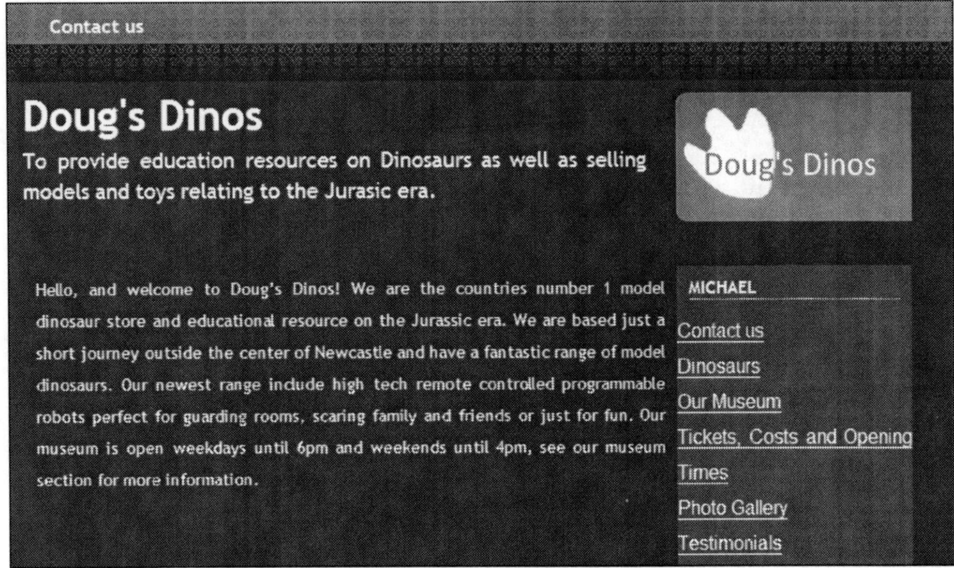

Doug quite likes the design, and has decided that he wants to have two themes on his site, the default theme, which we customized earlier in the chapter, and this new custom theme (once we have updated the template files for the other sections, and polished the design up a little). To go from template HTML file to this stage, which is a little rough round the edges only takes five minutes!

Summary

In this chapter, we looked into branding our site and we:

- Explored and customized the default themes
- Downloaded and installed new themes
- Created a custom theme

Now that we have a newly branded site with which Doug is really happy, it's time for us to look at Chapter 7—*Checkout and Taking Payments*, so we can begin to monetize our site!

7

Checkout and Taking Payments

We now have a great looking site for Doug to use. Along with his online product catalog, it is now time to look into the checkout process and take payments from customers. In this chapter, we will learn:

- How to finalize the store ready for customers
- How the checkout process works
- How to customize the checkout process
- How to process orders

This will allow us to start accepting payments from customers; however, we will need to do more to improve the process (such as more payment options; for now we will just set one up quickly so payments work).

Finalizing the Store Ready for Customers

Let's add a product to our shopping cart, place it as an order, and see what happens:

- Select a product.
- Click **Add to cart**.
- Click the **your shopping cart** link.
- Click **Checkout**.
- If we are not logged in, we need to enter an email address.
- Click the **Place your order** button.

The order is then placed.

What's Missing?

If you went through that process you might have noticed there were a few things missing, which prevent us from taking orders and payments:

- Our address was not taken.
- Our payment method and payment details were not taken.

We need to correct these problems so we can start to take payments!

Taking Addresses

In order to take addresses from customers during **Checkout** we need to enable the **Address** sub-module from the **E-Commerce Customer Interface** module, so let's enable that now:

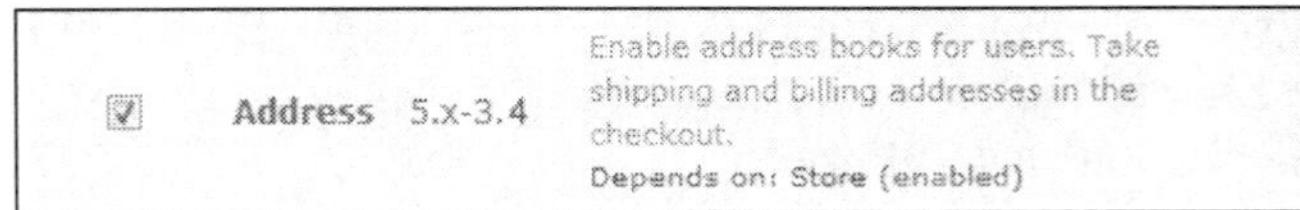

We are now able to take our customers' addresses (as we will see in a moment!).

Taking Payments

The reason we are not able to take payments is because we don't have a payment gateway installed. As we are going to look into payments in more detail in Chapter 9—*Taxes, Payment, and Shipping*, let's just look into the simplest payment gateway, which is called Cash on Delivery **(COD)**. This module can be used for transactions where the customer pays with cash or posts a cheque or pays with credit-card details over the phone. If we use this for telephone payments, we would need some form of payment processor where we can manually edit credit card information, such as PayPal's Virtual Terminal, so we can enter the details while the customer is on the phone.

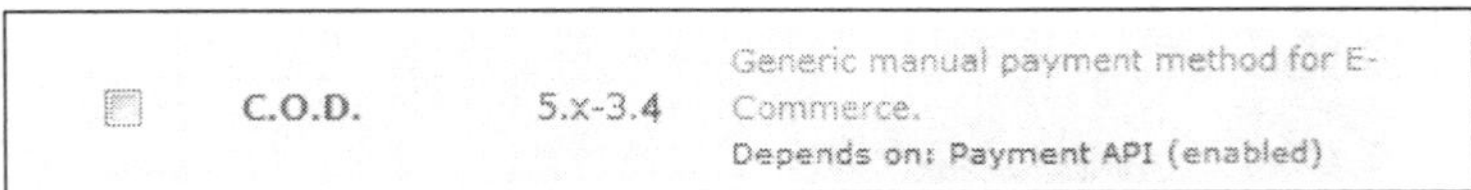

Once this is installed we can officially start taking orders and payments! Let's give it a try!

Let's Try Again

Now that we have provisions for shipping and payments, let's take another look at placing an order.

First, we need to add some products to our shopping cart and then click the **Checkout** button.

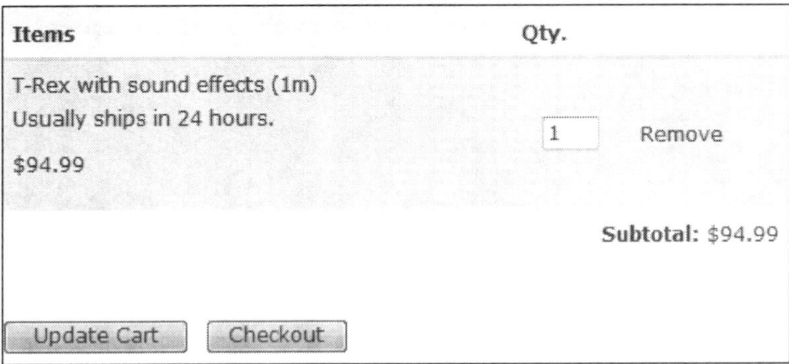

Next, we need to enter a new address because we don't have any postal addresses tied to our account in our "address book", so let's enter a postal address in the address form, and then click the **Create new address** button.

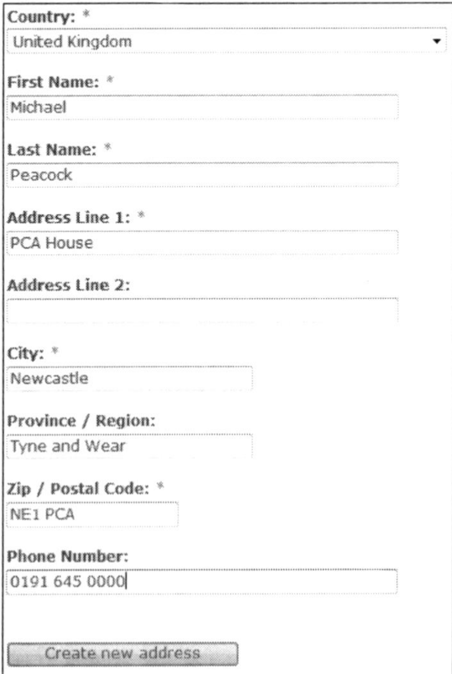

This saves the address to our address book, which is tied to our account; we can then select this address as our shipping and/or billing address. If we have an alternative address for either of these we can add it by clicking on the **add a new address** link next to the drop-down box of addresses.

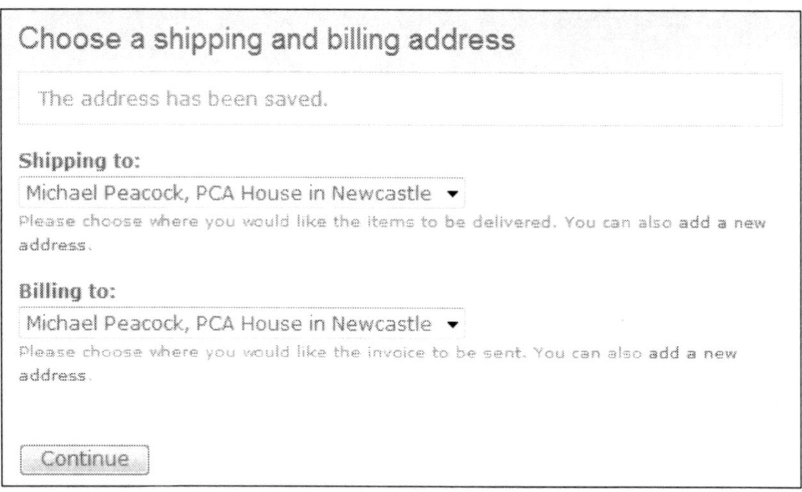

The confirmation page then confirms our:

- Email address
- Shipping address
- Billing address
- Payment details
- Order summary

Notice, that the addresses and payment methods were omitted when we first went through this process. We can also change the address from this screen by clicking the **(change)** link next to the addresses.

Shipping and billing address
Ship to: (change)
Michael Peacock
PCA House
Newcastle, TYNE AND WEAR NE1 PCA
United Kingdom
0191 645 0000
Billing to: (change)
Michael Peacock
PCA House
Newcastle, TYNE AND WEAR NE1 PCA
United Kingdom
0191 645 0000

There is only one payment option enabled in the system at the moment (as we will be looking at the rest in more detail in Chapter 9—*Taxes, Payment, and Shipping*) and this has no further options, so we have to leave that as it is. We can also make any last minute changes to the order before finalizing the order.

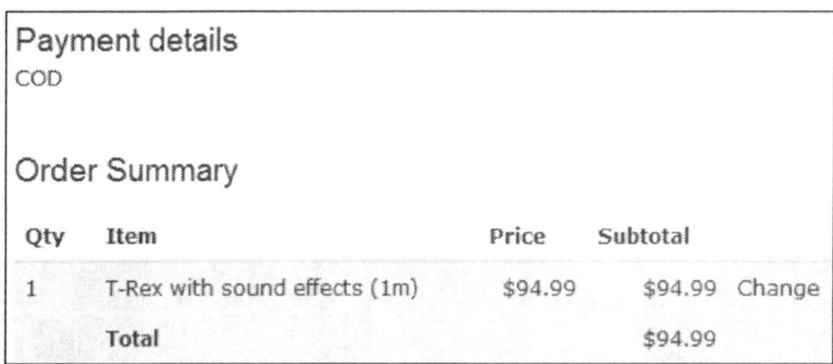

Once we submit this page we receive a confirmation note to tell us the purchase has been received.

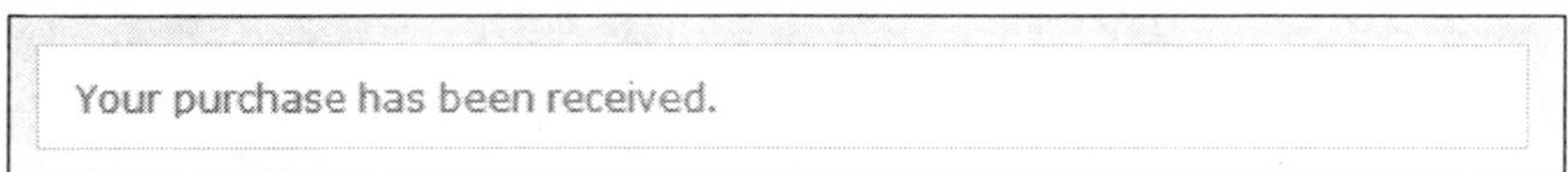

As we have set up the address and payment options, we also receive an email to confirm the order, which reminds us of our shipping address, billing address, and the purchases we made.

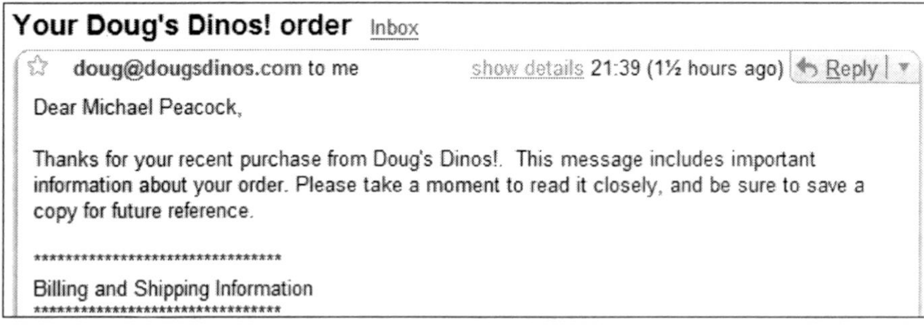

Unfortunately the payment options we have enabled are very primitive and essentially require us to communicate with the customer to handle the payment and arrange delivery or pickup; however, for now we are able to take orders!

How the Checkout Process Works

After setting up our store to accept orders with addresses and payment methods, let's review how this works:

- Select products to order
- Select billing and shipping addresses
- Confirm the addresses
- Select a payment method
- Confirm the order
- Place the order
- Receive confirmation email
- Order is processed by staff

The settings and options for some of these can be changed depending on the modules to which they are related.

How to Customize the Checkout Process

A number of parts of the checkout process can be customized including:

- The order of some of the checkout screens
- Price formatting
- Payment methods available (looked at in detail in Chapter 8—*Creating a Better Selling Experience*)
- How the payment method works
- The emails sent to the customer
- Global anonymous purchase policy
- Whether or not the site administrator is notified about transactions
- Overview text for a user's order history
- How a user adds a product to their shopping cart
- Continuing shopping after adding a product to the cart

Doug is not sure how he wants to customize the process, so let's take a look at how these options can be customized and see what he thinks!

Checkout Screen Order

With the modules we have currently installed, the order of the following pages can be configured:

- Anonymous user page (where the user enters their email address or logs in)
- User's address
- Payment method
- The cart

These settings are under **E-Commerce Configuration** in the **Screen order** page.

For practical reasons, however, the **ec_anon** and **cart** pages are restricted to being the first and last page respectively. This is because if the user is not logged in we first need to either get their details or ask them to login, and the cart itself must obviously be the last page.

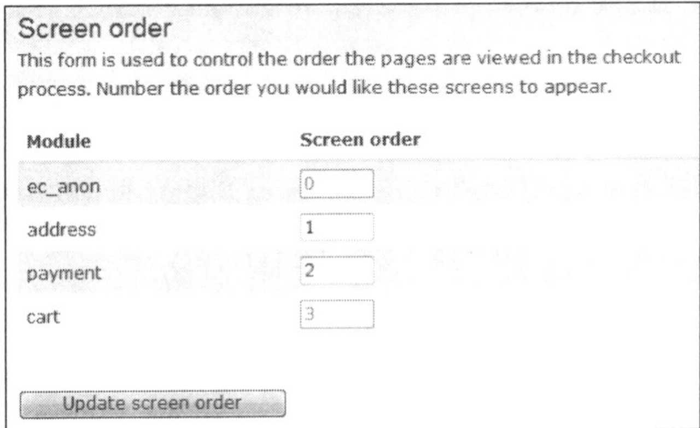

Doug is quite happy with the **address** being selected before **payment**, so let's leave those settings as they are and move on.

Price Formatting

Within **E-Commerce configuration** is the **Payment** section, which allows us to alter the format of prices as well as the currency used.

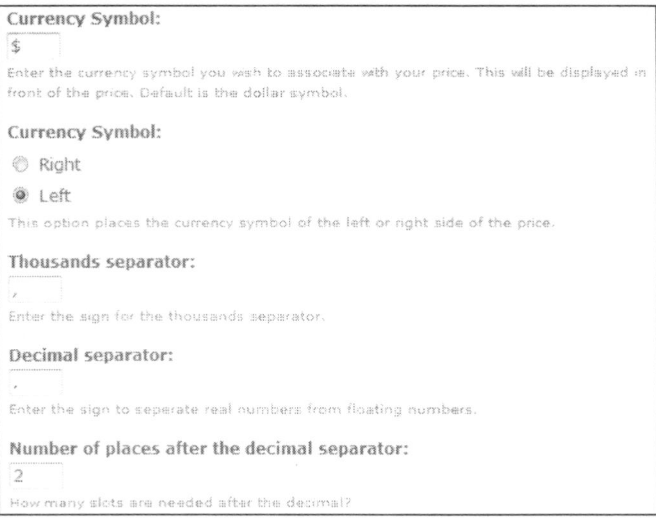

Although Doug's business is based in the UK, he is hoping to take a large number of orders for models from the US, and so wants us to leave the formatting unchanged and the currency as USD.

Payment Methods

The payment methods can be customized with the various payment gateway modules that can be installed; however, we will cover this in more detail in Chapter 8—*Creating a Better Selling Experience*, so let's leave it for now.

How the Payment Method Works

Within the **C.O.D.** section of the **E-Commerce configuration** section we have a number of configuration options for the payment method. There are:

- The title—We can see this as the name of the payment method when placing an order. As this payment method is generic we should consider renaming it to something like **cheque payment** or **telephone payment**.
- Thank You Page—We should also consider creating a **thanks** page for the user after the payment procedure.
- Marking the order once the payment has been made—In this case we don't, as the only way for it to be marked as paid is by an administrator.

- Marking the transaction workflow as completed—In the administration area, each order goes through a workflow of options including:
    - Received
    - Invoiced
    - Shipped
    - Awaiting customer response
    - Cancelled
    - Completed
    - Security violation

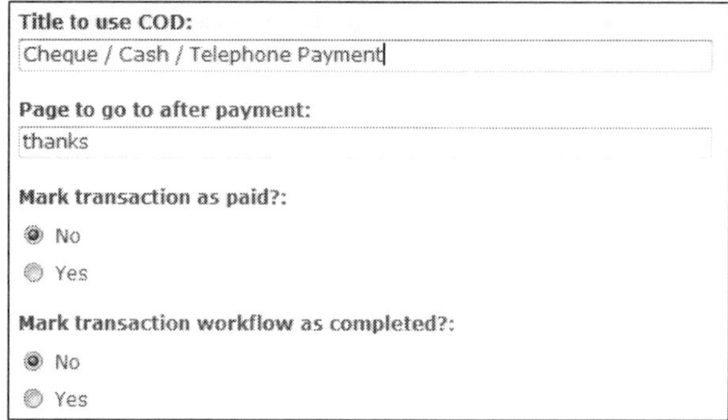

Doug wants to change the name from COD to something a little more meaningful, and he also wants the user to go to a special thanks page after completing their order.

Emails Sent to the Customer

At various points throughout the order process and the post-order process emails relating to their order are sent to the customer. Similar to the emails sent to users when they register, which we looked at in Chapter 5—*Customers and Staff*, we can edit and manage these emails. The email settings can be found in **E-Commerce configuration** under **Mail**.

name	type	op		
Default customer invoice	Customer invoice	view	edit	
Default email confirmation		view	edit	
Default expiration notice	Recurring product reminder	view	edit	delete
Default order cancellation notice	Transaction cancelled notice	view	edit	
Default processing error	Processing error notification	view	edit	
Default query to customer	Query to customer	view	edit	
Default renewal reminder	Recurring product reminder	view	edit	delete
Default welcome mail		view	edit	

The **Recurring product reminder** emails are not used by our current setup so they can be deleted; the other emails can be viewed and edited. For now, Doug is quite happy with the default emails, so we will leave them as they are.

Global Anonymous Purchase Policy

We looked into anonymous purchase policies in Chapter 4—*Creating Your Product Catalog* when we implemented our product catalog. In addition to the per product settings, we can also set this globally to one of:

- **Registered only**—Customers must log in or register to check out
- **Flexible**—Customers can register or log in or check out anonymously
- **Anonymous only**—Customers can log in or purchase anonymously but the option to register is never given.

Anonymous purchasing policy:
Flexible
This sets the site-wide policy for anonymous purchasing. This setting can be overridden by product settings.
- *Registered only:* Anonymous purchases are disabled. All customers must register or login before they can checkout.
- *Flexible:* Customers can choose to register, login or checkout anonymously.
- *Anonymous only:* Only anonymous purchases are allowed. Customers are never given the option to register during checkout. Customers will be given the option of logging in or purchasing

Doug likes the flexibility that comes with having a flexible purchase policy, as we discussed in Chapter 4—*Creating Your Product Catalog*, so let's leave it as it is.

Administrator Notifications

When orders are placed we can opt for the administrator to be emailed a summary of the order, this is particularly useful when manually processing orders, and these orders are infrequent so you may not need to visit the website on a daily basis.

This setting is found in **E-Commerce configuration** under **Store**.

Transaction notices:
- Disabled
- Enabled

Enable or disable transaction notifications. If enabled, the site administrator (*doug@dougsdinos.com*) will receive an email summarizing the status of all orders. The frequency of emails is dependent on how often the site administrator has scheduled to run cron jobs. Finally, The site administrator e-mail address can be changed in the general configuration screen.

Doug wants this feature enabled so he does not need to keep checking the system for new orders, so let's enable it for him.

> This setting depends on having set up a cron job to periodically call the `cron.php` file; this allows emails to be sent in groups periodically. For more information on setting up cron jobs, you should contact your web host. Typically it involves a crontab setting in your hosting control panel such as cPanel.

Order History Overview Text

Also in the **Store** area of **E-Commerce configuration** is the order history overview text; although it is not technically part of the checkout process, it relates to customer service and previous orders.

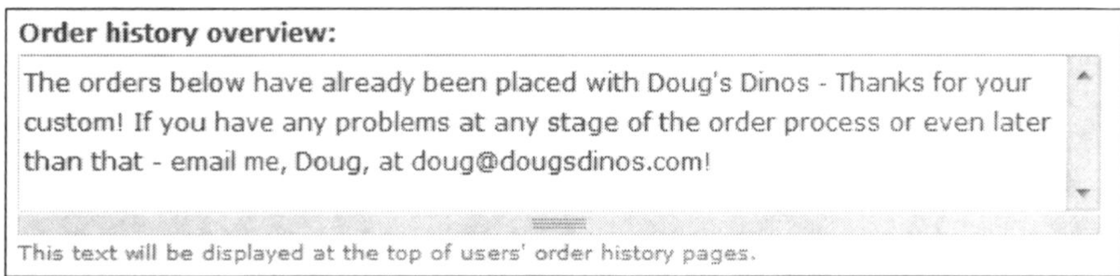

Doug wants to use this area to thank customers for their previous orders, and make them feel welcome to contact him whenever they need to, regarding anything about their purchases with his store.

This makes the order history page look quite friendly, as illustrated below:

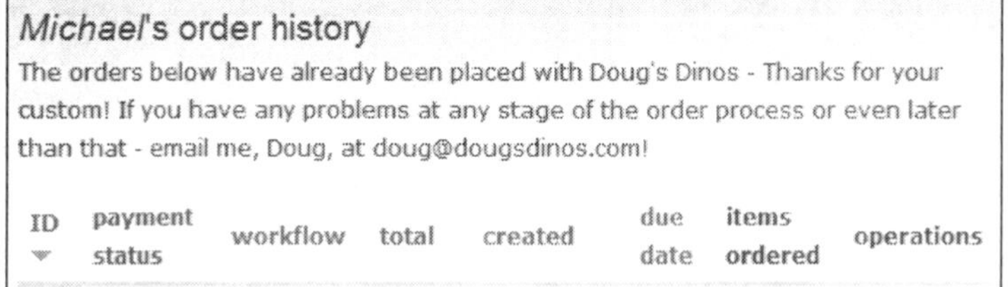

How Products are Added to the Cart

There are two options for users adding products to the shopping cart:

- Users can click a link, which adds the product to their cart.
- Users can enter the quantity of the product and then click the add to cart button.

These settings can also be found in the **Store** section of **E-Commerce configuration**.

Users adds product to cart using link.

If this field is unchecked a form will be placed at the bottom of the product view which will allow the user select the quantity and other information.

This form is quite useful as it encourages the user to order more than one of the product, whereas with the link a user must physically add the product to the cart multiple times, which can be inconvenient. Doug likes the idea of the form, so let's uncheck the box and save the settings.

We now have a small form at the bottom of each product page:

Continuing Shopping after Adding a Product to the Cart

When products are added to the cart we can either:

- Take the user back to the product listing
- Take the user to their shopping cart

This setting is from the **Store** within **E-Commerce configuration**.

User is directed to the shopping cart after adding item.
If left unchecked, the user will remain on the product page and a message will alert them that the item has been added to their cart.

This setting and the setting we looked at just before work well when they are oppositely set, so if the first box is unchecked this one works best if it is checked, something which Doug agrees with, so let's check this box and save our settings!

Processing Orders

So far in this chapter we have looked at how to set up our site to take orders, how to place orders, and how to customize the checkout process. Now let's have a look at actually processing the orders placed through the website.

Order Overview

In the **Administer** area, if we select the **E-Commerce** section from the menu, the page we are presented with contains an overview of order statistics including some monthly figures.

The **Orders** overview groups all of the orders in the system by their current payment status.

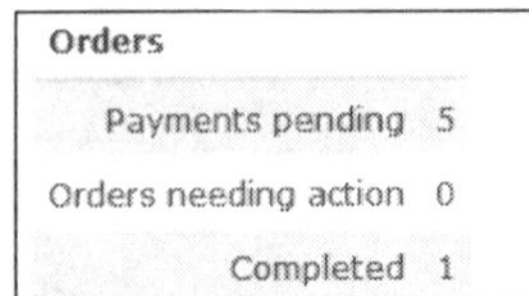

Each of the payment statuses in the overview is linked to a filtered listing of orders that have that specific status of payment.

Also on this overview page we have some monthly figures, which indicate how many orders we have had this month as well as how much we have taken in this month.

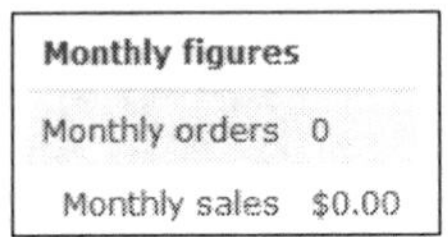

Since Doug's site have not yet taken any payments (we don't have payments properly set up yet) the monthly figures are currently zero.

Transaction List

From the **E-Commerce** menu, the **Transactions** page lists all of the transactions stored within the system.

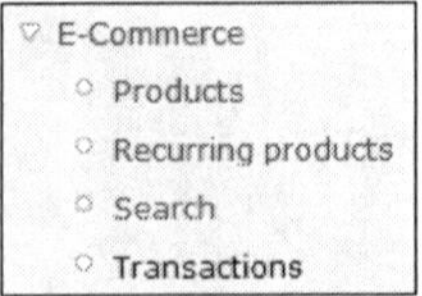

We can filter the list by each of the different fields for the order, as well as create new transactions. For each transaction the following information is displayed:

- Order ID number
- Customer name (and username)
- Payment status
- Workflow position
- Gross amount
- Date created
- Date changed
- Date due (for recurring payments)
- Number of items ordered
- Operations

5	Michael Peacock (Michael)	pending	received	$18.95	29/10/2007 - 22:39	29/10/2007 - 22:39	1 item	edit addresses items

We will look more into payment statuses and workflow information shortly, so let's take a look at the operations available.

The operations are:

- Edit
- Addresses
- Items

Edit

The edit page allows us to change the workflow and payment status of the order, the username and email address of customer, and the payment method. We can neither alter the gross amount nor the last modified date.

The ability to change these details is quite useful. For instance, if a user can no longer pay using a specific method we can change it for them, or if someone placed the order for someone else but cannot make the payment, we can transfer the order to another account to pay for it.

Addresses

Clicking the **addresses** link displays the billing and shipping addresses for the order; in addition to seeing these addresses we can also change them, which is useful if a customer contacts us to request a change of delivery address.

Items

The **items** link shows the items which are related to the order, and allows us to edit the individual items tied to the order.

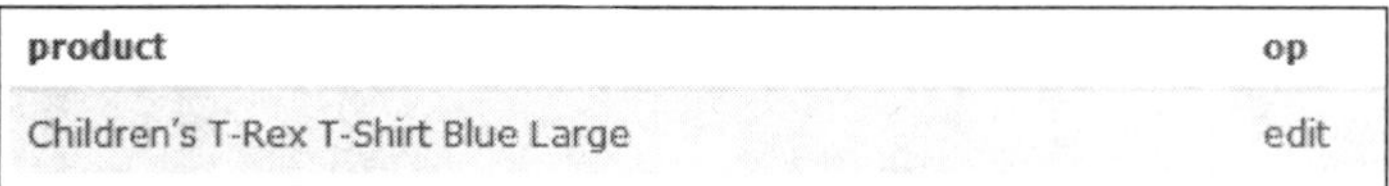

product	op
Children's T-Rex T-Shirt Blue Large	edit

Workflow

The workflow process indicates how the order goes through the system, and the workflow statuses available are:

- Order received
- Customer invoiced

- Order shipped
- Awaiting customer response
- Cancelled
- Completed
- Security violation

If we click on the workflow status of a particular transaction, we are presented with a number of operations including:

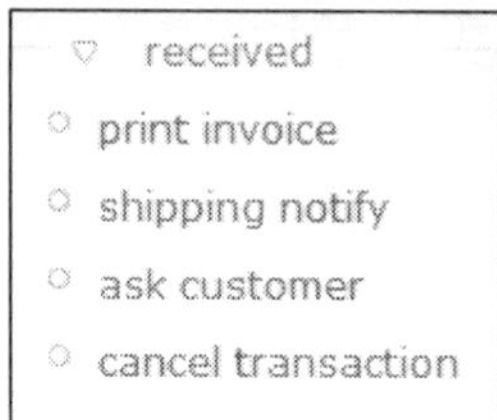

If we notify the customer that the order has been shipped (we can't do this yet, as we have not configured shipping options!) the workflow changes to **shipped**, if we need to send the customer an email (such as: We noticed you ordered a care package for your model dinosaur, but you have not purchased a model, do you want to continue with your order?) the status changes to **awaiting customer response**. Once payment is received by the payment gateway the status changes to **Completed**, and if we cancel the order it is marked as **Cancelled**.

Payment Statuses

A payment can have any of the following statuses:

- Pending
- Payment received
- Completed
- Failed
- Denied
- Refunded
- Cancelled

Currently, because of our payment gateway we have to manually edit the transaction to change the payment status; however, we will look into this in more detail when we look into the Payment API in detail!

Current Limitations with Our Store

Although we looked into taking orders and payments, we have the following limitations:

- Workflow is limited due to shipping and payment issues
- Payment status does not update
- The whole process is very manual

When we look into Chapter 9—*Taxes, Shipping, and Payments*, we will correct these issues and make massive improvements on our current store.

Summary

In this chapter, we have learned:

- How the order process works
- How to customize this order process
- How to place an order
- How to manage and process orders

Although we did not look into payment options in great detail, and are quite limited in that respect at the moment, we can at least use our store to receive orders and manually accept payments and update the orders accordingly. Now let's move on to creating a better selling experience before moving on to mentioned the topics covered in this chapter in greater detail.

8

Creating a Better Selling Experience

We have our newly branded site, and we can take a basic form of payment! In this chapter, let's look at creating a better selling experience for our customers.

In this chapter, you will learn:

- How to add a shopping cart
- How to add search features
- How to auto-create user accounts
- How to include images on our product listings
- How to provide discounts to customers based on their role
- How to enable coupons so customers can get discounts
- How to provide discounts on bulk purchases
- More about some of the other e-Commerce options and product types

Making Things Easier

Although Doug's store is relatively simple for his customers to use, it is missing three key features that would make their time on the website easier, these are:

- An overview of the shopping cart
- Search features
- Ability to auto-create user accounts

At the moment, without a search feature the only way for users to find products is by manually browsing through the website and stumbling across a product they like.

Adding a Shopping Cart

We can add a shopping cart to our theme so that customers can continue browsing the website but still know how much is in their shopping cart, and easily get to it later.

To add this block, we need to go to the **Blocks** section, which is under **Site Building** within the **Administer** area. Within the **Blocks** section, we need to ensure we have all our themes selected (or do this for each theme we are using) and then change the **Region** of the **Shopping cart** to the **left sidebar**.

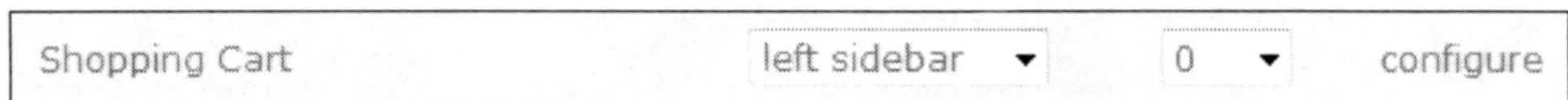

Once we click on the **Save blocks** button, the shopping cart block is displayed in our theme:

Adding Search Capabilities

Doug tested the website with a few friends and family members, and their main issue with it was the difficulty in finding products they wanted.

The first thing we need to do is install the **Search** module, which is grouped under the **Core - optional** section of **Modules** in the **Administer** area.

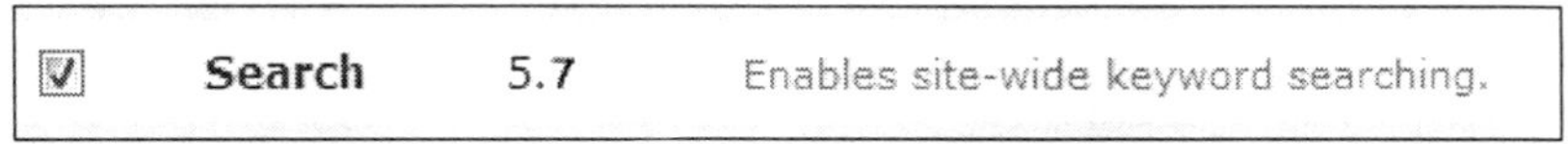

With the module installed, we now need to enable the **Search** feature from the **Blocks** section; otherwise the search box won't be displayed on the website. We can select this feature by going to **Administer | Site Building | Blocks**, then set it up in the same way as for the shopping cart and save the settings.

We now have a search box on our website under the header but above the main menu!

Let's try searching for one of our products, for instance T-Rex. Notice something? No results found! This seems quite strange as we have a product with T-Rex in the name, so why didn't we get any results?

The reason for this is that Drupal has not yet been indexed. Drupal uses a cron job to create the index of the site. Without the indexing done **Search** options cannot work. The **Search settings** under **Administer | Site configuration** allow us to specify how many pages are indexed per "cron run" and allow us to set the site to be re-indexed.

Cron Jobs

A cron job is a setting on your web host's server (if you have cPanel hosting, it is available under "crontab") that performs tasks at specific times. Drupal has a special page that performs various tasks; this can be called by a cron job so that it regularly opens the page and runs the tasks.

Indexing status

0% of the site has been indexed. There are 31 items left to index.

Re-index site

Indexing throttle

Items to index per cron run:

100

The maximum amount of items that will be indexed in one cron run. Set this number lower if your cron is timing out or if PHP is running out of memory.

> This setting depends on having set up a cron job to periodically call the `cron.php` file. For more information on setting up cron jobs, you should contact your web host. Typically it involves a crontab setting in your hosting control panel such as cPanel.

We can manually run the cron task, by opening the `cron.php` file in our web browser. In this case we just open: `http://www.dougsdinos.com/cron.php`.

Once we have opened this page, let's try searching for T-Rex again. This time we will get some results!

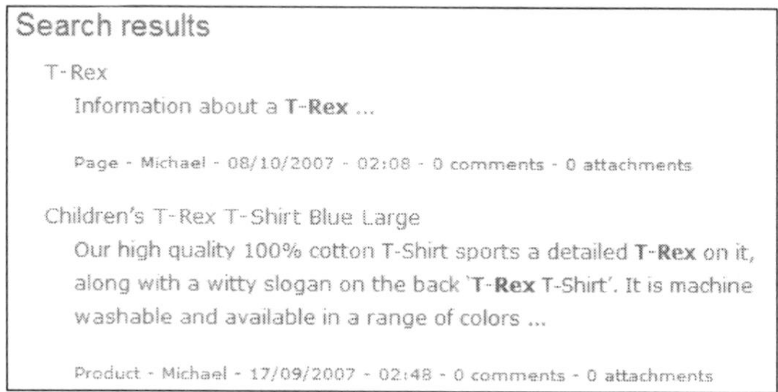

Customers will now be able to find products and other content on Doug's website much more easily!

Auto-Creating User Accounts

If a customer is not a user on our site, we can automatically create a user account for them once they have placed their order; this saves the inconvenience of using an anonymous purchase policy where the user has to log in or register, but it gives the user the added convenience of having their details saved for future orders.

This is something Doug wants to enable to make things easier for regular customers on this site. The first thing we need to do is install the module. The module is called **EC Useracc** and is listed in the **E-Commerce Uncategorized** group of modules.

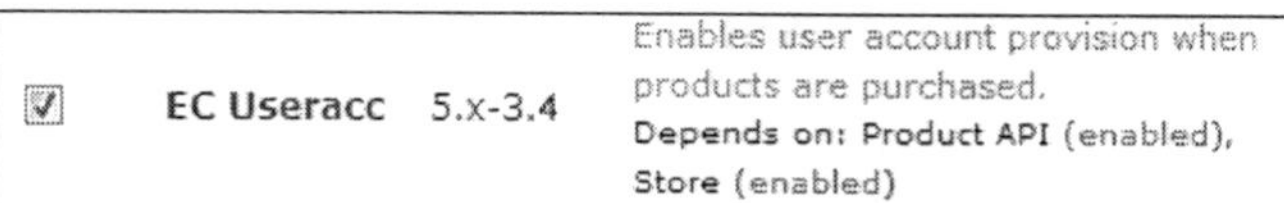

Now under **E-Commerce configuration** we have a new option called **User Account**; let's take a look at it. This has the following settings:

- Confirmation e-mail
- Welcome mail
- Days to confirm expiry

The **Confirmation e-mail** is to see if the customer wants to create a user account; this email expires after the number of days set in the **Days to confirmation expiry** setting has passed, and the **Welcome mail** is the email sent when the account is created. These emails can be configured on the **Mail** page.

These settings don't actually enable the feature though; we have installed the module and looked at the global settings, but to actually get it to work we need to set how we would like each product to work in relation to this module. If we go to edit any product, there is a new section, which was not there previously, called **User account provision**; this is what we need to change.

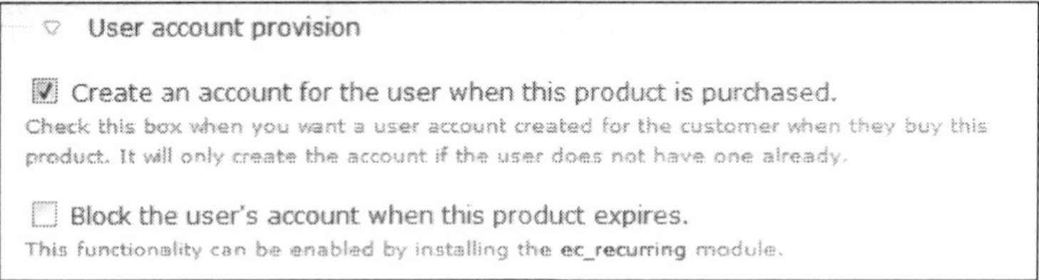

As Doug wants this feature enabled, we need to check the option **Create an account for the user when this product is purchased**. The other option, **Block the user's account when this product expires**, relates to using recurring billing in products (mainly non-tangible products i.e. services) such as a customer support contract or a magazine subscription.

Adding Images to Products

Doug is not happy with the products on his website as they don't have any pictures next to them, so he wants to upload some for his customers to know what they are buying.

There are quite a number of different methods for adding images and other related files to products and content types. First, let's have a look at the methods available:

- A built-in upload module
  - Listed as an attachment
  - Embedded into the description

- A third-party image module
    - Embedded into the description
    - As a product

Both these modules have their own merits and uses; the upload module can be used to upload files that are attached to a content element such as a product or a page. Attachments can be directly linked to or listed with the content.

> **CCK Module**
>
> Drupal's Content Construction Kit module along with Imagefield and Imagecache modules can provide a richer product view and improve a product's feature. If you are feeling adventurous you may wish to give them a try after looking at the options in this book!

A third-party image module can be used for uploading an image as a file in its own right; we can then embed this image into content (primitively using links and HTML tags) or we can edit the image to become a new content element, such as a page or a product and then turn it into the product we want. If we use this method then the image is automatically displayed in the product listing.

Built-in Upload Module

To enable this we need to install the **Upload** module, and then we can edit the product and upload the images.

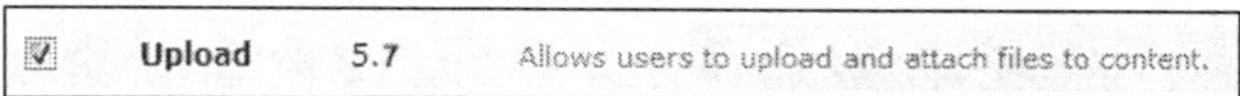

This module is not just for use in the e-Commerce section; we can use it for pages and other types of content to add images to the site.

Let's edit a product and also add a picture of that product. In the edit screen, we have a new section called **File attachments**; this is what we use to upload the pictures to the product. To try it out I'm just going to use the company's logo as the picture.

List as Attachment

To list the image as an attachment on the product page we need to leave the list box checked (as shown in the previous image) and then save the product. Now when we view the product we have a list of attachments at the bottom of the page.

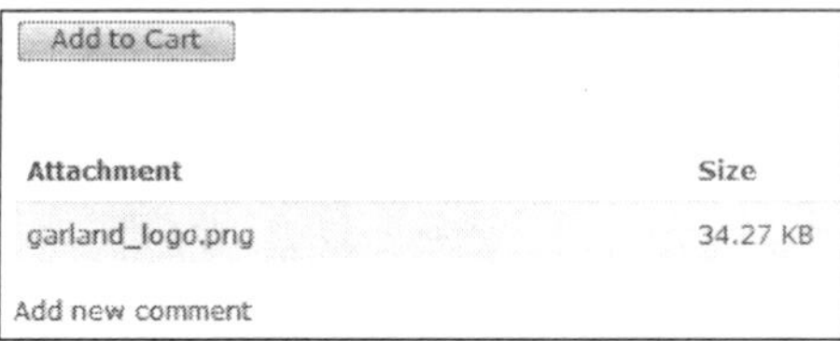
Add to Cart
Attachment
Size
garland_logo.png
34.27 KB
Add new comment

This is particularly useful for attaching files such as PDF fact sheets about the product in question.

Embed Image into Description

For images, having a list of attachments isn't very good, so let's embed the image into the product description using HTML.

If we go back to **Edit** the product, and scroll down to the attachments, the URL of the image is shown; we need to make a note of this: `http://www.dougsdinos.com/drupal-5.7/files/garland_logo_0.png`.

To use this image, we would add the following HTML in the **Description** section:

```
<img src='http://www.dougsdinos.com/drupal-
          5.7/files/garland_logo_0.png'
   style='float:left; padding: 5px;' alt='PRODUCT NAME' />
```

This adds the image, and allows text to wrap around it (but leaving some space) so it looks nice on the page, the end result is shown below:

Don't forget to select the correct input format! Otherwise Drupal will remove our HTML code when we create the product!

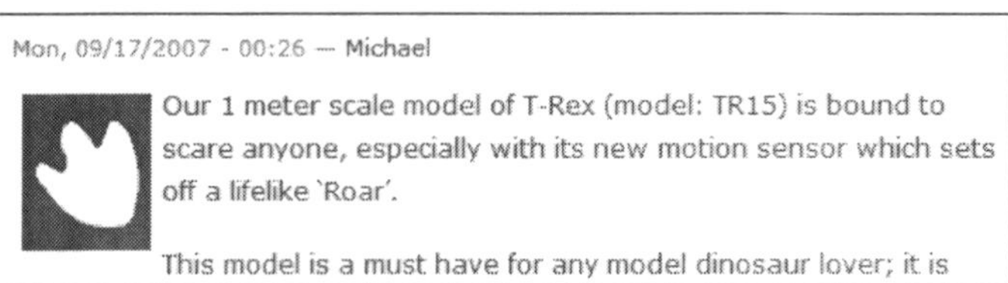
Mon, 09/17/2007 - 00:26 — Michael
Our 1 meter scale model of T-Rex (model: TR15) is bound to scare anyone, especially with its new motion sensor which sets off a lifelike 'Roar'.
This model is a must have for any model dinosaur lover; it is

Third-party Image Module

The **Image** module is one that we must download and install into our Drupal installation; it can be downloaded from the Drupal website: `http://drupal.org/project/image`.

Once we have downloaded the **Image** module package, decompressed the files, and uploaded it to our installation we need to enable the related modules within the package, including:

- Image
- Image Attach

We don't need the other sub-modules at this time, so let's enable these two for now.

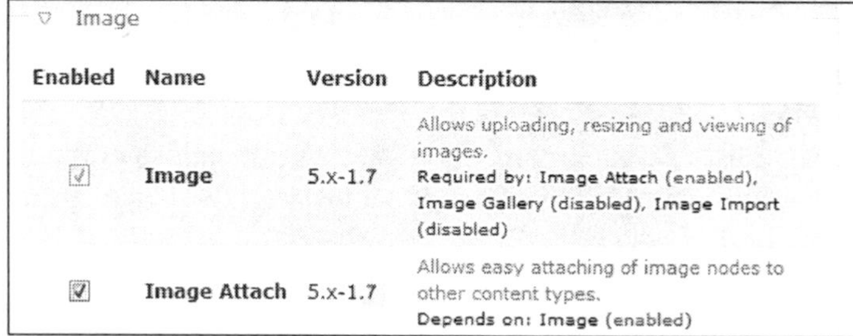

Image

Enabled	Name	Version	Description
☑	Image	5.x-1.7	Allows uploading, resizing and viewing of images. Required by: Image Attach (enabled), Image Gallery (disabled), Image Import (disabled)
☑	Image Attach	5.x-1.7	Allows easy attaching of image nodes to other content types. Depends on: Image (enabled)

Now that we have it installed, let's have a look at the module and how it works.

Within **Site configuration** there are two new sections, **Image** and **Image attach**. We are only concerned with the **Image** section. It has the following settings:

- The default path where the images are stored
- The maximum file size of images uploaded
- The sizes of the image, preview image, and thumbnail

For now, we shall leave these values as they are and upload an image.

Embed Image into Description

To upload the image, we need to go into **Create content** and select **Image**.

Image

An image (with thumbnail). This is ideal for publishing photographs or screenshots.

The **Submit Image** page asks for the following information:

- Title (required)

- Image (required)
- Description or body

We can also change settings for things like comments, menus, and author information and set the image to be a product (we will try that next). Once we have uploaded an image and entered the name of the image we are taken to the page containing the image. From here we can swap between **Original** view, **Preview**, and **Thumbnail**.

The best way to embed an uploaded image is to right-click on the thumbnail picture and copy the URL of the web address, and then do the same for the preview image. We can then add the HTML for the image and link it to the larger version of the image.

For the image I have just uploaded, the thumbnail link is: `http://www.dougsdinos.com/drupal-5.7/files/images/1847191118.thumbnail.jpg` and the preview link is: `http://www.dougsdinos.com/drupal-5.7/files/images/1847191118.jpg`. We can now create the HTML link for this and add it to the product page.

```
<a href='http://www.dougsdinos.com/drupal-
          5.7/files/images/1847191118.jpg'>
   <img src='http://www.dougsdinos.com/drupal-
          5.7/files/images/1847191118.thumbnail.jpg'
        alt='PRODUCT NAME' />
</a>
```

As a Product

The embedded option is not very practical because it involves looking up the image locations and creating the HTML code for the product. If we are creating a new product, we could create the image first, and then turn the image content into a product. To do this, we go through the process of creating the image as we did before, but we expand the product options and select a product type for the image.

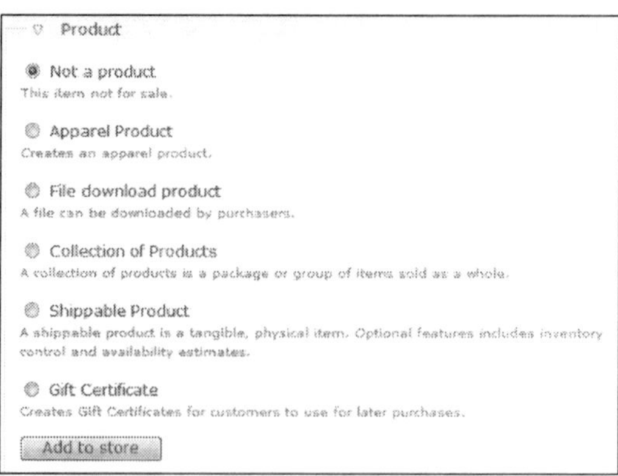

We select the product type, click **Add to store**, and then we can continue editing the product, using the **Title** and **Body** fields for the product name and description.

This method creates a neater product entry with the image already there for us, which is much neater and cleaner than the other methods.

CCK

The CCK module and other image modules mentioned earlier also provide the same effect; you can try them out!

Discounts

Many online stores offer discounts to customers by one means or another; we can use the following methods to offer our customers discounts when shopping at the store:

- Discounts based on the customer's role
- Coupons or gift certificates
- Discounts when customers purchase a certain number of items

The first two are built-in options, which just need to be enabled; the final option requires us to install a new module into our store.

Role-Based

Let's first enable the module in the same way we have enabled all of the other modules; the module is called **Role Discount**.

Once it is enabled there is now a new option under **E-Commerce configuration**, called **Role discount**. This page lists a text box alongside each of the roles in our store, for us to enter the discount for each respective role. Doug wants to offer a number of different discounts to his customers:

- Doug wants to offer a discount of $2.99 for customers who are new users to his site but have already registered.
- He wants to offer a discount of $15.99 to customers, who have already made a purchase, and thus are in the customers' role.

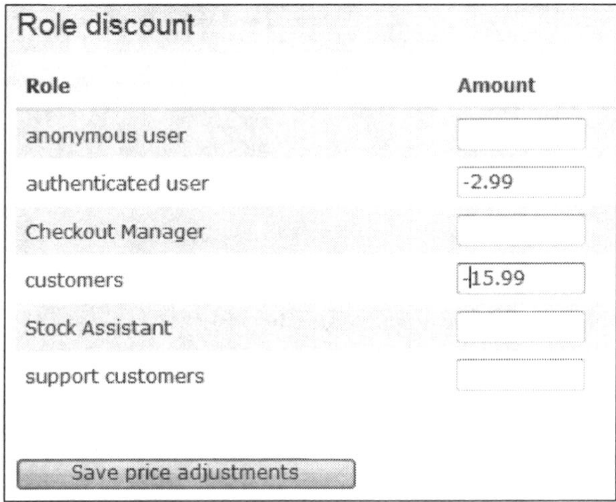

If we now go to the products page as a user who has been assigned the customers role, the price has automatically changed to reflect the discount. It does not inform us of the change, and as far as the user is concerned the cost has never changed unless they can recall it from before they logged in.

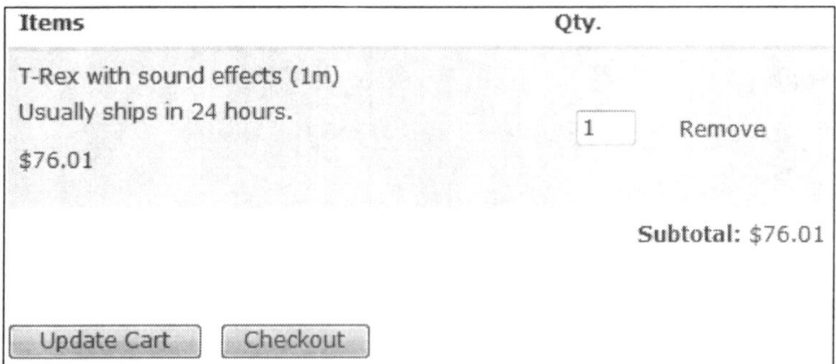

Coupons

With coupons, customers can purchase a gift certificate which entitles them to money off a future purchase.

To use the feature, we of course have to install the module; it is already built into the **e-Commerce** module, so we just need to check the box to enable it in the **Modules** page.

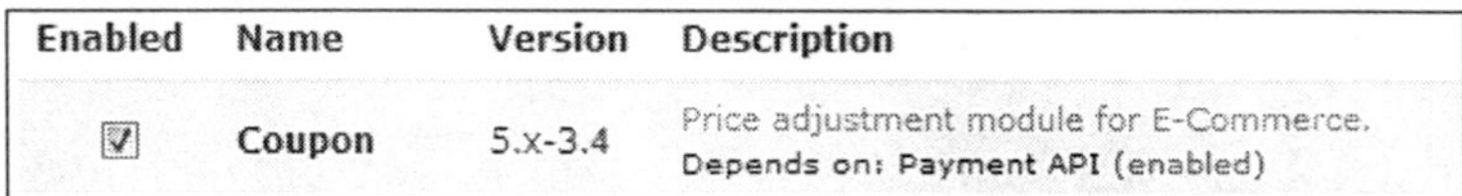

Depends on: Payment API (enabled)

Once it is installed we have a new product type, which is **Gift Certificate**. Let's create one and see how it works.

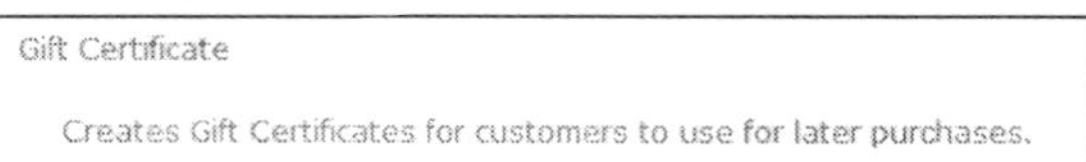

Gift Certificate
Creates Gift Certificates for customers to use for later purchases.

The options available are the same as with the other products; we can enter a name, a description, a price, as well as other options relating to the other modules we have installed such as the **Role assignments** or the **User account provision**. The difference with how this module works is that if we set the price to $0.00, then the customer can choose the amount for the voucher.

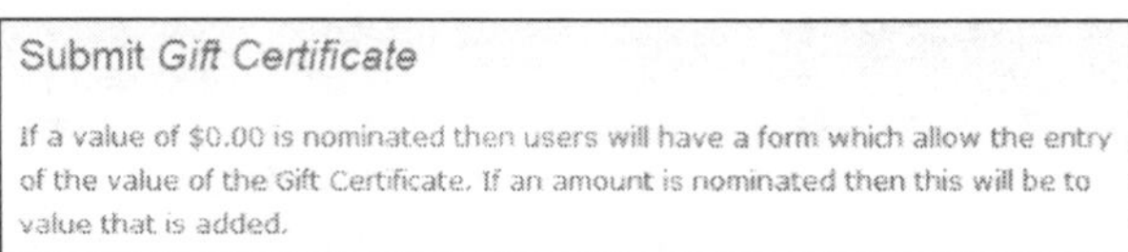

If a value of $0.00 is nominated then users will have a form which allow the entry of the value of the Gift Certificate. If an amount is nominated then this will be to value that is added.

Doug wants customers to be able to choose their own value of gift certificate so let's create a gift certificate with no value and then see it in action. We see the name and description and we see the **Amount** is a changeable textbox, where we can enter the amount we wish.

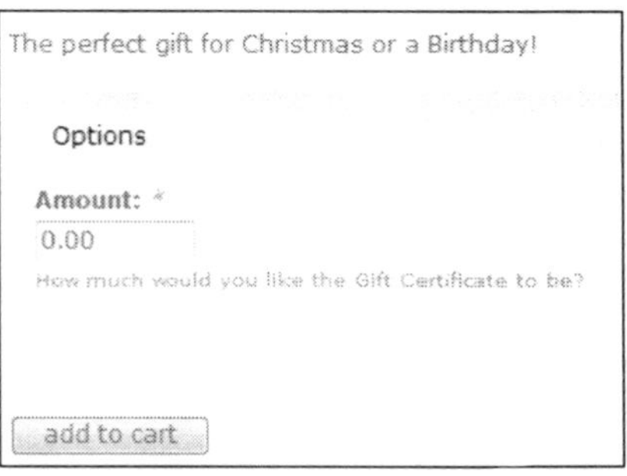

The perfect gift for Christmas or a Birthday!
Options
Amount: *
0.00
How much would you like the Gift Certificate to be?
add to cart

Bulk Purchases

The **Quantity Discount** module is a third-party add on, which can be downloaded from `http://drupal.org/project/quantity_discount`; let's download and install the module before setting it up.

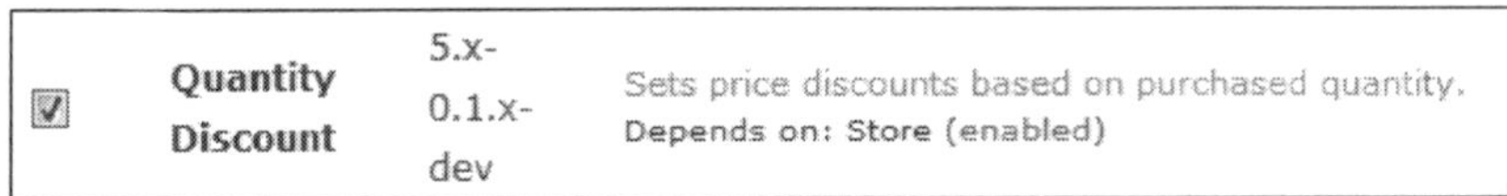

Once it is installed we have a new option under **E-Commerce configuration** called **Quantity discount**, within this we can define up to 15 discount rules, each containing up to six conditions for discount. For each discount rule we can set:

- A name for the discount
- Up to six conditions, each consisting of:
    - Minimum order quantity.
    - Operator (either percentage or fixed price reduction)—This defines how the adjustment should be applied.
    - Adjustment—This is the value of either the percentage or fixed discount.

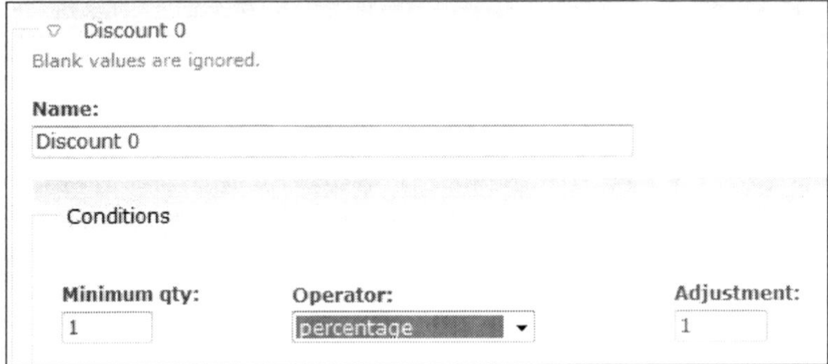

Since Doug has already introduced a number of other offers and discount initiatives, he does not want to use a quantity discount on his store; however, it is worth keeping this option in case he changes his mind.

When we create or edit a product we have the option to select a discount rule if any applies to the product.

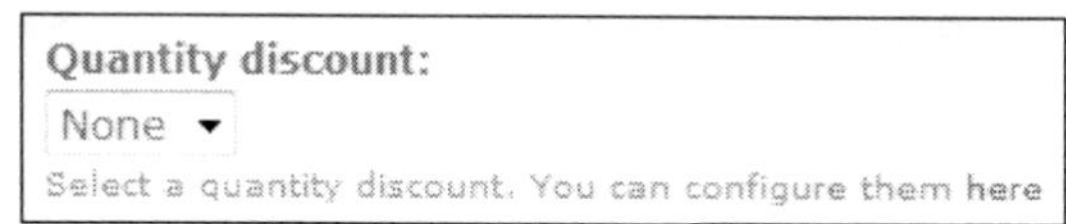

Other e-Commerce Options and Product Types

There are some other e-Commerce options that we can use to provide a better selling experience to our customers, as well as some different product types. Let's have a look at those now:

- Auction products
- Donate products
- Flexicharge

These three modules are included with the e-Commerce **Modules** and just need to be installed in the usual way.

Auction

If we want to, we can create products that act as auctions. There is only one setting related to auctions within the **E-Commerce configuration**, and that is the **Default Auction Length**. This setting is the number of days in the future that the expiry date will default too. Let's just try it with one day to see how the auction products work.

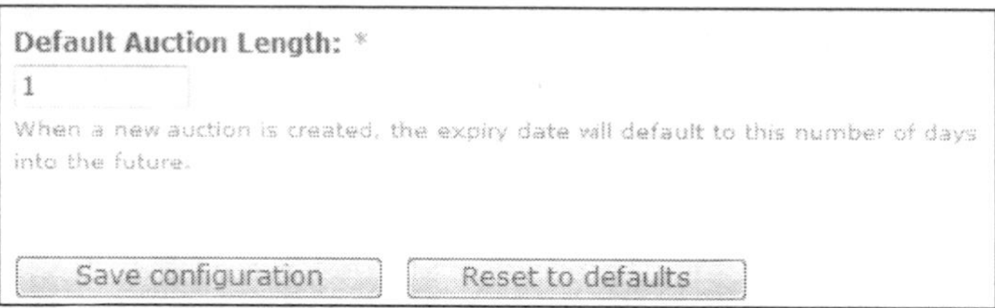

We also have the new product type when creating a new product; let's create a new auction.

Auction Item

A product that can be auctioned for a fixed period, and then sold to the highest bidder.

The only difference in the product's fields from the other product types is that there is the expiration date; the default date is one day ahead of the current day, as we observed in the default auction length setting. We can of course change this date as per our wish.

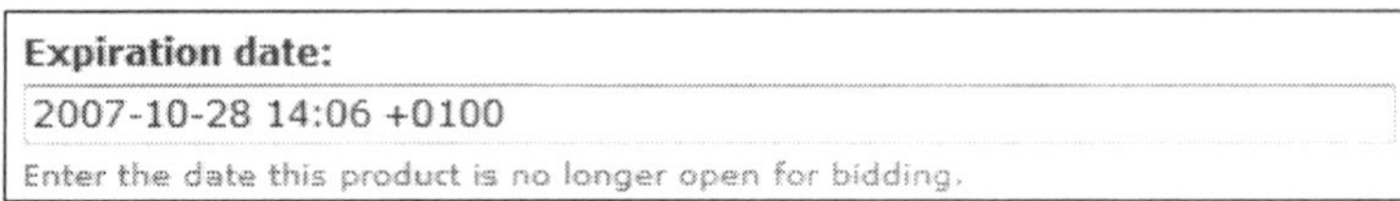

When setting the price on the auction product, we enter the minimum amount we would like for the product, as it acts as the initial starting bid.

When viewing the product we have just created, we can see where the current bidder is, who the high bidder is, and view the bidding history as illustrated below:

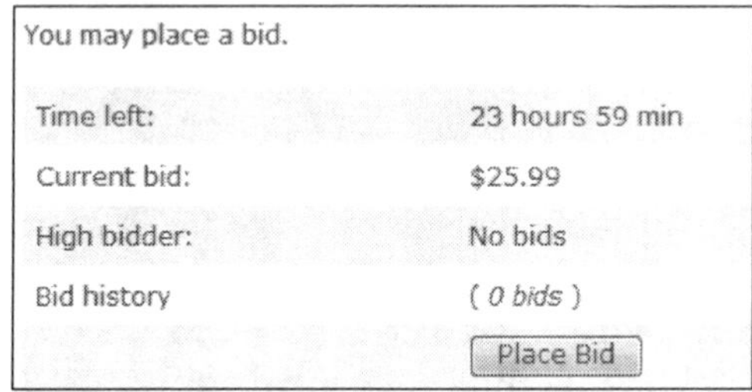

If we click the **Place Bid** button we are prompted to enter our bid (which is above the current high bid) and then to **Confirm bid**.

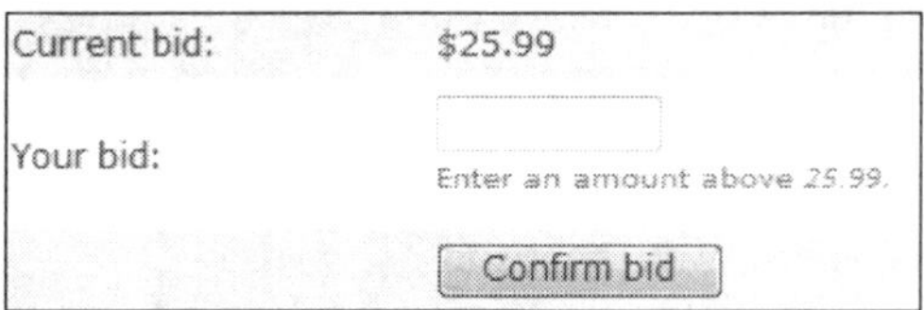

Donate

The **Donation** product acts like the other basic products except it is for neither a product nor a service and is classed as a financial contribution.

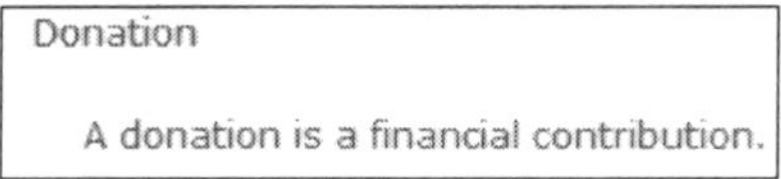

There are other third-party modules available that offer more features such as donation tracking.

Flexicharge

The flexicharge module allows us to create custom charges or discounts for particular conditions on an order. The charges are configured from the **Flexicharge** section of **E-Commerce configuration**. This page lists the **Currently configured charges** and the option to **Add a new charge**.

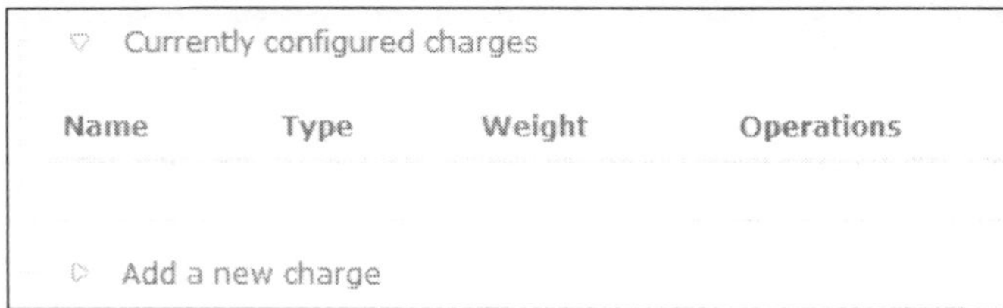

There are two types of flexicharge that we can create:

- Site-wide charge
- Simple shipping charge

We will look into simple shipping charges in detail in Chapter 9—*Taxes, Payments, and Shipping*. So, what does the **Site-wide charge** allow us to do and when is it useful? It allows custom charges to be added to orders, and can be useful in situations such as adding a payment processing charge or adding charges because a user is in a particular role.

When creating a site-wide charge we can set the following settings:

- Display label—This is the name or label for the charge.
- Operator:
    - Fixed amount added or subtracted from the cost
    - A percentage of the subtotal
    - A percentage of the total items
- Charge rate—This is the amount or percentage of the charge.
- Calculation order—This is the order in which this calculation is performed. It is useful when we have multiple charges applied to the same order.
- Options to:
    - Display a subtotal before the charge
    - Display a subtotal after the charge
    - Display the amount as included in the cost but not added to the subtotal
    - Ignore it if the charge is zero

- Product types—This charge applies to all the listed products.
- Roles—This applies to all the user roles that have the charge applied to their orders.

An example for these charges would be to add PayPal fees to an order; one charge would add the fixed charge to an order, and the other charge would add the percentage charge (since PayPal adds a fixed charge then adds a percentage charge) to an order.

In some countries adding PayPal charges violates their agreement. In the UK it is only permissible to add the charge to UK customers as long as you are telling them you are doing so. In the US and Canada this is a violation of their agreement—so don't use it in those countries!

Summary

In this chapter, we looked into improving our customers' experience by creating a better selling environment for our customers. In particular we:

- Added search facilities
- Set up our store to automatically create user accounts when a guest made a purchase
- Looked into the different ways to include images and files in our product listing
- Learned how to provide discounts based on:
    - User's role
    - Coupons
    - Number of purchases made
- Investigated other product types including:
    - Auction products
    - Donations
- Looked into flexicharges and their uses.

In the next chapter we will look into *Payments, Shipping, and Taxes* in greater detail, making it easier to take payments, and opening our site to more users, as well as integrating with a number of postal services.

9
Taxes, Payment, and Shipping

Our Drupal e-Commerce installation now sports a nice new theme, a product catalog, an improved selling experience for our customers, and a way for us to take orders. Let's now build upon this ability to take orders by looking into how Drupal e-Commerce handles taxes, payments, and shipping. Doug is very keen to look into this so he can take payments automatically and speedup the processing of online orders.

In this chapter, you will learn:

- How to work with taxes in Drupal e-Commerce
- How the electronic payment system works
- How to set up electronic payments
- How to use Drupal e-Commerce's shipping API modules

Taxes

Drupal e-Commerce has a very flexible Tax API that can be used to define a number of different tax rules based on a number of different conditions including:

- Location
    - State or province or region
    - Country
    - City
- Product type
    - Each product type that is available to our store

Before we can set up any tax rules, we first need to enable the **Tax API** module; this is done within the **Modules** section under **Site Building** from the **Administer** menu. Under the **E-Commerce Uncategorized** section we have the **Tax API** module; let's check the appropriate check box and click the **Save configuration** button to install the module.

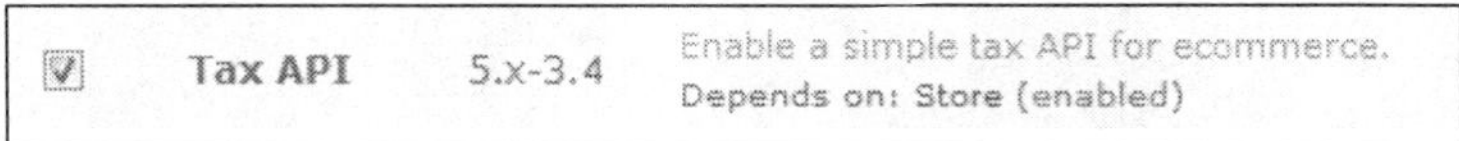

With the module installed we now have a new option under the **E-Commerce configuration** menu called **Taxes**.

If we go into this section we are taken to a page that lists the created tax rules (we don't have any yet) and also has a link to **Add tax**. Before we create some tax rules, let's think about the rules we might require.

Tax Rules

Doug's Dinos is a UK-based business so he needs to comply with the UK tax laws; however, his brother has just moved to the US and set up Doug's Dinos Inc, a small retail store based in California; this store sells the same products as Doug's own store in the UK and effectively acts as a US branch. They want to use the same website to sell products online so they also need to comply with the US tax laws wherever appropriate.

The tax rules here should be considered as a guide only, if you are unsure of the tax law in your country or state you should contact a tax advisor.

Tax Rules: UK

As Doug's Dinos is a VAT-registered company he must charge Value Added Tax on his products. All of Doug's products need to have VAT charged at the standard rate of 17.5%. Drupal also has provisions for donations to be made to the business, so depending on how these donations are used they may be classified as VAT exempt.

Unfortunately the tax rules within Drupal e-Commerce only allow rules to be applied onto product types, and not groups of products. This could be problematic if you offer products under both the standard and reduced VAT rate; however, it should be easy to accomplish by modifying the Tax API code. Most features from the **Tax** module can also be obtained using the **Flexicharge** module we briefly looked at in the previous chapter.

Rule: Add 17.5% to all orders excluding donations.

Tax Rules: California, USA

Doug's Dinos Inc needs to charge sales tax on all tangible goods but not on services such as its model repair service.

Rule: Add 7.25% to all tangible goods.

Tax Rules: Orders Placed Elsewhere

Tax for orders from other states and countries depend on a number of factors including the country or state fulfilling the order and the country or state of the customer. Doug will need to obtain professional tax advice to determine how to deal with these situations.

Creating the Tax Rules

If we click the **Add tax** link in the **Taxes** section we are prompted to select a **Type of Location to define the new tax rule for**. Let's start with the UK tax rule, and select **Country** from the drop-down list:

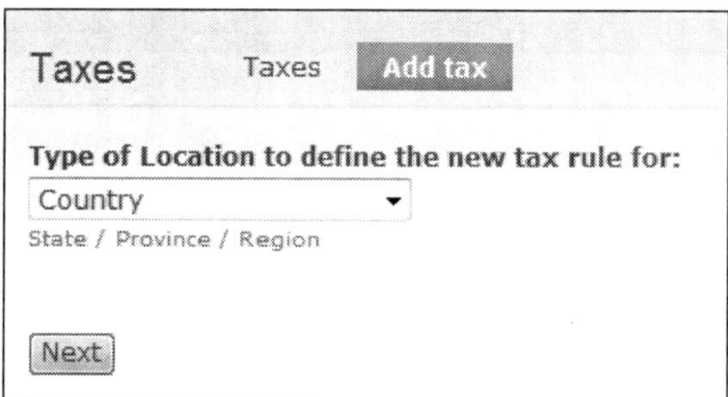

Then we need to click the **Next** button. We are now taken to a page with the final configuration options including:

- **Country** (a drop-down list of countries)
- **Adjustment** (the adjustment to be performed to the item's cost)
- **Product type** (the type of products to which the adjustment should apply)

Let's select **United Kingdom** for the country, enter **17.5%** as the adjustment, and then select all the product types except for **Donation**:

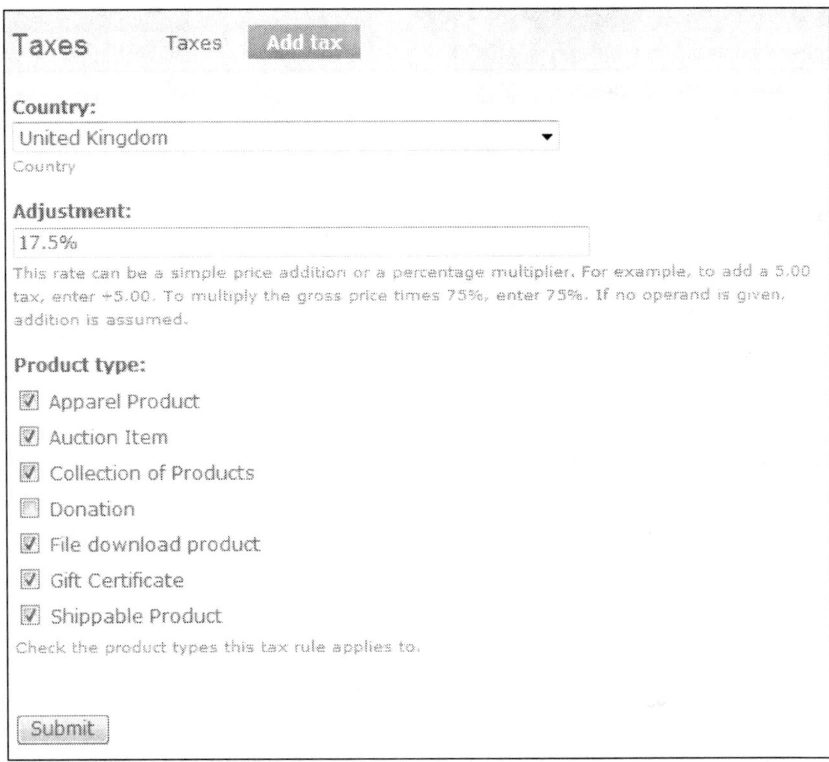

Next we need to click the **Submit** button; this then creates the tax rule and lists it on the **Taxes** page we were on earlier. Now let's create the rule for Doug's Dinos Inc. by clicking the **Add tax** link again, and this time selecting **State / Province / Region** as the **Type of Location to define the new tax rule for**.

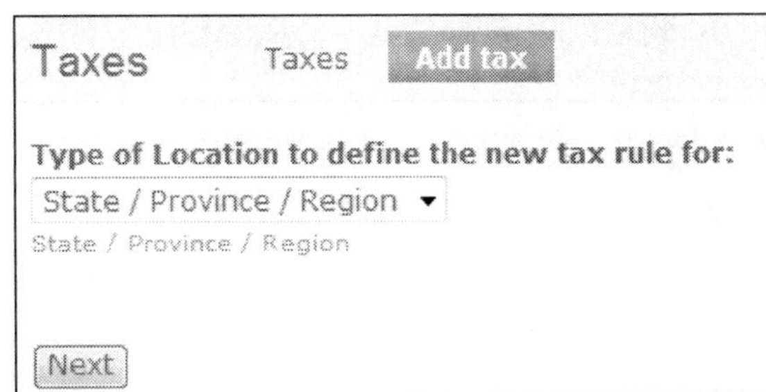

Once we have clicked the **Next** button we are again taken to the page with the tax options on it. The only difference to this from the previous tax rules we created is that we don't have a drop-down list for the states; we instead have a text box. This is quite a handy text box as it uses a collection of web technologies called AJAX to look up states that start with the text we type into the box. If we type C into the box, it will list all states beginning with C allowing us to easily find the one we want:

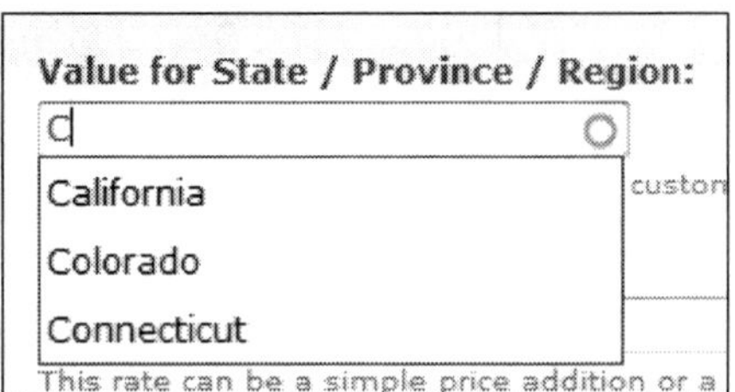

Once we select the state we want from the list, it then populates the text box with the abbreviated version of the state's name, in this case **CA**.

Next we need to enter **7.25%** as the **Adjustment** and then select the **Product types** we wish to apply the rule to and then click the **Submit** button.

The **Taxes** page lists these rules that we have created along with the options to **delete** or **edit** the rule.

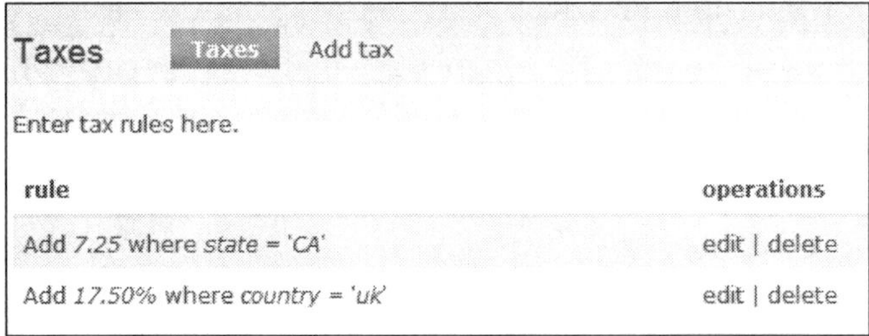

Further Options

The list of countries, regions, and states used by Drupal e-Commerce can be modified from the **Regions** section of the **E-Commerce configuration** menu. Within here we could create a group of states or locations, which is particularly useful if we need to apply the same tax rule to a large group of states.

Payment

At the moment, we have only installed and set up one payment option, **COD**, which is the Cash on Delivery option, which could also be used for posting a cheque, or making a payment using a credit card over the telephone. This is a useful payment option, but it is very limiting to have only this, and Doug wants to be able to take payments automatically and from as many people as possible, as easily as possible. In order to do this we need to install and configure a number of other payment gateways.

Before we install and set up these gateways let's first look at how they work, and also which ones are available to us.

How Payment Gateways Work

Payment gateways, or payment processors, handle the payment process for us working directly with banks and credit card providers to obtain the funds. The exact method of each gateway varies, so here I will explain the basic details of how the PayPal payment gateway works.

- The customer places an order on the website.
- The website creates the order and takes the customer to PayPal's website; in the background the website tells PayPal information such as the contents of the shopping cart, total cost, and the order's ID number.
- The customer either logs into their PayPal account to pay (which uses either funds from the customer's PayPal account or their bank account) or they enter their credit or debit card details. Credit card info is stored by the gateway and is never known to the store, which is good, as it provides added security to customers.
- PayPal verifies the details and charges the card or account.
- The customer is then returned to our website; if there is a problem with the payment or they cancel the order they will be taken to a "cancelled page", and if the payment is made, they will be taken to a "thank you" page.
- PayPal independently (so regardless of if the customer goes back to our site) sends a special command to our website containing information such as the amount paid, the order ID, and some authentication method to prove it really is PayPal.
- The website then checks the amount paid against the amount for the order; if they match then the order status is updated to paid.

Payment Gateways Available

There are eight different payment gateway modules available with Drupal e-Commerce; more of course can be added by downloading additional modules if they are available or by writing new modules.

Bank Integration Kits

Many banks have their own gateway methods that can be used, sometimes only for their cards, other times for any cards. Banks that offer these gateways generally provide integration kits to explain how to use their API and how to integrate the payment solution with your own website.

The gateways available are:

- Authorize.Net
- CCard
- COD
- Eurobill
- Eway
- iTransact
- PayPal
- WorldPay

Let's have a brief look at each of these:

The values for each of the payment gateways can be changed, you should consult the gateway provider for exact, and up-to-date information regarding the values required.

Authorize.Net

Authorize.Net's services are sold via a number of resellers and as such their costs vary depending on the reseller used. In order to utilize Authorize.Net, a special bank account called a merchant account is required; these in themselves can incur set up costs and per transaction costs, in addition to the set up costs and per transaction costs of the payment gateway.

Some resellers of Authorize.net offer their services on a monthly charge as opposed to charging set up fees and per transaction fees, whereas other resellers operate a per transaction charge.

A list of Authorize.Net resellers is available on its website: `http://www.authorize.net/solutions/merchantsolutions/resellerdirectory/`.

CCard

`www.ccard.com.au` is an Australian payment gateway; this gateway also requires a merchant bank account to interact with and applications to sign up to this gateway involve a paper-based application form, which can be downloaded from their website: `https://ccard.com.au/applicationkit.pdf`.

The fees for this gateway (in Australian Dollars) involve an annual $300 charge and a $0.20 charge per transaction. There is no minimum term to its service apart from a 30 day notice to disconnect from the service.

COD

The COD payment gateway is the gateway we installed earlier in order to test the checkout process. This gateway is useful (as we discussed earlier) for items where you do require cash on delivery, or where the customer is posting a cheque to you before their order is shipped, alternatively it could also be used for in-store collection or telephone-based credit card orders (although for these you would need a payment gateway with the capability of entering credit card details manually yourself, such as PayPal's virtual terminal service).

Eurobill

Eurobill can only be used to accept payment for digital content such as downloads or software, and is not permitted by law to be used for the processing of transactions that involve physical goods or products. Eurobill charges 14% of each credit card transaction and 10% for direct debit transactions. There are no setup fees, no monthly fees, and no set charges (only the variable charges) per transaction. More information on Eurobill can be found on its website: `www.eurobill.com/eu/`.

eWay

eWAY is another Australian-based payment gateway and is only available to Australian businesses. It has two pricing plans; eBusiness Saver and eBusiness Standard, both have the same set up costs of $599 Australian dollars, annual costs are $199 and $285 respectively, including the first year, and per transaction charges of $0.50. The only difference other than price between these two plans is that the eBusiness Saver plan requires you to include its logo and a hyperlink to its website on your website. A merchant account is required with your bank to use eWAY which incurs further set up costs and per transaction costs. More information on eWAY can be found on its website: `http://www.eway.com.au/`.

iTransact

iTransact is a US-based payment gateway; unfortunately its does not have its prices listed on its website and instead requests that you complete a simple online form to get a quote tailored to your needs: `http://www.itransact.com/merchant/prices.html`.

PayPal

PayPal is an International payment gateway owned by eBay Inc. It is one of the most popular payment gateways; it is used as the primary payment method for companies such as eBay and Skype. The fees charged depend on which country your business is based in and the total received monthly funds. There are no setup or monthly fees, and its per transaction costs range from 1.9% to 2.9% plus USD$0.30.

A merchant account is not needed to set up a PayPal account; this combined with the absence of set up or monthly fees make PayPal a very popular option. More information is available on PayPal's website: `www.paypal.com`.

WorldPay

WorldPay is a UK-based payment gateway owned by the *Royal Bank of Scotland Group*; it has set up costs of USD$399 and monthly fees of USD$50. Per transaction costs include a USD$0.40 charge plus from 3.25% to 5.25%. More information on its costs can be found on its website: `http://www.worldpay.com/usa/sme/content.php?page=pricing`.

Payment Gateways Overview

The table below gives an overview of the different payment gateway options that Doug has for his site:

Gateway	Setup cost	Recurring costs	Transaction cost	Other information
Authorize.Net	Varies by reseller	Varies by reseller	Varies by reseller	Easier to get a plan more suited to your business depending on the reseller
CCard	AUD$300	N/A	AUD$0.20	Australian only
COD	N/A	N/A	N/A	Cash on delivery
Eurobill	N/A	N/A	14% for credit card and 10% for direct debit	Non tangible goods only

Gateway	Setup cost	Recurring costs	Transaction cost	Other information
eWAY	AUD$599	AUD$199-285 (annual)	AUD$0.50	Australian only; lower cost option requires link to their website
iTransact	Contact them	Contact them	Contact them	Costs not public; must complete quote enquiry form
PayPal	N/A	N/A	1.9% to 2.9% plus USD$0.30	No merchant account needed
WorldPay	USD$399	USD$50 (monthly)	USD$0.40 plus 3.25 to 5.25%.	Fees vary on country

Doug's Choices

After reviewing the options available to him, Doug has decided to go with PayPal as his preferred payment gateway because of its low setup costs. It may be appropriate to choose another gateway later on (and possibly write a module for it) depending on the monthly volume of transactions as that may prove to be more cost effective, although from the gateways supported by default, PayPal also seems to be the most cost effective in the long term.

Configuring the Payment Gateway

Now let's set up and configure our store for the PayPal payment gateway, then let's have a brief look at the configuration involved in the other gateways.

This assumes we have already set up an account with our payment gateway and set up the account so that we can receive money.

To configure our store to use PayPal we need to go into the **PayPal** section within the **E-Commerce configuration** section in the **Administer** menu.

PayPal
Configuration for the PayPal payment gateway

This section provides us with eight different settings; let's see what they are and what they do:

- PayPal receiver email—This is the email address assigned to our PayPal account.
- PayPal processing URL—This is PayPal's web address for processing payments; this would only need to be changed if PayPal were to change its system to use a different URL.
- Successful payment URL—This is the page on our website where the customer should be taken to if their payment is successful.
- Cancel payment URL—This is the page on our website where the customer should be taken to if their payment is cancelled.
- PayPal IPN "request back" validation URL—If we use IPN where PayPal "pings" our website to let it know the transaction went through, we can send a request back to PayPal to prove this was valid; the address where we send this request is the request back validation URL. This will only be changed if PayPal changes its systems.
- Currency code—This specifies the currency that PayPal should use while processing payments.
- Debug Instant Payment Notification (IPN)—We may wish to check whether the IPN system within PayPal is working correctly with our website. If we enable the debugging of the IPN we will get an email each time it is used; this way we can keep a check on it.
- Minimum purchase amount—This is the minimum amount of a purchase before PayPal can be used as a payment gateway; this can be useful as with some low transactions such as $0.20 products PayPal would take the entire sum as the transaction fee.

At least one of these settings will require a new page to be created, this is for the cancelled payment page, so before we go and adjust these settings let's create the page for cancelled payments.

To create the page we just need to click **Create content** and create a **Page**.

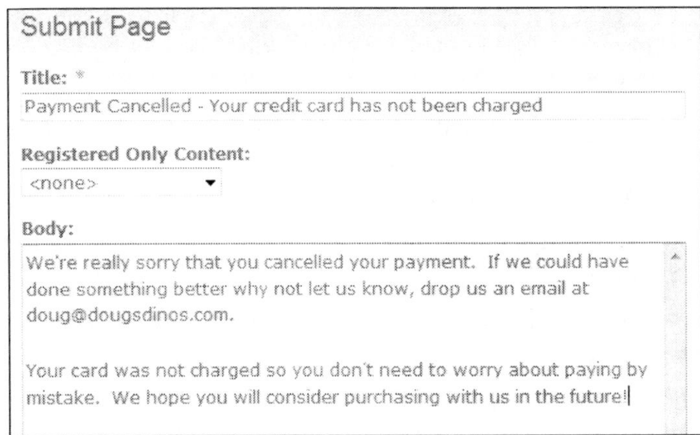

Doug wants a nice friendly page to make the visitor feel "welcome and wanted" even though they have cancelled their payment.

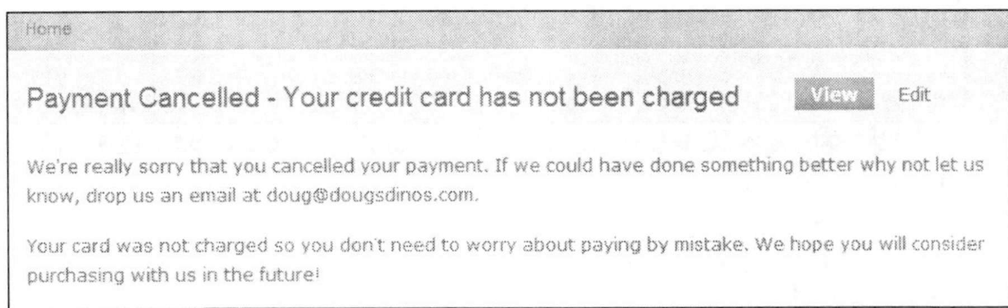

Now that we have created this page, let's make a note of the URL so we can add it to the appropriate setting. The part of the URL we need is `node/` and the following text:

From the URL we need to make a note of `node/39` for the cancelled payment setting.

Path Module

Drupal's core **Path** module can be used to create page URLs such as `Drupal-5.7/PAYPAL_CANCEL`.

IPN

In order to set up PayPal's IPN, which allows PayPal to notify our website that a transaction has gone through, we need to enter a special URL into PayPal.

PayPal

In order to use this module, you need to create an account with PayPal. Also, you can setup Instant Payment Notification (IPN) to track PayPal payments from your own website. The IPN URL of your site is:

http://dougsdinos.com/drupal-5.7/paypal/ipn

To set this up for Doug, we need to:

1. Log in to `PayPal.com`
2. Go to our Profile in PayPal
3. Under **Selling Preferences** select **Instant Payment Notification Preferences**
4. Click **Edit**
5. Check mark the box to enable IPN
6. Enter the URL from above into the relevant text box
7. Click **Save**

Instant Payment Notification Preferences

Activate Instant Payment Notification

Before activating Instant Payment Notification, please read the instructions to ensure that you can support the notification system.

☑ Instant Payment Notification integrates PayPal payment notification and authentication with your website's back-end operations. Check this box to activate Instant Payment Notification, and enter the URL at which you will receive the payment notifications below.

Notification URL:

:p://dougsdinos.com/drupal-5.7/paypal/ipn

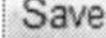

Settings

Now that we have set up IPN and have a page for cancelled payments, we can change the PayPal settings.

The first two settings are the **PayPal Receiver Email** and the **PayPal processing URL**.

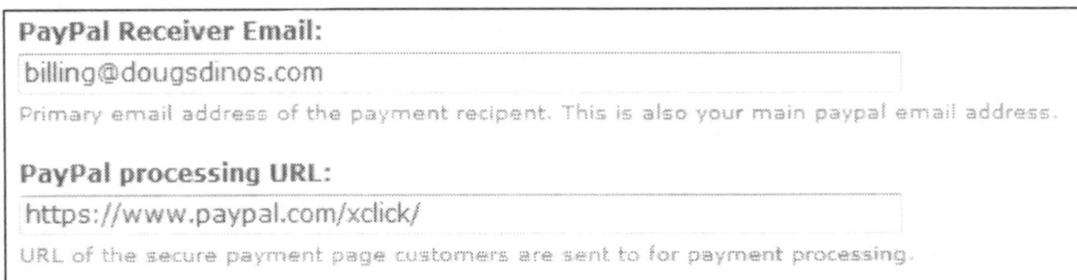

Doug set up a PayPal account using the email address `billing@dougsdinos.com`; he used a separate email address so that he can keep billing and payment issues separate from other emails. The processing URL can stay the same, as it only needs to change if PayPal changes its systems.

The next settings are the **Successful payment URL** and **Cancel payment URL**.

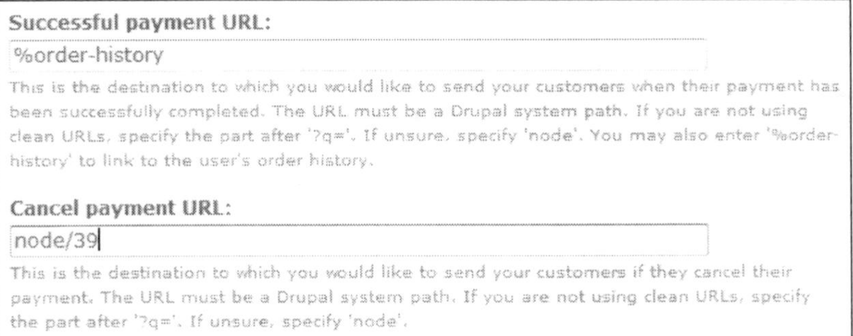

Doug likes the idea of taking the customers to the order history page once the payment has been completed, so let's leave that setting as it is. As for the **Cancel payment URL** let's use the page `node/39` we created earlier; now when customers cancel a payment they will be taken to this page.

The remaining settings are **PayPal's IPN "request back" URL** (which we don't need to change), the currency code, debug settings, and minimum purchase amount:

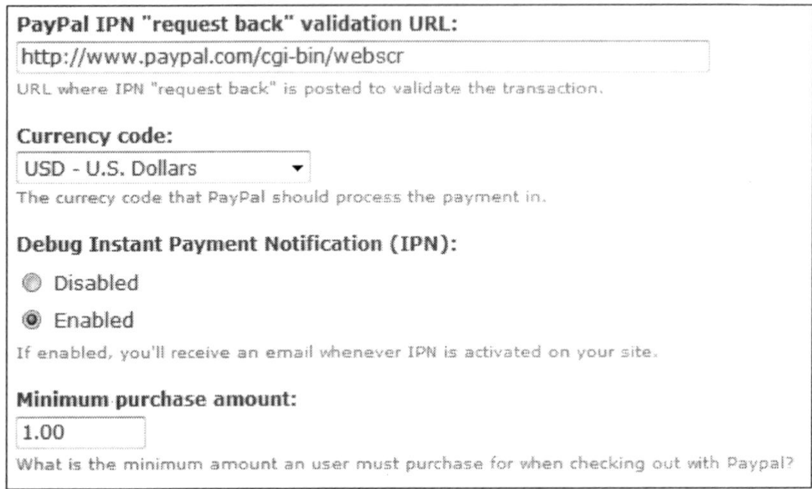

Doug wants to leave the **Currency code** as USD as he is hoping most online orders will be from US customers. He also wants to enable the debug options for IPN just to make sure everything works as it should. For the final setting, he wants the **Minimum purchase amount** to be reduced from five to one; this way any transaction that could entirely be consumed by PayPal fees cannot be purchased using PayPal, but also allows lower value products to be purchased using PayPal which is a convenience for customers.

Payment Gateway in Action

Now if we go and place an order, we have the option to choose the payment gateway. At the moment, we have the options of **COD** or **PayPal**. Let's choose **PayPal** and see how it links into our store:

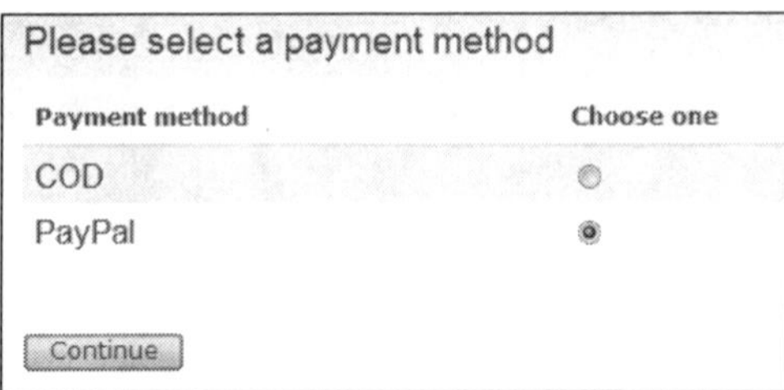

On the following page, which asks us to review the order, it confirms the payment method we wish to use and includes a link to change the method.

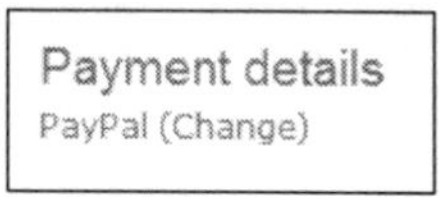

Payment details
PayPal (Change)

A Quick Look Back at Tax

Earlier in the chapter we set up various tax rules. We can now see the tax rules in action on the **Order Summary** page:

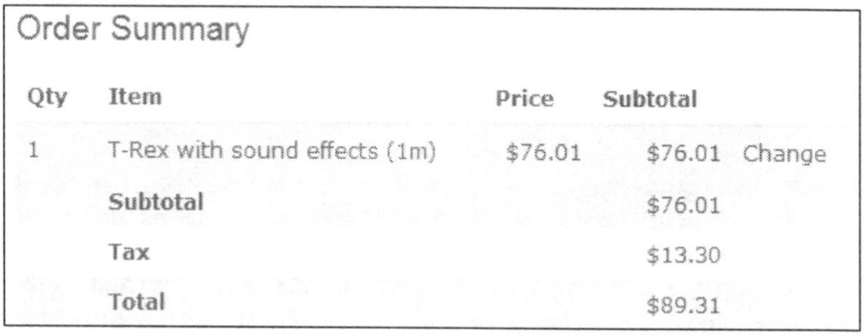

Order Summary

Qty	Item	Price	Subtotal	
1	T-Rex with sound effects (1m)	$76.01	$76.01	Change
	Subtotal		$76.01	
	Tax		$13.30	
	Total		$89.31	

Place the Order

If we now click on the **Place your order** button we will be taken to the PayPal website to pay for our orders.

If we cancel the payment, we will be taken to the cancel page we created earlier, and if we make the payment we will be taken to our order history page.

Settings for Other Gateways

Here we have focused on PayPal, so let's have a very brief look at the settings for using the other payment gateways.

Authorize.Net

The Authorize.net module has the following settings:

- Explanation or submission guides—This is a note displayed above the page where the customer enters their credit card details; this is used by default to warn customers about submitting the form twice, and how it can result in being charged twice.
- Login ID—This is our login ID with Authorize.net.

- Transaction key—This is the transaction key for the website set up to use Authorize.Net.
- Authorize.net processing URL—This is similar to PayPal's processing URL; we don't need to change this unless Authorize.net changes its systems.
- Successful payment URL—This is the URL the customer is taken to once they have successfully paid for their order.
- Authorize.net test mode—If we enable this then credit cards won't be charged and we can test to make sure the system works without having to do real transactions.
- Email Authorize.net receipt—This sets if Authorize.net should email the customer a receipt, in addition to the receipt the store sends them.

Ccard

The Ccard gateway does not require much configuration, only a few settings like:

- Ccard client ID—This is the ID provided by the Ccard gateway.
- Credit card payment page—This is the page on our store that contains the payment details, automatically done via Drupal e-Commerce.
- Thank you page—This contains the location of our thank-you page on our website.

Eurobill

Eurobill does not require much configuration either, just some details like:

- EuroBill username—This is our username for the EuroBill gateway.
- EuroBill site ID—This is the ID assigned by EuroBill to our site for reference.
- EuroBill security key—This is the security key provided by EuroBill to ensure that we are communicating with the EuroBill servers.

Unfortunately this does not allow configuration of thank-you pages or cancelled payment pages; these may be settable with the gateways own settings; for more information contact the gateway.

eWAY

Just like Ccard and Eurobill, eWay also does not require much configuration. The few available configuration options are:

- eWay client ID—This is our ID provided by eWay.
- Credit card payment page—This is the page on our store that contains the payment details, automatically done via Drupal e-Commerce.
- Thank you page—This contains the location of the thank-you page on our site.

iTransact

Only four of the six configuration options can be altered, as the final two require further development of the e-Commerce project for Drupal, and are there to serve as a place holder for the future features.

- iTransact client ID—This is the ID provided by the gateway.
- iTransact client password—This is the password for the gateway.
- Credit card payment page—This is the page on our store that contains the payment details, automatically done via Drupal e-Commerce.
- Thank you page—This contains the location of the thank-you page on our site.
- The CVV field is required.
- The Address field is required.

WorldPay

WorldPay has quite a number of configuration options, including:

- Installation ID—This is the installation ID assigned by WorldPay.
- Testing Mode—Sets whether the test modes are used or not.
- Currency code—This is the option where we enter the code such as USD or GBP for the currency we are using.
- WorldPay minimum amount—This is the minimum amount of the order before WorldPay should be available to the customer to use.
- WorldPay processing URL—This is the web address the customer is sent to on WorldPay's site to submit payment.
- Thank you page / World pay callback URL—This contains the location of the page on our site where the customer is directed to after:
    - Worldpay_callback—Payment completed message
    - Worldpay_callback—Order cancelled message
    - Worldpay_callback—Server validation check failed message
- Switching debug mode on.

Shipping

We can now take payment from a lot of potential customers with the payment gateway set up; now let's look at one of the final parts to the order process—shipping!

There are two methods for adding shipping charges within Drupal e-Commerce:

- Shipping API
- Flexicharge

Let's take a look at these two methods:

Shipping API

Firstly we need to install the **Shipping API** and at least one shipping module; by default there is only one shipping module, which is **Shipcalc**, a module containing APIs for UPS and FedEx. We install them from the **Modules** section from **Site building**:

The modules should now be installed.

If we now go to the **Shipping** section within the **E-Commerce configuration** area, we will see the following screen:

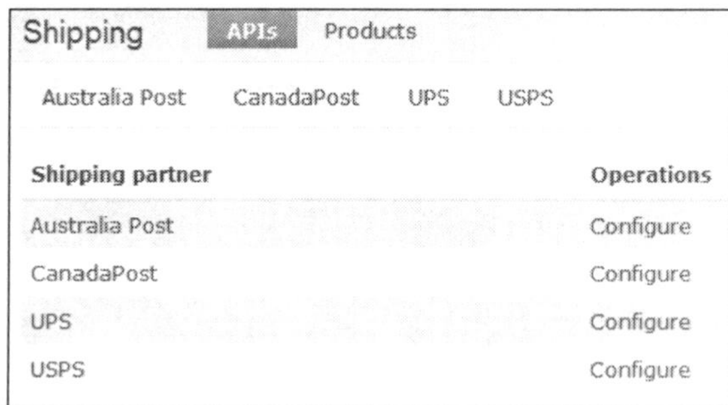

This area lists the shipping APIs that are installed; the module includes APIs for:

- Australia post
- Canada post
- UPS
- USPS

These APIs are used to calculate shipping costs, as they communicate with the appropriate companies to determine the cost.

To use the **Australia Post** module we need to enter our **Post code**, **Turn Around Time**, and the **Domestic Registered Post Cost**. **CanadaPost** requires a **Merchant ID**, which is obtained free when registering at: `http://www.canadapost.com/business/intsol/sb/ventureone/default-e.asp?source=web` as well as a **Potal Code** and **Turn Around Time**.

UPS requires us to register and obtain an API key, and **USPS** requires us to register too. To register for a UPS account we need to go to: `https://www.ups.com/servlet/registration?loc=en_US`, and then to this website to obtain a developer API key: `https://www.ups.com/e_comm_access/laServ?CURRENT_PAGE=INTRO&OPTION=ACCESS_LICENSE&loc=en_US`.

Once we have set up the APIs we need to set which shipping methods we want to use with which product type; we do this by clicking the **Products** link next to **APIs**.

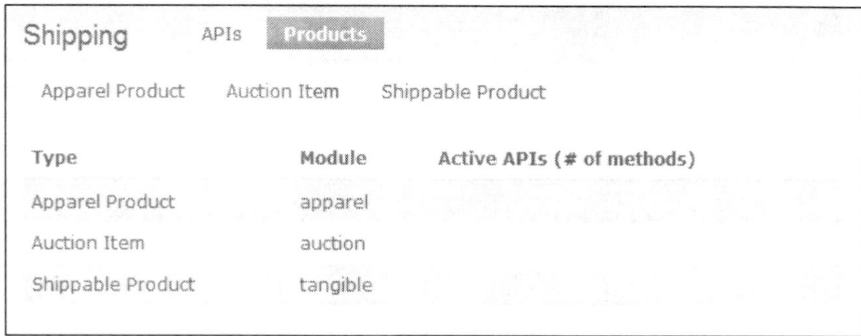

Next we select the type of products for which we want to enable the shipping APIs. This then lists all of the different shipping methods available; we can select the ones we want to enable for that particular product type.

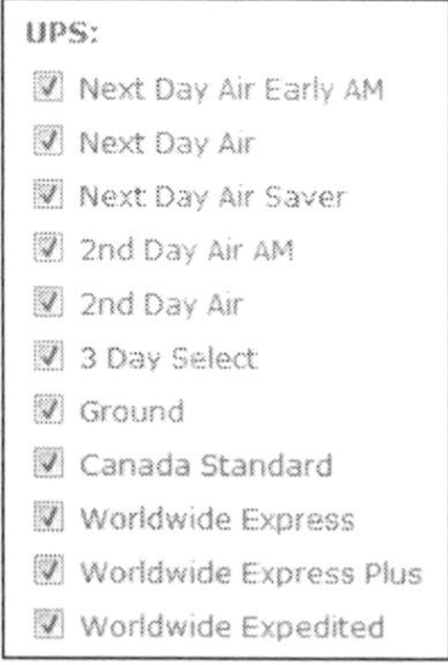

With the shipping options configured and installed, we now have some extra settings available for each product. If we create a new shippable product or edit an existing shippable product there is a new section called **Shipping methods**.

This new section includes all of the shipping APIs that allow us to select the available shipping methods (the same as when we were editing the shipping settings) as well as settings for:

- **Product Weight**
- **Product width** (in inches)
- **Product Height**
- **Product Length**
- **Product Width** (in inches)

Both values for width must be completed with the same value due to the way certain shipping companies use the data.

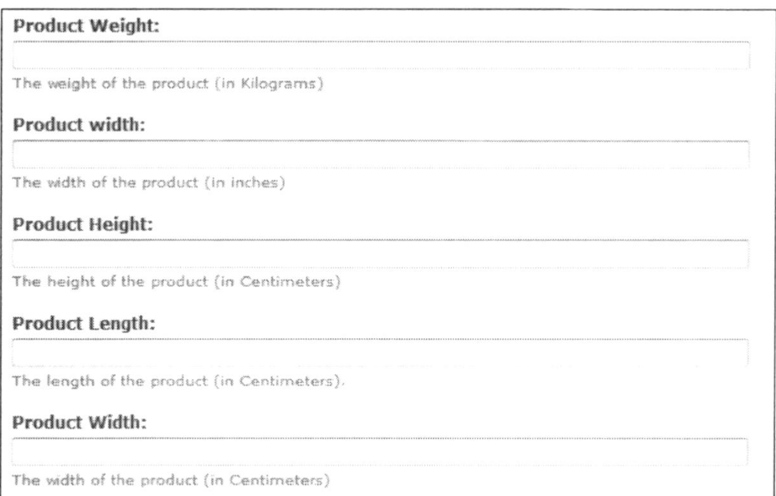

Product Weight:
The weight of the product (in Kilograms)
Product width:
The width of the product (in inches)
Product Height:
The height of the product (in Centimeters)
Product Length:
The length of the product (in Centimeters).
Product Width:
The width of the product (in Centimeters)

By setting these options for each product our store can link into the various shipping providers' API, send these details to it and obtain an accurate shipping cost to charge the customer. The cost is added to the order summary towards the end of the shopping process.

Flexicharge

Flexicharge is a simpler method of adding charges to orders, instead of linking in with shipping providers; it allows us to create simple rules that add charges to the order, similar to how the tax system works, although it supports more options. Let's take a look!

The **Flexicharge** settings are found under **E-Commerce configuration**, and on the Flexicharge page any charges previously set up are listed and there is the option to create a new charge, either a **Site-wide charge** (dependent on roles and products, and which can be used to reduce costs depending on conditions) or a **Simple shipping** charge. It is the **Simple shipping** charge we want, so let's create one of those.

The flexicharge page has a link called **Unallocated locations** along with options for:

- Enabling or Disabling a charge
- Base cost—A charge added to the item regardless of weight
- Cost per lb—Used to calculate shipping cost

This allows us to specify a standard shipping cost as well as a variable cost depending on the weight of the item, and of course we can enable or disable the charge at the check of a box.

These charges can be applied to a specific geographical region; we can even create a region and add countries or states to the region.

Doug wants to add a charge to a number of non-UK countries, so in order to create a charge for this we need to create the region. To create the region we need to follow the link to **Shipping regions and configuration**, which is in the same area as creating a new flexicharge.

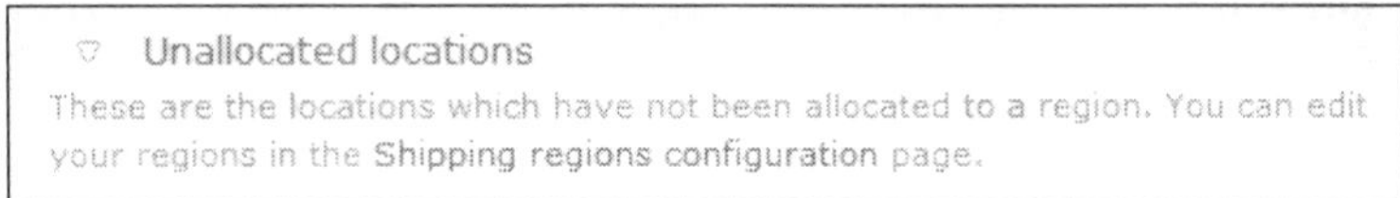

On the page to which we are taken to there is a link for **Add region**.

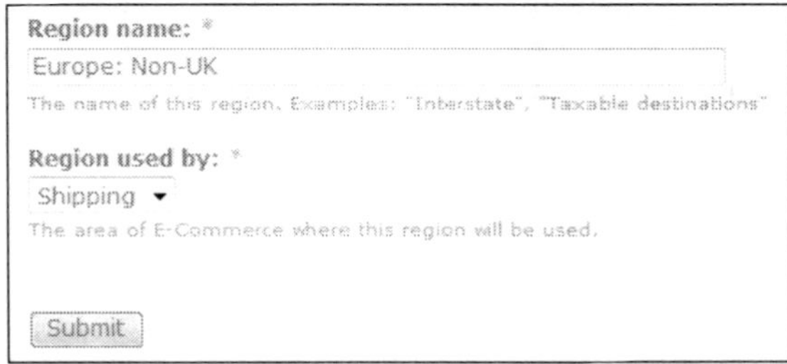

We can now assign countries to the region by clicking the **Configure** link next to the region. To assign a country to the region we click the radio button for **Europe: Non-UK** for each country we wish to assign to this region.

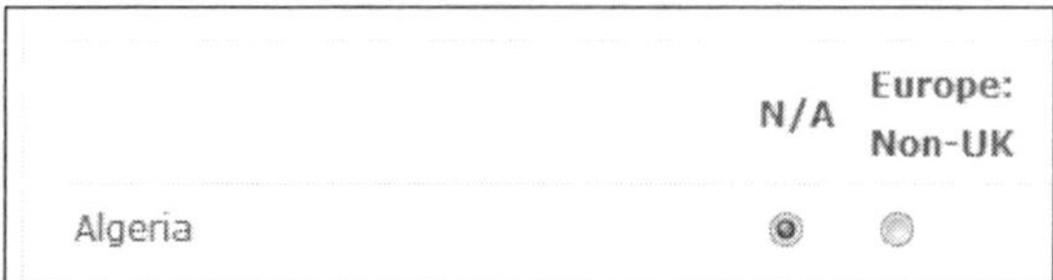

Now if we return to the flexicharge area and select the region, we can create a charge for those countries.

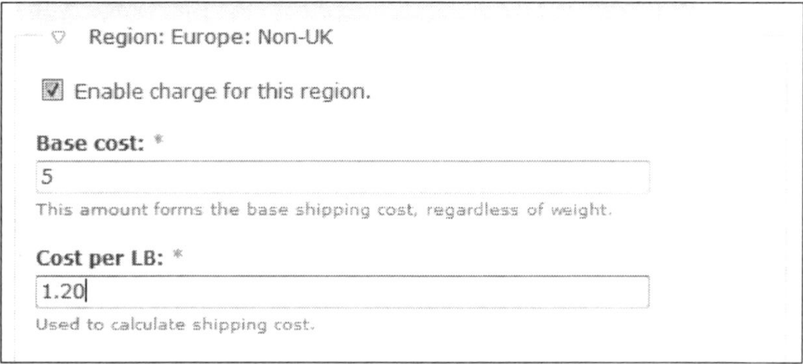

The charge above would add a cost of $5 to each purchase in that region and an additional $1.20 for every pound of weight.

[If creating this flexicharge results in an error, you may need to create a charge for all regions (all are on the same screen) at the same time, using 0 as the values.]

There is only one final thing to do in order for this charge to work fully, and that is assign weight to the products.

[Although there was a weight setting in the shipping modules earlier, if we are using a flexicharge, we need to set a separate weight setting (as flexicharge does not depend on having the shipping module installed, it cannot rely on using the shipping module's weight settings for each product).]

If we create a new product or edit an existing product, we should now have options for weight under a heading of flexicharge attributes.

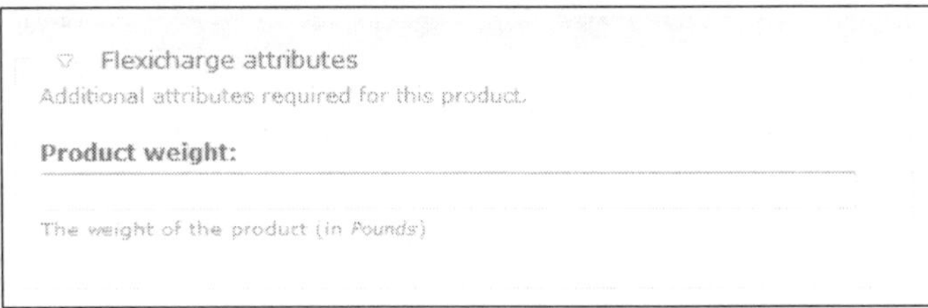

Now if we try to purchase a product that has a weight using a shipping address to which the flexicharge rule will apply, we should see an additional charge for the shipping.

Qty	Item	Price	Subtotal	
1	some test	$31.02	$31.02	Change
	Subtotal		$31.02	
	Tax		$5.43	
	Simple shipping		$11.00	
	Total		$47.45	

It works! So we can now use flexicharges to add shipping charges to orders.

Discounts

Don't forget, flexicharges can be used to create discounts too! This can be useful if we wanted to offer a discount on shipping when products are over a specific weight; this could be an incentive to customers put off ordering heavy or large products.

Summary

In this chapter, we set up Doug's website to accept payments online using PayPal as well as looking at how payment gateways work and which other payment gateways are available. We also set up tax rules, configured shipping rules, and APIs to add shipping costs to orders. We now have a completely functioning store! In the next chapter we will look at getting our store online, as well as securing and maintaining our store.

10

Securing, Deploying, and Maintaining Your Shop

Our store is now fully working and can handle taxes, payment, and shipping; let's now look at securing, deploying, and maintaining our store. If we are working on our store on our own computer and not online, a few things could not work correctly (such as the pingback requests from PayPal) so we will have to make a few changes.

In this chapter you will learn:

- The importance of security
- Drupal security
- About Secure Socket Layers
- Password and phishing security
- Deploying your site
- Handling orders (although we will look at it in more detail in Chapter 11—*Invoices and CRM*)
- Backing up and restoring your store

Importance of Security

We need to secure our store for a number of reasons including:

- To protect our website
- To protect our business
- To protect our customers

Drupal Security

Drupal is an open-source content management system which contains readable source. In terms of security this is both a good and a bad thing. It is bad because anyone can find security risks in the code with the code being readable, but conversely it makes it easier for someone to find a bug and get a security issue fixed.

Security Announcements

Drupal releases security announcements on a special dedicated section of its website which makes it easy to keep up with the latest security patches. This section is available at: `http://drupal.org/security`.

On this page there is also a mailing list sign-up box; by signing up to this we will receive emails each time a new announcement is released by Drupal's security team. There is also a link to the security team's own page within the Drupal site. They can be contacted with any security concerns regarding Drupal's code, so if you find a security issue somewhere, let them know and they can create a patch for everyone to use to secure their own Drupal installations.

> It is highly recommended that e-commerce sites utilizing Drupal subscribe to this list.

Securing Our Drupal Installation

Other than keeping up with any Drupal security announcements, there is little we can do to secure Drupal's code; however, there are some modules we can install that can help protect and secure our website. These modules are:

- CAPTCHA—This prevents automated "web bots" from using and submitting web forms in our website.
- Email verification—This performs some additional checks to see if an email address is a real email address.
- Legal—This is not specifically security related, but adds a terms and conditions box for users who sign up; this can inform them of the rules, regulations, and policies of the website.
- Log in security—This adds additional protection to user accounts and log in.

CAPTCHA

The CAPTCHA—*Completely Automated Public Turing test to tell Computers and Humans Apart* module installs a **Turing test** to prevent automated "web bots", such as the ones that automatically post spam messages onto forums, from submitting web forms on the website.

There are two kinds of CAPTCHA tests, ones utilizing text and ones utilizing images; a number of things need to be considered before using the image methods in the module, as it raises accessibility issues. For more information on those, and for alternative methods to the visual **Turing test**, have a look at the *World Wide Web Consortiums* working group note on the subject—`http://www.w3.org/TR/turingtest/`.

The module can be downloaded from the Drupal website: `http://drupal.org/project/captcha`. Once it has been downloaded, we need to uncompress the file, and put the `captcha` folder into the `modules` folder in our Drupal installation.

With the files in place, we now have a new group of modules called **Spam control** in the **Modules** section of the Drupal administration area. Let's check the boxes to install them!

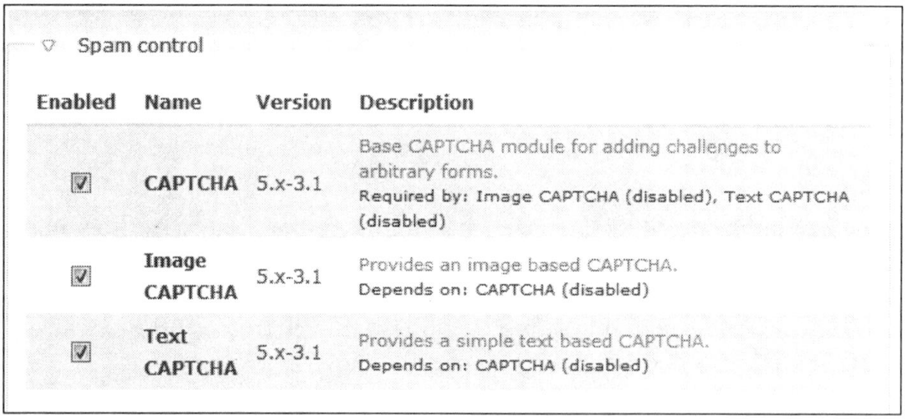

▽ Spam control

Enabled	Name	Version	Description
☑	**CAPTCHA**	5.x-3.1	Base CAPTCHA module for adding challenges to arbitrary forms. **Required by:** Image CAPTCHA (disabled), Text CAPTCHA (disabled)
☑	**Image CAPTCHA**	5.x-3.1	Provides an image based CAPTCHA. **Depends on:** CAPTCHA (disabled)
☑	**Text CAPTCHA**	5.x-3.1	Provides a simple text based CAPTCHA. **Depends on:** CAPTCHA (disabled)

We can now get to the **CAPTCHA** settings from **Administer | User Management** or (`http://localhost/drupal-5.7/admin/user/captcha`). The settings allow us to add a CAPTCHA element to the various different forms including the contact form, and registration forms and then set it if we want to challenge the user to prove they are human.

There are three different CAPTCHA "challenges" available with the module, they are:

- Math (this uses plain text, and does not have any accessibility issues linked to the image type)
- Image
- Text

There is an **Examples** tab on the same page to see how each of these works.

Math

The math CAPTCHA challenge presents the user with a basic math sum to complete, as shown by the example below:

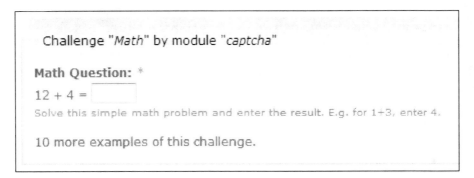

Challenge "*Math*" by module "*captcha*"

Math Question: *

12 + 4 =

Solve this simple math problem and enter the result. E.g. for 1+3, enter 4.

10 more examples of this challenge.

Image

The image challenge presents the user with an image containing a number of characters. We can select the font type and the level of noise or distortion in the background for the characters used from the **Image CAPTCHA** tab. The user must then correctly enter the characters from the image, which can in some cases be difficult to read, into a text box.

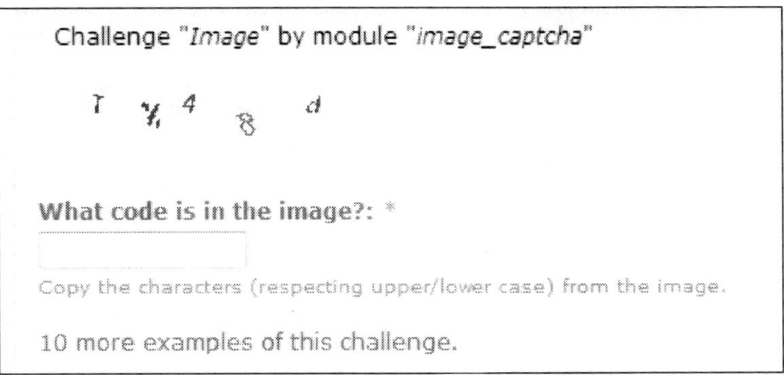

Text

This challenge provides a phrase and asks for a portion of the phrase to be entered into the text box.

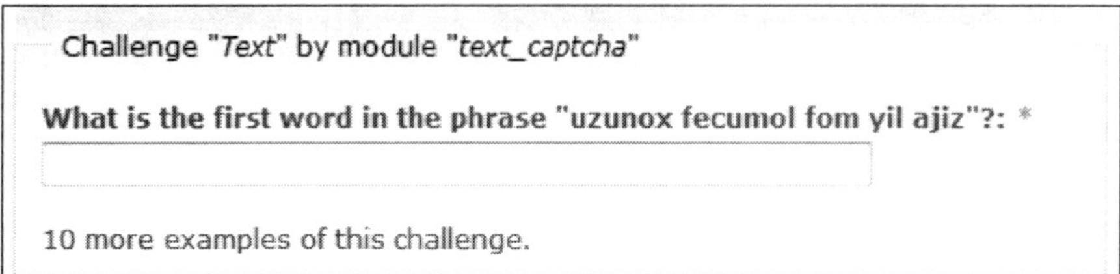

Challenge "Text" by module "text_captcha"
What is the first word in the phrase "uzunox fecumol fom yil ajiz"?: *
10 more examples of this challenge.

Setting it Up

Doug does not want to make the "challenges" inconvenient for his customers; he wants them to appear only on the contact and registration forms, and wants to challenge a user only once. He also wants to use only the Math challenge, as he always finds the image challenges on other websites frustrating.

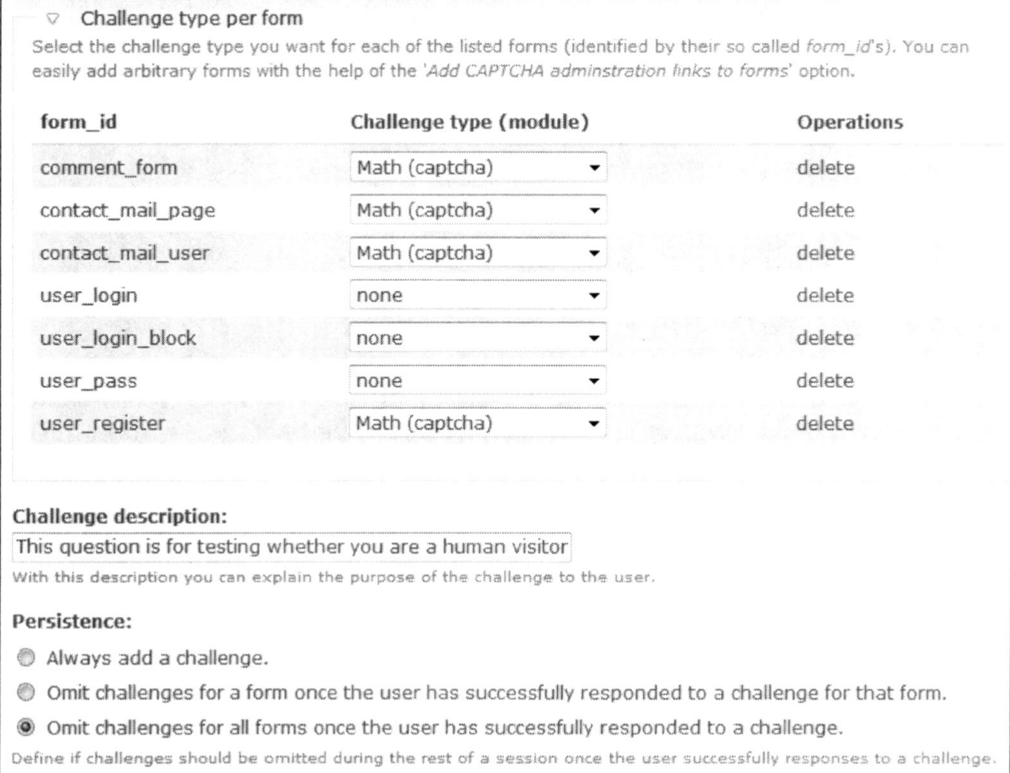

If we now log out, and try to register for an account we should be presented with the Math **CAPTCHA** challenge.

CAPTCHA

This question is for testing whether you are a human visitor and to prevent automated spam submissions.

Math Question: *

4 + 9 =

Solve this simple math problem and enter the result. E.g. for 1+3, enter 4.

If we enter the answer to the math question incorrectly we are presented with an error message indicating that the question was not answered correctly.

- Username field is required.
- E-mail address field is required.
- The answer you entered for the CAPTCHA was not correct.

Hopefully with these changes, Doug's Dinos will be protected from automated spam robots; unfortunately though, spam can still get through if it is submitted by a human, and of course spam bots are always evolving to try to beat the various CAPTCHA systems. So it is worth keeping an eye on the CAPTCHA module to see if it improves or changes.

Email Verification

This module performs additional checks on email addresses entered into the registration form to ensure the address is valid. Firstly it checks to see if the domain name within the email address is valid; then it contacts the SMTP server linked to the email address and sends it a number of commands to try and determine if the server acknowledges the existence of the email addresses. The module can be downloaded from the Drupal website from `http://drupal.org/project/email_verify`.

There are no configuration options with this module, so once it is installed—that's it!

Legal

The legal module displays terms and conditions to users who want to register on the website and will not accept their registration unless they agree to the terms. Although this is not directly linked with security, terms and conditions can be used to provide a disclaimer for content and to explain what is and is not allowed on the

website or that anyone violating the terms and conditions may be reported to their ISP. This may help legally when dealing with user-submitted content or disabling user accounts.

> You should seek legal advice regarding terms and conditions on websites in order to get accurate information on their use and enforceability.

The module can be downloaded from the Drupal website—`http://drupal.org/project/legal`. Once it is downloaded, decompressed, and uploaded into the `modules` folder we have a new module to enable in the **Modules** section of Drupal's administration area.

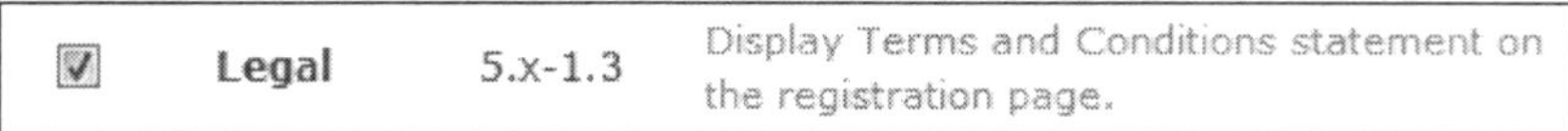

The settings for the **Legal** module can be found under the **Site configuration** section of the **Administer** area.

Legal
Display Terms and Conditions statement on the registration page.

The module provides us with the following settings:

- Style of displaying the terms and conditions—How the terms are displayed on a page.
- The terms and conditions themselves.
- Additional checkboxes—This would be useful if we were to enforce an age limit, and could act as an option for confirming whether the user is over a certain age.
- Explain changes—When changes are made to the terms, we should add a line explaining the changed areas for users who had signed up with the previous terms and conditions, so that they can get an overview of the changes made to those terms and conditions.

Doug only wants some basic terms and conditions with no additional checkboxes, so let's set that for him.

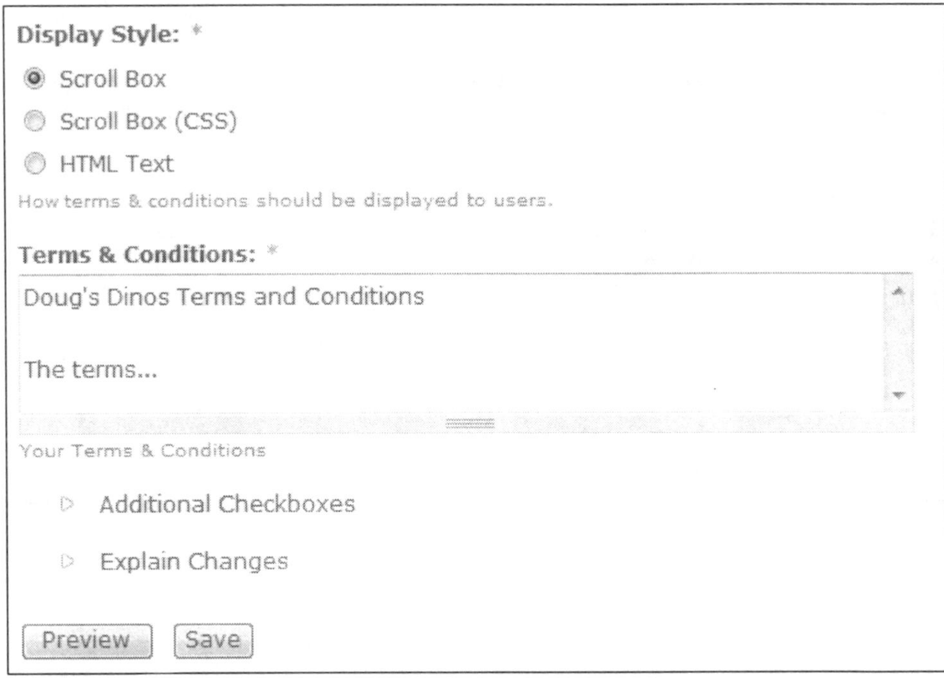

Once the terms and conditions are saved, we can see a preview of how they will be displayed.

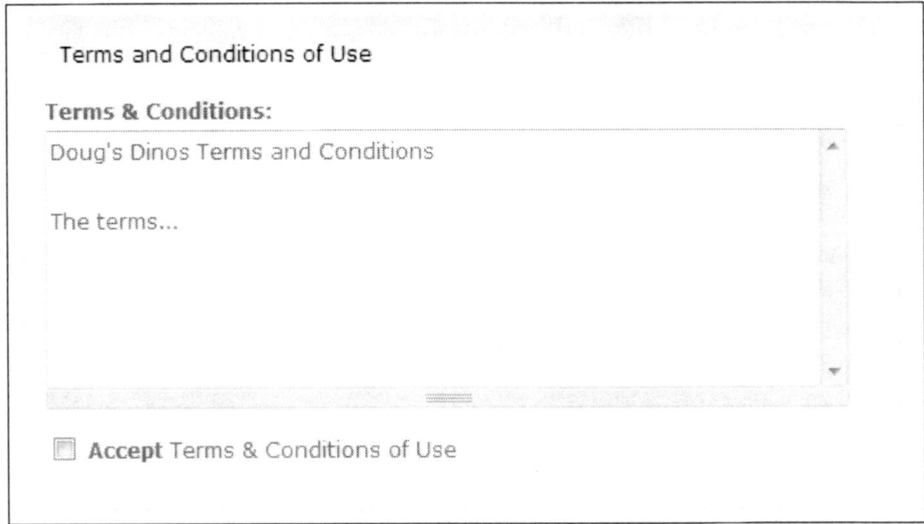

Login Security

The **Login Security** module provides features that it categorizes as soft and hard protections; soft protections just offer delays, which can help slow down attacks, whereas hard protections require an administrator to intervene to reactivate an account or allow access from a host. These are:

- Request time delay (soft protection)—This time delay is used when log in requests fail; to try to prevent, or at least reduce the effectiveness of brute force attacks.
- Block log in forms (soft protection)
- Block account on a number of failed log in attempts (hard protection)
- Block IP address on a number of failed log in attempts (hard protection)

Let's install this module; we need to download it from `http://drupal.org/project/login_security`, decompress the files, and upload them to the `modules` folder within our Drupal installation.

The final step to install the module is to check the **Login Security** box from the **Other** category on the **Modules** page.

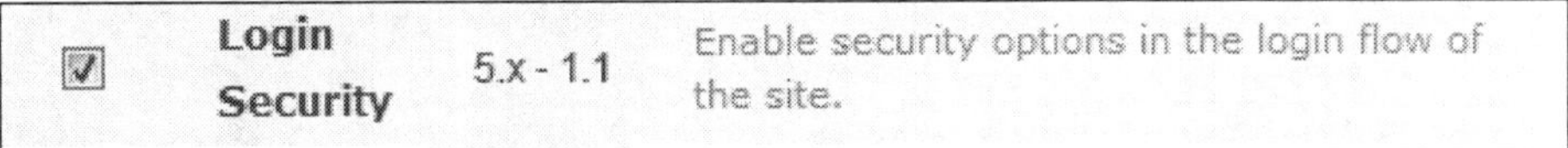

The settings for this module are in the **User settings** part of **User management**; the individual settings available are:

- Track time
- Login delay base time
- Maximum number of login failures before blocking a user
- Maximum number of login failures before soft blocking a host
- Maximum number of login failures before blocking a host
- Notifying the user after any failed login attempt
- Messages to be shown on each failed login attempt, for banned hosts, and when a user is blocked by their ID
- If an email should be sent to the administrator when a user is blocked, and the contents of that email

The **Track time** is the length of time for which failed logins are recorded; so if the maximum log in failures was three, and the track time was 1 hour, the three failed log in attempts would have to be within the one hour. The **Login delay base time** is a multiplier to define the delay the user has before being able to log in again from a failed log in attempt; this is multiplied by the number of log in attempts.

The soft host block would prevent that host from logging in once they had reached the limit, whereas the hard block would not allow them use the site at all—even anonymously.

Login Security settings

Track time:

0 Hours

Enter the time that each failed login attempt is kept for future computing.

Login delay base time:

0 Seconds

Enter the base time for login delay, computed as (base time) x (login attempts) for that user.

Maximum number of login failures before blocking a user:

0 Failed attempts

Enter the number of login failures a user is allowed. After that amount is reached, the user will be blocked, no matter the host attempting to log in. Use this option carefully on public sites, as an attacker may block your site users.

Maximum number of login failures before soft blocking a host:

0 Failed attempts

Enter the number of login failures a host is allowed. After that amount is reached, the host will not be able to log in but can still browse the site contents as an anonymous user.

Maximum number of login failures before blocking a host:

0 Failed attempts

Enter the number of login failures a host is allowed. After that number is reached, the host will be blocked, no matter the username attempting to log in.

▷ Edit notifications

The messages to display to the user as well as the email template to be sent to the administrator are stored within the expandable **Edit notifications** section.

Passwords

This may seem obvious, but password security is commonly overlooked by many people. Your Drupal password gives access to the administration area of Drupal, which could allow someone who obtained it to completely destroy the store as well as obtain and potentially abuse customer data.

Weak passwords can either be guessed or obtained by "dictionary attacks" on a user account; dictionary attacks are an automated process where a computer program tries words from a dictionary list in the hope that one of them is the password. We took steps to prevent this by installing the **Login Security** module; however, that does not mean we can safely use weak passwords. What makes a strong password?

- Mixture of letters and numbers
- Use of special characters i.e. @, /, \, etc.
- Being at least eight characters in length
- Being unique (don't use the same password for multiple things)
- If it includes a word (don't use the word itself as the password) the word should be spelled wrong
- Not contain personal information such as names, or date of birth

You might find substituting certain letters with numbers a good method to start introducing numbers into your password, but try to use most of those points above to use a secure password!

Phishing

As well as being aware of phishing yourself, it might be a good idea to promote understanding of phishing with emails sent out by your Drupal e-Commerce store. A number of large online retailers generally provide advice in their emails informing customers that their staff will never ask for specific pieces of information and that if they are unsure whether the links in an email are valid they should go to the homepage directly and navigate to the appropriate section.

With Drupal e-Commerce's email system it is very easy to add such notes to the ends of emails, including customer welcome emails, invoice emails, and confirmation emails. They can be changed from **Administer | E-Commerce configuration | Mail**.

Deploying

We have secured our installation, let's deploy it and get it on the Web!

What do we need, and what do we need to do, to get our website online?

- We need a web hosting account to store our shop.
- We need a domain name, and a web address to point to the website.
- We then need to upload our website to the hosting account .

Hosting and Domain Names

The Internet is saturated with web hosting companies and domain name registrars; most hosting accounts come with a control panel making it easy to administer an account (such as adding email addresses, changing passwords, etc.). Two of the most common control panels are cPanel and Plesk; if you do get a hosting account with cPanel (which is what the rest of this chapter assumes) you may find this book helpful: *cPanel User Guide and Tutorial* by Aric Pedersen ISBN 978-1-904811-92-3 published by Packt Publishing (`http://www.packtpub.com/cPanel/book`).

There are quite a few criteria when looking for hosting accounts such as the level of support offered, the amount of disk space provided, the amount of bandwidth (that's the data transfer from your site to your users), minimum contract term, uptime guaranteed, and of course the cost.

There are a number of popular hosting comparison and review websites around, including `www.webhostingtalk.com`.

Some popular web hosts include:

- 1&1 Internet Inc (`www.1and1.com`)
- A Small Orange (`www.asmallorange.com`)
- DreamHost (`www.dreamhost.com`)

Along with a host, you will also need a domain name e.g. `www.dougsdinos.com`. There are a large number of domain registrars around too; prices are quite competitive, and you should expect to pay less than USD$10 per year for a domain name. Some popular registrars include:

- Namecheap (`www.namecheap.com`)
- GoDaddy (`www.godaddy.com`)

Once you have a domain name, you will need to point it to your hosting account by updating its name servers with those provided by your host (contact your host for more information).

Getting the Site Online

We now have a domain name and a hosting account and can put our store online. This involves:

- Creating a user account for the database
- Creating a database and assigning the user account permissions to it
- Uploading the store
- Importing the database
- Altering some of the settings to use the database on the hosting account

Let's get started!

Setting Up the Database

We need to log in to our control panel, and go to the databases section in cPanel. This is the **MySQL** logo on the main page.

From the page that we are taken to we can create the database, create a user for the database, and assign the user to that database. Firstly we need to create the database.

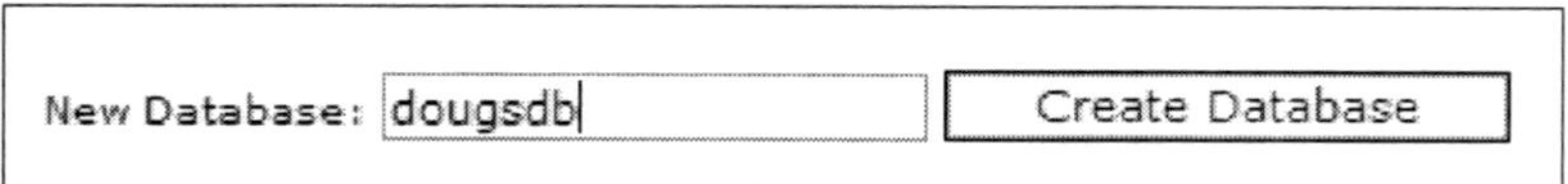

Next we need to create a user for the database.

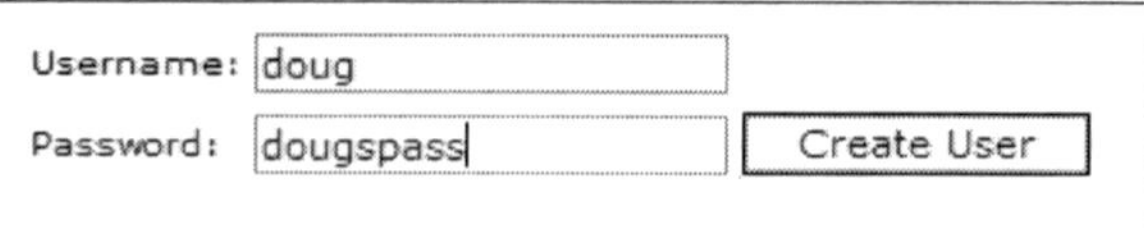

Then we need to assign the user to the database we have just created.

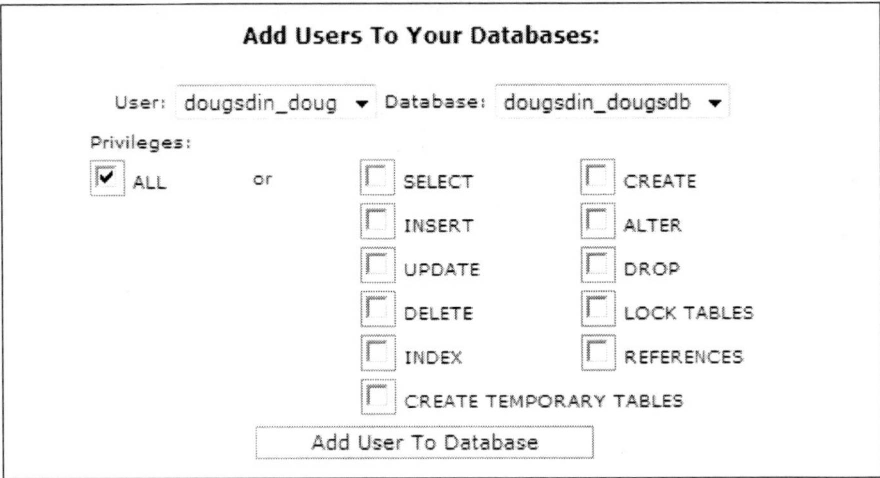

Now that we have a database and a user who has permission to access the database we can transfer the store's database to the new database on the hosting account.

We now need to export a copy of the database from our local installation of Drupal and then import this copy into the database we have on the web server. Our local copy of phpMyAdmin should be located at `http://localhost/phpmyadmin/`; from here we need to select the database from the list.

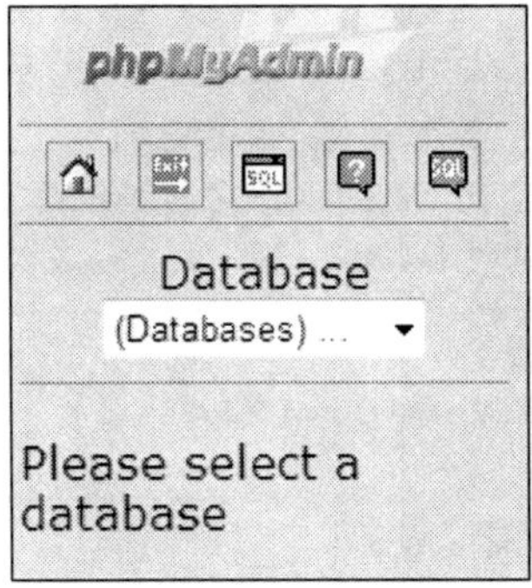

Once we have selected the database, we need to select the **Export** option from the top of the page.

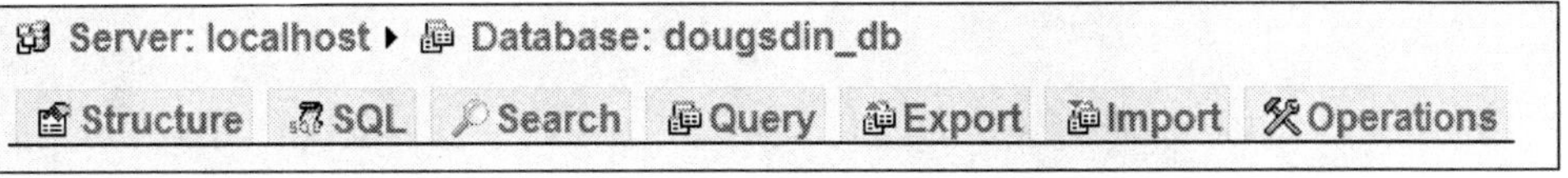

Within the export area, we need to select the database tables we want to export; obviously we want to export all of the data from the database so we click the **Select All** link to select all of the tables from the list.

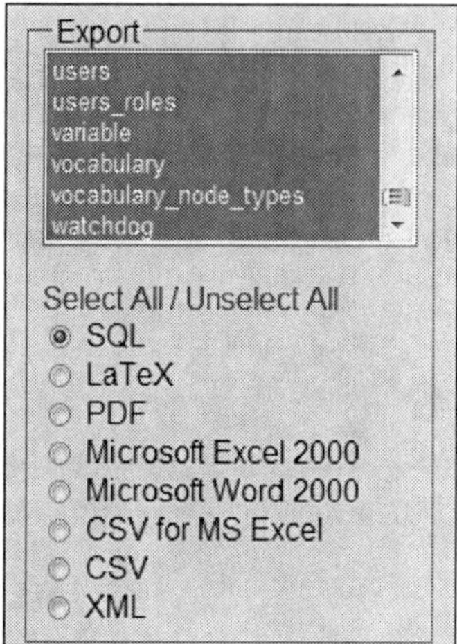

Then to actually save the data as a file, we need to check the **Save as file** box and click the **Go** button.

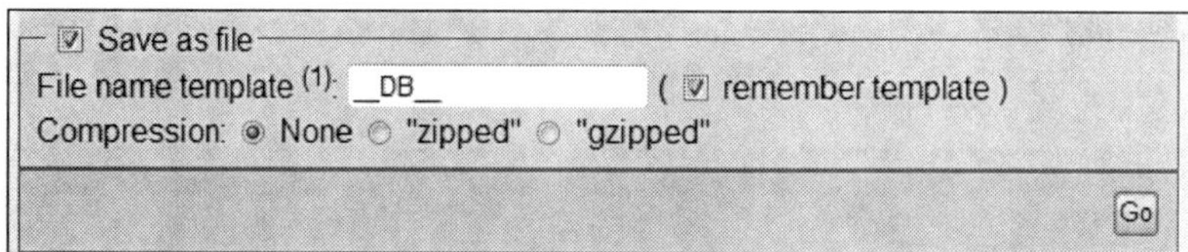

This should then download the data in an SQL file onto our computer. Now we need to import this data into the new database on the web server.

Firstly, we need to log in to our control panel, and select the MySQL logo to go to the database area. At the bottom of this page there is a link to the phpMyAdmin installation on the server—let's click that. Within phpMyAdmin we need to select the database we created earlier from the left-hand side of the page, and then click the **import** tab from the top of the page. On the import page there is a section with the heading **File to import**; we use the file **Browse** box to select the database file we downloaded onto our computer.

File to import
Location of the text file C:\Users\Michael\Downloa Browse... (Max: 51,200KB)
Character set of the file: utf8
Imported file compression will be automatically detected from: None, gzip, zip

Then we click the **Go** button at the bottom of the page; the page may then take few moments to process the data, but once it loads we have our new database set up with all of the information from our local installation.

Large SQL File

Some web hosting control panels have restrictions on the size of file you can upload, which can cause problems when importing a large database. If the database file is large it can be exported in parts, for instance we could create a file for a few tables. By importing these smaller files one at a time, we can bypass this problem.

Uploading the Store

Since we have the database set up and ready on our web server, we now need to upload the files from our local installation, otherwise we will just have a completely blank website!

To upload the files we need to use an FTP program; personally I prefer FileZilla—a free open-source lightweight FTP client (you can download it from `http://sourceforge.net/projects/filezilla/`).

With our FTP client, we enter the server's username and password to connect to the server, navigate to the `public_html` directory, and then transfer all of the Drupal files there.

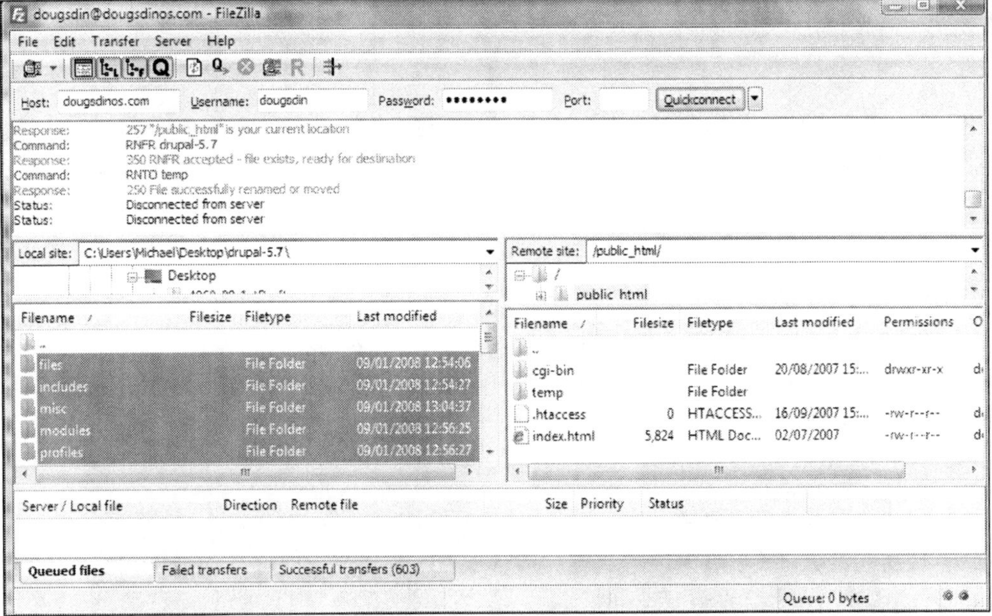

Tweaking the Settings

We have the database set up, and also have the files uploaded, but the files don't know about the new database yet, and so the website won't work. The database connection details are stored in a configuration file called `settings.php` in the `sites/default` folder. We need to edit this file, either using a PHP editor (such as Crimson Editor, or PHPEclipse) or something simple like Notepad.

Within this file we need to look for a line starting with `$db_url =`, and then we need to alter the line to contain the new username, password, and database.

For the database we set up earlier the line should now read `$db_url = 'mysql://dougsdin_doug:dougspass@localhost/dougsdin_dougsdb';`

```
 * Database URL format:
 *   $db_url = 'mysql://username:password@localhost/databasename';
 *   $db_url = 'mysqli://username:password@localhost/databasename';
 *   $db_url = 'pgsql://username:password@localhost/databasename';
 */
$db_url = 'mysql://dougsdin_doug:dougspass@localhost/dougsdin_dougsdb';
$db_prefix = '';
```

We have now successfully deployed our store online!

SSL

SSL stands for **Secure Sockets Layer**. It is a cryptographic protocol that provides secure communications on the Internet. It works by using encryption methods to encrypt data which is then transferred over the SSL connection. Standard web page requests are not in SSL and data sent from the client (browser) to the web server are sent in plain text, which could in theory be read by third parties. SSL connections encrypt this data so it cannot be read, and can only be read by the server. Wikipedia has a very detailed entry on **Transport Layer Security**, if you are interested in how SSL works and the technicalities of it—`http://en.wikipedia.org/wiki/Secure_Sockets_Layer`. The use of SSL in Drupal is not easy or available out of the box; there are a number of discussions on the Drupal website regarding setting up Drupal for SSL, including `http://drupal.org/node/60222`. Along with configuring Drupal you will also need to purchase and install an SSL certificate.

An SSL certificate is used to verify the identity of the server and is used when encrypting the data sent to and from the website. SSL certificates are available for a variety of prices, normally depending on the company that "signs" the certificate; this usually involves a trusted company verifying your own identity and then issuing the SSL certificate. Once you have the certificate you would then need to contact your host to get SSL set up on your hosting account, which would also require an additional dedicated IP address for your hosting account, which may incur additional charges.

Securing connections to your website is a very good idea; but you need to look into the costs and the efforts involved, and then weigh that against the advantages. If you are running a very popular store dealing with lots of sensitive data then it would almost be essential to set this up.

One of the advantages of the payment gateways used to make online payments is that they handle the card transactions, and they have secure websites, so at least that information is processed securely outside of our site.

Maintaining Our Website

With our store now online we need to look at maintaining our website on a regular basis, including making changes to the website and store, handling orders, and of course backing up, and if needs be, restoring our website from a backup.

Performing Maintenance

Content on websites often needs to change regularly, as does the content of our stores. Some changes, such as small content changes, can just be done there and then with the website online, whereas other changes such as a reorganization of the store or revamp of the product lineup would need the website to be taken offline to prevent customers purchasing products that are no longer being sold, or products with an old price associated with them.

Drupal has a maintenance option, which can be used to essentially block the website from the public, and display a message to visitors explaining that the website is down for maintenance.

This maintenance option is found under **Site maintenance** within the **Site configuration** section of Drupal's administration area.

Site maintenance
Take the site off-line for maintenance or bring it back online.

There are two simple settings in this area:

- **Site status**—This is used to set the status of the site i.e. **Online** or **Off-line**.
- **Site off-line message**—This is a message which is displayed to visitors if the website is in maintenance mode i.e. **Off-line**.

When Doug wants to perform maintenance on his website he wants to display a message to his customers telling them that the website is currently offline while the website is being improved and that it should be back online shortly.

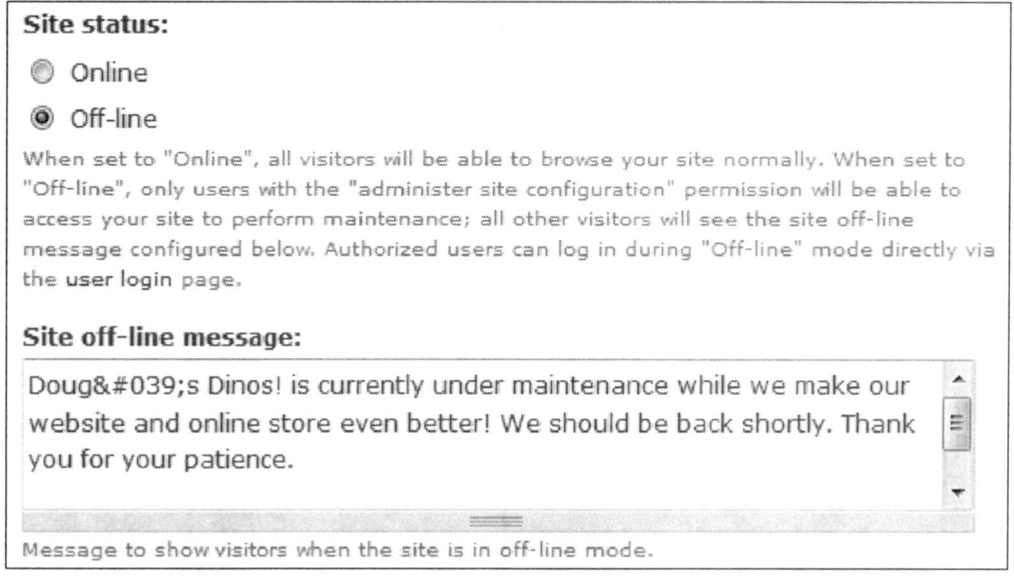

If we remain logged in and have a look at the homepage of the site, we can still access the site, but there is a small notice to remind us that the website is still in maintenance mode.

Operating in off-line mode.

However, if we logout and take a look at the homepage we get a completely different page, which contains the maintenance message.

Site off-line

Doug's Dinos! is currently under maintenance while we make our website and online store even better! We should be back shortly. Thank you for your patience. If you have any urgent issues please contact doug@dougsdinos.com

With this message we can easily make changes without worrying about customers getting confused or accessing content or products that are being updated.

> **Logging back in**
>
> To log back in to your Drupal website when it is in maintenance mode you need to go to the `user` page, so for Doug's Dinos we go to `www.dougsdinos.com/user`.

Handling Orders

If we go to the **E-Commerce** section in the **Administer** menu we have a small information box with some basic statistics about orders in the system.

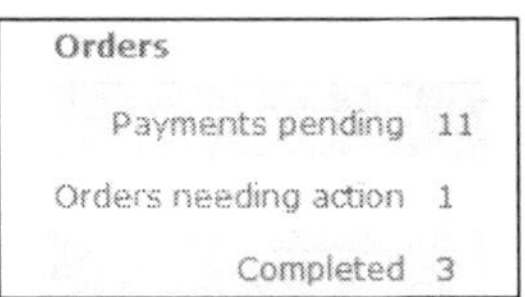

Each of the links in the box takes us to the list of orders with their status in the "order workflow". Orders go through a workflow starting from when the order is placed with pending payment, to payment made, to shipped, or cancelled. If we click the **Payments pending** link we will see all orders that still require payment. If payment is made manually, for example a cheque in the post, we would need to edit this transaction manually to set the transaction as paid.

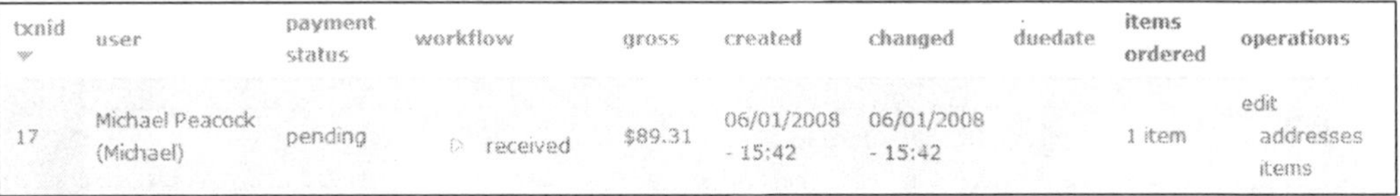

txnid	user	payment status	workflow	gross	created	changed	duedate	items ordered	operations
17	Michael Peacock (Michael)	pending	received	$89.31	06/01/2008 - 15:42	06/01/2008 - 15:42		1 item	edit addresses items

The **edit** link allows us to edit the **Payment status, Username, E-mail address**, and the **Transaction workflow** status.

On the transaction's list shown above, we can directly edit the workflow by clicking the status of the transaction's workflow; this presents us with a pop-out box with a list of status.

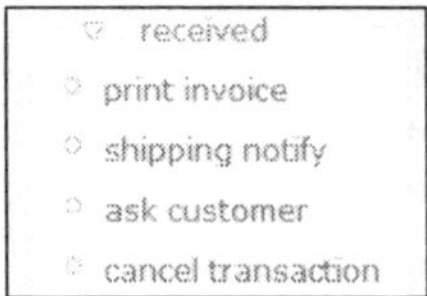

Here we can print an invoice, set the order as shipped, ask the customer a question, or cancel the transaction.

If we wish to ask the customer a question we are taken to an email screen where we can compose an email to the customer asking them any questions we have regarding their order.

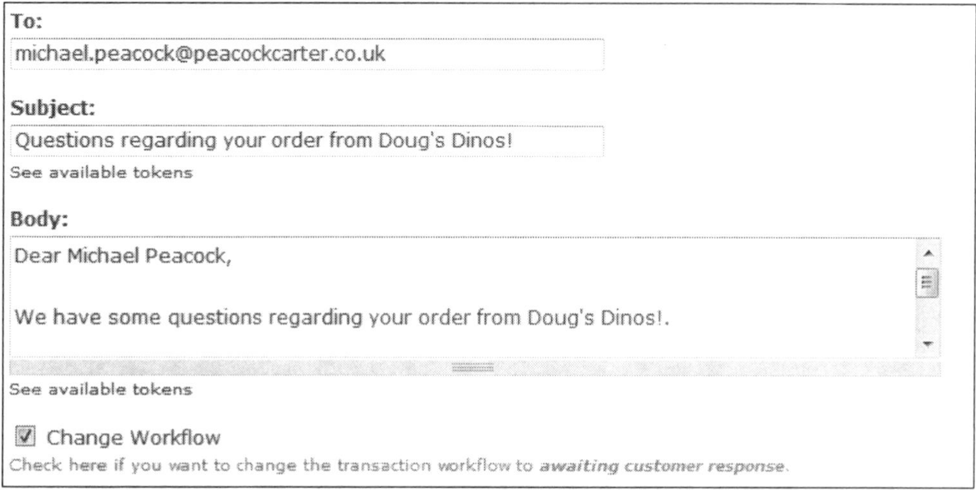

If we check the **Change Workflow** box then the workflow status will be set to *awaiting customer response* to remind us that we are waiting to hear back from the customer before sending out their order.

Backing Up and Restoring Your Store

It is very important to take regular backups of our store; if something were to happen to the website, the hosting account, or the web server our website is stored on, we could loose all sorts of data, including orders that we still need to fulfil but that have been paid, or information regarding payment on orders. This could cost the business a lot of money.

How regularly we need to take backups depends on how often we make changes to the website and how often we receive orders. Backups can of course be automated, but that is a little more complicated and relies on having access to cron jobs on your hosting account. Some hosting accounts include backups with several day retention policies. This is something else to consider when looking for a hosting provider.

Backing Up

cPanel provides an easy-to-use interface for backing up and restoring data. For more information on backing up using other hosting control panels, you should contact your host or the manufacturer of the control panel.

From the main page in cPanel there is a **Backups** link.

Within this section we have links to **Download a home directory Backup** as well as links to download the backups of the various databases on the account.

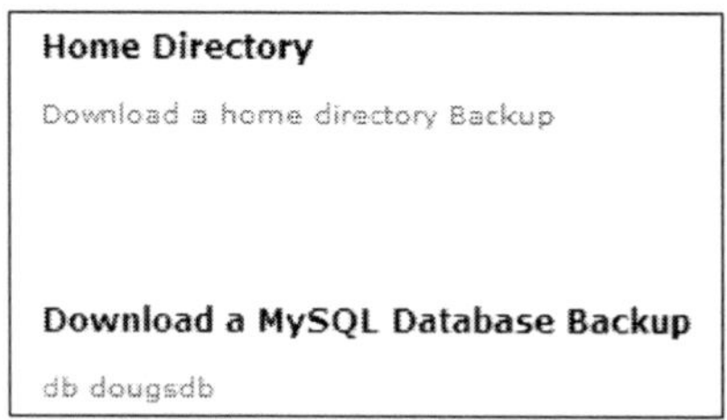

The home directory contains all of the files and settings, including any emails, logs, and statistics. The database will require more regular backups, however, as it is the data that changes the most and this is where all orders and transactions are stored.

Restoring

To restore a backup we need to go back into the **Backups** area of cPanel and on the right-hand side of the page there are upload boxes for restoring the home directory backup and for restoring the database.

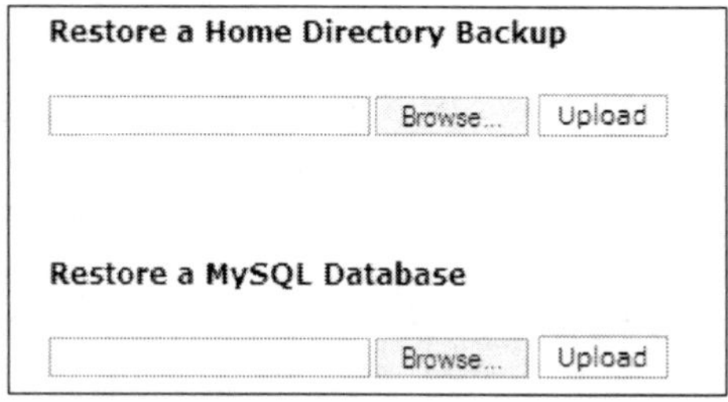

Once the files have been uploaded using this form the contents will be used to replace the existing home directory and the existing database.

Summary

In this chapter, we installed a number of modules to make our Drupal e-Commerce installation more secure as well as looking at keeping passwords secure and educating our customers about phishing. We also set up a hosting account, created a database, and deployed our website from our local installation into a live installation, which can accept orders and generate business.

Finally we looked into how to maintain our store, how to process orders (we will be looking more into order processing in the form of generating invoices and reports in the next chapter), and of course how to back up and restore our store.

11

Invoices and CRM

Our Drupal e-Commerce store is fully functioning and running live on the Internet, and we have secured it and looked into how to keep our store maintained as well as how to manage orders and transactions. Let's now look at generating invoices and reports for our store. In this chapter you will learn:

- How to print invoices
- How to customize the layout of these invoices
- How to create and manage invoices using the invoices module
- How to install CiviCRM, and integrate it with our Drupal installation

Printable Invoices

Within Drupal e-Commerce it is really easy to get a simple printable invoice from a transaction. From the orders list, we just need to click on a transaction's **workflow** status and then select **print invoice**.

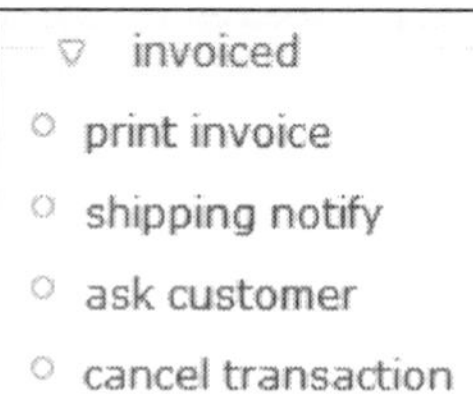

When we click this a simple web page containing the invoice is displayed. We can then print the invoice directly from the web browser; the simplistic design, size, and style of the invoice makes it easy to print on a single sheet of paper.

Doug's Dinos! Invoice

Shipping to	**Billing to**
Michael Peacock PCA House Newcastle, TYNE AND WEAR NE1 PCA United Kingdom	Michael Peacock PCA House Newcastle, TYNE AND WEAR NE1 PCA United Kingdom

E-mail: michael.peacock@peacockcarter.co.uk

Items ordered

Quantity	Item	Price
1	*T-Rex with Support plan*	$86.01
1	*some test*	$31.02
		Tax: *$5.43*
		Simple shipping: *$0.00*
		Total: *$122.46*

Payment Info

Ordered On: *Wed, 01/09/2008 - 23:58*
Transaction ID: *18*

The layout of the invoice is not particularly attractive, but for many it is fine. Thankfully, we can quite easily customize the design of the invoice by editing a single file.

Customizing the Invoice Design

Doug wants to change the design; he wants us to make the following changes:

- Add his logo to the page
- Add his contact details

- Move the order date and transaction ID to the top of the page
- Move the delivery and billing addresses to the bottom of the page

Before we make changes to the actual code that generates the invoice, let's first create a new style, and then make the appropriate changes. The reason we should do this is that since the invoice is generated on-the-fly from a function in the code (and not a template, which is easier to change) bits and pieces of the invoice design are spread across the code. If we make our design first, then we just need to copy bits of the design, and paste them into the code.

New Design Layout

The following design incorporates the changes Doug wanted.

Doug's Dinos

Doug's Dinos LTD, Some Address, Newcastle upon Tyne, NE1 123, T: 0191 645 0000

Date ordered: 10/01/2008
ID#: 00001

Item	Qty	Cost
T-Rex with support plan	1	$85.99
	Tax	$5
	Shipping	$5
	Total	$95.99

Delivery Address: Michael Peacock, PCA House, Newcastle, Tyne and Wear, NE1 PCA, UK.

Billing Address: Michael Peacock, PCA House, Newcastle, Tyne and Wear, NE1 PCA, UK.

contact email: michael.peacock@peacockcarter.co.uk

Doug likes the new design, so we will keep it. Let's take a quick look at the code used to create the invoice, and then we will look at moving the design into the module's code to generate invoices that look like this.

Code for New Design

The first bit of the code is the head, which contains the title of the page as well as style elements. As the style needed for the invoice is so minimal I've placed the CSS within the HTML file as opposed to including a CSS file. If a more extensive CSS was used, it would be better suited to its own file. Another book available with more information on Drupal's template system, and creating or changing themes within Drupal is *Drupal 5 Themes* by Ric Shreves ISBN 978-1-847191-82-3 published by Packt Publishing (`http://www.packtpub.com/drupal-5-themes/book`).

```
<!DOCTYPE html PUBLIC "-//W3C//DTD XHTML 1.0 Strict//EN"
  "http://www.w3.org/TR/xhtml1/DTD/xhtml1-strict.dtd">
<html>
 <head>
   <title>Invoice $txn->txnid</title>
   <style type="text/css">
      #invwrapper
      {
         margin: 0 auto;
         width: 500px;
         text-align: center;
      }
      #invheader img
      {
         align: left;
      }
      #invmain table
      {
         width: 500px;
      }
      .floatr
      {
         float:right;
      }
      .textr
      {
         text-align: right;
      }
      .textl
      {
         text-align: left;
      }
      .corporate
      {
         font-size: 13px;
      }
      .addressp
      {
```

```
            font-size: 12px;
        }
        #invmain th
        {
            background: #CC0000;
        }
    </style>
</head>
```

The next section includes the first changes Doug wanted to be made. We have added the logo, his contact details, and moved the order date, and transaction ID to the top of the page.

```
<body>
  <div id="invwrapper">
     <div id="invheader">
       <div class="floatr"><img
           src="http://www.dougsdinos.com/files/garland_logo.png"
           title="Doug's Dinos Logo" />
       </div>
     <h1>Doug's Dinos</h1>
    </div>
    <p class="corporate">Doug's Dinos LTD, Some Address,
              Newcastle upon Tyne, NE1 123, T: 0191 645 0000</p>
    <p class="floatr textr bpad corporate">Date ordered:
              10/01/2008<br />ID#: 00001</p><br /><br /><br />
```

Next we have the table containing the details of the order, and the charges added as well as the total cost.

```
<div id="invmain">
 <table border="1">
   <tr><th>Item</th><th>Qty</th><th>Cost</th></tr>
   <tr><td>T-Rex with support plan</td><td>1</td><td>$85.99</td></
tr>
   <tr><td> </td><td>Tax</td><td></strong>$5</strong></td>
   <tr><td> </td><td>Shipping</td><td></strong>$5</strong></
td>
   <tr><td> </td><td>Total</td><td></strong>$95.99</strong></
td>
  </table>
</div>
```

Finally we have the delivery and billing addresses, which are now at the bottom of the page where Doug wanted them.

```
<p class="addressp textl"><strong>Delivery Address:</strong>
       Michael Peacock, PCA House, Newcastle, Tyne and Wear,
       NE1 PCA, UK</p>
```

```
        <p class="addressp textl"><strong>Billing Address:</strong>
                Michael Peacock, PCA House, Newcastle, Tyne and Wear,
                NE1 PCA, UK</p>
        <p class="addressp">contact email:
               michael.peacock@peacockcarter.co.uk</p>
    </div>
  </body>
</html>
```

Adding the New Design to Drupal

We have made a new design for the invoice; now we need to take the design and add it to Drupal's code so the design applies to invoices it generated.

To make changes to the design of the printable invoice we need to take some code from the store's module file, and place a copy in the theme's template file. The module file is called `store.module` and is located in `sites/default/modules/ecommerce/store/`; we should use a PHP or text editor to edit the file. A PHP editor is best as they generally have better support for things like line numbers and syntax highlighting, which we may find useful.

Within this file we are looking for a function called `theme_store_invoice`, which is located on line 440. We need to copy this function, place it in the store's template file, and then make quite a number of changes to this function in order to change the style of the invoice as desired. The entire HTML of the invoice is stored and generated in this function, which is good, because it means we only have to look in one place.

Once we have copied the function, we need to open the `template.php` file that is located in the folder for the theme we are using, which is in the `themes` folder. Within this file, we should paste the function and rename it `phptemplate_store_invoice`.

> You may be wondering why we copied the code instead of just changing it directly. The reason is if the module is upgraded, we would then have to look into the code and reapply our changes.

The first part of the function does not need any alterations, as this is just building up data, and performing some minor style changes (such as making some elements bold), we need to start making changes from the line containing `if ($print_mode) {`.

This line and the eight following lines define the `head` of the HTML document, which contains a link to the style sheet. The conditional if statement wrapping the code just differentiates between viewing the invoice within Drupal or viewing it in a separate page to print off.

The use of `<<<EOD` and `EOD;` is a technique known as **heredoc** and is a specific "string literal"; in the instances following it is particularly useful to avoid the need to omit the " and ' characters.

```
if ($print_mode)
{
  $output .= <<<EOD
  <html>
    <head>
    <style type="text/css" media="all">@import url('$css');</
style>
    </head>
    <body>
EOD;
}
```

Our new code specifies a DOCTYPE for the HTML and a page title.

```
if ($print_mode)
{
  $output .= <<<EOD
  <!DOCTYPE html PUBLIC "-//W3C//DTD XHTML 1.0 Strict//EN"
   "http://www.w3.org/TR/xhtml1/DTD/xhtml1-strict.dtd">
  <html>
   <head>
    <title>Invoice $txn->txnid</title>
    <style type="text/css">
      #invwrapper
      {
         margin: 0 auto;
         width: 500px;
         text-align: center;
      }
      #invheader img
      {
         align: left;
      }
      #invmain table
      {
         width: 500px;
      }
      .floatr
      {
         float:right;
      }
      .textr
```

```
        {
           text-align: right;
        }
        .textl
        {
           text-align: left;
        }
        .corporate
        {
           font-size: 13px;
        }
        .addressp
        {
           font-size: 12px;
        }
        #invmain th
        {
           background: #CC0000;
        }
      </style>
    </head>
EOD;
}
```

In the code above I've just added the CSS inline, but we could have also edited the CSS file for the printable invoice, which is located in `sites/default/modules/ecommerce/store/invoice.css`, or the `style.css` file in the `themes` folder, which can override these styles.

Non-Printable Invoice CSS

The customer can also view invoices (for transactions and for invoices created using that module). The customer view of the invoice, however, does not import the styles we have included there (as the head part of the document is only included on the printable copy, as determined by the: `if ($print_mode)` section of the code). So we may need to edit the CSS file used by the main theme if we want to have the same design for customer invoices. The file we should add the CSS details to is `/sites/default/modules/ecommerce/store/store.css`.

The next bit that we need to change is the main content of the invoice; we need to change it from its original code:

```
$output .= <<<EOD
  <h1>
   $site_name
  </h1>
```

```
    <table cellspacing="5">
     <tr>
      <th align="left">$shipping_label</th>
      <th align="left">$billing_label</th>
     </tr>
     <tr>
       <td>$shipping_to</td>
       <td>$billing_to</td>
      </tr>
     </table>
     <p><strong>$shipping_method_label</strong>
                           $shipping_method</p>
     <p><strong>$email_label</strong> $txn->mail</p>
   <h2>
    $items_label
   </h2>
     $items_view
   <h2>
    $payment_label
   </h2>
     $payment_info
EOD;
```

to our new code:

```
$output .= <<<EOD
 <div id="invwrapper">
   <div id="invheader">
   <div class="floatr"><img
          src="http://www.dougsdinos.com/files/garland_logo.png"
        title="Doug's Dinos Logo" /></div>
   <h1>
    $site_name
   </h1>
 </div>
    <p class="corporate">Doug's Dinos LTD, Some Address, Newcastle
              upon Tyne, NE1 123, T: 0191 645 0000</p>
    <p class="floatr textr bpad corporate">Date ordered:
10/01/2008<br
              />ID#: 00001</p><br /><br /><br />
 <div id="invmain">
    $items_view
 </div>
    <p class="addressp textl"><strong>Delivery Address:</strong>
              $shipping_to</p>
    <p class="addressp textl"><strong>Billing Address:</strong>
              $billing_to</p>
```

```
    <p class="addressp textl"><strong>Delivery Method:</strong>
            $shipping_method</p>
    <p class="addressp textl"><strong>Payment Information:</strong>
            $payment_info</p>
    <p class="addressp">contact email: $txn->email</p>
</div>
```

Unfortunately this does not look exactly like the invoice design we made as a separate HTML file; let's take a look at the end result first, then have a look at why there are some slight changes.

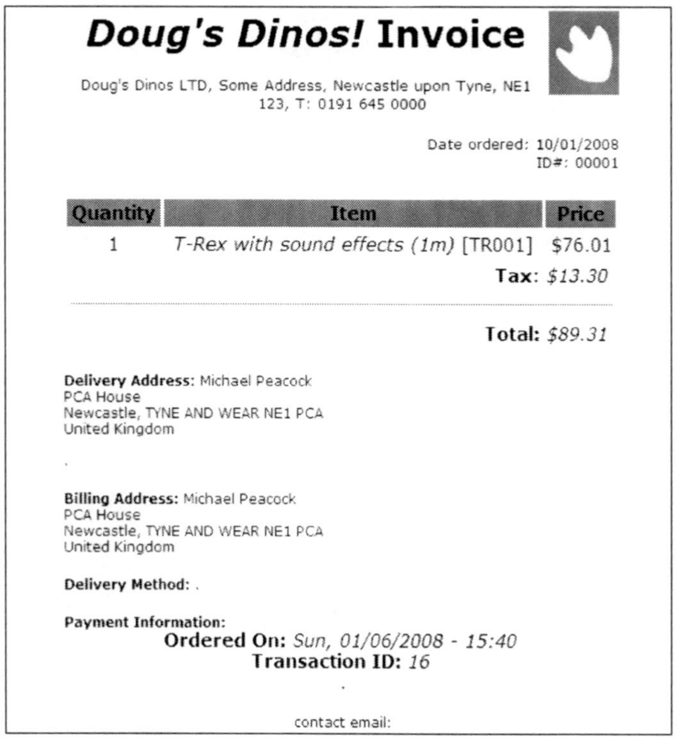

The main differences here are:

- The table of items
- Format of the delivery address
- Format of the billing address

These particular pieces of data are formatted by various functions within the e-Commerce module's theme system, the items within the transaction are automatically built into the table; however, its general appearance is still improved. The billing and delivery addresses are also formatted to include line breaks after each section of the address. It is possible to change this, but it involves digging

around other files and editing functions, which would make more difficulties if we were to upgrade the version of the e-Commerce module in the future.

Invoice Module

Doug wants to be able to take orders from certain regular customers and generate an invoice for them, and mark that payment is due in four weeks time. This can be done with the invoice module.

Installing the Invoice Module

The invoice module allows us to create and manage invoices for our customers, which can then be posted to them. The module is not enabled by default, so we need to go into the **Modules** section under **Site building** and enable the **Invoice** module.

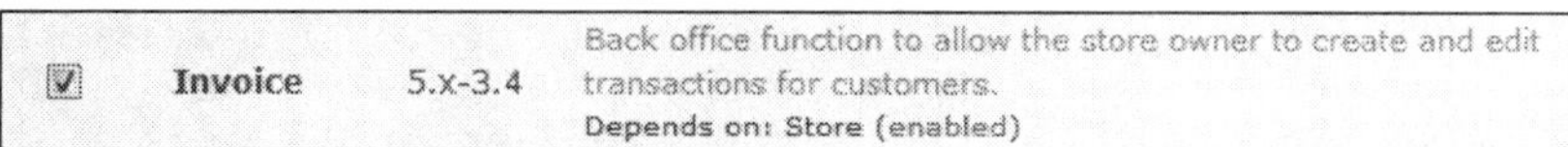

The module also provides us with some new settings within the **Invoices** section under **E-Commerce configuration**.

Invoice Module Configuration Options

These settings are for the **Order of the Invoice Screens** and for the **Invoice Terms**.

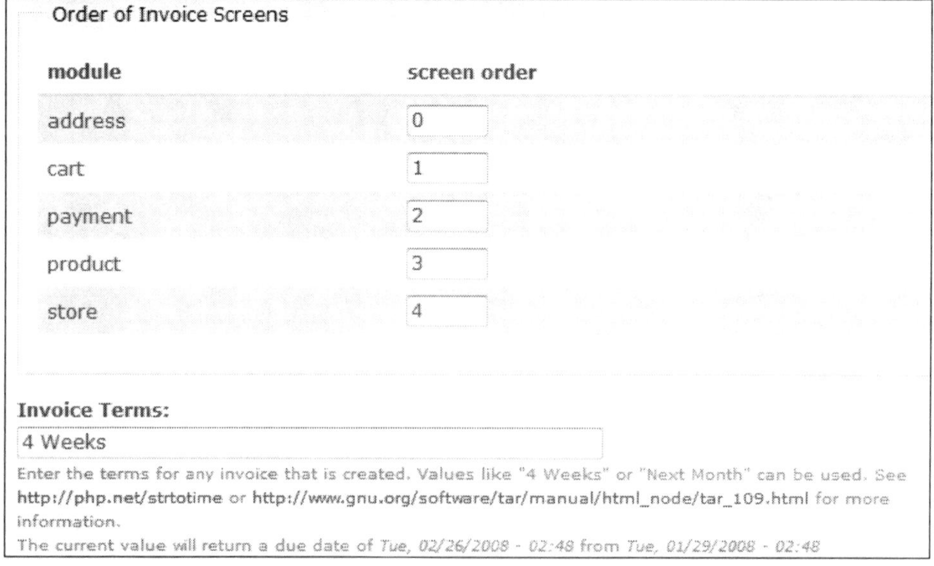

When creating an invoice we go through a number of screens before the invoice is created; the order of these screens can be configured here. The **Invoice Terms** define the maximum available time period until payment is due for a particular invoice. The PHP documentation link and the GNU manual link contain details on the format in which the invoice terms can be in.

Creating an Invoice

To create an invoice, we must first select a user (either from the user management area, or from a member's profile link); unfortunately there is no quick link to creating an invoice elsewhere.

If we go to the users list and then select a user from the list, on this page there is the **create invoice** link.

The next stage is to select the billing address where the invoice would be posted; we can select an address from the addresses stored for that user, or we can add a new address by clicking on **add a new address** link. Once we have selected an address, we click the **Continue** button to move on to the next stage.

The next stage is to add products to the invoice; we can do this in two ways: either enter the ID of the product (a handy pop-up window listing product names and IDs can be found by clicking on the **list of all products** link) or by entering the name of the product and selecting the ID from the list. If we enter the name of a product, the web page looks up all products starting with that word or those letters and lists them, so we can select the one we want. When we select the one we want it adds the ID number into the **Product Ids** field.

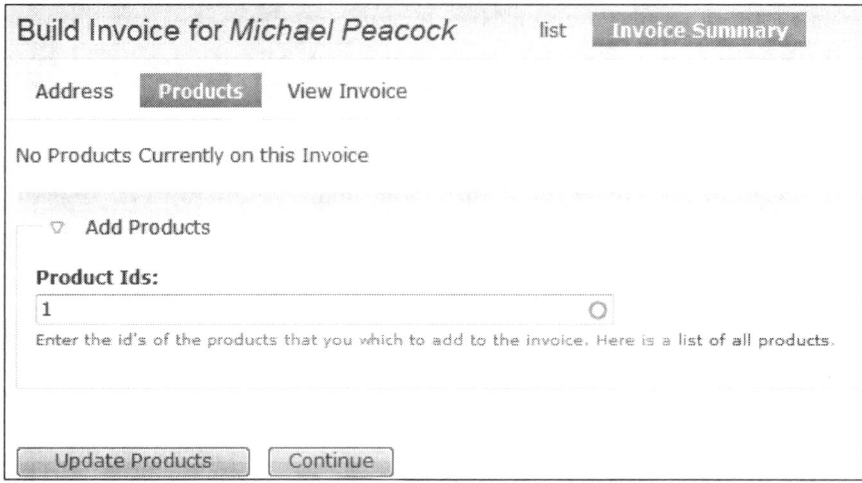

To add more products we can click the **Update Products** button and then add more products to the invoice; once we are finished we can click the **Continue** button.

The final section allows us to review the invoice in a summary form, make any changes to the addresses, and select if we wish to process the payment now, or if we want to just save the invoice as it is.

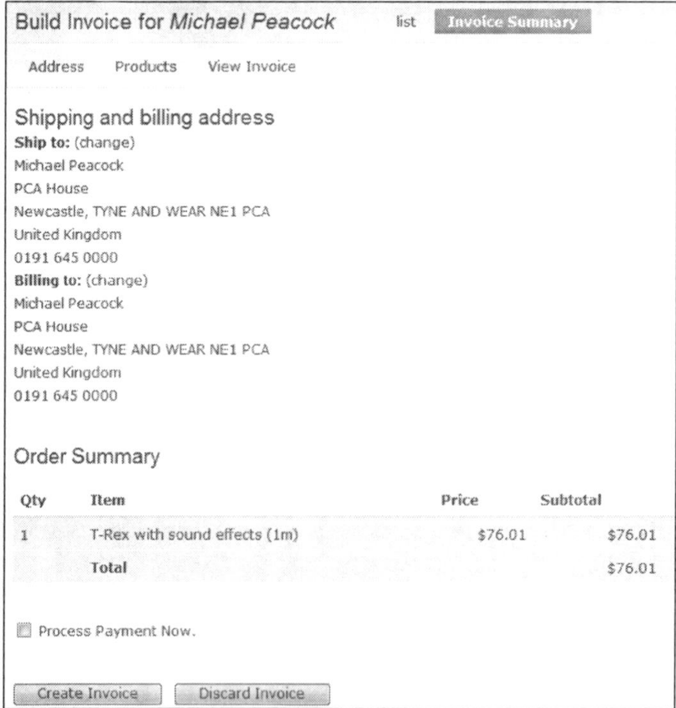

If we do check the **Process Payment Now** button then the next page will ask us to pay for the invoice now; otherwise the invoice will be saved on the user's account.

Managing Invoices

Under the **E-Commerce** link in the **Administer** menu is a link for **Pending Invoices**; within this page are any pending invoices on the system. We can see the invoices, edit them, and delete them from here.

Pending Invoices

Invoice	Created	Changed	Last Changed by	Operations
	Thu, 01/10/2008 - 00:52	Sun, 01/27/2008 - 17:08	Michael	edit delete
Michael	Tue, 01/29/2008 - 03:05	Tue, 01/29/2008 - 03:05	Michael	edit delete

If we were to edit an invoice we can edit the billing address, products within the invoice, and of course view the invoice.

All invoices are stored as transactions, and since installing the invoice module we also have an additional column in the **Transactions list**, which is for the **duedate** of the invoice.

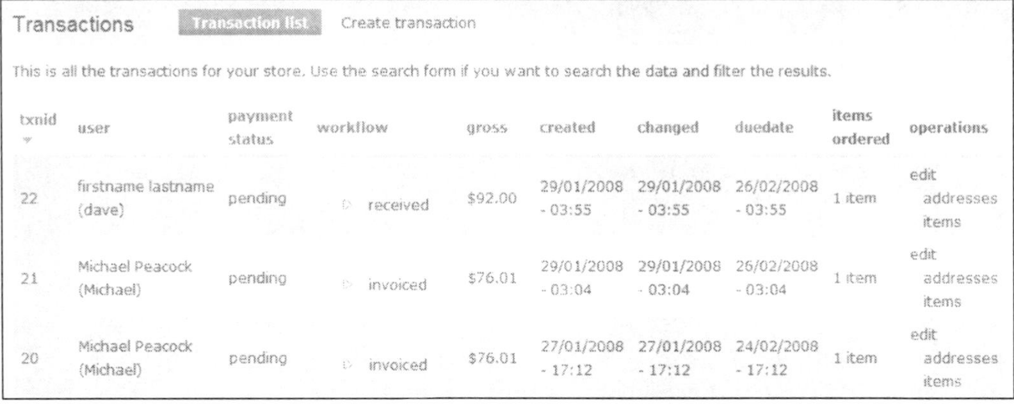

Transactions Transaction list Create transaction

This is all the transactions for your store. Use the search form if you want to search the data and filter the results.

txnid	user	payment status	workflow	gross	created	changed	duedate	items ordered	operations
22	firstname lastname (dave)	pending	received	$92.00	29/01/2008 - 03:55	29/01/2008 - 03:55	26/02/2008 - 03:55	1 item	edit addresses items
21	Michael Peacock (Michael)	pending	invoiced	$76.01	29/01/2008 - 03:04	29/01/2008 - 03:04	26/02/2008 - 03:04	1 item	edit addresses items
20	Michael Peacock (Michael)	pending	invoiced	$76.01	27/01/2008 - 17:12	27/01/2008 - 17:12	24/02/2008 - 17:12	1 item	edit addresses items

We can also filter the **Transaction list** using the **Search** option based upon transactions that have been **invoiced**, as well as by the **duedate** of the invoice.

Invoices for the Customer

Customers can either view their invoice from their own invoices where they can view all of their orders from **View your order history** or view their pending invoice from the **edit pending invoice** link.

History

Blog

View recent blog entries

Member for

19 weeks 4 days

Orders

View your order history

Invoice

edit pending invoice

CiviCRM

CiviCRM is a *Customer Relationship Management* application, although its primary design is to serve advocacy, non-profit, and non-governmental groups. It can, however, be integrated with either Drupal or Joomla! So let's have a look at what integrating CiviCRM can do for us.

CiviCRM does not integrate, apart from sharing a few settings with the e-Commerce functionality of Drupal; however, it can still be useful for online stores, particularly with regular customers or regular follow-ups.

Doug wants to use CiviCRM to record communications with customers, such as technical support phone calls, logging meetings, and scheduling bookings for groups that arrange to visit his museum and store.

Installing CiviCRM

The CiviCRM download page, `http://civicrm.org/download`, links us to SourceForge to download the latest version. The version we have used is `civicrm-1.9.13019-drupal-php5.tar.gz`.

The installation method we are going to use is the web-based automated installer, that requires at least PHP 5, Drupal 5, and MySQL 4 with InnoDB support. If you are not sure that your web hosting has the correct versions, contact your web host.

We need to extract our newly downloaded CiviCRM archive, and upload this to our Drupal website. The extracted folder `civicrm` needs to be uploaded to the `sites/all/modules` folder on our site. CiviCRM is a large application, at about 30MB once extracted, so it may take a little while to upload. A quicker way to upload would be to upload the ZIP file, and extract it using a command-line interface, if available; more information on that is available on the CiviCRM website.

If your store utilizes page caching, an additional step is needed to prevent CiviCRM pages being cached; see `http://wiki.civicrm.org/confluence/display/CRMDOC/Automated+Installer+for+Drupal` for more information.

Once uploaded, we need to go to the automated installer, which is located at `http://www.dougsdinos.com/sites/all/modules/civicrm/drupal-5.7/install/index.php`. The installer tells us there is an error, informing us that **Your database settings don't appear to be correct. Please check the Database Details below for specific errors**. This is because we have not told CiviCRM our database connection details.

CiviCRM Database Settings

MySQL server:	localhost
MySQL username:	dougsdin_db
MySQL password:	••••••••
MySQL database:	dougsdin_db

Drupal Database Settings

MySQL server:	localhost
MySQL username:	dougsdin_db
MySQL password:	••••••••
MySQL database:	dougsdin_db

Once we have entered the connection details we need to click the **Re-check requirements** button.

Once that has been checked we can click the **Install CiviCRM** button to install CiviCRM.

Installing without the Automated Installer

Your web server may not have the correct version of PHP or MySQL to use the installer, or it may not support InnoDB format for the databases. If that is the case we can manually install CiviCRM.

We need to open PHPMyAdmin and select the database we want to use, such as our Drupal database, and then click the **Import** tab at the top to allow us to perform some SQL commands to set up the database. From this page we need to browse to the `civicrm_41.mysql` file from where we extracted CiviCRM on to our local computer, which should be in the folder `civicrm/sql/`, then we need to click **Go** to perform the import.

Next we need to import the data into the new tables that have just been created; we just follow the steps above but select the file `civicrm_data.mysql` to import.

Finally, we need to edit the configuration file for CiviCRM. Let's open the sample configuration file from our computer, edit it, and then upload it to our store; the sample file is called `civicrm.settings.php.sample`.

Within this file we need to edit the following lines:

- 44 (Drupal's database connection)—We should use the connection string from Drupal's settings file.
- 90 (CiviCRM's database connection)—If we are going to use Drupal's database for CiviCRM data (we don't have to) we should also put Drupal's connection string here.
- 134 (CiviCRM path)—This is the file system path to CiviCRM on our server.
- 135 (CiviCRM template compiler path)—This is the system path to CiviCRM's template compiler.
- 169 (Our site's URL)—This is `http://www.dougsdinos.com/`.

More information and help on the values of these settings is available in the comments of the configuration file itself.

The configuration file then needs to be saved with a new name of `civicrm.settings.php` and uploaded to the `sites/default/` folder in our site.

Setting up CiviCRM

CiviCRM is now uploaded and set up, and ready to use. Let's enable the module and get it up and running!

To enable the module we just need to check the **CiviCRM** box in the **Modules** page and then click the **Save configuration** button at the bottom of the page.

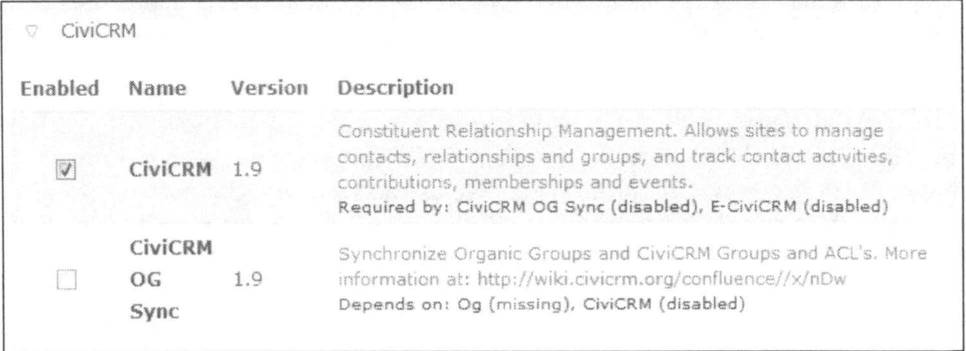

If there are any problems with our settings file, they will be pointed out to us now, so we can correct them and try again.

There is now a new option on the menu called **CiviCRM**.

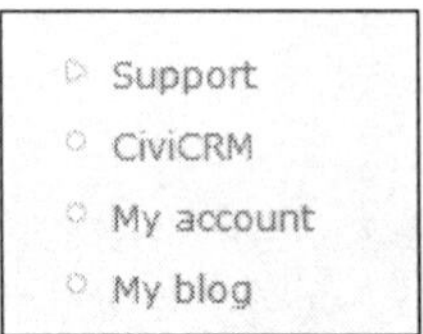

The main page for **CiviCRM** contains a **list of scheduled activities**, which is currently empty, as well as a **Menu** and **list of shortcuts** on the right-hand side.

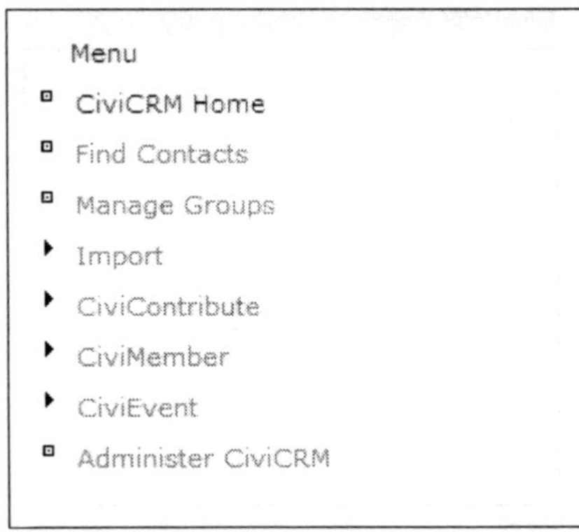

We need to click the **Administer CiviCRM** link to perform some initial settings and tweaks.

The first thing we need to do is **Synchronize Users to Contacts**; this is because contacts in CiviCRM are not the same as users in Drupal, but obviously if Doug wants to use customers from his store in CiviCRM then we will need to perform this synchronization routine, and perform it regularly too.

When we click on this link a pop-up will ask us to confirm the task, so we need to click **OK**.

A confirmation message confirms that the users have been converted to contacts in CiviCRM.

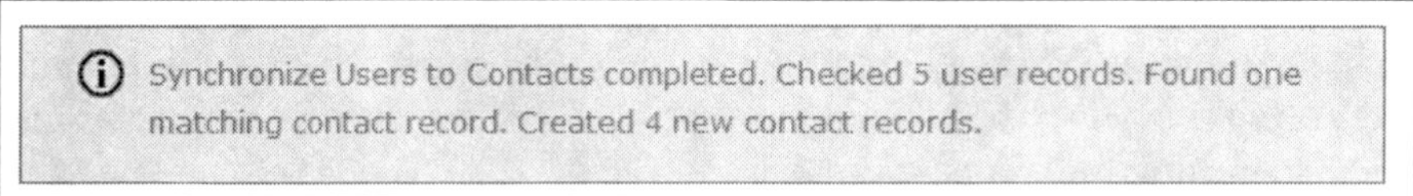

Synchronize Users to Contacts completed. Checked 5 user records. Found one matching contact record. Created 4 new contact records.

Using CiviCRM

CiviCRM is a large system, and would need a book of its own to explain how to use all of its features. We will just have a look at some of its features here. Doug's main use for CiviCRM is to log and schedule meetings and calls with some of his more corporate clients, as well as log incoming technical support calls. This way he can look up a customer and see all phone calls made and received relating to that customer.

If we click the **Find Contacts** link on CiviCRM's **Menu** we can then search for contacts within the system; once we find a customer we can schedule and log meetings, and calls with them.

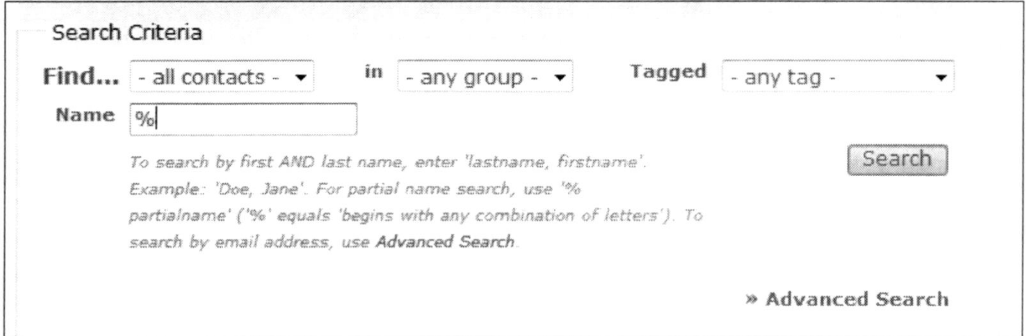

The results are then displayed in a list on the next page.

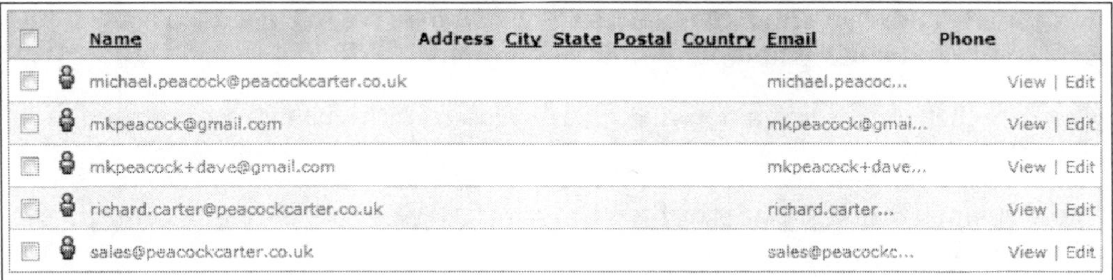

If we then click on the **Name** of a contact (which is currently their email address from the synchronization) we will be taken to that contact's profile where we can manage their details, and log meetings and calls.

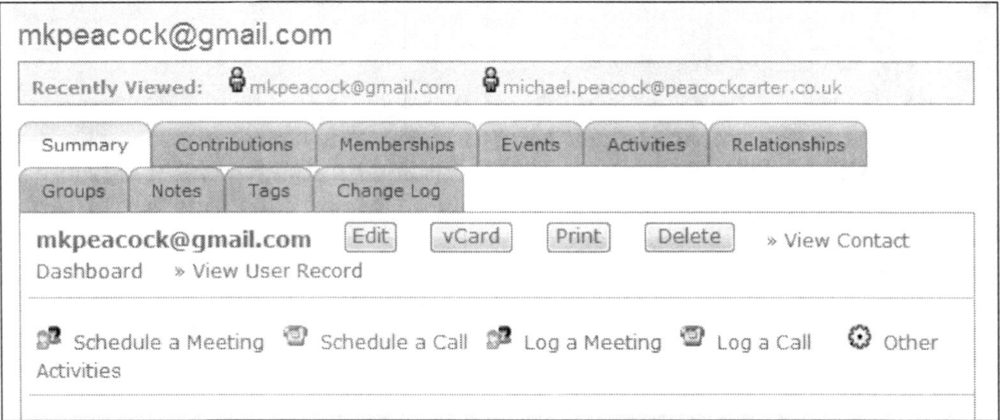

The profile is divided into tabs, each of which contains more information on the contact, such as relationships to other contacts (useful if multiple contacts from an organization are customers; we can record that one is the employer of the other), notes on a customer and so on.

The links just below the tabs allow us to log and schedule meetings and calls with that customer. Let's look at logging a call.

The first few options allow us to enter a subject for the call, the telephone number used to make a call (or the number used to call us), as well as the date and time. There is even a calendar link so we can select the date from a calendar.

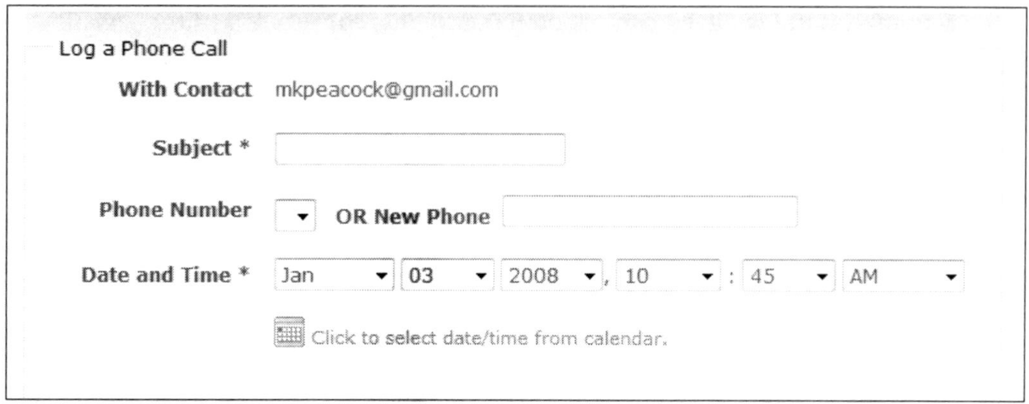

The final options allow us to specify the duration of the call, the call status, and a text box for details on the call.

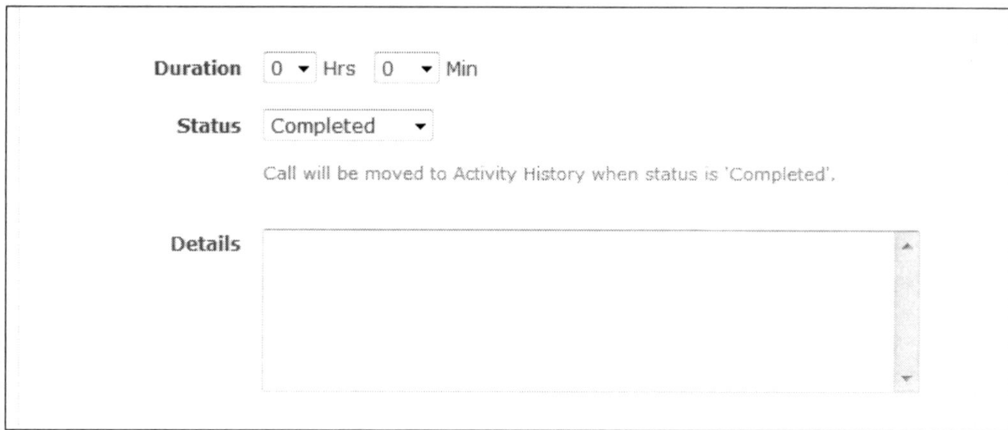

With the call **Status** we can specify whether the call was completed, or scheduled, in case the contact was unreachable or if a message was left for them.

This will then add an **Activity Type** to the contact's profile.

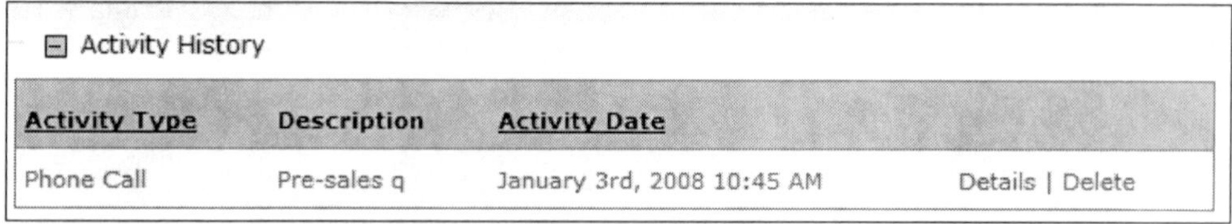

If the activity has not yet been completed it is added to the dashboard for CiviCRM under **Scheduled Activities**.

So with CiviCRM Doug can manage all contacts with his customers, which can allow him to ensure support contracts are cost effective, and schedule meetings, as well as have a nice list of meetings and calls that need to be made in the near future.

Summary

In this chapter we took our fully functioning live e-Commerce store and:

- Customized the printable invoices
- Installed the invoice module
- Looked at how the invoice module works and tried it out
- Installed CiviCRM to allow Doug to manage appointments and log phone calls with customers

In Chapter 12 we will look at *Marketing Your Business*!

12
Marketing Your Business

We have our store up and running, but there isn't any point in having an online store without customers. Marketing our business and store is the key to generating new business so let's have a look at it. However, even some simple site-based features and enhancements can improve our businesses marketing so we will also have a look at that.

In this chapter you will learn about:

- Advertising programs
- Advertising on websites and newsletters
- Things to watch out for when advertising on other sites, or accepting adverts on your website
- Viral marketing
- Using newsletters to market your business
- How to improve traffic with SEO

The Basics

When it comes to marketing a business there are loads of different methods and advertising mediums; the Internet provides many of them such as websites, blogs, newsletters, and emails. By promoting our business and website on the Web we can hope to drive more visitors and more traffic to our website, and thus increase our sales.

Update your Corporate Stationary

One thing that a lot of existing businesses that set up a new website forget to do is promote their website on their company's stationary. Update your business cards, letterheads, invoices, and promotional material with your web address. By doing this your existing customers, suppliers, and those receiving your correspondence will know about your website! I know from experience a number of clients who have commissioned a new website, requested no Internet marketing and not updated their stationary and wondered why no one was going to their website. The reason was that nobody, not even their existing customers and some of their staff knew it was there!

Advertising

There are many different advertising programmes available on the Internet ranging from simply purchasing some advertising space on a website, to using professional advertising networks and search engines.

Buying Advert Space

Some websites offer to sell advertising space on their site, and in some cases this can be a great way to generate new traffic and business. Things to bear in mind while considering buying an advertising space on a website are:

- Does the website compete: If the website you are advertising on is a competitor then it isn't a good idea to place an advert there!
- Is it relevant: It wouldn't make sense for Doug to advertise on a florist's website, but it makes sense to advertise on websites aimed for kids, or toy-related websites.
- What their statistics are like: There is no point in advertising on a website that nobody visits, so always ask for information on their statistics. One common pitfall here is hits versus visits. Some websites selling space may just try quoting large figures at you, typically X thousand hits per day. A hit is a single file request so if you load a webpage with 10 images that's 11 hits that website has just had. A visit is someone visiting the website and loading a number of pages and files, then going on elsewhere; that counts as a single visit.
- Are they reputable: Try to make sure the website is reputable; if it operates bad practices some will see an advert as a sign of affiliation or endorsement, which wouldn't look good!

Professional Advertising Networks (PPC)

Some companies, particularly search engines, operate PPC advertising networks; this stands for Pay per click. Let's have a brief look at how PPC advertising generally works. First we sign up with the network, and submit information about the website, the business, and billing information. Then we select keywords that we want to target. These are keywords that someone may type into a search engine; the advert would then be displayed down the side. Alternatively some website owners monetize their website by displaying adverts from PPC advertising networks so if their website contains related keywords, the advert might be displayed in their advertisement box. Then we would enter how much we would pay, at most for each click on an advert to our website relating to that keyword. The higher the cost the more likely it would be displayed, and more prominently it would be displayed.

We may also set up a limit, or a monthly limit, so that once our bill for that month reaches $50 the advertising campaign stops for that month. We would then be charged for each time someone clicks on one of our adverts; the cost would be up to the maximum amount we selected for the keyword, depending on the search itself, and the position relative to other advertisers.

One potential issue with these schemes is fraudulent clicks, where someone repeatedly clicks an advert in order to generate money for the site displaying the advert. Networks have technologies in place to detect this, with severe penalties, so it's worth checking which networks do and don't penalize; after all we wouldn't want to pick a network that leaves us vulnerable to wasting our marketing budget!

Useful Links

Google's Advertising Programmes: `http://www.google.co.uk/intl/en/ads/`

Yahoo! Search Engine Marketing: `http://sem.smallbusiness.yahoo.com/searchenginemarketing/index.php`

Microsoft Search Advertising: `http://advertising.microsoft.com/search-advertising?s_int=277`

Product Search

Some websites and search engines allow you to search specifically for products as opposed to other information; an example of this is Google's Product Search, which searches specifically for products. With this it is possible either to submit a single product to the search engine, or to create a data feed (such as an RSS feed for our store) that automatically updates with new products, which allows the search engine to automatically update its own listings. More information can be found on Google's Information for Sellers page: `http://www.google.com/base/help/sellongoogle.html`.

Directories

Business directories can often be a good way to advertise a website; they are normally designed with SEO in mind so they are often found when looking for one particular business or type of business. There are generally a few types to be aware of:

- Automatic directories: There are a number of automatic directories that crawl the Web similar to search engines and "scrape" business information to create listings; others rely on staff to perform the search and enter businesses. These can be fairly good, but it's important to look for any existing entries on the business and edit them to make sure the information is up to date.
- Free directories: There are also quite a few free directories relating to specific industries or geographical areas.
- Paid directories: There are paid directories too, sometimes combined with the free directories, where you pay to get extra information. Be careful with these, as there can be a number of disreputable directories trying to scam businesses for money. The Yellow Pages (in the UK and US) have free basic listings on their website, but you must pay to display more information, categories, and a web address. In some cases this can be well worth it; try contacting such directories to discuss free trials, promotions, or cancellation periods to give it a try. Don't sign up for a long commitment, try it, see how well it improves the business, and then consider committing for a longer term.

Newsletters

There are two sides to newsletter marketing; advertising in a newsletter, and creating a newsletter. We will look at creating a newsletter later on in this chapter; first let's look at advertising in newsletters.

Essentially the same rules apply that did when looking for websites to advertise on. It is of course more difficult to find newsletters to advertise in; however, there are some websites dedicated to connecting newsletters with potential advertisers, such as Carsonified's Amigo: `http://heyamigo.net`. This website allows us to create an advert, and manage its cost and budget, through its own PPC system.

Things to Watch Out For when Buying or Selling Adverts

Buying or selling advertising space to either advertise your website or make some additional money is often quite a good thing to do; however, in certain circumstances it can do a lot of harm.

Search Engine Penalization

Most search engines use a number of different metrics to determine where a website is positioned in a list of search results. Some search engines, such as Google have a metric (Google's is called Page Rank and factors in other things too) that is based on in-bound links, where a website link from one site to another acts as a vote.

Some websites and businesses use this to their advantage, and offer to pay for advertising space on other websites (normally ones that have a high ranking). This way of both the buying and selling of advertising is not something that many search engines like, and Google even has an online tool to report websites that do this, which will result in their rankings being penalized.

Of course, there is nothing wrong with buying and selling advertising space, and in fact one of Google's core businesses revolves around advertising space. The solution is to alter how the link is structured.

A traditional link is structured as follows:

```
<a href='http://www.packtpub.com'>PacktPub</a>
```

If this was a paid advert on our site (or if we were buying the advert space on a site) we should structure the link like so:

```
<a href='http://www.packtpub.com' rel='nofollow'>PacktPub</a>
```

The 'nofollow' attribute signals to search engines that we don't wish for the link to count as a vote towards that website's rankings, and so if this was an advert, we would not be penalized by search engines for buying or selling it on a website.

It is important to note that there is nothing wrong with providing links to other websites without the `rel='nofollow'` attribute. The penalization really only comes from adverts that are bought or sold and don't contain this, as it is classed as a trick to fool the rankings.

Things to keep in mind:

- Only purchase adverts, or buy adverts from reputable websites.
- **Always** use `rel='nofollow'` for adverts you are displaying on your website that you are paid to display, and for adverts you have on other websites.
- Beware of emails offering to pay to put adverts on your website; they probably don't have the `rel='nofollow'` attribute.
- Don't risk your search engine rankings!

Social Network Marketing

Most social networking websites available have provisions for user information and profile data, including website addresses. We can add our URL to MySpace profiles, Facebook profiles, Twitter accounts, and so on, to try to provide that extra promotion to our site.

Facebook has a new addition to its website that allows business to create their own profile page, advertising the business, its contact details, opening hours, as well as hosting a discussion forum, photo gallery, and other features. We can of course create a profile for our business and share the profile among our friends. Users of Facebook can also become fans of businesses, promoting the businesses among their own friends too.

Viral Marketing

Viral marketing is a relatively new marketing concept, which revolves around utilizing social networks. One particular example of viral marketing is utilizing video sharing websites such as YouTube and promoting videos there that advertise the business or its products. This technique (at least in that particular example) is probably more suited to large businesses with large marketing budgets who are trying to promote a brand. Information on using YouTube in particular was recently posted on a technology blog called TechCrunch, `http://www.techcrunch.com/2007/11/22/the-secret-strategies-behind-many-viral-videos/`.

Newsletter Marketing

Earlier we had a brief look at advertising within a newsletter; the other side to newsletters is of course creating one of our own to promote the business to existing customers and other interested subscribers.

There are a couple of aspects to setting up a newsletter:

- Subscriber lists
- The newsletter itself

Subscriber Lists

There are a few options for keeping and maintaining a list of subscribers to a newsletter:

- Drupal module
- Server-based solution
- Hosted solution

There is a Drupal module available for mailing list management, which allows us to embed a subscribe form on the website to request email addresses of interested visitors to sign up to the mailing list. Unfortunately the module does not handle creating the newsletters, it only distributes them to a list. There are some other server-based software solutions that can be used, including mailman and phplist. The final option is a hosted solution, where a third-party company manages the mailing list on our behalf, such as SafeSubscribe or Constant Contact. Hosted solutions like this provide extra security to those joining the list with regards to spam and privacy.

The Newsletter

With regards to the newsletter itself, this depends very much on the nature of the business, and the intentions of the newsletter. Some general tips for newsletters and their content:

- Don't send newsletters too often, otherwise subscribers will get sick and unsubscribe.
- Address each subscriber by their name, wherever possible.
- Keep them fresh; don't repeat the same content from previous newsletters. Only send a new newsletter when there is new and fresh content available.

- If the newsletter is in HTML format, make sure there is a text version too that can be read, not all users have HTML enabled on their emails or include a link to the newsletter on a webpage; this way if there is a problem with the email they can click the link and read it online.
- Don't attach files; link to them, this also saves cluttering up inboxes!
- Add something unrelated to some newsletters. I've seen some that I actually enjoy receiving; these contain something quirky and unrelated at the bottom, such as websites the author found interesting this month, and it also shows a personal touch.
- Always ensure there are unsubscribing instructions in the newsletter.
- Appeal to both customers and potential customers with public newsletters (obviously just appeal to customers if it is a customer-only newsletter).

Improve Traffic with Search Engine Optimization

SEO can be a real traffic booster, as it makes our site more visible to search engines, easier for them to read, and makes our site seem more important and more relevant.

There are two main aspects to SEO; on-site and off-site SEO.

On-Site SEO

On-site SEO relates to making optimizations on the website itself. This improves visibility and readability for search engines.

Meta

Meta tags are tags stored in the head section of an HTML document, typically for information such as keywords, description, and author of the website. This is not regarded very highly by search engines anymore, but it is still worth doing, particularly if different pages and sections have different metadata.

Sitemap

Google has released some webmaster tools, one of which allows us to create a list of the pages within our site, rank them in importance, and specify the frequency that those sections will be updated. This is then saved as an XML file and stored on the website; Google can then read it and see which content it should check regularly and which content it should check rarely; this helps keep the website more relevant to search engines.

Links

A very simple trick is to make use of relevant sentences in keywords for hyperlinks and their titles; let's take an example of a products page. A poorly optimized link would be:

```
To view our products <a href="products/">click here</a>.
```

The link has no context and no meaningful information; a more meaningful and search-engine friendly link would be:

```
Why not view our
<a href="products/" title="View our Dinosaur Products | Doug's
        Dinos">list of dinosaur products</a>
```

All these small changes do make a difference!

Staying Fresh

Keep content up-to-date! If the content on our website is always the same, or rarely changes, search engines (and visitors!) will stop coming to the website. Frequent updates cause the search engines to pay more attention to the site.

Blogs

Having a blog as part of a website can help keep it fresh, and it's a whole new area to try to attract and retain visitors that will help promote the main site. Many businesses are finding it effective to set up company blogs, with posts' content relating to the business and personal thoughts of some of the executives.

Off-Site SEO

Off-site SEO is a large area, particularly useful for specific keywords to obtain a specific ranking in search engines. It relies on promoting the website on other websites, hence off-site.

As we discussed earlier, one of the metrics for a website's position in search results is its in-bound links. Commenting on websites, blogs, forums, video posts, profiles and so on with web links can increase a website's ranking. This should always be done with care, consideration, and courtesy. Spamming websites with comments is a very bad practice; however, relevant and appropriate comments with a link back to our site, on relevant websites and articles is a good start. Many companies specialize in this form of SEO, so if it is something you are serious about, it is worth looking around to see what they can offer.

Summary

In this chapter we looked into marketing our business online, and the various techniques available, ranging from improving our site, to purchasing advertisements, as well as looking at some useful pointers on advertising and newsletters. Now it is over to you: *Good luck with your store*!

A
Installing WAMP

In order to install Drupal e-Commerce on our own computer, we need a development environment in which to run it, including:

- A web server
- PHP
- A database server (MySQL)
- Various PHP and web server libraries to utilize additional features

WampServer is a package providing all of these, and more, for Microsoft Windows systems.

Installing WampServer

Now we know what we need to install, let's get started!

Downloading WampServer

Firstly, we need to download the software from the Internet. WampServer is available at `http://www.wampserver.com/en/download.php`; from here we click the **DOWNLOAD WampServer 2.0** link, which then takes us to SourceForce to download the application.

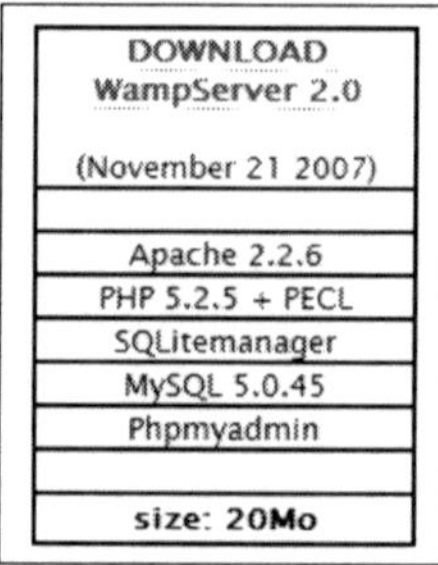

Installing WampServer

Once it is downloaded we need to install the software; first let's open the file we have just downloaded; we may need to agree to some security dialogues before Windows allow us to install the software.

You must be logged in as an administrator to install WampServer.

The first window to be displayed warns us that we shouldn't try to upgrade from a previous version of WampServer and that we need to uninstall any old versions; let's click **Yes** so the installation can continue.

Next we are presented with the installation splash screen; we need to click **Next**.

Next we need to read and agree to the license agreement for the software. Once we have read it we need to select **I accept the agreement** before clicking the **Next** button.

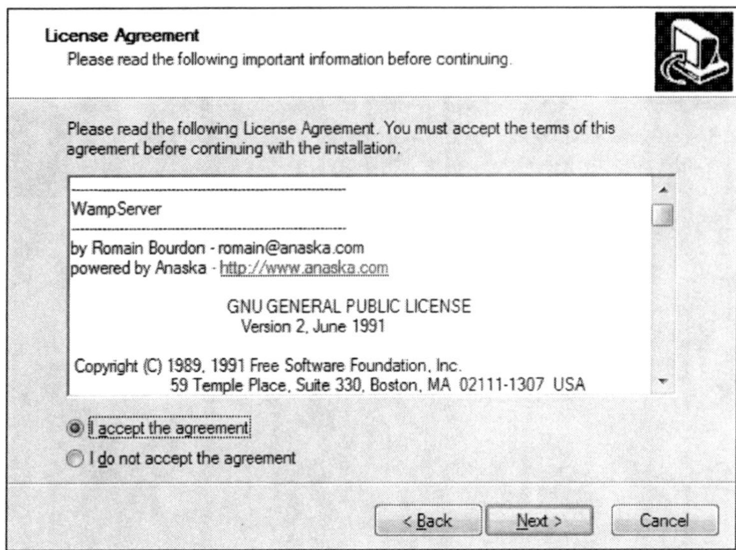

Now we need to select the location where we wish to install WampServer. If we are happy with the default location we should click **Next**, otherwise we should change the location first.

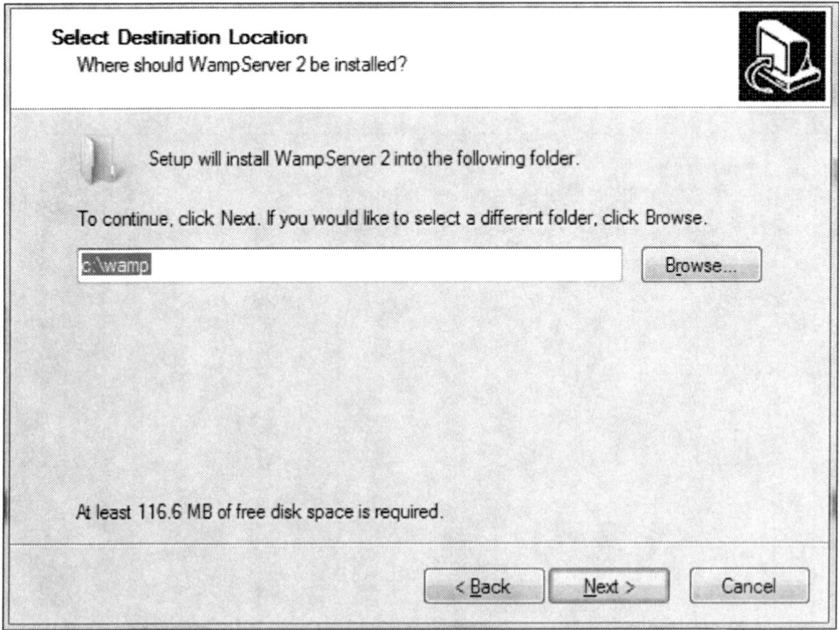

Next we have the option to add a shortcut to WampServer to our desktop and to the Quicklaunch toolbar before clicking **Next**.

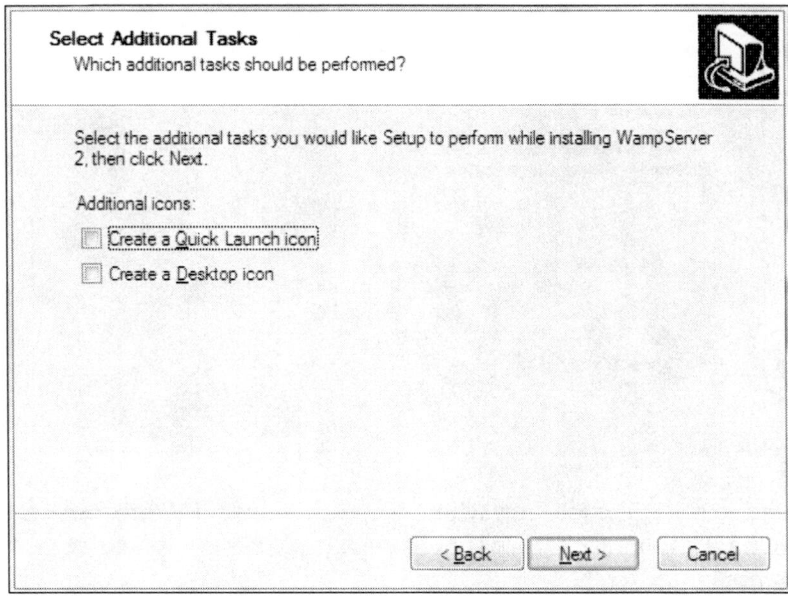

Before WampServer actually begins installing we are shown an overview of the options we have selected; provided everything is fine we can click **Install**, otherwise we need to click **Back** and make any relevant changes.

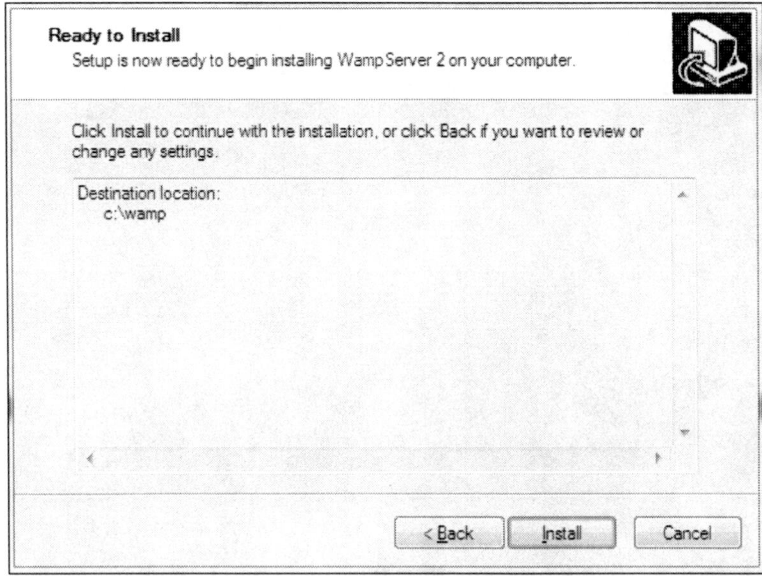

WampServer will then install on our computer.

Once the installation has completed we are asked to confirm our primary web browser; by default it has selected Internet Explorer. If we are happy with that we should click **Open**, otherwise we should browse for an alternative browser first. Next the installation will ask for details on PHP mail; on most installations we won't be able to send mail from PHP scripts as we have no mail server installed so just click **Next**.

We now have WampServer installed; if we click **Finish** WampServer will start.

Apache not starting?

If WampServer has not started, the icon in the system tray will be red or orange; this is likely because something else might be utilizing the computer's port. Apache runs on port 80 programs such as Skype also do this, so you may need to close other applications before trying to start WampServer.

WampServer Overview

When WampServer is running it is displayed in our computer's system tray alongside the clock. Clicking the icon displays a menu where we can configure our server, and start or stop various services.

Putting the server online would allow web pages on our computer to be accessible to other computers on our network, and potentially via the Internet. We can quickly start, stop, and restart the services, configure each of them, quickly open the folder containing our website's files, and quickly open our website or database manager in a web browser.

Configuring WampServer

Within the WampServer menu the Apache, PHP, and MySQL options allow us to configure the various services. We can install modules and add-ons to the different components, or we can edit the configuration files for them.

There are two main features that need to be enabled:

- GD for PHP
- Rewrite_module for Apache

Configuration Files

The files `my.ini`, `php.ini`, and `httpd.conf` are the configuration files for the three services; although we shouldn't need to edit these for our website, it is important to know where they are, in case we do need to change them later, as they have a lot of control on how the software works. More information is available on their respective websites.

GD2

PHP's GD2 module is a graphics library that allows PHP to easily manipulate and manage images, including resizing images, recreating images, adding watermarks to images, and so on. Drupal has a number of image features that require an image module to be installed with PHP. By default GD2 is installed with WampServer, but it is important that we check this and also that we know where the setting is.

PHP's modules are enabled and disabled by clicking the WampServer logo in the system tray, selecting **PHP** and then **PHP Extensions**.

From here we can enable or disable the GD2 extension.

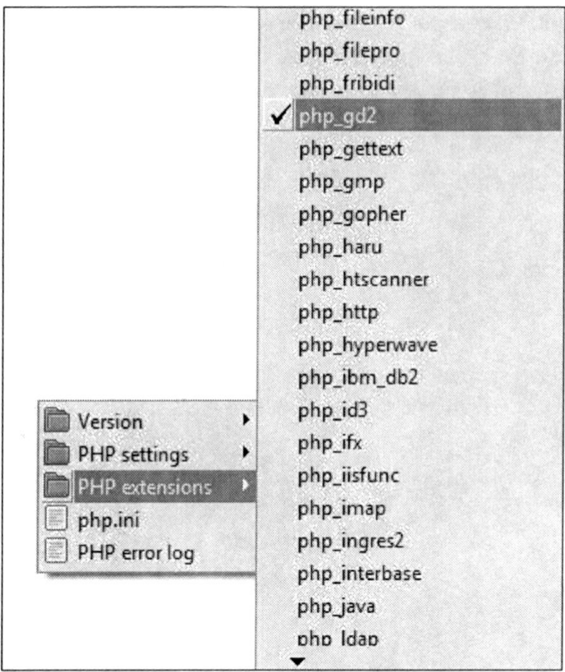

Rewrite Module

Apache has a module called `rewrite_module`, which allows it to rewrite URLs, in particular to make them more friendly by rewriting URLs such as `/home/about` to `index.php?section=home&page=about`.

A number of Drupal's modules make use of this feature if it is available, so let's enable it! It can be enabled from **Apache modules** within the **Apache** menu.

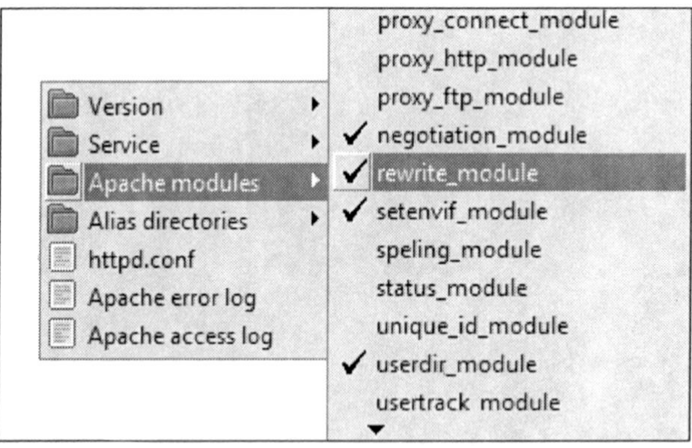

Summary

We have now installed the Apache web server, the PHP interpreter, and MySQL database server using the WampServer package. We have also ensured various options are enabled for Drupal e-Commerce to utilize later on.

Index

D

E

F

G

I

L

M

N

O

P

R

S

T

W

X

Packt Open Source Project Royalties

When we sell a book written on an Open Source project, we pay a royalty directly to that project. Therefore by purchasing Selling Online with Drupal e-Commerce, Packt will have given some of the money received to the Drupal e-Commerce Project.

In the long term, we see ourselves and you—customers and readers of our books—as part of the Open Source ecosystem, providing sustainable revenue for the projects we publish on. Our aim at Packt is to establish publishing royalties as an essential part of the service and support a business model that sustains Open Source.

If you're working with an Open Source project that you would like us to publish on, and subsequently pay royalties to, please get in touch with us.

Writing for Packt

We welcome all inquiries from people who are interested in authoring. Book proposals should be sent to `authors@packtpub.com`. If your book idea is still at an early stage and you would like to discuss it first before writing a formal book proposal, contact us; one of our commissioning editors will get in touch with you.

We're not just looking for published authors; if you have strong technical skills but no writing experience, our experienced editors can help you develop a writing career, or simply get some additional reward for your expertise.

About Packt Publishing

Packt, pronounced 'packed', published its first book "Mastering phpMyAdmin for Effective MySQL Management" in April 2004 and subsequently continued to specialize in publishing highly focused books on specific technologies and solutions.

Our books and publications share the experiences of your fellow IT professionals in adapting and customizing today's systems, applications, and frameworks. Our solution-based books give you the knowledge and power to customize the software and technologies you're using to get the job done. Packt books are more specific and less general than the IT books you have seen in the past. Our unique business model allows us to bring you more focused information, giving you more of what you need to know, and less of what you don't.

Packt is a modern, yet unique publishing company, which focuses on producing quality, cutting-edge books for communities of developers, administrators, and newbies alike. For more information, please visit our website: `www.PacktPub.com`.

Drupal 5 Themes

ISBN: 978-1-847191-82-3 Paperback: 250 pages

Create a new theme for your Drupal website with a clean layout and powerful CSS styling

1. Learn to create new Drupal 5 Themes
2. No experience of Drupal 5 theming required
3. Set up and configure themes
4. Understand Drupal 5's themeable functions

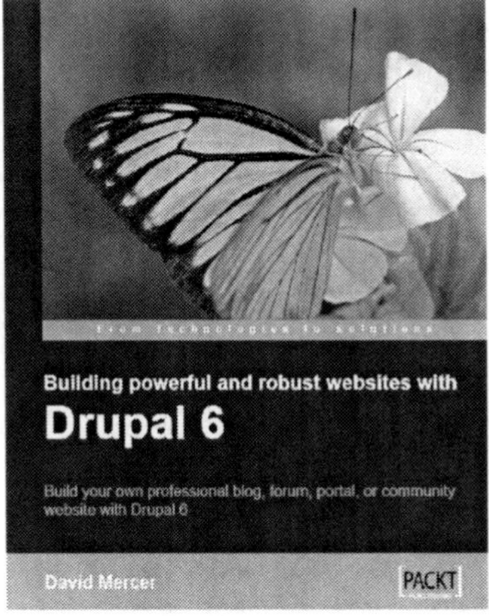

Building powerful and robust websites with Drupal 6

ISBN: 978-1-847192-97-4 Paperback: 330 pages

Build your own professional blog, forum, portal or community website with Drupal 6

1. Set up, configure, and deploy Drupal 6
2. Harness Drupal's world-class Content Management System
3. Design and implement your website's look and feel
4. Easily add exciting and powerful features
5. Promote, manage, and maintain your live website

Printed in the United States
122399LV00004B/61-62/P

9 781847 194060